A STAIN IN THE BLOOD

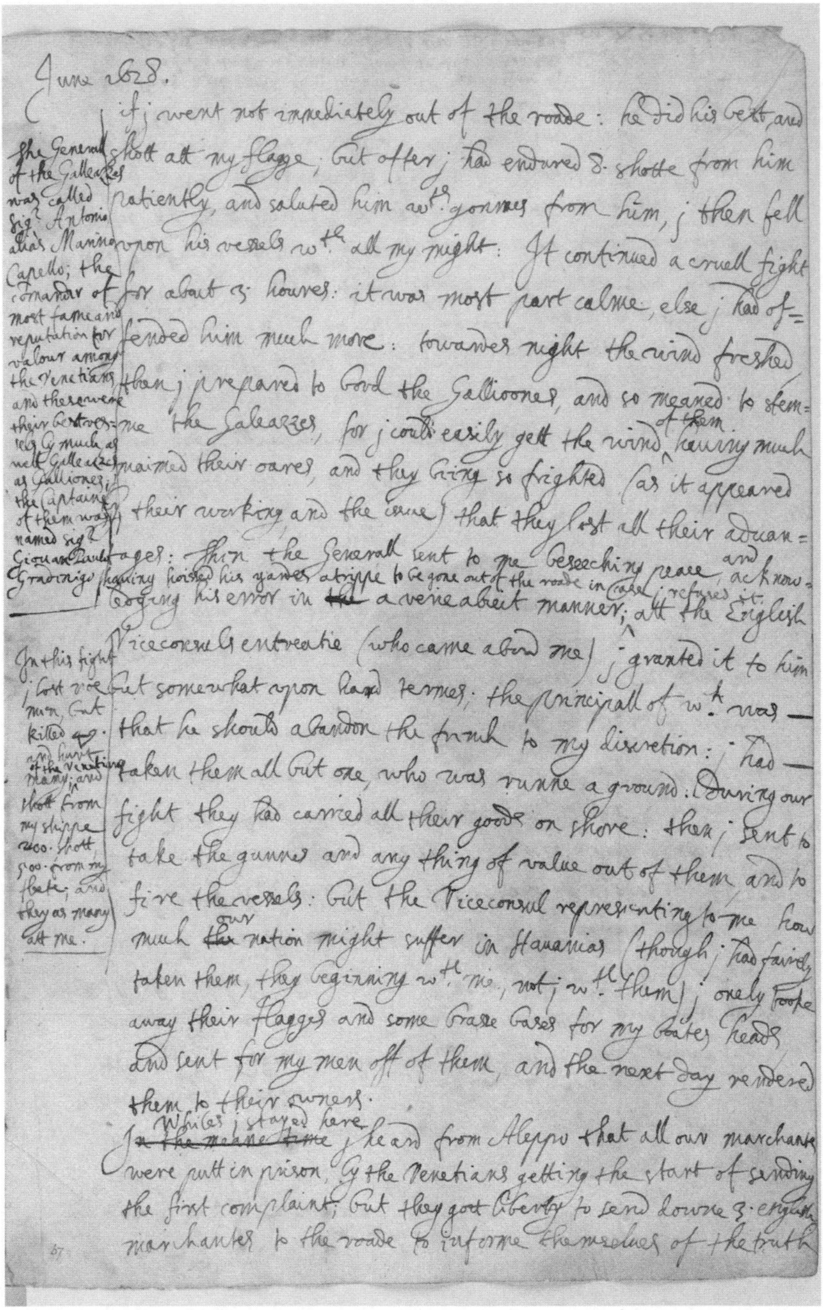

June 1628.

if j went not immediately out of the roade: he did his best, and
the Generall shott att my flagge, but after j had endured 8 shotte from him
patiently, and saluted him w.th 3 gonnes from him, j then fell
upon his vessels w.th all my might: It continued a cruell fight
for about 3 howres: it was most part calme, else j had of=
fended him much more: towardes night the wind freshed
then j prepared to bord the Gallioones, and so meaned to stem=
me the Galeazzes, for j could easily gett the wind of them,
hauing much maimed their oares, and they being so frighted (as it appeared
their working and the issue) that they lost all their advan=
tages: then the Generall sent to me beseeching peace, and acknow-
ledging his error in a verie abiect manner; all the English
Viceconsuls entreatie (who came abord me) j granted it to him
but somewhat upon hard termes: the principall of w.ch was
that he should abandon the prush to my discretion: j had
taken them all but one, who was runne a ground: During our
fight they had carried all their goods on shore: then j sent to
take the gunnes and any thing of value out of them and to
fire the vessels: But the Viceconsul representing to me how
much our nation might suffer in Hauanias (though j had fairly
taken them, they beginning w.th me, not j w.th them) onely tooke
away their flagges and some brase cases for my boates heads
And sent for my men off of them, and the next day rendered
them to their owners.

Whiles j stayed here j heard from Aleppo that all our marchants
were putt in prison, by the Venetians getting the start of sending
the first complaint; but they got liberty to send downe 3 english
marchants to the roade to informe themselves of the truth

[left margin notes:]
the Generall
of the Galleyes
was called
Sig.r Antonio
alias Marino
Capello; the
comandor of
most fame and
reputation for
valour among
the Venetians
and therefore
their Lieutene-
ry; as much as
well Galleazzes
as Gallioones;
the Captaine
of them was
named Sig.r
Giovan Paulo
Gradonigo

In this fight
j lost noe
men, but
killed ...
on hurt
& the venting
many; and
shott from
my shippe
1000 shott,
500 from my
boate; and
they as many
att me.

The page from Kenelm Digby's journey describing the sea battle that he fought at the
Turkish port of Scanderoon

A STAIN IN THE BLOOD

The Remarkable Voyage of Sir Kenelm Digby

Pirate and Poet, Courtier and Cook,
King's Servant and Traitor's Son

Joe Moshenska

WILLIAM HEINEMANN: LONDON

1 3 5 7 9 10 8 6 4 2

William Heinemann
20 Vauxhall Bridge Road
London SW1V 2SA

William Heinemann is part of the Penguin Random House group of companies
whose addresses can be found at global.penguinrandomhouse.com.

Copyright © Joe Moshenska 2016

Joe Moshenska has asserted his right to be identified as the author of this
Work in accordance with the Copyright, Designs and Patents Act 1988.

First published by William Heinemann in 2016

www.penguin.co.uk

A CIP catalogue record for this book is available from the British Library.

ISBN 9780434022892

Typeset in 12.5/16.5 pt Fournier MT Std
Jouve (UK), Milton Keynes
Printed and bound by Clays Ltd, St Ives plc

Penguin Random House is committed to a
sustainable future for our business, our readers
and our planet. This book is made from Forest
Stewardship Council® certified paper.

For Rosa
Socia itineris mei

CONTENTS

CONTENTS

LIST OF ILLUSTRATIONS

CAST OF CHARACTERS

The Digby Family

Digby, Everard (c.1578-1606). Kenelm's father: tall, handsome, elegant and multi-talented, with a weakness for convoluted schemes and a tendency to place too much faith in his friends.

Digby, George (1612-77). Son of the Earl of Bristol, he has spent much of his childhood in the Spanish court and is fluent in its language and customs. Shares many of his distant cousin Kenelm's enthusiasms from literature to astrology.

Digby, John (1605-45). Kenlm's younger brother. Shorter and more heavily built than his older sibling, John lacks something of Kenelm's appetite for learning but more than makes up for it with immense physical strength and prowess with a blade.

Digby, John, later Earl of Bristol (1580-1653). Kenelm's distant relative and patron. One of the king's most valued diplomats, entirely au fait with the delicate ins-and-outs of court life, he brings Kenelm along on the young man's first trips into Europe. Transformed in *Loose Fantasies* into **Aristobulus.**

Digby, Kenelm (1603-65). The protagonist: a young man of many talents and with a voracious appetite for knowledge and new experiences, struggling to find his place in the world and escape the memory of his father's treasonous death. Transformed in *Loose Fantasies* into **Theagenes.**

Digby, Mary, née Mushlo (c.1581-1653). Kenelm's mother: she was originally more pious than her husband and inspired his conversion to Roman Catholicism. Following his execution she has devoted herself to a devout and cloistered life. Transformed in *Loose Fantasies* into **Arete.**

Digby, Venetia, née Stanley (1600-33). Kenelm's childhood sweetheart, of great beauty, fine character, and rare intelligence. She constantly finds herself beset by rumour and gossip of the most base and malicious sort. Transformed in *Loose Fantasies* into **Stelliana.**

Dyve, Lewis (1599-1669). Stepson to the Earl of Bristol, he is more interested in the women of Madrid than in the political and religious debates to be found there. Transformed in *Loose Fantasies* into **Leodivius.**

Stanley, Sir William (date of birth unknown, d.1629). A spendthrift Catholic gentleman, father of Venetia. Transformed in *Loose Fantasies* into **Nearchus.**

Others

Allen, Thomas (c.1540-1632). An aged and hugely learned Roman Catholic antiquarian and book collector, based in Gloucester Hall, Oxford, around whom a circle of brilliant young mathematicians frequently gathered.

Aubrey, John (1626-97). An eclectic polymath and pioneering biographer who pieced together detailed lives of Kenelm and Venetia among many others.

Bristol, Earl of. See **Digby, John, later Earl of Bristol.**

Buckingham, Duke of. See **Villiers, George, later Duke of Buckingham.**

Capello, Antonio (dates uncertain). A grizzled and experienced Venetian captain, he has been given command of the galleasses and galleys near the port of Scanderoon and tasked with ensuring that trade there continue uninterrupted.

Cervantes, Miguel de (1547-1616). After losing a hand in the Battle of Lepanto and spending years enslaved in Algiers, he produced a series of magnificent works crowned by his novel *Don Quixote*.

Charles I. See **Stuart, Charles.**

Coke, Sir John (1563-1644). An adept administrator who had devoted his life to expunging ingrained and widespread naval corruption. He is the client of Fulke Greville, poet and politician, one of the last great Elizabethans.

Contarini, Alvise (1597-1651). Venetian ambassador to England, he reports court gossip and political events back to his masters, the Doge and Senate of Venice, and defends the Venetian Republic's interests in England.

Dallam, Thomas (c.1575-c.1630). An expert organ maker who, in 1599, made a voyage to Constantinople with a gift from Elizabeth I to the Sultan, and kept a detailed voyage of his travels.

Drake, Sir Francis (1540-1596). To the English, the greatest naval hero of the Elizabethan age, and heroic defeater of the Armada; to the Spanish, a scurrilous and godless pirate.

Frizell, James (dates uncertain). The Levant Company's semi-official agent in Algiers, he knows both the opportunities and dangers of North African life, and is the first to suffer for the offences of English ships.

Galileo Galilei (1564-1642). The greatest astronomer and scientist of the age, renowned for his discovery of the moons of Jupiter. More controversial for his suspected support for Copernicus's heliocentrism, and the revival of ancient atomism.

Heliodorus (dates uncertain, 3ʳᵈ-4ᵗʰ Century CE?). An ancient Greek writer of whose life little is known. His great work, the rambling and complex novel *Aethiopica*, was rediscovered in a Hungarian monastery in 1526. Inspired later writers from Cervantes to modern novelists.

Howard, Thomas, Earl of Arundel (1585-1646). An austere and cultured nobleman, a rival and sworn enemy of the Duke of Buckingham, and the greatest collector and connoisseur of ancient and modern European art in England.

Howell, James (c.1594-1666). A well-travelled and curious young man who has witnessed the workings of Venice and Madrid. One of Kenelm's closest and most loyal friends, with a rather ill-advised tendency to intervene in duels.

James I. See **Stuart, James.**

Jonson, Ben (1572-1637). The greatest poet and playwright living in England, growing corpulent in his old age and surrounding himself with young acolytes and imitators, on the look out for a dashing young patron.

Laud, William (1573-1645). The rising star in the English church, becoming Bishop of London in 1628 and Archbishop of Canterbury in 1633. His love of ceremony and religious splendour matches King Charles's, and he is fascinated by Greek and Arabic learning.

Matthew, Tobie (1577-1655). The charismatic son of an archbishop and a convert to Catholicism, who has spent much of his life enjoying the pleasures of Florence surrounded by friends and admirers.

Medici, Maria de' (1575-1642). A member of the famous Florentine dynasty who married King Henri IV of France in her youth, following his death she entered into a series of schemes and plots, some directed against her young son, Louis XIII. Transformed in *Loose Fantasies* into **The Queen of Attica.**

Napier, Richard (1559-1634). A priest, chemical physician and expert astrologer, given to speaking with Angels. His book-lined rectory at Great Linford is not far from the Digby home of Gayhurst.

Nicholas, Sir Edward (1593-1669). Buckingham's secretary and loyal servant, who will do everything he can to thwart a young adventurer's ambitions when his master commands him.

Petty, William (1587-1639). The Earl of Arundel's agent in the Levant, he will stop at nothing to obtain the most rare and valuable pieces of ancient art.

Raleigh, Sir Walter (1554-1618). A heroic poet-adventurer during Elizabeth's reign, he fell from favour once King James made piece with Spain. After years of imprisonment in the Tower of London, where he conducted chemical experiments, he was finally executed.

Roe, Sir Thomas (1581-1644). Following a globetrotting earlier life that took him to Guyana and India, he spent the years 1621-8 as King James's ambassador to the Sultan's court in Constantinople, departing mere weeks before Kenelm's arrival at Scandcroon. A fervent Puritan.

Sidney, Sir Philip (1554-86). One of the great heroes of the Elizabethan age, the consummate courtier and author of the masterpieces *Arcadia* and *Astrophil and Stella*, he died young while fighting in the Low Countries.

da Sosa, Antonio (dates uncertain). A Portugese priest, he spent many years as a slave in Algiers at the same time as his countryman Miguel de Cervantes, and wrote at length of his impressions of the city.

Spenser, Edmund (c.1552-1599). The author of one of the greatest, longest and most complex of Elizabethan poems, *The Faerie Queene*, a sprawling romance mixing imaginative digression, political commentary and arcane philosophy.

Stradling, Edward (c.1600-1644). A Welsh gentleman from a well-known and cultured family, he is second-in-command on Kenelm's voyage and shares his love for abstruse verse.

Stradling, Henry (exact date of birth unknown, d. c.1649). An officer and younger brother to Edward.

Stuart, Charles, later King Charles I (1600-49). A nervous and hesitant young man, who grew up in the shadow of his charismatic older brother Henry and his father's favourite, George Villiers, before his travels in Spain allowed him to form his own convictions and determine the kind of king he intended to be. Transformed in *Loose Fantasies* into **The Prince of Morea.**

Stuart, James, King James I & VI of England and Scotland (1566-1625). A monarch who sees himself as a philosopher and strives to be the peacemaker of Europe, overcoming violent religious divisions in part through carefully chosen dynastic marriages for his children.

George Villiers is the latest of a series of beautiful young men to capture his affections. Transformed in *Loose Fantasies* into **The King of Morea**.

Van Dyck, Anthony (1599-1641). A Flemish painter and expert portraitist, he first visited England in 1620-21 and returned in 1632, when he quickly became Kenelm's close friend and the most renowned artist in the court.

Villiers, George, later Duke of Buckingham (1592-1628). The beloved favourite of King James I and closest friend of James's son, Charles. Devastatingly handsome and elegant but with a short temper and propensity to take political manoeuvres as personal insults. Transformed in *Loose Fantasies* into **Hephaestion**.

Wake, Sir Isaac (1580-1632). English ambassador to Venice during the period of Kenelm's voyage. An urbane diplomat with a taste for lavish spending.

Winthrop, John Sr. (1588-1649). A Puritan who, after becoming increasingly disillusioned by the direction of English religious change, is determined to emigrate to New England. Founder of Connecticut.

Winthrop, John Jr. (1606-76). A pious young man with a passion for alchemy and the arcane learning of eastern lands, he decided to travel into the Mediterranean in search of secret wisdom before traveling with his father to New England. Later governor of Connecticut.

Wotton, Henry (1568-1639). Former English ambassador to Venice, an expert on Italian art, architecture and customs, and first biographer of the Duke of Buckingham.

Wyche, Peter (exact date of birth unknown, d.1643). Thomas Roe's successor as King James's ambassador to the Sultan's court in Constantinople.

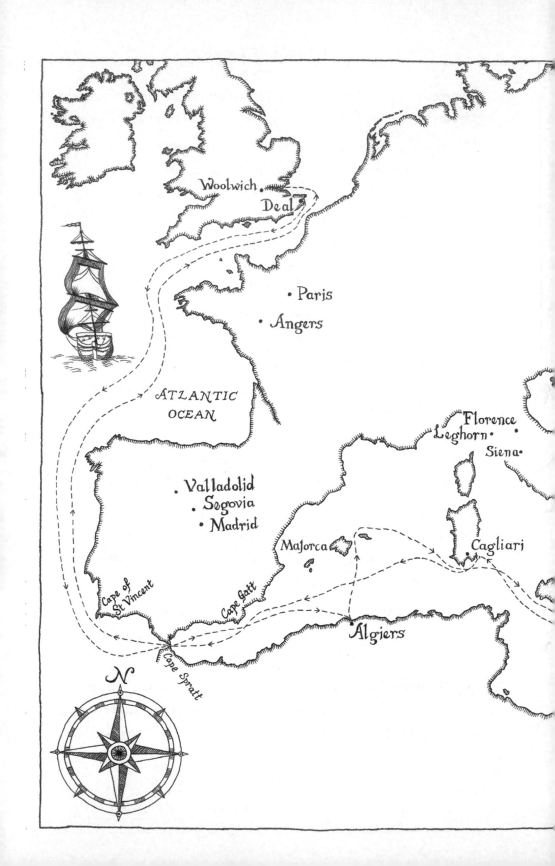

Woolwich

Deal

Paris

Angers

ATLANTIC
OCEAN

Florence
Leghorn
Siena

Valladolid
Segovia
Madrid

Majorca

Cagliari

Cape of
St Vincent

Cape Gatt

Algiers

Cape Spratt

N

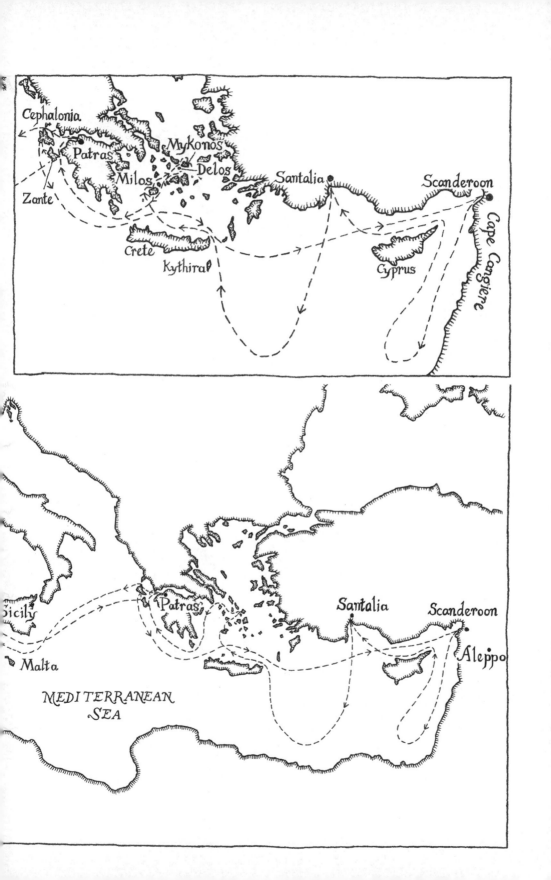

PREFACE

5 June 1665
London

I

Just before dawn on 5 June 1665, a terribly sick man sat in his chambers on the north side of Covent Garden Square and readied himself for a long journey. Approaching his sixty-second birthday, Sir Kenelm Digby had outlived many of those closest to him, and for some months he had realised that his own days were drawing to a close. His mind was as active as ever, but his body was failing: the imposing frame that had seen him loom over his contemporaries had been bent double by spasms of pain running through his abdomen and his long limbs. He had drawn up his will, written in his gorgeous, looping handwriting, and as June began he prepared to depart from London. The large and rambling set of rooms in which Kenelm sat, and which he steeled himself to leave behind, were packed with reminders of what he had lost, and of what he had experienced and achieved. The sumptuous foreign furnishings, such as the 'spanish tables', richly patterned Turkish carpets, tapestries and damask-clad chairs dotted throughout, were a mark not only of cosmopolitan taste, but of a lifetime spent zigzagging between England and the furthest corners of Europe. Five years previously, following the restoration of Charles II to the throne, Kenelm had been one of many notable English exiles who returned to England from Paris, but even among this nomadic crowd he was distinguished by his restlessness. He had seen the splendours of the Spanish court as a boy of fourteen on his first foreign jaunt; he had sampled the intellectual and artistic delights of Tuscany and Rome, mixing with scholars, cardinals, and even the Pope; he had ventured through the colder expanses of Northern Europe, exploring Germany and even the fringes of Scandinavia. His had been a life made up of travels, of incessant enquiry and discovery, but this appeared likely to be his final journey.

As dawn broke, a knock at the door announced the arrival of George Hartmann, Kenelm's steward and assistant. Hartmann explained that a horse-drawn litter was waiting for his master in the elegant arcade that ran beneath his building facing on to the square. As Hartmann left his master to his final preparations, Kenelm slowly rose and surveyed the splendid walls of the great room in which he stood. Looming over him, their dark depths gradually revealed by candlelight and the first hint of the summer sun, were a number of imposing paintings, to which Kenelm had clung throughout his travels. He cherished them in part for the hand that had executed them – that of his dear friend Anthony van Dyck, who had electrified the English court in the 1630s with the poise and lustre of his compositions – and in part for what they depicted. There were a series of intense religious scenes – Christ taken down from the Cross, St John the Baptist in the wilderness, Mary Magdalene transported with ecstasy by the singing of a heavenly choir – an immediate reminder of Kenelm's piety, and of the religion into which he had been born. This was the religion for which, when Kenelm was a tiny boy, his father had been willing to commit treason and suffer an appalling death – he was hanged, drawn and quartered in the churchyard of St Paul's Cathedral; the religion in which Kenelm's mother Mary had insisted on raising her two sons in the face of overwhelming hostility; the religion to which his wife Venetia had remained faithful until the dreadful night in 1633 when she died suddenly in her sleep. The solemn glow of the paintings was not just comforting for Kenelm, however, but chastising. He had never rested comfortably with the faith in and for which his parents, his brother and his wife had lived and died; he had struggled to bring his idiosyncratic mind into line with its orthodoxies and its authorities.

There, in the midst of these pious scenes and frozen in place by the magic of van Dyck's brushstrokes, was Venetia herself on her deathbed, her features as still as marble. Her head was propped on her wrist as if she was only slumbering, and her left eye was very slightly open, holding out the impossible promise that she might still wake. Nearby, resting on a low table, lay other chilling relics, the plaster casts of her face, hands and feet taken in the hours after her body was found, as if she could be extracted from time, her fragments petrified and retained. A mile away, in Christ Church on Newgate, stood the funeral monument that he had ordered to be built after her death, but here in his rooms he had constructed a different kind of shrine.

Around these paintings, and framing their pious glow, loomed numerous shelves of books, all that remained of the magnificent

3

Kenelm's wife Venetia, painted on her deathbed in 1633 by Anthony van Dyck

collections that had once been his. Some he had lost amidst the turbulence of the times – he had left a splendid library behind in London once before which was destroyed by Parliamentary troops, while the bulk of the new collection that he had painstakingly assembled while in exile remained in Paris, too bulky and expensive to transport. He had not only lost books, however: in the words of his first biographer, John Aubrey, Kenelm 'was very generous, and liberall to deserving persons.' He gave volumes away to his friends, to those he admired, and especially to the great libraries that sprang up in his lifetime: an astonishing treasure trove of medieval manuscripts, a bequest from his own teacher and mentor, to the Bodleian in Oxford; and an expensive set of theological tomes to the newly founded Puritan institution of Harvard in distant New

England. Even after so many books had been lost and given away, though, the shelves that lined his London chambers still held thousands. These were not merely dusty authorities for Kenelm, but living, breathing presences. 'My books,' he wrote, '[are] my faithful and never failing companions.' Even their covers became miniature memorials, the spines stamped with a monogram in which the letters 'K', 'D' and 'V' were intermingled, Kenelm and Venetia Digby entwined together in perpetuity.

In pride of place were the books that Kenelm himself had written, giving full rein to his expansive mind. The Earl of Clarendon, who knew him well, wrote that Kenelm possessed 'such a volubility of language, as surprised and delighted', and Aubrey called him 'master of a good and gracefull, judicious stile': words flowed unstoppably from Kenelm's mouth and from his pen throughout his life. Among the shelf of volumes that he had authored were musings on the mysteries of theology; his philosophical magnum opus, the *Two Treatises* on the nature of body and soul, in which he explored the fundamentals of the physical and metaphysical

The monogram stamped on to the binding of many of Kenelm's books

realms; and, most recently, his botanical treatise *A Discourse Concerning the Vegetation of Plants*, which he had read before the newly formed Royal Society two years previously following his election as a fellow. On the shelf below his own writings, his eyes rested on those of the great men whom he had befriended and with whom he had conversed and debated: the philosophical musings of René Descartes and Thomas Hobbes; the dizzyingly complex work of Pierre de Fermat, the greatest mathematician of the age; and the writings of Ben Jonson, including a magnificent series of poems dedicated to Venetia's memory, which Kenelm had helped to edit following the playwright's death. Below and beyond the achievements of his illustrious friends, Kenelm surveyed the hundreds of other volumes by writers ancient and modern: huge tomes and tiny pocketbooks, printed texts and meticulously hand-written manuscripts, poems, tales of adventure, great works on religion, philosophy and science, written in English, French, Italian, Spanish, Greek, Arabic and Latin. These were pages in which Kenelm had not only felt the thrumming and the pulsing of the past, but had also found the inspiration and the resources for the life that he had lived.

Footsteps echoing up the stairwell announced the imminent arrival of his most trusted servants, two men named George Hang-master and Mr Aurelius, who were coming to help Kenelm descend to the waiting litter and out into the London morning. He turned from the shelves and shuffled slowly towards the doorway, glancing as he went into the adjoining chambers. In them he glimpsed the sparkle of polished tin, copper and glass as the rising sun entered his well-stocked kitchen. He employed two cooks – George Hang-master's wife Anne, and another named Mrs Brooks – but he had also passed many happy hours labouring in here himself. Wherever he had travelled, Kenelm wasted no opportunity to sample strange and unfamiliar delicacies, and to learn new recipes and techniques which he transcribed and sought to replicate. Now, he surveyed the tools he had assembled for these attempts: pie-plates, syllabub dishes, brass and iron kettles, countless ladles, forks and tongs, scales, graters, colanders, brewing tubs and many more, by means of which a dazzling array of ingredients could be combined, transformed, and sampled. His chambers were also fitted out with a well-equipped and fully functioning laboratory, and he could not depart without peering into this room for a final time. It was here, right up to his final days, that Kenelm had continued to practise the chemical and alchemical experiments that were also a lifelong obsession: here he heated his furnaces until they would melt sand into glass, from which he deftly fashioned cutting-edge wine bottles and artificial gemstones; here he scorched the bodies of crayfish, in the hope that he could later resurrect them from their ashes. Much of Kenelm's equipment did double duty in the kitchen and the laboratory, and there was no firm line for him between cookery and chemistry, nor between alchemy and science: all were overlapping ways of understanding, transforming and enjoying the minute and messy particulars of the world around him.

The footsteps arrived at his door, and a tentative knock informed him that the time for departure had arrived. As he limped from his chambers, he paused by the 'greate writeinge chayre with whings' next to his desk, in which he had passed much of the preceding weeks setting his affairs in order. Sitting for a brief moment, he snatched up the tiny oval portrait of his wife, made for him in Paris decades before, from which Venetia stared with an impassive and unchanging gaze, surrounded by finely wrought loops the colour of emerald and sapphire and tiny white figures bearing swags of fruit and flowers. It was fashioned from gold and painted with enamel, and on the back, in Latin, were inscribed words which painfully reminded Kenelm that no earthly journey he might undertake would have his wife at its end. 'He tries to snatch a ghost from the funeral pyre and fights a great battle with death,' they read. 'Everywhere he searches for thee – O, the bitterness of it – on a piece of metal.' As he thrust this memento into his inner pocket with one twisted hand, with the other he reached into the bottom-most drawer of the desk, rummaged beneath a pile of papers, and pulled out a small and unprepossessing volume. Unlike those that lined his shelves, it had no rich binding or embossing; though he had once intended to present it to the world, this work had become Kenelm's most intimate secret, and it contained the pages on which he had striven to record and to transform his memories, his life, his entire character. A glance at the first page confirmed the title he had once given it, and which he had perused countless times since in private moments: *Loose Fantasies*. He slipped it into his pocket, and hobbled out into the morning air.

II

The sixty-two years of Kenelm's life encompassed one of the most eventful and dizzyingly transformative periods in the history of England, and of the wider world. He was born on 11 July 1603, four months after the death of Queen Elizabeth I and the ascension of James VI of Scotland as James I of England. In 1618, when Kenelm was fifteen, the King's daughter and son-in-law ill-advisedly

A miniature portrait of Venetia, made for Kenelm in France

agreed to be crowned as monarchs of the eastern European region of Bohemia, thus triggering an all-out religious and political conflict that would devastate much of the Continent for three decades. Changes in England were no less violent and dramatic: James died in 1625 and was succeeded by his son Charles, who faced a revolutionary challenge to his kingship in the Civil Wars of the 1640s, and was executed as a tyrant in 1649. After a decade of republican rule, largely overseen by the Lord Protector, Oliver Cromwell, Charles II was restored to the throne in 1660, some five years before Kenelm's final journey. In a time of repeated upheavals and starkly polarised divisions, Kenelm was one of the few men able to adapt repeatedly to changing circumstances, flourishing amidst the turmoil and winning admiration from all sides in the political, religious and intellectual disputes erupting around him.

The chaos and strife engendered by the age through which Kenelm lived, however, also prompted an astonishing efflorescence in the realms of human thought and endeavour, as men and women strained to come to terms with the horrors and the emerging possibilities that they witnessed. Kenelm observed the birth of modern science and medicine, in Galileo Galilei's radical new account of the heavens and William Harvey's argument for the circulation of the blood, and the beginnings of modern philosophy. He experienced an age in which religion was not only becoming violently polarised, but assuming novel forms, from newly founded pious orders to radical utopian sects: a response both to scientific developments, and a rising awareness of the differing religions that proliferated around the world, from China to the indigenous people of North America.

It was a period in which the corners of the earth were increasingly linked by stable trade routes, bringing the exotic splendours of Asia and the Americas into European homes and marketplaces. But if the revolutions in all these areas seemed to point towards a rational and enlightened future, Kenelm also lived during an epoch fixated on, and saturated by, the past: deepening studies of Latin, Greek, Hebrew, Arabic, Syriac and Aramaic opened up new vistas on ancient and distant worlds; the authoritative texts of antiquity and Scripture remained authoritative but were opened up to new forms of scrutiny and scepticism; the rise of archaeology and antiquarianism opened up new appreciations of historical distance and difference; and the most dusty and obscure of scholarly disputes could assume urgently topical and controversial significance. Amidst these wider currents of change, both drawing upon them and influencing them deeply, was the great flourishing of art and literature through which Kenelm lived: he was born into the England of Shakespeare, Donne and Jonson, and by the end of his life Milton, Marvell and Dryden were in the midst of their greatest achievements. He walked through the great cities of Europe whose squares and palaces were being transformed by the creations of Rubens, Velazquez, Poussin and Bernini.

This was an age of reason and superstition, of tolerance and sectarian hate, of fanatical certainty and unmoored scepticism, of stifling authoritarianism and creative freedom, of an iconoclastic desire to open a new future and a nostalgic urge to cling on to tradition. It was an age in which fact and fantasy could blend, intermingle and inform one another – an age when the richest imaginings often assumed something of the solidity of history, and the events of a single life could be elevated from mundane happenings to the lofty heights of myth.

Kenelm Digby, more than any other individual, encapsulates within a single life and character both the sheer thrilling variety of this period in history, and its deepest and most compelling contradictions. He lived his life in constant contact with the harsh facts of political and religious struggle, and of personal loss; yet he also strove constantly to shape these harsh states of affairs through the power not only of his actions, but of his imagination. As well as an omnivorous reader he was an inveterate teller of stories, especially his own. Determined to achieve his ambitions, and to free himself from the burdens of his past, Kenelm realised that the only way to do so was by reinventing himself, making his own life into a compelling tale in which the disparate strands of his identity could be woven together. He was a mutable and kaleidoscopic figure, dancing deftly between an astonishing array of spheres, and living a life that expressed the deepest tensions of the age; yet he knew that he remained utterly singular, in his activities and in his character, and sought every means by which he could display this uniqueness to the world.

These were endeavours that preoccupied Kenelm for his entire life. The small, unprepossessing book that he stuffed into his pocket and took with him when he left Covent Garden in 1665 represented his most daring act of self-transformation, one that had taken place nearly four decades before, during a year-long voyage into the furthest reaches of Europe. Written in the sweltering heat of a Greek island in August 1628, with the noisy festivities of his Muslim hosts, his officers and his crew echoing in the distance, it was the story of his remarkable voyage, but also of his earlier life, of the travails and intimacies of his love for Venetia, of his deepest hopes and desires. He rewrote his own life as a romance, a tale of noble heroes and virtuous heroines, unsettling sorcerers and nefarious seducers, pure virtuous love and unadulterated wickedness. He renamed himself 'Theagenes', and his beloved Venetia became 'Stelliana', while England became 'Morea' and London 'Corinth', and every other person and place that had mattered to him assumed a similarly altered guise. He fused the tale of his life with the tales from the books he loved, creating a work in which no reader would be able entirely to disentangle fact from fantasy.

The story of Kenelm's voyage of 1628 stands at the centre of his own story, reflecting and shaping not only his own personal history, but that of the nation. Until he left for the Mediterranean, Kenelm and those who were dearest to him had been harried,

The handwritten key that a later hand added to the *Loose Fantasies*, explaining the people and places that Kenelm renamed as he wrote

chastened and limited by the stories that others told about them — the rumour, gossip and sheer lies to which they fell victim. Above all, he risked being defined by 'a stain in the blood' — the legacy of a crime for which his father had been condemned to die, and whose bitter memory threatened to overshadow all of Kenelm's ambitions and his promise. Kenelm embarked upon his journey to the Mediterranean in order to free himself from these burdens; but he travelled, above all, so that he could find the freedom to reinvent himself, the freedom to live out the greatest story that he would ever tell.

This book, like Kenelm's own life, centres around his voyage of 1628. It begins with his own past — with the events, the hopes and the fears that shaped his early years, and that led him ultimately to take to the seas. By then following Kenelm into and around the Mediterranean, it becomes possible to witness the formation of his mind and his character: during his travels he drew upon his unique range of previous experiences, and fused them with the events and sensations from his travels into something entirely new. As he made his return voyage and re-entered English life following these adventures, Kenelm never ceased looking back on his voyage, striving to understand what he had experienced and who he had become, and to present his achievements to the world in the most compelling manner. Although his striving both for self-understanding and for success was a lifelong endeavour, this part of his story ends in 1633, with the death of Venetia. This dreadful event marked another decisive break in his life, dividing it into a before and an after; but the way in which he strove to come to terms with this personal tragedy, and the habits of mind and action that remained with him until the end of his life, show how fully he remained the man that he first became during his remarkable Mediterranean voyage.

Excursus: The Brazen Head

Fryer Bacon reading one day of the many conquests of England, bethought himself how he might keep it hereafter from the like conquests, and so make himself famous hereafter to all posterities. This (after great study) he found could be no way so well done as one; which was to make a head of Brass, and if he could make this head to speak (and hear it when it speaks) then might he be able to wall all England about with Brass. To this purpose he got one Fryer Bungey to assist him, who was a great Scholler and a Magician, (but not to be compared to Fryer Bacon). These two with great study and pains

so framed a head of Brass, that in the inward parts thereof there was all things like as is in a natural mans head.

Then called Fryer Bacon his man Miles, and told him, that it was not unknown to him what pains Fryer Bungy and himself had taken for three weeks space, only to make, and to hear the Brasen-head speak, which if they did not, then had they lost all their labour, and all England had a great loss thereby: therefore he entreated Miles that he would watch whilst that they sleep, and call them if the Head spake. Fear not, good Master (said Miles), I will not sleep, but harken and attend upon the head, and if it doe chance to speak, I will call you.

At last, after some noise the Head spake these two words, TIME IS. Miles hearing it to speak no more, thought his Master would be angry if he waked him for that, and therefore he let them both sleep.

After half an hour had passed, the Head did speak again, two words, which were these: TIME WAS. Miles respected these words as little as he did the former, and would not wake them, but still scoffed at the Brasen head, that it had learned no better words.

Then the Brazen-head spake again these words: TIME IS PAST. And therewith fell down, and presently followed a terrible noise, with strange flashes of fire, so that Miles was half dead with fear. At this noise the two Fryers awaked, and wondered to see the whole room so full of smoke, but that being vanished they might perceive the Brazen-head broken and lying on the ground: at this sight they grieved, and called Miles to know how this came. Miles half dead with fear, said that it fell down of it self, and that with the noise and fire that followed he was almost frighted out of his wits. Fryer Bacon asked him if he did not speake? Yes (quoth Miles) it spake, but to no purpose.

From *The Famous Historie of Fryer Bacon . . . Very Pleasant and Delightfull to be Read* (London, 1627).

Part I

Time Is
Time Was
Time Is Past

I

1603–1620
Buckinghamshire – Madrid – Oxford – France

I 'A Foul Stain in his Blood'

The very first time that ever they had sight of one another, [they] grew so fond of each other's company, that all that saw them said assuredly that something above their tender capacity breathed this sweet affection into their hearts ... It was the perfect friendship and noble love of two generous persons, that seemed to be born in this age by ordinance of heaven to teach the world anew what it hath long forgotten, the mystery of loving with honour and constancy, between a man and a woman; both of them with the vigour of their youth, and both blessed by nature with eminent endowments, as well of the mind as of the body.

'Alas,' said Stelliana, 'be not so unjust as to tax him with what thou knowest he cannot remedy.'

'Nay, but,' said Faustina, interrupting her, 'let not passion blind you altogether . . . Theagenes hath hardly escaped, by his mother's extreme industry, with the scant relics of a shipwrecked estate, and from his father hath inherited nothing but a foul stain in his blood for attempting to make a revolution in this state.'

'Methinks, Faustina,' replied Stelliana, 'you speak in his prejudice with more passion than you can accuse me of in loving him . . . for although it be the custom of these times to lay a punishment beyond death upon those that conspire against their prince or their government, that so by making it extend to their posterity, it may, peradventure, deter some . . . from attempting upon their own sacred persons and from making innovations in the laws; yet it seemeth to be with this condition, that if the son in himself deserve the contrary, he shall be esteemed and cherished according to his own merit, in which the father's offence is then drowned; so that it rather becomes an incitation for him to do virtuous and worthy actions, than any stain or blemish.'

On the night of 5 November 1627, aged twenty-four, Kenelm paced restlessly across his chambers in London as he strove to shut out the sounds of the outside world. He was 'a goodly handsome person', but now an expression of fear and indignation distorted his fine features, his slightly bulbous brow furrowing; his mouth, surrounded by a neat reddish beard, twisting as he muttered his frustrations to himself. He was hugely tall and heavily built, his long legs carrying him across the confined space of the room in just a few strides, his hands clenching and unclenching into great fists. For the past few months, Kenelm had devoted himself with single-minded focus to practical preparations for a voyage that he was determined to undertake. He had been negotiating a fair price for his ships, scouring the city for able seamen to crew them, and stockpiling barrels of gunpowder, water and salted beef. All the while he had worked energetically and adaptably to circumvent the obstacles that threatened to delay his departure, or to prevent it altogether. He had become increasingly convinced that these were not mere mishaps, but surreptitious attempts by the most powerful man in the land – the Duke of Buckingham, the King's closest friend and advisor – to derail his carefully laid plans. But Kenelm was not deterred, and had convinced himself that he could prevail and set out as planned. He was determined to leave behind the memories and damaging rumours that he knew would haunt him for as long as he remained in England, and sail towards new and thrilling possibilities.

As the sun set on 5 November, however, and the city began to vibrate with flickering shapes and raucous noises, Kenelm realised that, for this night at least, there would be no escape from the darkest of the doubts that echoed in his mind. Throughout the course of the day, Londoners had stacked up great heaps of wood and refuse in any available open space; now, at nightfall, the inhabitants stood ringed around each of the piles while torches were thrown on and they ignited with a low roar like a great breath being let out across the city. As they did so, the bells of every church, from the smallest parish chapel to the tall tower of St Paul's Cathedral, began to ring with a joyous jangle that cut through the winter streets. The crowds, tumbling from the taverns and holding cups of liquor aloft, screamed their approval, breaking into spontaneous songs and chants and cavorting through the midst of the city.

The festivities marked the anniversary of the Gunpowder Treason of 1605, the dark scheme from which King James I had been so miraculously delivered just two years into his reign, when a group of disillusioned Roman Catholics had tried and failed to blow up the Houses of Parliament. Every year throughout the two decades and more since the foiling of the plot, its memory had been drilled into the collective consciousness of the nation by a deluge of sermons and printed histories, until it was as established a cornerstone of the annual calendar as Christmas. In the months that Kenelm had fought to arrange his departure, he had steeled himself to endure once again the yearly ordeal in which his compatriots were repeatedly and gleefully exhorted: remember, remember the fifth of November. The nation seemed as one to offer to God 'Thankfull remembrance of thy great and wonderfull deliverance' from 'our Enemies, the Papists', and their 'hellish powder'. 'For which deliverance, upon the 5. of November, 1605., we sung praise, and expressed our joy, with Boonfiers and praises to thy holy name.' The memory of the event, scored ever deeper into the minds of men, women and children across the country who were urged to mark it 'yearly and forever', confirmed their status as a nation specially chosen and protected by God who had 'snatcht us like Brands from the mouth of the Furnace', and it bound them together as one.

For Kenelm however, the night of 5 November brought not effusive celebration, but the flooding back of the darkest recollections of his childhood. He had been forced to endure the cackling and collective glee that erupted around him each year, for as long as he could recall; but in 1627, as he prepared for his voyage, the peals of bells and laughter and the smell of smoke drifting in through his tightly shuttered windows forced him back into himself with particular urgency, back to the very dangers and memories that made him so determined to leave England behind. He was desperate to set out for the Mediterranean, to begin the voyage that he had expended such effort in planning; but the festivities that thrummed so loudly in the background made him realise that he could not simply escape from the events that had inspired his journey. He would have to look back into his own past, more fully than he had previously forced himself to do, before he could embark upon the creation of a new present for himself.

The botched attempt to blow up Parliament in November 1605 had been followed by an equally ill-fated attempt over the ensuing days to incite rebellion in the Midlands, in which a forlorn gang of plotters 'wandred a while through Warwickshire to Worcestershire, and from thence to the edge and borders of Staffordshire', looking for sympathetic Catholic households and dragging a cart of weapons along with them. Among their number, towering over his fellow conspirators by more than a head, was a striking man in his late twenties named Sir Everard Digby. He had rushed from his family's home at Gayhurst in Buckinghamshire to join the ragged procession, leaving behind his wife Mary, and his two infant sons – Kenelm, who was a little over two years old, and John, who had been born just a few months previously. The conspiracy quickly collapsed, and Everard was taken prisoner after trying to hide in the woods.

Brought from the Tower to his trial for high treason, Everard managed even to impress the judges who condemned him to death: he breezed into the courtroom dressed in a loose taffeta gown and a suit of black satin, and delivered a long discourse in which he insisted that he had acted not from treacherous hatred but only due to 'the friendship and love he bare' for Robert Catesby, one of the chief conspirators. He then made an impassioned plea that his wife and sons not be punished for his crime, and, uniquely among the condemned plotters, he openly 'confessed that he deserved the vilest death, and most severe punishment that might be'. 'Those who were present at his trial,' one witness reported, 'could not restrain their wonder.' Once the sentence which he demanded had been duly handed down, 'Sir Everard Digby bowing himself towards the lords, said, if I may but hear any of your lordships say, you forgive me, I shall go more cheerfully to the gallows. – Whereunto the lords said, God forgive you, and we do.' On 20 January 1606, Kenelm's father was dragged by horses through streets lined with spitting and screeching householders to a gallows that had been erected in the churchyard at St Paul's. His magnificently composed behaviour continued beneath the gibbet, where Everard clung doggedly to his self-appointed role as insouciant courtier, offering cheery greetings to all of those present, 'as he was wont to do when he went from Court or out of the City, to his own house in the country'. He managed to display 'warmth of feeling, and even light-heartedness' while staring death in the face, and a dreadful death it was, inflicted upon him 'with more than usual cruelty', brutally butchered while he was 'completely conscious and alive'. His valour and defiance, though, persisted until his very last breath. He was hanged almost to the point of death, before the public executioner cut open his chest and ripped out his heart, holding it before the crowd and proclaiming 'this is the heart of a traitor': the dying man somehow managed to gasp out the words, 'Thou liest.' Once the breath had finally left his body the executioner sliced off his genitals, opened his belly, and struck off his head, to be disposed of at the King's pleasure. The crowd watching this grisly spectacle, even those who had bayed for Everard's blood minutes before, 'marvelled at his fortitude' and talked 'almost of nothing else'.

According to family lore, the infant Kenelm, who was miles away in the family home of Gayhurst when his father met this awful fate, leapt from his nurse's knee and cried out 'Tata, Tata,' at the exact moment of Everard's death. Whether or not this deep intuitive connection did indeed exist between them, Kenelm was haunted by his father's memory. As he grew, it became increasingly clear to Kenelm, and to all those who knew his father, just how closely the pair resembled one another. Everard had impressed all those who met him, and was admiringly called 'as complete a man in all things that deserved estimation or might win affection, as one should see in a kingdom'. He was 'a gallant Gentleman, and one of the most handsomest men of his time' – even 'accounted the handsomest Gentleman in England'. Unusually tall, 'of stature about two yards high', and 'skilful in all things that belonged unto a gentleman', Everard astounded and dazzled all he encountered with his 'countenance so comely and manlike'. As Kenelm grew, he became increasingly aware of the impact that his own height, good looks and dazzling physical presence had on those around him, and he gradually realised that he was becoming ever more like his father. If Everard was tall and strong, Kenelm was likewise 'Gigantique' and endowed with a 'great voice', developing into 'a Person of extraordinary strength', powerful enough to lift a fully grown man and the chair in which he was sitting above his head using just one arm.

Kenelm was too young to recall his father's arrest and imprisonment, but Everard's memory was unavoidable, and his spectre threatened to overwhelm his son's life from the outset. While awaiting trial in the Tower of London, Everard had written a letter placing an impossible burden on his infant child. 'Let me tell you, my son Kenelm, you ought to be both a Father and a Brother to your unprovided for Brother and think, that what I am hindered from performing to him by short life . . . so much account yourself bound to do to him, both in Brotherly affection to him, and in natural duty to me.' Kenelm grew to be haunted by this sense of responsibility, of stepping into Everard's shoes, and he also developed an anxious awareness that he might have inherited from his father more than just his impressive physique and charisma. He had grown up in a Protestant England, a nation vocally committed to the harsh justice of the Old Testament God, who insisted upon 'visiting the iniquity of the fathers upon the children unto the third and fourth generation'. When, at his trial, Everard implored the judges to allow his wife and infant sons to inherit his goods and not leave them destitute, the prosecutor, the ferociously Protestant Attorney General Sir Edward Coke, spitefully intoned the words of Psalm 109: 'Let his children be fatherless and his wife a widow; Let his children be continually vagabonds, and beg; Let his posterity be cut off, and in the generation following let their name be blotted out.' Fortunately for Kenelm, Coke's cruel hopes were frustrated: Everard had taken the precautionary step of bequeathing his property to his son before embarking on the plot, and King James mercifully stopped short of beggaring the entire family. The Earl of Clarendon thought that Kenelm 'inherited a fair and plentiful fortune, notwithstanding the attainder of his father', and his mother ensured that he received around 'three thousand pounds per Annum', a significant sum. Although, in the aftermath of the Gunpowder Plot, ordinary Catholic homes across the country had been raided, treasured religious paraphernalia confiscated and destroyed, and families taunted and targeted,

Kenelm's family escaped the worst of this persecution despite his father's direct involvement. Mary was left relatively unmolested to devote herself to the same Roman Catholic religion for which her husband had died, and to raise her sons within its confines. Most remarkably, she was permitted to keep on living in the family home of Gayhurst, which was no small matter. It was a large and beautiful house that Mary's father, William Mushlo, had begun building in 1597, and when she and her husband had inherited it Everard threw himself into completing it with characteristic gusto until it rose to three elegant storeys of stone, with a classically pure and perfectly symmetrical outline, decorated with tastefully selected pillars and friezes. Mary was allowed to raise her sons in the midst of her disgraced husband's finest achievements.

Kenelm may not have been held as fully responsible for his father's crime as Coke had hoped, but his obvious resemblance to Everard was still unsettling. He never stopped agonising about 'the blackest and horridest plot that ever was hatched . . . who had my unhappy father involved in the ruines of it'. Everard was a traitor, but he was also a compelling and deeply impressive figure who managed to earn pity even from those who should have loathed him, and the awe-struck stories that circulated about his execution proved the enduring power of hearsay and gossip in the making of a reputation. For all his crimes, as a man he embodied much of what Kenelm hoped to be. Even his role in the Gunpowder Plot was remembered by the sympathetically minded as an error of judgement rather than a sin – an appalling slip by a man too invested in his friendships, and too susceptible to the lure of grandiose schemes. In his philosophical writings, Kenelm was fascinated by the nature of hereditary characteristics, observing 'that even in particular gestures, and in little singularities in familiar

Gayhurst in Buckinghamshire, the home in which Kenelm was raised

conversation, children will oftentimes resemble their parents, as well as in the lineaments of their faces'. Throughout his early years he clung on to the hope that he might prove to the world that he was not his father reborn, even as he remained fully aware of the traits and 'little singularities' that he could not have helped inheriting. He would have to emulate his father's undeniable bravery and magnetism, while compelling the world to remember him in a very different way.

Mary Digby had understandably retreated from public life following her husband's trial and execution, cloistering herself away in Buckinghamshire at the family home, Gayhurst, and devoting herself to prayer and lamentation. Her husband might have been willing to die for his faith, but she was the more deeply pious of the two: they had both been won over to the Roman Church by the prominent Jesuit John Gerard, but it was Mary who was much keener to discuss 'Catholic doctrine and practice' while her husband was busy hunting and hawking, and he converted some time after her and thanks in large part to her persuasions. She arranged for Catholic tutors who would school her two sons in the religion to which she continued to cling, hoping that an inconspicuous and provincial life would keep them safe from the suspicious eyes of those who remembered Everard all too well. One of the men who taught Kenelm was the Jesuit John Percy, sometimes known as Fisher, who had been instrumental in the conversion of Mary and Everard; after the discovery of the Gunpowder Plot he had gone into hiding in the nearby village of Harrowden, but he surreptitiously rode over the hills to Gayhurst to hear Mary Digby's confessions, and to school her sons. Percy was steeped in theology and an expert in religious polemic, and he was the first to open Kenelm's eyes, from a young age, to the realities of the confessionally divided world around him. When he was not having his faith formed by Fisher, Kenelm devoted himself to honing the other skills expected of the elder son of a gentry family; his mother ensured that he had some training in horse-riding, swordsmanship and dancing, and that he learned to speak French and Italian. He also undertook some activities less expected of a young gentleman, constantly nosing around the kitchens and watching the cooks at work, and spending hours observing the birds in the dovecote that stood just to the south of the kitchen, on the corner of its herb and vegetable garden. Before long he could ride by himself through the fields that undulated around Gayhurst, hunting game in the surrounding woods, or finding a quiet spot in which to sit with a book. Despite the shadow under which he still lived, Kenelm's early childhood was happy and fairly sheltered, though not protected from the terrifying diseases to which all children were prone: he suffered a 'great and dangerous sicknesse' at the age of two and a half, another at the age of eight, and a 'desperate and mortall sicknesse' that overtook him shortly before his twelfth birthday and 'continued a prettie while'.

Not long after he survived this last bout, when Kenelm was just entering his teens, the wider world intruded in a different and altogether more delightful way. Not far from Gayhurst lived a middle-aged couple named Francis and Grace Fortescue, who had recently taken in a relative of theirs: a girl named Venetia Stanley. She was three years older than Kenelm, and even at a young age the pair had much in common. Both had already endured the death of a parent: Venetia's mother, Lucy, had died when she was only a few months old. Sir Edward Stanley, her father, 'retired himself to a private and recollected life' and grieved for the loss of his wife, appreciating her fully only once she had departed. Devoting himself wholeheartedly to his new status as a mourning widower, Stanley sent Venetia and her sisters to the country to live with the Fortescues. Venetia's parents, like Kenelm's, were Roman Catholics, and so were her hosts: Grace Fortescue, like Mary Digby, was 'a grave and virtuous lady', and the two women paid frequent visits to one another in their shared piety, allowing the two young people to meet and talk. While the Digbys were respectable enough members of the gentry, Venetia came from rather loftier stock. 'The greatnesse of her heart and minde,' Kenelm observed, 'was aequall to her birth, the noblest and the highest that ever I knew; her minde was sutable to the blood that ranne in her vaynes, which I may boldly and safely say, was inferior to no subjectes upon the earth.' Her grandfathers were the Earls of Derby and Northumberland, great noblemen. 'Two such rivers, running with so pure streams . . . I am sure few subjectes bloods in Christendom can boast of.' Venetia's bloodline may have been lofty, but it was not beyond reproach: her maternal grandfather Thomas Percy, seventh Earl of Northumberland, had been centrally involved in the attempt to place Mary, Queen of Scots, on the throne in the early 1570s, and was publicly and unrepentantly beheaded in York. Venetia's blood might be pure and noble, but it too was not without the stain of family treason.

In his most enthusiastic moments, Kenelm allowed himself to believe that in some cases 'there is a naturall appetence and inclination to love, betweene two, even at first sight', and that this was so with him and Venetia, as soon as he saw her dark hair and eyes, and her pale skin with the 'litle moule upon her cheeke'. He felt transformed by meeting her, and it seemed to mark the end of his youth, the end of one stage in his life and the beginning of another. 'Till I saw and knew and loved her and was loved by her,' he rapturously wrote, 'my palate relished such pleasures as other men delight in; but ever since that time, I have looked upon the pleasing entertainments of my most boiling youth with such valuation of them as I did then upon the fond toyes and sportes that delighted me in my childish yeares.' Caught up in the first flush of passion, Kenelm idealised the older and more mature young woman and placed her on a pedestal. 'Miracle of woman,' he considered her, 'so like an Angell she looked as I had much adoe to keepe my selfe from kneeling downe to her.' He was overwhelmed, and coped in part by transforming the captivating and challenging young woman whom he had encountered into a bland encyclopedia of the virtues that she possessed: 'true magnanimity, courage, sweetnesse of disposition, candor and ingenuity, integrity, constancy, stayednesse, discretion, solid judgement, and all other vertues of an heroyke mind'.

Kenelm never relinquished this urge to view himself and Venetia as the hero and heroine of the perfect love story, but he was also sufficiently self-aware to aim affectionate mockery at those who 'paint out nothing but perfections and excellencies' when describing their beloveds. 'Their language,' he wryly noted, 'is all in the measure and cadence of Romanzes.' He was attracted by such ideals, but became ever more aware that they bore little re-semblance to the messier reality of two people falling in love, which was a process more unsettling and delightful. As he got to know Venetia, he formed a more realistic and sensitive appreciation of her qualities. Chasteningly, he came to realise that the instant explosion of strong feeling that he felt for her was not immediately reciprocated: older and less impetuous, she 'was slow in coming to this height of affection; and I thinke defended her selfe all she could against it'. He found her intriguing precisely because getting to know her was not a straightforward matter. 'She was not easie to contract a familiaritie with any, though she was most pleasingly affable to all.' He came to value Venetia's more cautious and ruminative manner, which usefully complemented his own impulsiv-ity and eventually developed into a stable and enduring love. 'When it had taken fire, never flame burned clearer.' What began in 'the first violence and heate of a passionate and extreme love', gradually grew into 'a solide vigorous and peacefull friend-ship'. Kenelm increasingly appreciated Venetia's virtues not only as lofty abstractions, but for their place in everyday life. She was possessed of a 'strange calmnesse', so different from his own excitable state. This serenity was enlivened by an irrepressible cheerfulness, 'inclined rather to mirth and free conversation than to thoughtfulnesse and melancholy retiredness', but she tempered her sociable impulses with 'modesty and circumspection'. She was compulsively truthful, and 'knew not how to tell a lye so much as in jest or sport'. She had a playful side, though, and a taste for risk: she was a keen gambler, often winning considerable sums at the card-table that she would not keep to herself but send 'to some poor religious houses beyond the seas'. Playing late into the night took its toll, for she was not a morning person: though she forced herself to rise early each day for two hours of prayer and meditation, it 'was a great mortification to her, for she loved much her sleepe and rest'.

As his appreciation of these idiosyncrasies grew with their increased familiarity, Kenelm came also to value Venetia's intelligence and habits of mind: her fine memory, making her 'soddainely apprehensive of any thing that was taught her which afterwardes she never forgate', and the sharpness of her reason and her judgement. He particularly admired, and hoped to emulate, her brilliant talent for adapting herself to changing circumstances. 'Her mind was composed of so aequall a temper as it could bend it selfe wholly to whatsoever the present occasion required.' He listened with 'exceeding delight' when she spoke confidentially to him of other people's characters and actions, making 'admirable strong observations', and often changing his mind about those whom he had known far longer than she had. He respected her as a judge of people, and believed that he could 'learne more from such naturall collections and discourses of wisdom than from the studied eloquence of Philosophers'. While he remained tempted to view her as simply perfect, he came to love her precisely for her ability to combine in her character a rich mixture of contrasting tendencies. 'Majesty and sweetnesse, awefulnesse and mildenesse, gravity and gentlenesse, were strangely mingled in her behaviour and presence.'

Kenelm fell ever more deeply in love with these facets of Venetia's character as he got to know her, but he frankly admitted to himself that he might never have come to know of them had he not first been riveted by her beauty. 'A faire outward shape,' he admitted, 'is a powerfull invitement to draw one to examine what guest dwelleth in that beautiful pallace.' All who saw Venetia from this young age agreed that she was startling – 'an extraordinary beauty', Clarendon called her, while Aubrey described her as 'a most beautifull, desireable Creature', gushingly praising her 'lovely sweet-turn'd face, delicate darke browne hair', oval face and brown eyes, and her cheeks, just the colour of a damask rose 'which is neither too hott, nor too pale'. Kenelm was equally prone to mask Venetia's beauty in syrupy clichés and generalities – she was 'the goodliest, the loveliest and the sweetest creature that ever I saw' – but as with her virtues, while they were falling in love he came to appreciate her appearance all the more because it was not flawless, and because he knew its peculiarities better than any. Her face was striking, but he could not stop gazing on it precisely because it was difficult to determine what made it so. 'It was not immediately winning at first sight,' he admitted. Her growing reputation meant that many came to her 'with the great expectation of a miraculous beauty' and were disappointed, since 'it was the second or third sight of her before all her excellencies were discerned'. In the early years that he spent with her he had the chance to familiarise himself with the minute details of her face, from the high forehead with skin so fair that 'the blewnesse of her vaines' was visible at her temples, and as they grew he would come to know all the 'specificall differences and markes upon her bodie'.

Like him she was much taller than average, with long limbs that she moved 'with wonderfull grace and dexterity'. Her nose was long and straight with somewhat flared nostrils, but her mouth and ears were small, the latter 'so admirably made and finely turned that it was a full delight and a satisfying beauty to looke upon them alone'. There was something unsettling and thrilling to Kenelm about Venetia's physical form. Her body seemed to shimmer elusively even as he got to know it better than anyone, eluding him altogether or revealing hidden depths and further levels of complexity that mirrored the layers of her character. Her hair was 'tending to browne', but so fine that 'I have often had a handful of it in my hand and have scarce perceived I touched anything'. Likewise her flesh was 'firm, and yet so gentle and smooth as it seemed to escape ones touch'. It seemed at first like the alabaster skin of the elusive women whom Kenelm had encountered in countless poems and tales, but 'if you looked heedfully to it you might discerne the upper superficies of it to be extreme pure and white, and that under it there shone a most lively and fleshly ruddiness'. Likewise her eyes were not simply brown, as Aubrey believed: only Kenelm had stared into their depths with enough intensity to realise that they were 'composed of a mixture of all that is best'. At times they seemed green, at others sea-blue, but finally their beauty was too mobile for any such fixed label. 'In a word, some thing there was that I cannot describe, for these colours express it not.'

35

As Kenelm became ever more wonderingly aware of the mingled riches of Venetia's character and her beauty, his mother became increasingly concerned, and began 'with watchful eyes, armed with longing, hatred, and jealousy, continually [to] observe all passage' between the pair. While Venetia's religion and her lineage made her an attractive match for Kenelm, she was, unfortunately, exceedingly poor. She should have been heir to a vast estate from her Percy and Stanley ancestors – 'as great a share of inheritance as any woman in England these many yeares' – but unfortunately it had passed first into the hands of her father, with considerable latitude as to how it should be used. Sir Edward had 'suffered his daughters to be abused and plainely cheated of what should have come to them by their mother', due not to malice but extreme haplessness and gullibility: he had 'a generous and large heart', Kenelm admitted, and was 'a foe onely to himself and his children'. Distracted by grief for his late wife, Sir Edward had allowed much of his fortune to slip away, and was embroiled in interminable legal battles over the remainder. Mary Digby had only barely extracted a reasonable inheritance from the ruins of her husband's treason, and it was imperative for the survival of the family that her elder son make a good marriage to a respectable woman of fortune.

Kenelm was unwilling, for the sake of such mundane worldly concerns, to suppress the love that grew every day until it had possessed him in his very being. He made every effort to continue seeing Venetia, resorting when necessary to secretive and illicit means. His mother could not stop them participating together in the hunting parties that roamed near Gayhurst. These frenzied rides revealed Venetia to Kenelm at her most vivacious and exuberant, freed from the strictures that usually governed the behaviour of demure young ladies: on one such venture, he looked on admiringly as Venetia, 'coming in to the death of the partridge before any of the company, with admirable agility and with out helpe of any bodie leaped of from her horse to save the hawke from a dogge that else had killed her'. 'By Heaven,' he reflected, 'I never saw any thing so lovely as she looked then . . . The lively red and heate that the hard course had putt her in and the sparkling of her spirits in her eyes and her earnestnesse to succour the hawke, and her nimble bestirring her selfe and the confidence she came with all to the angry faucon.' She was magnetic in such moments, fearless and adept, more inadvertently herself than in the quiet moments they were able to snatch elsewhere. While preparing for another expedition, this time in pursuit of a stag glimpsed in the forest around Gayhurst, Kenelm managed to slip a note into Venetia's glove, asking her to leave the main hunt with him the following day. When the moment came, she veered off suddenly as if her horse were bolting, and 'ran so furiously away that everyone that saw her was in much fear in her behalf' but could not keep pace with her. The pair rendezvoused in 'a wild place' where the rest of the company could not find them, and there, beneath a tree where 'we sheltered ourselves against a shoure of raine', he openly declared his love for her and, for the first time 'joining his lips fast to hers, all other language was stopped between them both, whilst their souls ascending to the very extremities of their tongues, [and] began a mystical discourse'. Venetia eventually ended the kiss, 'like one starting out of a profound sleep that were broken by some affrighting dream', and moved to flee the grove in which they stood; Kenelm threw himself on his knees, and begged forgiveness for his forwardness.

This fervent and waterlogged kiss was a fittingly dashing

expression of the passion that had been building in Kenelm, and now burst uncontrollably forth. When he saw Venetia leaping nimbly from her horse, he could not help marvelling that 'if the ancient poets had ever seen such a sight, Diana would have been more beholding than she was in their eyes'. He refracted her instinctively through the prism of the antique writers whom he revered. The whole episode bore an uncanny resemblance to the most famous love scene in all of ancient literature, from Virgil's *Aeneid*, in which Dido and Aeneas consummated their own love while separated from a hunting party and taking refuge from a storm. Mary Digby's role as the overbearing mother, striving to thwart her son's pure affections, gave a folksy, fairy-tale feel to this lofty scene. As Kenelm grew into his early teens, he developed the deep love of reading that he would retain throughout his life, and which encompassed everything from the pious theological tomes that he studied with John Fisher to the stories of love and adventure that he devoured in his spare moments. Already, as he ventured out into the world around Gayhurst and into the world of ideas, these books were starting to inform his deep sense of who he was. In his early years and in the first throes of his love, Kenelm was already living a life where fact and fiction blurred, shaped by the tales that he avidly consumed.

The untroubled childhood that he had been allowed to lead, and the deepening love for Venetia that occupied ever more of his thoughts, encouraged Kenelm to hope that he might escape the shadow of his father's legacy, and grow into a very different kind of man. In one respect, at least, they were very unlike one another:

Everard was 'skilled in all things that became a gentleman', and 'very cunning at his weapon', but he was no great scholar, his reading restricted mostly to books of Catholic spirituality. Kenelm's brother John more closely followed their father from a young age in his mixture of fervent piety and expertise in 'martial affairs': he was so devout that 'hee seemed even with his nurses milke to have sucked piety and devotion', but, as Kenelm affectionately noted of his younger sibling, 'he is not an enemy of study, though he be not naturally addicted to it'. Kenelm, by contrast, was an addict from his early years, his deep love of books swiftly apparent: he inherited his father's conversational charm, but fuelled his own loquaciousness with the words and ideas of the books he read. It became clear that his sharp mind and fast-expanding knowledge had quickly outstripped the Catholic tutors to whom Kenelm's mother had entrusted his education, and she set about seeking a more suitable guide for his youthful studies.

The man who was selected for this task was named Richard Napier, and he was based in the village of Great Linford in Gloucestershire, which lay only a few miles from Gayhurst. Napier was perhaps not an obvious choice, since he was an ordained Protestant minister, 'a Person of great Abstinence, Innocence, and Piety' whose 'Knees were horny with frequent Praying' and who harboured anti-Catholic views in line with his vocation. As well as a priest, though, Napier was a physician – indeed, one of the most admired and sought-after doctors in the country – and his medical practice brought him into contact with people of widely varying religious persuasions and social status. He had known the Digbys since before Kenelm's birth, visiting Gayhurst and treating Everard and other members of the household, and he could be trusted. The bright young man and the learned doctor-priest quickly bonded over their shared bibliomania: Napier's library was 'excellently furnished with very choice books', and Kenelm borrowed 'whole cloak-bags' crammed with them, slinging them over his shoulder as he rode through the fields back towards the family home. Napier observed, with affectionate admiration, that Kenelm was 'addicted to all maner of learning'. The pair became close friends, and before long Kenelm was addressing his teacher with the familiar nickname by which he was generally known, 'Parson Sandie'.

Napier opened his young charge's eyes to more than just the shelves of his library. He owed his renown as a doctor in large part to his unrivalled expertise in astrology, while he was also fascinated by alchemy and employed it in the preparation of chemical recipes. He meticulously scrutinised the bodies of his patients, but believed that such examination had to be complemented with equally careful attention to the arrangement of the stars in the heavens. Napier also believed that he did not conduct his cures unaided, but with the assistance of benevolent spirits: and not just any common-or-garden spirits, for 'he did converse with the Angel Raphael', who was particularly helpful in medical matters and 'told him, if the Patient was curable or incurable'. In the Rectory at Great Linford, Kenelm was first introduced to the mysteries encoded in the stars, and inducted into the smoke and fire of chemical transformation. He also learned from Parson Sandie that to devote oneself to such pursuits did not involve unthinking superstition and credulity. To identify the right herbs and minerals and then to transform them into effective medicines required the same skills practised by a botanist or a chemist; likewise, the astrologer gazed at the heavens with as much attentiveness as the astronomer, and the two activities overlapped and aided one another. Parson Sandie helped Kenelm for the first time to locate himself firmly within the universe. He cast his young pupil's horoscope, showing the exact configuration of the planets at the moment of the young man's birth, and made certain predictions regarding his life and character: the sextile of Mercury and Venus helped to explain Kenelm's love of literature and art, while Venus in Gemini pointed towards striking encounters with women of the sort that he was already experiencing. Kenelm learned to apply the skills that Napier taught him in order to understand not only himself, but also Venetia's character and her physical form, observing that 'all such specificall differences and markes upon her bodie as I have read . . . do belong to those that are borne under the dominion of Venus'. To read the role of the heavens in this fashion did not mean giving up responsibility for one's life, or seeing one's character as determined from birth: casting a horoscope required intense self-scrutiny, each detail of a life carefully recalled and ordered. With Napier, Kenelm discovered not only the mysteries of the heavens, the alchemist's limbeck and the spirit world, but also new ways in which to tell and retell his own life story that intermingled with his growing love of adventurous tales.

II 'The Entertainments of the Mind'

Theagenes, although the great strength and well-framing of his body make him apt for any corporal exercises, yet he pleaseth himself most in the entertainments of the mind, so that having applied himself to the study of philosophy and other deepest sciences . . . he is already grown so eminent, that I have heard them say, who

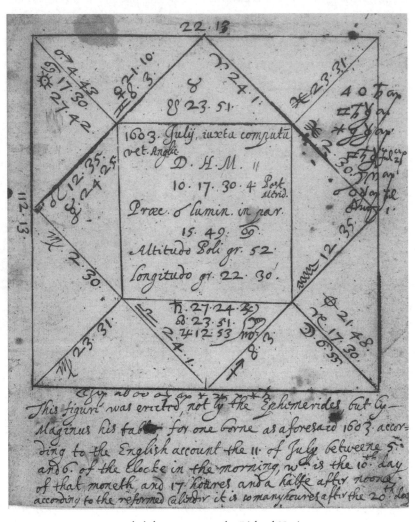

Kenelm's horoscope, cast by Richard Napier

have insight that way, that if a lazy desire of ease or ambition of public employments or some other disturbance do not interrupt him in this course, he is like to attain to great perfection: at least I can discern thus much, that he hath such a temper of complexion and wit, that his friends have reason to pray God that he may take a right way, for it cannot keep itself in mediocrity, but will infallibly fall to some extreme.

He had obtained leave to travel into foreign parts for two or three years, that course being usually followed in the education of the youth of quality and eminency in Morea, that by so conversing with several nations, and observing the natures and manners of men, they might enable themselves with good precepts, drawn from experience, and by variety of observations upon sundry and new emergent occasions, learn to banish admiration, which for the most part accompanieth homebred minds, and is the daughter of ignorance: 'Of which fair pretences,' said Theagenes, 'I will make my benefit to get free out of these dangers, and then I will stay so long abroad until riper years may in me challenge the disposal of myself. Then shall I come home free from these fears that now hold my soul in continual anguish.'

Theagenes took his journey into Attica ... coming one masque-night to the court with the company that importuned him to go along with them, [he] was by one of the ladies, that had known him at Athens, taken out to dance; in which he behaved himself in such sort, that whether it were the gracefulness of his gesture ... or whether the heavens had ordained he should be the punisher of the Queen's past looser affections, she felt at the first sight of him a secret heat creep through her veins, which soon grew

*so violent that it made her forget her own greatness, and languish so
in melting desires, that she almost died in thinking what happiness
it would be . . . to die a loving death in the arms of him whose
name she knew yet not.*

Kenelm's horoscope also showed Jupiter and Mars in affliction at
the moment of his birth, which predicted foreign adventures and
unusual pursuits. By 1617, when he was nearly fourteen years old,
these seemed unlikely given the relatively cloistered life that Mary
Digby had chosen for her sons' protection. He had expanded his
experiences and his mind through his time with Venetia and with
Parson Sandie, but had as yet seen little of the world. This changed
with the arrival in his life of another new and powerful influence.
If Kenelm's childhood was quiet and private, then during the same
years his relative, John Digby, had grown to ever increasing prominence. Despite their shared surname they were in fact quite distant
cousins, but word of Kenelm's precocious intellectual talents
brought him to his relative's attention. Guilt may have played a
role in provoking John Digby's interest: he himself had first come
to the notice of James I in the aftermath of the Gunpowder Plot,
when he was sent to inform the King that the plotters' plan to
seize his daughter Elizabeth had failed. The same conspiracy that
propelled Everard towards the scaffold catapulted John Digby into
public life, and by 1607 he had been knighted. His obvious talents
enabled him to take advantage of the tectonic shifts under way in
English politics, and particularly the increasingly close connections
that were developing with Continental Europe. Within a year of
assuming the throne in 1603, the year of Kenelm's birth, King
James had ended the long war with Spain that defined Elizabeth I's
reign, and made peace. Diplomatic relations were restored, and

Kenelm's relative John Digby, Earl of Bristol

in 1611 John Digby was sent to Madrid as the first English ambassador for many decades.

James was determined to establish stable relations with the great European powers, and even harboured hopes of brokering peace and achieving religious unity across Europe. His most powerful means for doing so was the pursuit of carefully chosen marriages for his children. Fervent English Protestants who were appalled at the new rapprochement with the Catholic enemy invested their hopes in James's eldest son Henry, Prince of Wales, who combined religious seriousness with cultured sophistication and martial skill: but to universal despair, in November 1612, aged only eighteen, he fell ill of typhoid fever and died. Early in 1613 James's daughter Elizabeth, who shared her deceased brother's religious convictions, married the Protestant Frederick, Elector Palatine, and in order to maintain his balanced stance James began to consider marrying his younger son Charles, a shy and awkward boy with little experience of public life, to a Catholic princess. It was in part this possibility that John Digby was sent to Madrid quietly to investigate, and though his own Protestantism inclined him personally to oppose the marriage, he proved an effective and discreet servant to the Crown. He familiarised himself with the Byzantine structures and glacial pace of Spanish diplomacy, the reverence and formality that the King and his chief ministers expected; he learned how to balance the opposed factions at court and their respective priorities, and developed a network of informers; he perfected his own Spanish and won the respect of King Felipe III and his most powerful advisors. As John Digby embedded himself in Madrid like no Englishman before him, he moved progressively upwards in King James's estimation. Having been summoned back to England to deliver a full update in 1616, by early 1617 John Digby was preparing to return again to Spain: it was then that he visited Gayhurst and proposed that young Kenelm join his retinue. The idea may originally have been Mary Digby's – it seemed a perfect way for her son to gain more worldly experience and get to know his powerful relative, while removing him from Venetia's company.

A month past his fourteenth birthday, in July 1617, Kenelm arrived in Spain, his first experience of the foreign lands which he knew only through books. It was also his first time setting foot in a Catholic country: after a childhood spent celebrating Mass in the secret confines of Gayhurst, surrounded by prying eyes and hostility and the haunting memory of his father's execution, here was the religion of his birth being practised publicly, and amidst gorgeous splendour. Kenelm was afforded a remarkable degree of independence, and during eight months of travel he was even permitted to break away from the main body of the embassy in order to accompany a number of other young men on a sightseeing tour to Valladolid. This city had been the royal capital in the sixteenth century, and again early in the seventeenth: it boasted a rich array of palaces and churches, as well as the English College, where Catholic priests were trained before being sent on missions into England. For the first time, Kenelm could interact with people who shared his religion in public discussions, not clandestine gatherings behind the walls of Gayhurst; he could wander through the city's churches and relish the gory splendours of baroque sculpture, like the bleeding, supine Christs in the churches of San Pablo and San Martín, created by the local master, Gregorio Fernández. Finally, these sights and conversations buzzing in his mind, he rendezvoused with John Digby in Madrid.

After returning from Spain Kenelm decided, with his mother's full approval, to interrupt the course of his and Venetia's love once again, and relocate to Oxford where he could devote himself fully to his studies. He arrived in the autumn of 1618, soon after his fifteenth birthday – not unusually young by the standards of the time. His particular college, Gloucester Hall, was carefully chosen as a safe haven for young Catholics. Kenelm was able to pursue his studies there without formally matriculating – thus he 'did not weare a gowne there', as Aubrey noted – since this would have required a public declaration of loyalty to the Church of England. He might have departed from the family home, but this was still not a place in which Kenelm could openly be himself, and his life continued to be carefully regulated and scrutinised.

Within the walls of Gloucester Hall, however, he discovered new freedoms of the mind. The main attraction that the college held for him was the presence of one of the most eminent Catholic intellectuals in the country, Thomas Allen. There was a remarkable convergence between his wide range of expertise and Kenelm's own emerging interests, and the young man quickly became one of Allen's favourite and most trusted students, while 'a great friendship' sprang up between them. In the time that they spent together, the intellectual explorations that Kenelm had begun to undertake with Parson Sandie's guidance were thrillingly widened and enriched. There was an extraordinary degree of continuity in his education: Allen was 'the best astrologer of his time', and as practised as Napier in the casting of horoscopes. This was only one facet of his voracious learning, the fruits of a long life spent as 'an unfeigned lover and furtherer of all arts and sciences'. Already an old man in his late seventies when Kenelm arrived at Gloucester Hall, Allen had published almost nothing but he revealed to his young charge the other ways in which ideas could be exchanged and debated directly. Though he had resisted public employment and controversy in favour of 'the sweetness of a retired life', he was no brooding hermit but was 'generally acquainted' and 'a very cheerful, facetious man', proving that immense learning could sit side by side with quick wit and a sense of humour. He would ride into the country to visit friends and patrons during the university vacations, and 'every body loved his company, and every Howse, on their Gaudie-dayes, was wont to invite him'. He was scarcely less sociable during term-time, when a group of brilliant young minds would gather in his rooms in Gloucester Hall and debate the most up-to-date questions in philosophy, and especially in mathematics – he was considered 'the very soul and sun of all the mathematicians of his time'. For the fifteen-year-old Kenelm, used to exploring such abstract ideas in solitude or solely with the guidance of Parson Sandie, it was thrilling to be part of a passionate and quick-witted cohort. These gatherings were an electrifying glimpse of the intellectual life that he aspired to live.

If Kenelm had grown up feeling that his family's shameful history was a deep threat to his own hopes and aspirations, then Allen's example also showed him that the immediate present could be enriched rather than overshadowed by the past. He offered Kenelm a link to history in more than one way. His advanced age meant that he had met and mingled with great figures of a bygone age: he had cast the horoscopes of two of the great Elizabethan heroes, Sir Philip Sidney and Robert Dudley, Earl of Leicester, and had also taught Sidney mathematics. While Allen entertained his young charge with stories of these men, his bookshelves opened up for Kenelm the entire history of human achievement. Napier's rectory had given Kenelm access to an excellent provincial library; now he could wander freely within one of the finest private collections in England. Allen owned hundreds upon hundreds of rare and beautiful manuscripts, some heavy and replete with gorgeous illumination, others humble and moth-eaten, all crammed with the most astonishing range of writings. There Kenelm could sample the riches of Chaucer and other medieval English poets, of abstruse scholastic philosophy, of medicine and law, of the great ancient mathematicians from Euclid to Ptolemy, and seemingly endless others. He could also dive even further than he had with Parson Sandie into the deep waters of alchemy, astrology and other occult pursuits, in which Allen's collection was unrivalled. Even as he enjoyed these forays, however, he became aware of the strains that they placed on his master's reputation. Allen's library contained the finest collection to be found anywhere of the writings of Roger Bacon, the thirteenth-century friar who was alternately lauded as a prophetic genius and derided as a sorcerer. Allen lent these volumes to many of his young admirers, including Kenelm, who read them avidly, but as a result of his enthusiasm Allen himself 'was accounted another Roger Bacon, which was the reason why he became terrible to the vulgar . . . who took him as a conjuror'. The aged Allen – with his white beard, his nose buried in dusty and incomprehensible tomes, performing smoky experiments and creating optical illusions with the curved mirror that he had inherited from the philosopher-magus John Dee – perfectly fit the public image of a terrifying magician, especially since, as Aubrey put it, 'in those darke times Astrologer, Mathematician, and Conjurer were accounted the same thing'. His

Thomas Allen, renowned mathematician and conjuror of spirits,
who taught Kenelm at Oxford

servant, a man named John Murtagh, enjoyed mischievously stoking these rumours, telling 'Freshmen and simple people' that sometimes when he went to attend on his master in his rooms at Gloucester Hall, 'he should meet the Spirits comeing up his staires like Bees'. Murtagh may have made light of these popular fears, but for Kenelm they showed that the occult practices in which he was increasingly immersing himself were no guaranteed route to respectability. He was already seeking to make his way in the world despite the foul stain in his blood; he could hardly afford to dabble too openly in the darker arts.

Kenelm lingered in Oxford for over a year, from 1618 to 1619, enjoying the company of Allen and the circle of bright young things who clustered around him, and losing himself in the endless pages of his master's library; yet he already felt he had imbibed enough wisdom for the time being, and was itching to return to the wider world that he had tantalisingly sampled in Valladolid and Madrid, and the religious and artistic riches to which such travel had opened his eyes. He had kept his love for Venetia alive during his Oxford jaunt, snatching moments with her whenever possible during the long university vacations that divided the Michaelmas, Hilary and Trinity terms, when he would return to Buckinghamshire; but now his desire to expand his travels would mean seeing whether their deep connection could survive extended separation. Naturally his mother was delighted, and more than happy to support his desire to experience foreign climes. It was a bold moment at which to go abroad. Late in 1619 James I's son-in-law, the strongly Protestant Frederick, had foolhardily accepted the Crown of Bohemia after Archduke Ferdinand of Austria had been deposed, a move sure to outrage all of Catholic Europe. Even the most pessimistic could not have anticipated that these events would trigger a devastating and messy struggle that would drag on for three decades. While pious English Protestants rejoiced, the whole nation waited anxiously to see how the massed armies of the Habsburgs and their allies would respond to this affront. Kenelm, who had thoroughly enjoyed his first taste of elite European politics as a fourteen-year old, decided to experience this Continental turmoil for himself. His earlier months in Spain had exposed him all too briefly to forms of art and religion for which he felt a glow of instinctive affinity, as well as some glimmers of what life looked like at a great royal court. He was determined to expand and deepen the experiences that he had so far acquired.

Even after Kenelm had formed this resolution to travel extensively into foreign parts, organising his departure was no simple feat. He needed to obtain a document confirming that he had leave to travel: unlike a modern passport, permission was required to leave England, rather than to enter a foreign country. English people had never stopped coming and going from the Continent even during Elizabeth's more insular reign, and sometimes they did so for the oddest reasons: the Earl of Oxford, when 'making of his low obeisance to Queen Elizabeth, happened to let a Fart: at which he was so abashed that he went to Travell, for 7 yeares. At his return the Queen welcomed him home, and said "My Lord, I had forgot the Fart." ' While such travels had become more common during James's reign, for many suspicious Protestants their effect was even more noxious and offensive than this unfortunate episode of flatulence: as one bishop put it, all travel 'southward, into the jaws of danger' inescapably risked 'corruption of religion, and depravation of manners'. To leave the country was not merely to waste time: it was to risk a total and terrifying transformation. To such suspicious types, Kenelm's religion was already corrupted: their fear when it came to young Catholics of his ilk was that they would be further radicalised by their co-religionists abroad, and return ready to foment treasonous conspiracies. The previous year, in 1618, Kenelm's younger brother John had confirmed this sort of anxiety by choosing to depart for the English College at St Omer in Flanders, the famous Catholic seminary, where he could complete his education; the decision to leave devastated their mother, whose 'bowells yearned at the thought of her departure from hym, yet she sacrifized her private content to his greater future good'. Whether through his own efforts or his mighty relative John Digby's intervention, Kenelm was nonetheless able to negotiate his departure in the final months of 1619. By the end of March 1620 he wrote excitedly to Parson Sandie that 'I have now dispatched all my businesse and am to begin my journey tomorrow', and in April he made the short hop across the channel to Calais, with the intention of travelling onward to Paris.

Though he would eventually spend much of his adult life in the French capital, Kenelm's first visit was brief and fraught. The city was in the midst of a horrific outbreak of plague, and so Kenelm instead travelled onward to Angers, a city around a hundred miles to the south-west, 'inferior to none in all that country for wholesomeness of air, beauty of buildings, pleasure of situation, abundance of provisions, and courtesy of persons of quality that inhabit there'. After arriving, Kenelm realised that he had wandered into the midst of a political crisis so convoluted that it could easily have been lifted straight from the baroque plot of one of the revenge tragedies that were so popular on the London stage. The old King, Henri IV, had been assassinated by a Catholic fanatic in 1610, and his son had ascended to the throne as Louis XIII a few months before his ninth birthday. Until the boy-king reached his maturity, Kenelm discovered, 'the power and management of affairs remained with his mother, who, being a woman of great judgement and strong parts, carried business with a high hand'. This was Maria de' Medici, the Italian princess whom Henri had married in order to forge a useful dynastic alliance. Her early life in Florence among the rest of the Medici clan had given her first-hand experience of the plots and schemes through which a court could be successfully run. She made a serious error of judgement when, already viewed with suspicion by her French subjects, 'she cast the beams of her favour upon a gentleman of her country', another Florentine named Concino Concini, who became the Queen Regent's favourite and effectively shared her power. To be ruled by one Italian was bad enough, but two was more than the French nobility could bear. In 1617 Louis, now of age, led a rebellion against his mother: Concini was stabbed to death in the Louvre, and Maria was exiled to the city of Angers. When Kenelm arrived there in 1620, she was continuing to plot against her son, and these bitter familial and factional struggles divided the nation.

Kenelm had left England precisely to experience the hurly-burly of European politics, but he could never have expected to blunder into it so swiftly, or for it to become so thrillingly and so terrifyingly personal, as it did when he arrived in Angers, and swiftly captured Maria de' Medici's attentions. Kenelm was approaching his seventeenth birthday, and the mere sight of his handsome features and his long limbs as he pirouetted about the floor at a

Maria de' Medici, Queen Regent of France

court dance was enough to distract the Queen Regent from the power struggles with her son in which she was embroiled, and kindle a fire in her breast. She summoned the young man to her bedchamber, where she led him into a dark corner and declared, 'I was never truly happy till the first hour that I saw you.' Kenelm was understandably dumbfounded. No sooner had he left Venetia behind for an extended period than he found himself fending off another woman's blunt affections – and not just any woman, but one of the most powerful figures in France. He needed to maintain his faithfulness to Venetia, but avoid offending the Queen, and so he tried at first to appear oblivious or obtuse, behaving 'as if he had not comprehended the tenor of what she spoke', and took her passionate outpourings for mere civility. Maria, though, would have none of it, and baldly insisted, 'If you be resolved to contest or struggle with me, this bed is a fitter field for our wars.'

Kenelm was trapped in an impossible situation, torn between infidelity and offending a formidable woman. Fortunately for him, the violent political backdrop forced itself into the foreground at just the right moment: as he was dithering uncertainly about how to respond to her advances, 'many disordered troops of soldiers' charged the Queen's palace. The simmering tension between Maria de' Medici and her son was now boiling over; Louis XIII had run out of patience with his mother's plots, and his armies launched an assault against her followers and their gathered troops. After a brief but fierce battle, the young King's forces prevailed; his mother knelt before him and pledged allegiance to her son, and they were formally reconciled. This was not the end of the carnage in Angers, however: the Queen's demobbed soldiers, angry at their lack of pay, proceed to sack the town, 'and committed many murders'. Kenelm witnessed this scene of chaotic horror with deep disquiet, but he also realised that it presented him with an opportunity to extract himself from a difficult bind, and he resolved to seize it. Amidst the many men slain, he 'caused his servants to give out that he was one, himself lying concealed, in the mean time, in a friend's house: he hoping, by this means, to free himself from the trouble of the Queen's love, and from the danger of her fury'. He did what any sensible and honourable young man might do in order to protect his own life and reputation: faked his own death, and fled the country.

This tragedy of an untimely death amidst French political carnage was a compelling tale that not only convinced the Queen, but also winged its way further afield. As soon as he could, Kenelm wrote letters home to Venetia, 'to advertise her of his health, and to prevent the rumour of his death, which . . . might come to her ears'. Unfortunately, however, all of the letters went astray: some through sheer ill fortune, and others that 'were industriously intercepted and suppressed by his mother, who was jealous of his affection'. When the false news of Kenelm's death reached Venetia's ears, she was at first entirely numbed, before collapsing, devastated, into a storm of lamentation, and she 'spent many days without any diminution of sorrow'.

Venetia had initially remained unwavering in her love for Kenelm after his departure, maintaining the life of 'continual martyrdom' that she had determined to live while he was gone. The circles in which she moved and the experiences available to her, though, began to change markedly in his absence. Kenelm had complacently assumed, as he rode off to Great Linford to cast horoscopes and conjure spirits with Parson Sandie, or gallivanted off to Spain and enjoyed the patronage of his illustrious relative, or swapped witticisms and mathematical theorems with Thomas Allen and his disciples at Gloucester Hall, that Venetia would wait dutifully for him in quiet seclusion. But this was not so: she too had lost no opportunity to sally forth into wider society with an impatience to leave behind her provincial home, for 'as private as that place was, it seems her beauty could not lie hid'. When she first came to London she made a sensational entrance into court circles: 'the young Eagles espied her' and she was 'commonly courted, and that by the Grandees'. Richard, third Earl of Dorset, was particularly forward in his affections, but it was another, unknown and unscrupulous nobleman who saw an opening in her grief at Kenelm's supposed death. He wasted no opportunity to offer her comfort and sympathy, and Venetia gradually allowed him to visit her in private to talk, though she unequivocally insisted that since Kenelm's demise, 'her heart was also dead to all passionate affections'. Soon, though, their frequent and private encounters set tongues in the court wagging, and rumours began to fly which 'made a false construction of her actions'. Before Venetia even realised it, she had been lured into a deeply comprom-ising position: her new, sophisticated friends convinced her that since she had 'submitted herself to the world's censure' through her intimacies with this man, 'she could not now retire from him without much dishonour'. Gradually they wore down her resolve and, in her belief that her true love was lost for ever, 'a cold and half constrained consent' was wrung from her and Venetia agreed to become engaged to her devious suitor. When word of her betrothal reached Kenelm on his travels, it wrenched his soul. Collapsing in 'a torrent of fury', he tore from his arm the bracelet of her hair that Venetia had given him as a keepsake, 'and threw it into the fire that was in his chamber'.

Travelling independently for the first time, through countries where no one knew him, Kenelm was no longer defined by the stain left in his blood by his father's infamy, and was free to make himself the hero in a new kind of story. He never tired of telling the tale of Maria de' Medici's attempt to seduce him, and embellishing it with ever more salacious details. His formative years had made him acutely aware of the inescapable effects of rumour and insinuation: the spiteful gossip that came with being his father's son; the unmerited whispers that Venetia was beginning to attract; even the reputation for illicit sorcery ignorantly attributed to his mentor at Oxford. Forced to make his way through life amidst these half-truths, he resolved to spin some jaw-dropping tales of his own, which made it impossible to tell where the truth ended and something else, something so compelling and enjoyable that it seemed obviously preferable to the simple truth, began.

2

1620–1623
Florence – Siena – Madrid

I 'The Garden of the World'

*He transported himself over the sea into Ionia, intending to spend
some time in that pleasant climate, where the sun seemed to cast more
propitious beams than upon any other place. For in the fruitfulness
of the soil it may well be termed the garden of the world; and the
cities of it, which are many, being every one under a several lord,
the territories of them are so small, and the means of extending
themselves, by doing great actions abroad, so little, that those who
have noble minds must apply themselves to contemplative and
academic studies, wherein their spirits working upon themselves,
they are so refined, that for matters of wit, civility, and gentleness,
these parts may be the level for the rest of the world to aim at.
Here Theagenes resolved to detail himself some time, as well to
give himself content of noble and learned conversation, as also
to practise such exercises as befit a gentleman to have learned,*

*and are the worthiest ornaments of a mind well fraught with in-
terior notions, to attain to perfection, in which here is complete
conveniency.*

*It was his fortune to fall into the company of a Brachman of India,
who shaped his course the same way that he did; which man (as
his name giveth him out to be) was one of those that the Indians
held in great veneration for their professed sanctity and deep knowledge of the most hidden mysteries of theology and of nature . . .
With this man then, Theagenes (whose mind yet was not altogether
out of love with intellectual notions) entered into much familiarity,
whereby he had daily much cause not only to admire his wisdom,
but withal his grave conversation was mingled with so much grace
and with such attractive sweetness, that he grew very affectionate
to him.*

On 5 November 1627, Kenelm was jarred from his memories
by gleeful howls coming from directly below his window.
He bent and peeped through one of the wooden shutters, and saw
that a new feature had been added to the raucous festivities: the
crowd hoisted aloft a life-sized effigy of the Pope, with tattered
red robes and limbs of straw, and another of Satan himself, sporting
horns and a leering grin: the gathered throng tossed these man-
nequins into the nearest blaze, where they exploded into flames
and drew a huge cheer. Kenelm recalled with weary bitterness the
denunciations of the Gunpowder Plot that had seeped into his
consciousness over the years, in which the culprits were decried
as not only an affront to all things English, but to humanity itself:

'the quintessence of Satan's policy', one particularly indignant preacher had called the plot, 'the furthest reach and stain of human malice and cruelty, not to be paralleled among the savage Turks, the barbarous Indians, nor, as I am persuaded, among the more brutish cannibals'. It was largely thanks to pronouncements like this, Kenelm reflected, that he had always felt like an alien in the country of his birth simply by virtue of what, and not who, he was; sinking again into reminiscence, he recalled again just how liberated and at ease he had felt during his first extended travels into Europe, where to be a hopeful young Catholic made him not an inhuman savage or a traitor's son, but resoundingly normal.

Once he left the internal strife of France behind towards the end of 1620, and with rumours of his death still echoing around Angers, Kenelm longed above all to see Italy. He could have travelled south to Nice or Marseilles, and taken a ship to the Tuscan port of Livorno, but instead he chose to follow the French post-route along the upper Loire to Lyon, then continue through the Alps and through the Mont-Cenis pass towards Turin, eventually entering Tuscany from the north. Kenelm had hoped that France would provide him with the opportunity further to broaden his intellectual horizons, but plague and political strife had put paid to his plans. The internal struggles between the French King and his mother were as nothing compared to the fracture-lines that were appearing across Europe: in November 1620, a few months after Kenelm arrived in Italy, the armies of the Elector Palatine, James I's son-in-law, were routed by the Catholic armies at the battle of the White Mountain outside Prague. Frederick and his

English wife, nicknamed 'the Winter King' and 'the Winter Queen' for the brevity of their reign, fled into exile in the Hague, and the rest of the Continent braced itself for the next convulsion of what was becoming an all-out religious war. The ripples of the conflict were yet to reach Italy, though, and for Kenelm his arrival in Florence represented a welcome respite both from the anxieties he faced at home, and his travails in France. He settled contentedly into a new life and quickly familiarised himself with Florence, with its 'streets very long, streight, large, and faire . . . beautified with many stately Pallaces' that English visitors so admired. He felt both a thrilling sense of novelty, and the satisfaction of having arrived in a place where, finally, he could feel at home. All sophisticated people agreed that this country 'hath beene always accounted the Nurse of Policy, Learning, Musique, Architecture, and Limning [painting], with other perfections, which she disperseth to the rest of Europe'. Italy might have been the cradle of modern civilisation, but since the English Church had broken with Rome under Henry VIII it also came to be viewed by Kenelm's countrymen as the source of every depravity and vice. It taught young Englishmen, as one satirist put it, 'the art of atheism, the art of epicurising, the art of whoring, the art of poisoning, the art of sodomitry'. Even those who admired it had to admit that Italy 'is able to turn a Saint into a Devill, and deprave the best natures, if one will abandon himselfe, and become a prey to dissolut courses, and wantonnesse'.

Before he had left England, his relative John Digby had arranged for Kenelm to meet a man named Sir Tobie Matthew, who had told him what he should expect to find in Florence, and gave him letters of introduction to his friends there. Matthew, twenty-five years Kenelm's senior, had first travelled into Italy as a young man and become a high-profile defector to the Catholic Church: his father was the Archbishop of York, second only to Canterbury in the hierarchy of the English Church, and the conversion and subsequent ordination of such a luminary's son was a sensation. English Protestants lamented 'the fall of Mr. Tobie Matthew . . . from God's only saving and single truth, to this idolatrous church', a conversion which he did 'not only plainly but boastingly profess'. Matthew spent most of the decade after 1609 loitering in Florence, and as one of James I's ambassadors reported, 'There is in that town at the present a certain knot of bastard Catholics, partly banished and partly voluntary residants there, whereof Tobie Matthew is the principal; who with pleasantness of conversation, and with force of example, do much harm.' Matthew himself had returned to England in 1617, where he enjoyed scandalising all and sundry with his religious beliefs, while advertising his virtuosity in languages by translating the essays of his friend Sir Francis Bacon into Italian. The 'knot of bastard Catholics' who had clustered around him remained in Florence, though, and after he and Kenelm struck up a friendship Matthew ensured that the young man was welcomed into their circles. They were the perfect guide to the sights of the city: its 'large *Piazzes*', and the 'many statues' that they contained, as well as 'the most magnificent and admirable Fabrick of the *Duomo*' looming above them. They included men like George Gage, Matthew's closest confidant and lifelong companion, who was an equally staunch Catholic as well as a particular connoisseur of painting. These were men who had perfected the art of living their lives in various shades of grey, publicly asserting their identity as English Catholics yet drifting effortlessly between languages and nations, successfully shaping themselves to the exigencies of particular situations, and interacting cheerfully both with those whose beliefs they shared and those with whom they disagreed. They were sophisticated lovers of art and poetry, and wove these passions effortlessly into their political ambitions. Perhaps most importantly, they refused to let the political and religious complications in which they found themselves entangled get in the way of enjoying life or of immersing themselves in its intellectual, artistic and sensual pleasures. Growing up in England, Kenelm had felt the pull of conflicting loyalties and opposed parts of himself: his fidelity to his parents' religion and his desire to live a public life; his love of arcane learning, and his fear of the attacks to which its pursuit might open him. Arriving in Florence, he found himself for the first time in a city where he might not be forced to make excruciating choices about the kind of man he wanted to be, or the kind of life he wanted to lead.

The Medici family who had ruled Florence and much of the surrounding region since the fifteenth century – and one of whose members had thrown herself so startlingly at Kenelm in France – had long employed every effort to advertise their magnificence and discernment. They surrounded themselves with beautiful objects and the artists who created them, and promoted the 'many famous men in matter of learning' whom the city had produced, in current and former ages: from the three greatest writers of the Italian middle ages – Dante, Petrarch and Boccaccio – to the infamously cynical political thinker Niccolò Machiavelli. Nothing that Kenelm had seen in England, which was decades behind Southern Europe when it came to appreciation of painting and sculpture, could have prepared him for the dazzlingly crammed chambers of the Medici treasury. He had perused the extensive private libraries of his teachers, Napier and Allen, but the 'very faire and beautifull Librarie' built by the Medici in the church of San Lorenzo was on a different scale altogether, with its gorgeously carved roof 'of Cedar very curiously wrought with knots and flowers', and its magnificent collection of 9,000 leather-bound volumes.

It was not just the scale of public culture in Florence that astounded Kenelm, but its range. His Italian was already excellent before he arrived, honed with a private tutor at Gayhurst, but in this region, 'where the prime Italian dialect is spoken', he had the chance to perfect it, not only in conversation but by reading its greatest poets. He bought a learned commentary on Dante's *Divine Comedy*, but his prized possession was a stunningly beautiful manuscript of Petrarch's poems, replete with intricately patterned illustrations and illuminations. He pored over every line with care, but the pages that spoke to him most personally contained a fragment of Latin prose in which Petrarch described his grief at hearing of the death of his beloved Laura in 1348 during the Black Death. Petrarch described her as 'renowned due to her own virtues, and famous due to my poems', advertising his success in elevating his beloved to the level of a timeless ideal, beyond the vagaries of fortune. The passage mattered so much to Kenelm that he copied it by hand in its entirety, and kept it with his most treasured papers.

Kenelm arrived in Florence at a moment of intense intellectual ferment, for three years previously, in 1617, the city's greatest and most famous thinker, Galileo Galilei, had moved back to the region and rented a villa just outside the city, where he was still living

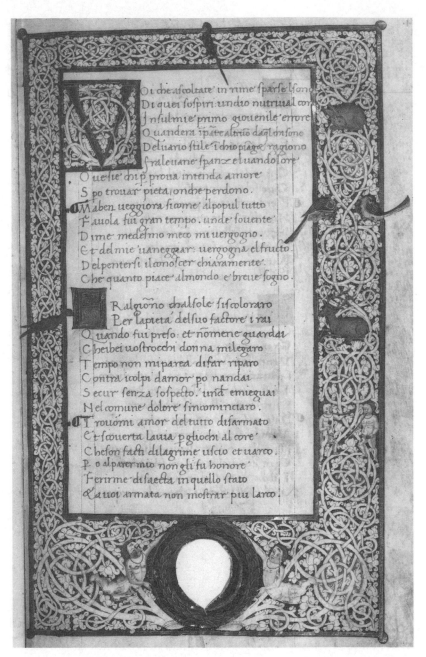

The ornate manuscript of Petrarch's poems that Kenelm bought in Siena

when Kenelm arrived. After 1618, Galileo had been drawn into a
new set of intellectual quarrels by the ominous appearance in the
heavens of three previously unobserved comets. The proper way
to interpret their appearance led him and his supporters to clash
with the Jesuits, his persistent foes and the defenders of orthodox
church doctrine, and especially with a member of the order named
Orazio Grassi, a noted mathematician. While the Jesuits had generally sought to hang on to the belief that the cosmos was unchanging
and eternal, and tried to explain away any apparent novelties,
Grassi accepted that the comets proved celestial change; but he
argued that this was not in itself enough to displace the Earth as
the stable centre of the universe, and insisted instead that it
supported the account of the great Danish astronomer Tycho
Brahe, who claimed that the planets rotated around the Sun while
the Sun in turn circled the static Earth. In response, Galileo
advanced the somewhat surprising argument that comets were not
celestial bodies at all but optical illusions, 'wandering simulacra'
that existed only in the eye of the beholder. Unlike his great
discoveries of the preceding decade, on this point Galileo turned
out to be utterly in error: but while Kenelm was in Florence the air
was thick with these discussions, and all participants in the debate
appreciated the vast questions, concerning the nature of the cosmos
and the position of the earth within it, that were at stake. Galileo,
in collaboration with his followers, began to prepare a grand
polemic which, while wrong in its account of comets, would
put forward the magnificent and novel claim that the entire
universe is a book 'written in the language of mathematics, and
its characters are triangles, circles, and other geometric figures'.
Learned Florentines debated these questions excitedly, and Kenelm,
whose mathematical training with Thomas Allen had equipped

him well to follow them, pored over Galileo's works. He was particularly thrilled to realise that in Florence, his keen interest in the cutting edge of mathematics and emerging science need not conflict with his continued pursuit of more esoteric arts. The city's Medici rulers extended their patronage not only to great philosopher-mathematicians like Galileo, but to alchemists and practitioners of chemical medicine. Even astrology, which was generally frowned upon by the Church as an impious way of laying claim to a foreknowledge that belonged only to God, was widely practised in the city, and the most eminent churchman in Tuscany, Maffeo Barberini, was said to be devoted to its lore. It was widely accepted that astrology could be abused by wicked necromancers and conjurors; but this merely confirmed its efficacy, and many orthodox churchmen sought to develop a properly humble and pious form of the art that would not impinge upon God's proper knowledge of the future. Kenelm delighted in the continued availability of these occult sciences, and in November 1620, a few months after arriving in Florence, he obtained a rare twelfth-century manuscript on the nature of geomancy: the art of divining the future from natural shapes that appeared in the earth, or from patterns of apparently random dots made on paper. It was the terrestrial counterpart to astrology; and, like the careful taking of horoscopes, it required an intense scrutiny of the natural world and all of its resplendent details. It reinforced Kenelm's belief that mysteries of the highest significance could reside in the tiniest and most mundane of particulars, if only one knew how to look.

If Florence enabled Kenelm to continue his youthful interests in the occult arts, it also allowed him to see, for the first time, that there were no hard and fast distinctions between cookery, alchemy

The treatise on geomancy, the art of divination from seemingly random patterns, that Kenelm obtained in Florence

and medicine: all were ways of transforming the substances that made up the world and the human body through flame and friction, and through acts of ingenuity and technical skill. Helping a sauce to thicken or quickening a syllabub with lemon peel was no different to Kenelm from the startling alterations of matter that he effected with furnace or limbeck, and a successfully executed dish was just as much of a marvellous metamorphosis as the transmutation of mercury or sulphur. Nothing that had emerged from the kitchen of his Buckinghamshire home, or that had been slopped in front of him in hall during his student months at Oxford, could have prepared him for the wonders of Italian cuisine. Italians were notorious for the seriousness with which they took their cooking, as the great essayist Michel de Montaigne recalled of his own travels in the country: after posing an innocent question to a former Cardinal's steward, he received in return 'a discourse on the science of guzzling, delivered with magisterial gravity and demeanour as if he had been expounding some great point in theology'. Tobie Matthew had languorously enjoyed the delights of Florentine cuisine, as part of the decadent lifestyle with which he enjoyed scandalising his English friends. 'I live in Florence,' he wrote in a letter home, 'in an excellent coole terrene, eat good melons, drinke wholesome wines, looke upon excellent devout pictures, heer choyse musique'. For Kenelm, such straightforward pleasures were not enough: he longed to understand the 'science of guzzling' that Montaigne had mocked, and did all he could to be initiated into the secrets of Tuscan cookery. He was most fascinated not by its delicacies, but by the ways in which humdrum, everyday ingredients might be elevated and transformed.

His favourite recipe of those which he sampled, and which he meticulously transcribed, was for 'Sucket of Mallow Stalks'. The mallow, an edible green plant with shiny, wavy leaves, was eaten relatively seldom in England but gobbled avidly across the Mediterranean. Like many vegetables, including artichokes, aubergines and spinach, it had first arrived in Europe from the Muslim lands to the east, where it was known as *khobbeiza*. As Kenelm observed, 'In Italy these tender stalks of Mallows are called *Mazzocchi*, and they eat them (boiled tender) in Sallets [salads], either hot or cold, with Vinegar and Oyl, or Butter and Vinegar, or juyce of Oranges.' He detailed the careful processes by which this Italian vegetable should be prepared, peeling the stalks like string-beans and boiling them until tender, then putting them into 'a high Syrup of pure

Sugar . . . whiles it is boiling hot, but taken from the fire'. The stalks, he explained, should then be removed while the sugar is reheated, and returned to the scalding syrup, with this process repeated as many as nine times until they have absorbed all the sweetness they can. Kenelm suggested serving them 'dry, but soft and moist within', like sweetmeats. He was fascinated by this incremental process of alchemical transformation, in which a common plant, practically a weed, gradually assumed a new and elevated form, and was imbued with tantalising sweetness. The sugared mallows that Kenelm admired were not simply tempting nibbles, but had a more practical role. 'In Italy they eat much of them, for sharpness and heat of Urine, and in Gonorrhoea's to take away pain in Urining'. This lowly plant was all the more magical because it could be made not only delicious, but salubrious: when treated with the proper knowledge and care it was a common herb, sweet treat and medicine all at once.

Even to acknowledge these additional benefits, though, was to recognise the more dangerous temptations of an extended sojourn in Italy, and the suspicions that it was likely to provoke in the eyes of Kenelm's compatriots when he chose finally to return home. Nervous English moralists had long warned that young men travelling in the peninsula were 'free in Italie, to go whither so ever lust will cary them', and the culinary and sexual delights of the country were often correlated directly, with young adventurers warned to protect 'your body from distemperature, either by over eating, drinking, violent or venereall exercise'. Tuscany tempted Kenelm with these kinds of pleasure as well. Decades later, following his death, an account of his life written by the Anglican memoirist David Lloyd coyly alluded to Kenelm's 'entertainments of the Ladies of the several nations that he travelled in', specifically mentioning his journey to 'Florence, and most of the states of Italy: of one of the princes whereof, it is reported, that having no Children, he was very willing his wife should bring him a Prince by Sir Kenelm, whom he imagined the just measure of perfection'. While Venetia was entering London life and attracting the attention of its young rakes, Kenelm was attracting intense attention of his own in Italy. The young man who had inadvertently seduced a queen with a mere turn about a dance floor was not too lost in new worlds of learning to bedazzle the lords and ladies of Florence, even if, he insisted, he kept their temptations entirely at bay.

During his first months in Florence in 1620, Kenelm busied and distracted himself with reading, conversing with his new friends, and eating his way around the city, but as the year 1621 began he started to crave a more active form and a more public forum for the ferment of ideas that were beginning to take shape in his mind. That year was also a time of turmoil in Italy: at the end of January the Pope, Paul V, died after a fifteen-year reign, and he was followed to the grave a few weeks later by Galileo's patron, Grand Duke Cosimo II de' Medici, who succumbed to tuberculosis at only thirty years of age. The jostling for power that inevitably followed the deaths of such powerful figures prompted Kenelm to avoid spending all of his time in Florence. He began making the onerous forty-mile journey on horseback to Siena, a town that he admired for its splendour of an altogether different sort: if Florence sprawled grandly on its plain beside the Arno then Siena was a medieval jewel tucked into the Tuscan hills, all steep flights of stairs and zigzagging alleys, with the great black-and-white chequered *Duomo* towering over the whole and the sloping terracotta *Piazza del Campo*, fanned out like a scallop shell, at its heart. The city, which had been an independent republic until it was absorbed into the Medici territories in the sixteenth century, had a rich tradition of learning, and the Italian spoken there was said to be the fairest and purest in the whole peninsula.

If these attractions made Siena an ideal place for Kenelm to spend some time more sedately, he also had more specific goals in mind. He had become aware in Florence of the countless learned academies that had sprung into existence across Italy during the preceding decades, and discovered that they were a particularly important part of civic life in Siena. These academies sought to emulate the famous, semi-mythical gatherings of cultured minds from the ancient and more recent past – Plato's academy in Athens, and the Florentine academy of the fifteenth century, led by the philosopher Marsilio Ficino and centred around Lorenzo de' Medici, known as 'the Magnificent', which was devoted to interpreting Plato's wisdom. These academies held meetings at which their members delivered learned orations or read poetry, centring on certain topics of particular interest – the nature of the ancient languages, Hebrew, Greek and Latin, and the relative merits of Latin and the modern Tuscan tongue. As long as matters of political and theological controversy were avoided, however, almost any topic could be discussed: the Sienese academies pursued 'universal knowledge' and considered 'all disciplines and all liberal arts' within their remit, as long as the speeches delivered were 'virtuous'. Almost as much as virtue, though, these academies delighted in learned jokes and witticisms, and particularly enjoyed wordplay of all sorts, including linguistic games in which words with similar-sounding first syllables were exchanged. The *dubbi* or doubtful questions that they debated included such light-hearted topics as 'whether black or blue eyes are more to be esteemed in a beautiful face' and 'whether the fire of love is aroused more by seeing the beloved's smile or tears'.

On one of his first forays to Siena in 1620, carrying letters of introduction from his friends and contacts in Florence, Kenelm was granted admission to one of the city's pre-eminent learned gatherings, founded in 1577, the *Accademia dei Filomati* (the 'Academy of the Philomaths', or lovers of knowledge). Italian academies were famous for the practice of granting pseudonyms to members, often playing anagrammatically upon their real names, and the *Filomati* were no exception. Kenelm was delighted to be dubbed '*Il Fiorito*', the little flower, a name which referred flatteringly to his youth and good looks and his potential for intellectual flourishing, as well as alluding to the fleur-de-lis that appeared in the Digby family coat of arms. At the meetings of the *Filomati*, Kenelm had found a place where he could give free rein to his emerging speculations, and try out for the first time a version of his public self, freed from any prejudice based on his family history or his own youthful pursuits. As learned gentlemen, its members were concerned with the sustenance not only of the mind but of the body, and the meetings at which orations were delivered featured equally fulsome outpourings of food and wine, allowing Kenelm to further his appreciation of the country's cuisine. While the *Filomati* liked to claim that they were more sober than other academies, they still threw lavish feasts, especially during the city's carnival, when the series of rich courses would be interspersed with dancing, oratory and moralising warnings against just the sort of excess in which the guests were indulging. Some banquets even had their own equivalents of the *dubbi* debated at usual meetings, known as *cicalate* or 'chats', which focused on culinary topics such as 'In praise of Salad' and 'On the similarity of watermelon and pork'.

Kenelm rejoiced in this new arena where his diverse and developing interests could be effortlessly fused. On no fewer than four occasions between 1621 and 1622, *Il Fiorito* stood before the rest of the *Filomati* and delivered long orations, in fluent Italian, that revealed the staggering range and breadth of thought of which he was already capable, still a year short of his twentieth birthday. The first was on the beauties and complexities of human language itself, especially the majesties of speech and the mysteries that lurk within written words; the second, delighting in mischievous paradox, was on the happiness of misers, despite all appearances to the contrary; the third, returning to loftier realms, was on secret modes of writing among the ancients; the fourth discussed the way in which the human soul inhabited its body, a topic that gripped Kenelm throughout his life. He gave voice through his speeches to the deep philosophical, theological and arcane interests that he had already begun to develop before leaving England, and continued to augment and refine in Florence; but, for the first time, he publicly laid claim to the ideas that he expressed with a swagger and a wit that was all his own. Kenelm's first oration, delivered late in 1620, was the most daring, as he sought to make his mark on his new acquaintances with a tour de force of abstruse learning and erudition. He began with the general observation that *ragione* and *sapienza* – reason and wisdom – 'are of two sorts: one animated by the living voice, which proceeds from the chest through the tongue and through the other instruments necessary for speech, in articulate and distinct words; the other is writing . . . of which the hand is the instrument'. From this basic starting point, Kenelm went on to discuss the various ways in which words can embody and reveal deep mysteries and hidden meaning, quoting liberally in Greek and Hebrew as he went. As the speech progressed, Kenelm launched himself from this discussion of language into even grander speculations, describing the light of God that lies behind all meaning and, like the sun, shoots forth 'shining sparks of divinity'. Not only did he demonstrate to his fellow *Filomati* a precocious grasp of languages and his taste for theological speculation; Kenelm also displayed his deep knowledge of poetry and philosophy, both ancient and more recent. He quoted several lines of '*vostro Poeta*', Dante, which described the divine flame that lies at the centre of all creation, and ended with a series of descriptions of light as the basis of all cosmic change from great ancient Roman astronomers, philosophers and poets. As Kenelm drew his meandering tour de force to a close, the *Filomati* rose to their feet and hooted their approval of this young Englishman who had mastered such a dazzling medley of ideas with such ease and wit.

Kenelm also endeavoured to gain the respect of the *Accademia* in other ways, by proving that he was no less comfortable with a sword in his hand than a book. In 1621, one of his new Sienese friends, Bonaventura Pistofilo, dedicated his book *Oplomachia* to Kenelm: this treatise, by a man from a family of eminent scholars, was on the proper use of weapons, and Pistofilo chose *Il Fiorito* as his dedicatee precisely because Kenelm had 'in the manner of Pallas joined splendour in arms with worth in letters'. This was the first time that Kenelm had been publicly praised in this fashion, and it gave him a tantalising glimpse of the accolades that might follow, were he to successfully live the life to which he aspired.

Kenelm spent the remainder of 1620 and the first half of 1621 pleasurably, making frequent journeys between Florence and Siena and availing himself of the contrasting pleasures of both cities. In the summer of 1621, his enjoyment was interrupted when he was exposed to another side of Italian life that intrigued and terrified English visitors – the inhabitants' fiery tempers and speed to take offence. Kenelm had enjoyed the urbane dinners with the *Filomati*,

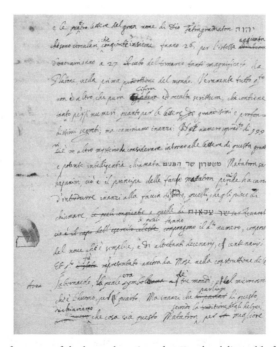

A page from one of the learned orations that Kenelm delivered before the *Accademia dei Filomati* in Siena

Kenelm's portrait, from the book dedicated to him in Siena

but in June he found himself at a more raucous feast, and following an initial misunderstanding and a harsh exchange of words, 'a Captaine quarrelled with him, and with his sword strucke him dangerously on the head'. There was uproar in the hall as all those present leapt back in horror and then crowded forward to glimpse the fate of the young English visitor: but somehow Kenelm '(with admiration of all) received no wound'. If this seemed to suggest that a higher power was looking out for Kenelm's safety, as he allowed himself to wonder, such fantasies were dispelled when 'the smallpockes broke out upon him in great abundance, and held him a long time dangerously sicke'. For a time Kenelm's life hung in the balance, but slowly, with the help of his friends among the *Filomati* and the chemical treatments available in Florence, he

78

overcame his sickness without even suffering permanent disfigurement. This brush with death changed Kenelm's focus for the remainder of his time in Italy. He continued to enjoy the learned discussions in Siena throughout the year 1622, but he began to get increasingly restless, moving between spheres within which he felt comfortable, but which were cloistered from the wider world. He had been interested in medicine since his studies with Parson Sandie, but now receiving successful treatment for smallpox made him determined to delve into the art in new depth. Furthermore his travels through the peninsula, and his reading, had started to draw his mind further eastward: studying for the orations delivered before the *Filomati* had led him to explore Ancient Greek and Hebrew for the first time, and now he longed to learn more about the lands in which these languages originated, as well as others more mysterious still – Arabic, Chaldean, Syriac. His youthful studies with Napier and Allen had first piqued his interest in the wisdom of these distant places, which were often lauded as the cradle of medicine. A physician like Parson Sandie routinely employed many of the drugs that were imported via the eastern Mediterranean from the countries that lay far beyond: he was particularly fond of an Arabic concoction known as *confectio hamech*, whose powerfully purgative qualities aided those with troubled minds. Beyond these specific substances, men like Napier and Thomas Allen, who were interested not only in mathematics but in the occult arts of alchemy and astrology, attributed their origins to these semi-mythical eastern lands. Many writers believed that the three wise men, who came from the east and attended Christ's nativity having read of it in the stars, embodied the celestial wisdom of Arabia, while the invention of alchemy was often attributed to a legendary figure named Geber, 'King of the Arabs'.

Even Greek sages like Plato, Pythagoras and Hippocrates were rumoured to have gained their wisdom by travelling through the 'land of Araby'. During Kenelm's youth, a secret society, the Brotherhood of the Rosy Cross, had spectacularly announced itself as the guardian of true wisdom in Europe. According to the widely circulated life of the Rosicrucians' mythical founder, Christian Rosenkreuz acquired his learning when he 'went to Damascus' and 'became by chance acquainted with the wise men of Damascus and Arabia, and beheld what wonders they wrought, and how nature was discovered unto them'. Rosenkreuz supposedly 'sailed over the whole Mediterranean sea'. 'This is the place where he did learn his physic, and his mathematics.'

The more Kenelm learned in Italy, the more he was convinced that he too would have to travel eastward if he were to further the studies and the personal transformations that he had begun. His intentions were reinforced by the strangest of his Florentine encounters, early in 1623. He met 'a religious Carmelite that came from the Indies and Persia to Florence', and 'had also been at China'. On his travels, this man had acquired a secret recipe, 'which he had learnt in the Oriental parts, and he thought there was not any who knew it in Europe but himself, and that it deserved not to be divulged'. The recipe allowed its possessor to concoct a powder, which could be used for the cure of wounds. It was not to be placed directly on the injured part, however: instead, it was to be applied to the weapon that had inflicted the wound. Were this done properly, no matter the distance from the victim, the hurt would be sympathetically remedied and restored to perfect health. The Carmelite was so nervous of sharing his powerful secret that he refused to divulge it even to the Grand Duke himself. Some months later, though, Kenelm 'had opportunity to do an important courtesie to the said Frier, which induced him to discover unto me his Secret'. As a result, he became its sole possessor: 'the same year he returned to Persia; insomuch that now there is no other knows this Secret in Europe but my self'.

The recipe with which the Carmelite entrusted Kenelm was not unique: there were many supposed versions of the 'weapon-salve', as it was generally known, present across Europe, and it had become one of the most hotly debated topics between those who believed in the presence of occult forces in the universe that might legitimately and piously be harnessed, and those who saw this as demonic sorcery or mere legerdemain. Kenelm took up a more complex position. He concocted and refined his own version of the salve according to the Carmelite's instructions, which he called 'the Powder of Sympathy', and became convinced of its effi- cacy. He insisted, however, that it worked 'naturally, and without any Magick', and insisted that 'we need not have recourse to a Daemon or Angel' in order to explain it. Rather than accepting it as an inexplicable wonder, he brought to bear upon it the resources of his expanding mind. The cutting-edge mathematics and emerging scientific debate to which he had been exposed, first in Oxford and even more resoundingly in Galileo's Florence, were leading him towards the conviction that the physical world consisted entirely of material atoms that moved chaotically in a void, but were amenable to mathematical explanation: this was a position becoming increasingly common among scientific pioneers, including Galileo, even though it seemed difficult to reconcile with God's active role in the world. Kenelm uniquely sought to blend this world view with the sense, derived from his culinary pursuits as much as from his alchemical training, that the things of the world could be strangely and startlingly active and alive: they could enter into sudden connections and transform one another in unanticipated ways. The atoms in which he believed were not pallid and inert, but charged through their vacuum 'like Cavaliers mounted on winged Coursers', and it was their vivacity that allowed the remarkable cures to take place: he believed that when the powder of sympathy entrusted to him by the Carmelite was applied to a bloody cloth and left near a fire, the atoms of heat and light, aided by the powder, would dislodge the atoms of blood, releasing them into the air. Meanwhile, because the bleeding wound released an 'abundance of hot fiery spirits, which gush forth as a river out of the inflamed hurt', this outpouring would create 'a kind of current of air drawn round about the wound': this airy vortex of fiery spirits would meet with the atoms of blood and vitriol released from the cloth and draw them back towards the wound, repairing and making it whole.

There was, for Kenelm, no intrinsic difference between the secret with which the Carmelite entrusted him, and other processes which seemed able inexplicably to occur over large distances: magnetism, which caused inert metal objects to leap and cavort, and to display preferences and antipathies, almost like living creatures, or heat and light, which could work their effects across vast expanses of space. These were the opaque forces that appeared to bind the universe together, and that seemed both magical and rational at once: he longed to disentangle them in greater detail. He found himself drawn painfully in two directions at once: homeward towards Venetia, to see if the dark rumours of her betrothal to another man had any truth to them; and further eastward, into the lands that the Carmelite had seen, to discover other secrets, pursue yet more daring travels, and further expand his developing mind. As he wavered between these possibilities,

Kenelm's mind was made up for him by an external intervention. While he had first been settling into his extended stay in Florence and Siena, the upwardly mobile John Digby had returned from his embassy to the Holy Roman Emperor at Vienna, and swiftly been dispatched back to Spain, where he resumed his ambassadorial duties in February 1622. In September of that year, his continued diplomatic prowess had so impressed the King that James elevated him to the rank of a great lord, naming him first Earl of Bristol. Early in 1623, the 'fame' of Kenelm's actions in Siena reached Bristol's ears in Madrid: whether or not he had truly believed for the past three years that the young relative had died in the turmoil of French civil war, he was delighted to hear that Kenelm was flourishing, having identified the young man's promise from an early age, and done what he could to nurture it. He sent word to Tuscany, urging the younger man to join him in Madrid, where 'he had plentiful means to put him in a way of benefiting himself, and making himself known in great actions'. This was too tempting a prospect for Kenelm to resist – an arena to continue the presentation of his learning and virtues to the world that he had begun in Italy, under the benevolent gaze of a powerful patron. He would have to defer for now his desire further to investigate the secret lore of the East, and refuelling the flickering flame of his and Venetia's love would also have to wait. He had been happy in Florence and Siena, but after nearly three years the time was right to depart. Early in 1623 he made his way to the port of Livorno, and boarded a ship bound to Spain, sailing for the first time across the waters of the Mediterranean.

Even as he bid farewell to the Italian coast, however, Kenelm was not quite done with the arcana to which his experiences there had exposed him. As the vessel on which he had set out made its way through the waves, Kenelm made the acquaintance of one of his more striking fellow passengers. This man was another traveller from the distant east: 'a Brachman of India, who shaped his course the same way', and was well-versed in learned secrets. As Kenelm sailed gradually towards the Spanish coast in the Brahman's company, the pair engaged in a series of conversations. The Brahman proved particularly expert in the astrological lore that had long fascinated Kenelm, but he startled the young man by asserting unequivocally that 'the heavens and stars govern this world, which are the only books of fate: whose secret characters and influence but few, divinely inspired, can read in the true sense that their Creator gave them'. Kenelm objected that such an assertion 'overthroweth quite the liberty of the will', prompting the Brahman to a rapturous account of divine wisdom, and the paradoxical way in which the human soul can combine 'an entire liberty together with a constrained necessity'. He moved from these mysteries, much like those that had preoccupied Kenelm in his oration on the soul before the *Filomati*, to the provocatively bald insistence 'that angels and devils do interpose themselves in our ordinary familiar actions'. The Brahman even claimed that, 'by abstracting my thoughts from sensual objects and raising my spirits up to that height I could', he had been able to conjure up 'a real and obedient apparition', which he had imprisoned in 'a hallowed book' that he always carried with him. Kenelm was shocked, but curious: he could not help but wonder whether it might be possible to harness this mysterious man's dark arts and learn the truth of Venetia's actions, so that he would no longer have to torment himself with speculations. He began telling the Brahman of the rumours he had heard of his distant beloved, and his mysterious new acquaintance immediately 'drew out of his bosom a little book enclosed in a leaden cover, and the leaves of it made of the thin and membranous skin of unborn lambs, which were inscribed with various figures or pentacles' and began murmuring to himself the strange sounds of its 'magical characters'.

No sooner had the Brahman finished than Kenelm saw a lady appear before him on the deck of the ship on which they stood, sitting 'in a pensive posture' with her face half concealed. She turned towards him, revealing a countenance so beautiful that he 'doubted whether it were a goddess or a human creature'. He stood frozen in a wondering trance, but the Brahman approached the figure and asked it to come closer: only then did Kenelm recognise the lady as the perfect image of Venetia – her high forehead, the eyes that changed colour as one gazed into them, the face that became more striking each time one looked upon it. He tried desperately to lay hold of the apparition, but 'when he thought he had taken her by the hand, he found that he grasped nothing but air, which discourteously fled from his embraces'. He began instead to question the spirit, which explained to him the full story of Venetia's misfortunes – that she began to give in to her suitor only because she falsely believed Kenelm to be dead, and that she had gone astray only through 'want of experience, that made her liable to censure'. Kenelm stood wondering at these words, 'irresolute which way his belief should sway': the spectral Venetia told him that, as proof that what she spoke was the truth, he should know that within days of his arrival in Spain he would find himself surrounded by armed men, yet escape unscathed while killing one of their number. At that exact moment the Brahman slammed shut the book, and the spirit vanished.

Two wise men from the east, in possession of secrets: one who had been in Persia and China, and who entrusted to Kenelm alone a recipe that would provoke him to probe the mysterious forces binding the universe together; the other with privileged knowledge of the stars and the spirit realm, and able to harness them through his powers. Kenelm may indeed have met these two men, or two men like them; or they may have been distillations of the kinds of people he encountered and the experiences that he underwent in Italy, personifications of the distant lore that he hoped one day to encounter for himself. Both men could equally have waltzed straight from the tales of adventure that he read so avidly, in which the heroes frequently encountered wizards and magi, anchorites and prophets, both benevolent and malevolent: figures like Shakespeare's Prospero, who also dwelled in the Mediterranean and possessed magical books with which he controlled spirits. It was through these two figures, real or imagined, that Kenelm chose to crystallise the lessons and the delights of his years in Italy. He left the country emboldened and empowered, far more confident of his standing in the world and his ability to make his own way within it, regardless of the foul stain that remained in his blood. Now, he began to realise, he had the power independently to pursue the arts into which he had been inducted by his first teachers in England, develop them through his own talent and initiative, and fuse them with his wildest and most expansive imaginings into something entirely novel. Gazing westward as the ship made its way across the Mediterranean, Kenelm saw the coastline of Spain creep gradually into view on the horizon: on these waters, he was beginning to believe, he might be able to forge a story that was all his own.

II 'Wise and Prudent Negotiation'

Aristobulus having, through his wise and prudent negotiation, concluded the marriage between the King of Morea's son and the King of Egypt's sister, had wrought into the treaty thereof conditions of so much advantage for his side, that Hephæstion, who was the old King's favourite, doubted that if he alone had the honour of it, he should gain thereby so much strength that he might in time be able to contest in greatness with him, who had ever a jealous eye of his rising, and did himself subsist only by his master's favour. Wherefore, perceiving now that any delay would make it too late to prevent these fears, he resolved to make use of the King's affection towards him, and taking that business out of the hands of Aristobulus that he had so much laboured in with happy success, to attribute to himself the honour of effecting it. Whereupon he procured for himself an extraordinary commission of embassage, with full power to do what he thought fit in this treaty (which, to colour his actions, he pretended to be full of difficulties); and to strengthen his proceedings, and to have a favourable witness of what he should do, he carried the prince alone with him into Egypt, who loved him as much, if not more than his father, where, after a laborious and dangerous journey, they arrived safe.

But all the glories of the court and beauty of the ladies there, which shined continually with so many stars, could not make him forget or sweeten his quarrel to womankind in general, for Stelliana's sake: which gave occasion to the Earl of Arcadia ... to speak thus one day to him.

'When I look upon you, Theagenes, methinks I see enough that telleth me your abilities might win you the affection of any lady; but when I consider how you daily pass by the fairest faces without seeming to have any sense of the divine beams of beauty that shine there, I begin to doubt that the fault proceedeth from your mind, which, I understand, hath been trained up continuously in scholastical speculations, and hath always conversed with books at such times as you have not exercised your body in the use of arms and managing of horses, and such other disciplines as become a gentleman and a soldier; so that I see there may be excess in the best and most commendable things, for these, that in a moderation may be esteemed chief ornaments, do beget either a dull stupidity or a rude barbarousness in those that adore them too affectionately; and I doubt much that from one of these two causes doth proceed your having no mistress here, where so much beauty reigneth.'

Which when he had said, accompanying his words with smiles, Theagenes answered him in this manner: 'You should not censure me before you are certain that I have no mistress, and feel not in my breast the heat of love's flames; which you cannot collect from my concealing them, since you may have a familiar example in the deepest waters, whose streams slide away with least noise.'

Kenelm arrived in Madrid in February 1623, and made his way to the Earl of Bristol's ambassadorial residence on Calle de las

Infantas. Bristol was delighted to see the young relative whom he had first shown around the city as a wide-eyed fourteen-year-old on his first journey abroad: the tall and suntanned young man who arrived, fresh from three years of living independently in Italy, was a different creature indeed. Kenelm was quickly provided with 'a convenient house near the Ambassador's'. He found himself in stimulating company: he was impressed by Bristol's son George, a precocious boy of ten who had been born in Madrid and was entirely bilingual, and also struck up a firm friendship with the Earl's stepson, Lewis Dyve, who was four years his senior. From Dyve he learned everything he could about the tortuous and clandestine negotiations in which Bristol was immersed. It had been a decade since King James had first sent the Earl to Madrid discreetly to investigate the possibility of marrying Charles, the Crown Prince, to the King of Spain's sister, the Infanta Maria. Since that time the negotiations had proceeded tentatively and intermittently, with neither side willing to commit to a firm alliance with a nation of opposed religion who had been an enemy for so many of the preceding years. After the outbreak in 1618 of the war that threatened to consume all of Europe, James wanted assurances that the Spanish would restore his exiled daughter and son-in-law to their rightful lands in the Palatinate, which they had lost after their ill-fated Bohemian adventure and which was now overrun with Catholic troops. If this was the price that the English King demanded for his nation's allegiance and his son's hand in marriage, the Spanish wanted Charles himself to become a Catholic: failing this, they insisted that any children of the union should be raised in the Roman fold, and demanded vastly improved treatment for English Catholics. For years, Bristol had wheedled, pussyfooted and cajoled his way around Madrid, learning the ways of the court and keeping a keen ear out for faraway events in the Vatican, since any proposed marriage would need papal approval.

During the three years that Kenelm spent in Italy, he had focused on the development of his own mind and talents, happy to keep safely away from the terrible war that was unfolding on the other side of the Alps and maintain a comfortable distance from the grand events of European politics. Now, arriving in Madrid, he was thrust into their front line. As Dyve familiarised him with the ins and outs of the marriage negotiations, Kenelm discovered just how alluring and dangerous the city in which he had arrived could be. The two men strolled through the streets one evening soon after Kenelm's arrival, talking of Bristol's latest efforts, and 'the night slided so insensibly away while they were in their pleasing conversation' that they found themselves at midnight on a silent street, beneath a clear moon. Suddenly they heard the tremulous sound of 'a rare voice, accompanied with a sweet instrument', and the 'soul-ravishing harmony' drew their eyes up to a window where a beautiful woman was singing 'in a loose and night habit'. While they stood, dumbstruck, fifteen men burst from the shadows, swords drawn, and charged at them. Dyve fought one of the men off fiercely, and swiftly departed the scene. Kenelm would not flee, but 'resolved rather to die in the midst of his enemies, than to do anything that might be interpreted to proceed from fear'. He managed at first to fend them off without wounding any of the men, wondering inwardly what offence he could have caused so soon after his arrival in Madrid, and tried to fight his way back towards the safety of Bristol's residence. One man managed to sneak behind him, though, and raised his sword to deliver a blow: Kenelm deftly 'avoided it with a gentle motion of his body, and gave him such a reverse upon the head, that . . . it divided it in two parts, and his brains flew into his neighbour's face'. The rest of the gang scattered into the night. Kenelm had been praised for his prowess in arms in Siena but never forced to bear them in anger; here in Madrid, he discovered the grim messiness of the active life that he craved. He had no time to pause and consider what he had done; no chance to linger over the horribly gory reality of taking a life for the first time, as he sprinted through the quiet streets towards the ambassador's house.

The next day, Kenelm discovered that he had been swept up into the skirmish entirely by mistake: it was Dyve who was the intended target, having previously been overfamiliar with the lady singing at the window, leading her jealous husband to set up this trap. Because he had acted in self-defence, Kenelm was able to escape any punishment for the death he had inflicted. It was only after the dust had settled and Bristol had helped smooth matters over that Kenelm realised the significance of what had occurred: the prophecy of the spirit conjured by the Brahman while he was en route to Madrid had been proven true. In fact the prediction was not entirely accurate, for while Kenelm had escaped with his life he was not unscathed, having 'received a wound in his right hand . . . by a mischaunce'. He banished this inconvenient detail from his mind: if he could hang on to the conviction that the first part of the spirit's prophecy was accurate then he could allow himself to believe that the apparition's description of Venetia's continued fidelity was also true. If the fracas had been a terrifying ordeal for Kenelm, not least because it forced him to recognise his own talent for violence, it had also allowed him to display his courage and prowess, and word of his behaviour 'was daily carried and related by sundry mouths, who were filled with many other high commendations added to the fame of his valour'. Finally, rumour was working in his favour, burnishing rather than demeaning his standing in the world. So far did word of his bravery carry that it finally reached Venetia in England, confirming that her beloved was in fact alive and well: but rather than being elated she mourned in a new way, for having entered into an engagement with another man while believing him to be dead: 'if before she lamented the loss of him', she 'had now as much reason to renew the lamentation of her own misfortunes', and while Kenelm's reputation soared in Madrid Venetia 'remained in clouds of sorrow'.

Within a few weeks, though, Kenelm's valiant display was all but forgotten: the whole of Madrid had something far more extraordinary and exciting to discuss. In the early hours of the morning of 7 March, the Earl of Bristol was rudely awoken by a servant reporting the arrival of two strange visitors, who had announced themselves as John and Thomas Smith and demanded to see the ambassador immediately. Bristol made his way sleepily downstairs and was met in the hallway by two bearded men: or rather, when he peered at them more closely, by two men who seemed to be wearing rather obvious false beards. Removing their fake facial hair with a flourish, the pair revealed their true identity, leaving Bristol 'in a kind of astonishment'. The two faces were instantly recognisable, but these were the last people that he expected to meet without warning in Madrid. The elder of the pair, who had identified himself as Thomas, was in his early thirties. Standing before the Earl, tall, slender and elegant, and carrying himself with a brash confidence befitting a man who, as King James's favourite, was effectively the most powerful individual in England, was George Villiers, Marquis of Buckingham. If Buckingham strode into the ambassador's hall as though he owned the place, then the younger companion, who styled himself John and was a decade younger and much shorter, licked his thin lips with nervousness. Behind the beard of John Smith, Bristol was still more stunned to see the King's sole surviving son and heir, Charles, Prince of Wales, whose marriage he had spent the past decade striving to arrange.

The pair began explaining themselves to the ambassador, and the daring and wrongheadedness of their scheme became increasingly apparent. As the negotiations to marry Charles to the Infanta had dragged interminably on, the impatience of the young Prince had grown. He had been sent a painting of the Princess who was to be his bride, and convinced himself that he was in love with her: she appeared in his dreams, and he rehearsed the ways in which he would woo her. Charles had lived a cloistered and frustrating life, watching impotently as more powerful figures eclipsed him in the eyes not only of the wider world, but also of his own father. First there was his brilliantly talented elder brother, Henry, in whom such great hopes were invested, and who bore the burden of being heir to the throne with seemingly effortless ease; then, when Henry prompted universal lamentation by succumbing to his sudden dreadful illness and it seemed as if Charles's moment to take centre stage might have arrived, George Villiers came roaring on to the scene. James was always happiest when he had a beautiful young man by his side, to be his closest friend and confidant, and, as the gossips gleefully insisted, his bedfellow. In 1614, two years after Henry's death, a faction at court sought to displace the then favourite – Robert Carr, Earl of

Somerset – from his pre-eminent position by introducing the King to the suave and fetching young Villiers. They had no idea of the forces that they were unleashing. His flowing speech and skill on horseback and the dance floor soon caught James's eye, and by 1615 Villiers had replaced Somerset in the King's affections, and begun a rise that astounded and terrified his contemporaries. No royal favourite had ever acquired so much power so quickly, or knew how to wield it so effectively: within a few short years James had named Villiers his cupbearer, knighted him, and made him a gentleman of the bedchamber, master of the horse, and finally, in 1619, Lord Admiral. Though he was not born into a great family – his forebears had lived 'rather without obscurity, than with any great lustre', as his first biographer put it – the favourite also shot up through the ranks of the nobility, with James naming him

George Villiers, Duke of Buckingham

in turn as Baron of Whaddon and Viscount Villiers, then Earl and Marquis of Buckingham. His rapid rise was compared to that of a 'prodigious comet' tearing ominously through the fixed fabric of the heavens, its exorbitant course threatening to undo the firm order on which English society was based. No other figure inspired such extremes of admiration and loathing, and Buckingham collected scores of followers and dependants as well as a slew of enemies.

At first, Charles counted himself among the latter: he hated and resented the man who loomed largest in his father's affections, and quarrelled openly with Buckingham. James made no secret of his feelings, loudly and tactlessly declaring to his privy councillors that 'he loved the Earl of Buckingham more than any other man'. Gradually, though, Charles's feelings changed: he began to look up to the older and much more worldly man, and admire Buckingham's resplendent talents and the charisma that he himself resoundingly lacked. Buckingham had good reason for directing the full force of his magnetism at the Prince, for James was ageing and ailing: usually when a king died the favourite lost what power he had acquired, but, if he could charm the son as he had the father, then Buckingham could cap his unlikely rise to eminence by surviving a change of reign. When he saw Charles pining for the Spanish Princess on whom he had never clapped eyes, he seized his chance and 'discoursed how gallant and how brave a thing it would be for his highness to make a journey into Spain and to fetch home his mistress . . . These discourses made so deep an impression upon the mind and spirit of the Prince (whose nature was inclined to adventures) that he was transported with the thought of it, and most impatiently solicitous to bring it to pass.' Despite James's opposition and tearful recriminations, the pair resolved to depart incognito from England and travel overland through France, with only one servant to assist them. They had convinced themselves that, by making this grandiose gesture, they would be able to break the deadlock, bring an end to years of fruitless discussion, and carry the Infanta triumphantly back to England where she and Charles would be wed.

Bristol was utterly shocked by the unannounced arrival of these illustrious visitors, but there was little that he could do other than welcome them, and find them beds for the night. The next morning, he summoned Kenelm, Lewis Dyve and his other most trusted underlings, and told them what had happened. Word of the new arrivals spread quickly through Madrid, and Kenelm had the opportunity to meet the Prince and the Marquis for himself, and was frequently at their side during their first weeks in Madrid as they made their presence known to King Felipe and his court. Kenelm regarded Buckingham with a mixture of fascinated admiration and profound nervousness. He was struck, first of all, by his magnetism and his beauty: the Marquis was the very 'touchstone' of 'composure . . . symmetry and gracefulnesse'. Beyond his looks, Buckingham was also everything that Kenelm hoped to be: a man who had risen to the pinnacle of English society based solely on his force of personality and talent for self-presentation, and who had forced the world to take note of his actions, irrespective of his lineage. As Clarendon observed, Buckingham 'was a very extraordinary person; and never any man, in any age, nor, I believe, in any country or nation, rose, in so short a time, to so much greatness of honour, fame and fortune, upon no other advantage or recommendation than of the beauty and gracefulness and becomingness of his person'. Furthermore, the Marquis's own religious and political convictions were profoundly unclear, but these merely augmented his ability to adapt to emerging circumstances. From the moment that he arrived in Madrid, however, Buckingham's behaviour was a great concern to Bristol, and to Kenelm: it was clear that the Marquis now considered himself to be in charge of the marriage negotiations. Bristol had spent years familiarising himself with the Spanish style of diplomacy, and learning the ways of its intensely formal court, in which every ritual of deference and respect had to be carefully observed: Buckingham brashly and wrongly assumed that his impulsive charms would work as well here as they had in England. The Marquis quickly began to resent Bristol's attempts to maintain control of the negotiations: he blamed the Earl for the long delays, and viewed all of his allies, including Kenelm, with profound suspicion. Buckingham, though, had no reason to moderate his behaviour: if some in England thought that he had left his position in the court vulnerable by leaving the King's side, James assuaged any such doubts by taking the extraordinary step of naming his favourite the only living Duke in England while he was in Madrid, and elevating him above the entire nobility at a single stroke.

If Kenelm soon realised that Buckingham, the man he so admired, viewed him as a potential enemy, then he found the Prince himself to be a far more relaxed and agreeable presence, and began to enjoy his company. Charles was relishing his adventure: he had never been abroad before – nor had any heir to the English throne since the days of Henry VIII – and he had in common with Kenelm the feeling of profound liberation that came with leaving England behind and being his own man, not his father's son. He had passed incognito through France and braved the notoriously rocky and dangerous roads of the Spanish countryside. In the absence of servants he had even taken care of his own dinner: near Bayonne, when Buckingham tried and failed to catch a goat to eat and chased it haplessly around a field, Charles drew a Scottish pistol and shot it dead from the saddle of his horse. In the weeks and months following his arrival in Madrid, he realised that he was also free for the first time to develop and test his own beliefs and tastes, and to consider the kind of king that he hoped one day to be. To travel without warning or a grand retinue into another monarch's dominions was a staggering breach of etiquette, but, once Felipe and his counsellors recovered their composure, Charles was treated with every courtesy – largely because his Spanish hosts wrongly but understandably assumed that his decision to travel to Madrid was a signal of his willingness to become a Catholic. Where Buckingham was impatient with Spanish ceremoniousness, Charles was deeply impressed: unlike the messy and boisterous court that his own father had transplanted from Scotland when he assumed the English throne, this court operated according to a carefully maintained set of rules and protocols, in which everyone knew their place and just how to behave. King Felipe reinforced his power not through ostentatious moments of display but by remaining invisible to his people: this was a kind of kingship that operated through withdrawal and restraint, an idea which suited Charles's more retiring inclinations. Nobles dressed in sombre colours, and advertised their greatness not with garish clothing or jewels, but through their magnificent collections of paintings and sculpture. Charles had tentatively continued his elder brother Henry's interest in European art, but now he was exposed to it directly and on a lavish scale: he and Buckingham both began avidly to obtain all the notable artworks they could, and the Prince bought and was given numerous works by the great Titian, and had his portrait painted by Diego Velázquez, the foremost Spanish master. He also showed a new boldness in his religious convictions, proving to his hosts' disappointment that he had no intention of converting by debating the finer points of theology with eminent Spanish divines: he did a good job, arguing against any scriptural basis for the Pope's authority. At the same time, he publicly signalled for the first time a commitment to religious ritual and ceremony that would have appalled his more puritanical subjects at home: the priests that were sent after him to Spain were ordered to carry out services in a manner 'as near the Roman form as can lawfully be done', in order to emphasise the potential for the two nations to be reconciled, and these were conducted in the chapel at the Earl of Bristol's house.

Kenelm watched the Prince with acute interest as he increased in confidence, and Charles liked immensely the confident and worldly younger man. Kenelm also began to be directly involved in the ongoing marriage negotiations, and was a useful asset: when Bristol needed to negotiate with the papal representative in Madrid, Bishop Innocenzo de' Massimi, he recognised that 'an acceptable messenger doth much advance any business' and chose to send Kenelm, whose fluent Italian and friendship with some of the Bishop's relatives in Tuscany made him an ideal choice. He and the Prince had time not only for the politics, art and religion of Madrid, but also its more esoteric attractions and sensations. It was 'whiles I wayted upon the Prince of Wales (now our gratious Soveraigne) in Spaine', Kenelm later recalled, that the pair were introduced to the younger brother of the Constable of Castile, who had been born entirely deaf and dumb. Despite these disadvantages, he had been taught to communicate and to understand speech by a priest named Juan Pablo Bonet. Kenelm and Charles were intrigued, and put him to the test: the man proved capable of repeating sounds not only in English but also in Welsh. Kenelm was able to continue the observations of remarkable phenomena that he had begun in Italy, but now he could extend his fascination with natural wonders and strange customs in the company of the heir to the throne. The interest he had developed in Florence in the way that physical atoms permeate through the world was now supported by the striking new customs that he encountered:

> *When they that are curious in perfumes, will have their chamber filled with a good scent in a hot season, that agreeth not with burning perfumes, and therefore make some odoriferous water be blowne about it by their servants mouthes that are dexterous in that Ministery, (as is used in Spaine in the summer time) ... every one that seeth it done ... is well satisfyed that the scent which recreateth him, is the very water he saw in the glasse extremely dilated by the forcible sprouting of it out from the servants mouth.*

These scents wafted through the air from the mouths of Spanish servants became for Kenelm an encapsulation of the way in which all matter moves through the universe, and, as his familiarity with Charles deepened, he was also able to derive his ongoing philo-sophical ruminations from the pleasing quirks of Spanish life.

What most deeply caught Kenelm's attention as he spent time in the Prince's company in the middle months of 1623, however, was the way in which Charles's adventurous journey with Buckingham and his continued courtship of the Infanta were coming to be understood. When James had heard of the pair's safe and secretive arrival in Madrid, false beards intact, he wrote a gushing letter in which he addressed them as 'my sweet boys and dear venturous knights, worthy to be put in a new romance'. The King's tone was echoed by Edward Conway, the Secretary of State, who described the escapade in a letter of his own as 'a voyage of the Knights of Adventure', and by the Duke of Savoy, who 'said that the Prince's Journey thither was, *un tiro di quelli Cavellieri antichi che andavano cosi per il Mondo a diffare li incanti*, That it was a Trick of those ancient Knight Errands who went up and down the World after that manner to undoe Enchantments'. According to these flattering accounts, a hare-brained scheme that could easily have been dismissed as a juvenile prank, and which was of enormously risky political significance, was instead elevated to the level of a lofty and dignified tale of heroism and wonder.

Even after arriving, Charles continued to act as if he were living out the plot of a romance. He was eventually allowed to meet the Princess about whom he had fantasised so intensely, but he did so only briefly and in a public setting, as propriety demanded, since their betrothal was not yet confirmed. Undeterred, he cooked up another daring scheme, and brought Kenelm along. Charles had heard that the Infanta liked to gather may-dew at Casa de Campo, a summer house of the King's, so he made his way there and 'got on top of the wall, and sprung down a great hight', which caused the Princess either to run off with a shriek (according to English reports) or decorously to ignore him and walk calmly on (as the Spanish had it), while her aged guardian begged the Prince on bended knee to leave lest he lose his head for admitting Charles to her presence. The idea for this attempt was not entirely

Charles's own: he had bought books as well as paintings in Madrid, including a popular tale titled *La Celestina* which had an opening scene in which the protagonist, Calisto, approaches his beloved Melibea in a garden to which she has retired and professes his love, only to be rebuffed. Charles, Kenelm wonderingly realised, had not only tried boldly to woo his beloved: he had also perfectly enacted the beginning of one of his favourite books.

Kenelm strove in turn to emulate the Prince's exuberance and ease in politically fraught circumstances. His cheerfulness was increased because he found himself once again in the midst of a circle of like-minded young men, cosmopolitan in their inclinations and uncertain of their place in the world, many of whom would become dear and lifelong friends. Tobie Matthew, whose Spanish was nearly as good as his Italian, had travelled down to Madrid to lend Bristol his shadowy diplomatic assistance; Kenelm was delighted to see him, and to update him on the happy years he had passed in Florence among Matthew's erstwhile companions. He also met an energetic young man named James Howell, who had stopped off in Madrid on his way back from Venice, where he had been trying to learn the secrets of glass-making. He attached himself to Bristol's retinue, and he and Kenelm struck up an immediate rapport. Kenelm was also introduced to Wat Montague, son of the Earl of Manchester, who was almost exactly his age, and was using his first taste of freedom from his overbearing and fierily Protestant father to put his own beliefs and convictions to the test in foreign surroundings. These and many more men had flooded from England to Spain once word of Charles's presence there spread, and by July of 1623 Howell could refer to 'that confluence of English gallants, which upon the occasion of his Highness being here, are com to this Court'. One of the men who had come was the elegant and charming Henry Rich, Earl of Holland, who one day teased Kenelm that he was too committed to the life of the mind to care anything for earthly renown, and needed to find a woman who would draw him away from drier and dustier pursuits. Kenelm defended the 'soul-ravishing delight' of reading as no lifeless thing, but nonetheless agreed to pursue a mistress as a wager, just to prove the Earl wrong: accordingly, he began to court 'the greatest lady' he could find, who was named Doña Anna Maria Manrique. Unfortunately, however, his attempt to indulge in the same games of adventurous love that Charles was busy playing came with a human cost: his 'personated affection won such a real one' from the lady that she was soon besotted with him.

These were carefree times, for Kenelm and for the Prince whom he had befriended, but they quickly soured. As the long and sweltering summer months dragged on in Madrid, the pleasures to be found in such frivolous pastimes began to wear thin. It became horribly apparent just how fully Charles and Buckingham had miscalculated. Not only had their arrival failed to break the deadlock and bring the marriage negotiations to a swift end, but the Prince's presence in Madrid had effectively eliminated his power, making him a prisoner in the gilded cage of the Spanish court, unable either to leave or to affect the course of events. Buckingham, meanwhile, was flailing. The Duke's arrogant manner managed to cause wide offence, and gained him no advantage. His counterpart in the Spanish court, the King's favourite and chief advisor, the Count Duke Olivares, was a far more canny and seasoned operator, and able to run rings around the younger and more impulsive man. As Buckingham became ever more frustrated, his disdain for the Earl of Bristol ripened into sheer loathing: he accused Kenelm's relative of obstructing any progress just to prove that only he could conduct the negotiations. A particularly unseemly squabble occurred when Buckingham instructed Bristol to leave a coach in which he and the Prince were riding in order to make room for Olivares because they had secret business to discuss: Bristol refused, recognising the command as a deliberate slight, only to be ordered out of the coach by Charles, who took his close friend's side.

After they had endured enough of these frustrations, the Prince and the Duke concocted a devious scheme that would enable Charles to depart. Though he had no intention of doing so, the Prince told the Spanish that he would agree to the revised conditions of the marriage treaty, and left a letter with Bristol, giving him permission to act as a proxy so that the marriage could take place in his absence. Having enacted this charade, in September 1623 Charles and his large retinue were allowed to leave the city, with Kenelm among their number. He left with mixed emotions: he still had an immense sense of gratitude and obligation to Bristol, who had supported him and taken him seriously, and he felt deep disquiet in leaving him behind and joining a party containing Buckingham, who had become so openly malicious towards the Earl. Nonetheless, he was determined to return to England, having been away for more than three years. His and Venetia's love, which had once seemed so solid and so central to who he was, had been stretched and frayed until he could not even be sure how much remained: each had heard rumours of the other, but he needed to go back and determine what their shared future might hold. Furthermore, the intimacy that he had developed with the Prince offered the hope of the respectability that he craved – the best chance yet to expunge the memory of his father's treason.

Kenelm's departure left Doña Anna Maria Manrique, still besotted with him, 'wedded to sorrow and despair'. Howell forwarded him a message from her and another noblewoman on whom Kenelm had left an impression, and wrote that she 'told me this was the first Letter she ever writ to man in her life'. He assured Kenelm that 'you are much in both these Ladies Books, and much spoken of by diverse others in this Court'. Though he had made his mark in Madrid, as he left the city Kenelm was more interested in the final wonders of Spain that he might witness before departing. The travelling party stopped at Segovia, a town around fifty miles from the capital, which housed the royal mint 'where the handsomest Coin in all the Kings Territories is made', and Charles gleefully threw a dish of specially minted silver coins into the air. More than the gold and riches on display, Kenelm was struck by the technical ingenuity of a remarkable machine 'or rather multitude of severall engines, to performe sundry different operations', which were harmonised into the single task of producing a coin: one part beat the silver or gold ingot to the requisite thinness, another printed a figure on it, another stamped out the shape of the coin, and the whole contraption moved and shook with an integrated singularity of purpose that made it resemble a living creature. It was as they left Segovia that Charles dispatched a messenger back to Madrid with a curt message for Bristol: the Prince had no intention of adhering to the agreement into which he had entered, and he told the Earl that he was not under any circumstances to deliver his proxy for the marriage, which he had left only as a pretext to enable his departure. Fuming at the thwarting of their hopes and their failure to outfox the Spaniards, Charles and Buckingham led Kenelm and the rest of the party northward to the coast, where they boarded ships bound for England. 'The winds and the seas seemed to rejoice in the Prince's return, and to delight in the glorious navy that was committed to them.'

3

1623–1627
London

I 'That Heaven of Perfection'

*Not many days after, Theagenes having occasion to make a journey
into the country, came to take his leave of Stelliana in the morning,
somewhat earlier than she used to rise . . . He then being in the
chamber, and the servants retired, went to the bed side, where
the courtains were yet drawn, which opening gently, he might
perceive that Stelliana was fast asleep . . . He remained a while
like one in a trance, admiring that heaven of perfection, and accusing
that fortune which made him see so near him the happiness which
he could never attain; but at length being transported beyond himself
by his silent thoughts, he concluded not to omit that opportunity,
which chance gave him, of laying himself in the same bed by her
naked side, which he was sure he could never gain by her consent.
So then he made himself unready with the greatest haste and the
least noise that might be, and put himself between the sheets in the*

gentlest manner that he could; but yet the stirring of the clothes half waked Stelliana . . . For as she rolled herself about, the clothes that were sunk down to the other side, left that part of the bed where she now lay wholly uncovered; and her smock was so twisted about her fair body, that all her legs and the best part of her thighs were naked, which lay so one over the other, that they made a deep shadow where the never satisfied eyes of Theagenes wishes for the greatest light.

The small fleet carrying the party back from Spain landed at Portsmouth on 5 October, and Charles and Buckingham set off immediately to see King James at his palace near Royston in Hertfordshire, where he had hoped to go hunting but was instead lying ill. Kenelm would have joined them, but he too fell sick for a time, and when he recovered in late October he made his way instead to London. Finding himself back in England after a little over three years away, Kenelm was deeply unsure of where he stood in relation to the country of his birth, which was undergoing baffling and rapid changes. At first, though, the signs were extremely promising. Charles continued to trust and value him following their time together in Madrid, and as soon as the Prince returned to London from Royston he named Kenelm a gentleman of his bedchamber, admitting him to the circle of his most intimate friends. Soon the King had recovered sufficiently to return from the country to his palace at Whitehall, and on 28 October Kenelm received the public confirmation of his worth and respectability that he so craved, when, on the Prince's recommendation, 'he was knighted by the king' for the services he had rendered in Madrid, and James conferred the 'marke of honour . . . with his owne hand and sword'. Even at this triumphant moment, however, the ceremony nearly went horribly wrong: the King, Kenelm later discovered, could not bear to look upon a naked blade, an aversion he had acquired *in utero* when his pregnant mother survived an assassination attempt and watched as her secretary was butchered before her eyes. When he came to place the sword-point on Kenelm's shoulder, 'he could not endure to look upon it, but turned his face another way, insomuch, that . . . he had almost thrust the point into my eyes, had not the Duke of Buckingham guided his hand aright'.

Having achieved a mark of his restored family honour despite this near mishap, Kenelm was able to turn his mind to Venetia, for if he was now more optimistic about his standing in the world he was still deeply unsure of where he stood with her. He was desperate to see her for himself and find out, but did not know where she was to be found. Soon, though, on an unseasonably sunny day when 'many persons of quality came out in their coaches into the fields to refresh their spirits with sucking in the free and warmed air', he caught a glimpse of her riding past in a carriage and staring pensively into the distance. 'After so long absence her beauty seemed brighter to him than when he left her', and he immediately realised that 'he did unjustly in censuring her before he heard her defence from her own mouth'. Before long he managed to arrange a private meeting and, for the first time in several years, the pair stood opposite one another, overwhelmed and unsure of what to say. Kenelm had been a youth of sixteen when they had seen each other last, full of bravado and ambition but with little to show for it, and Venetia had been cloistered away in the home of her Buckinghamshire guardians: now he had seen the great cities and courts of Europe, and she had experienced the allures and the dangers of London society. The young couple who had snatched a kiss beneath a tree during a rainstorm suddenly seemed to belong to a different lifetime altogether.

Kenelm quickly established the fact that concerned him most: Venetia was no longer betrothed to another man, as her erstwhile lover had continued in his philandering ways and broken off the engagement. Even with this obstacle removed the pair quickly quarrelled, each blaming the other for the misunderstandings that had separated them; but as the weeks passed, Kenelm persisted in arranging private meetings between them in which each could explain the actions that they had undertaken during their long separation, the misunderstandings that had arisen, and their enduringly pure motives. Slowly, as their conversations proceeded, they set their bitterness aside and began to re-establish their former closeness. Kenelm, though, was impatient and impetuous, trying too quickly 'to satisfy his looser desires, and prosecuted his suit with all the vehemence and subtlety that an earnest and well experienced lover could use'. He thought that the amorous games he had played in Angers, in Florence and in Madrid could be played here as well, but he had misread Venetia entirely, and she dismissed him from her presence. Kenelm retreated, and for a time contented himself with rebuilding the 'high and divine friendship' that had once existed between them. He continued to visit her frequently, but struggled to contain his rekindled desires. He even dared to enter her bedchamber while she was asleep, gazing at her naked body and climbing into bed with her, before she awoke in horror and berated him at length for his presumptuousness, pointing out 'how apt others might be to misconceive of her honour upon such an occasion'. Kenelm leapt, shamefaced and naked, from her bed, and vowed never again to do his love for her a disservice by being so forward and so improper. For the

time being, Kenelm found it impossible to recapture the easy
intimacy that he and Venetia had once shared: he vacillated between
lingering suspicion of her behaviour in his absence, and wildly
over-the-top expressions of his affection.

Still struggling to rekindle his relationship after more than three
years of absence, Kenelm strove to distract himself from Venetia
by continuing the forays into high-level political life that he had
begun in Spain. He decided to try and make his mark upon the
learned men of the nation, and further impress the King and
Prince, by concocting some of the sympathetic powder whose
secret he had acquired in Florence. The opportunity arose in
1624 when his friend James Howell, who had made his own way
back from Madrid not long after Kenelm, tried to intervene to
stop a duel and had his hand badly sliced through 'the Nerves,
and Muscles, and Tendons'. Kenelm came to assist: he sent for the
garter on which Howell's hand had first bled, and, without his
friend realising, he dipped it into a basin into which he had secretly
dissolved his powder. As soon as he did so, Howell, 'who stood
talking with a Gentleman in a corner of my Chamber, not
regarding at all what I was doing . . . started suddenly, as if he
had found some strange alteration in himself'. When questioned,
he announced, 'I feel no more pain; methinks that a pleasing kind
of freshnesse, as it were a wet cold Napkin, did spread over my
hand.' When Kenelm removed the garter from the water after
dinner and dried it before the fire, though, 'Mr Howells servant
came running, and told me, that his Master felt as much burning
as ever he had done, if not more, for the heat was such, as if his
hand were 'twixt coals and fire'. Kenelm removed the garter,
treated it again with the powder, and the deep wound was fully
healed in six days. He proudly announced his amazing feat at

court, and 'all the circumstances were examined': not only 'by one of the greatest and most knowing Kings of his time, *viz*. King James of England' but 'also by his Son', the Duke of Buckingham, and several learned men. The audience included the King's 'first physician', the Frenchman Théodore de Mayerne, who became Kenelm's friend and shared his chemical interests, and the greatest English philosopher of the age, Lord Francis Bacon, who was so struck by Kenelm's achievement that he added a chapter on sympathetic cures to his book on natural history. James was immensely impressed and asked for the secret of the cure, but he also 'drolled with me first, (which he could do with a very good grace)', and joked that Kenelm was 'a Magician and a Sorcerer'. The mere fact that Kenelm could enjoy such jests showed how far he had come: the accusations of demonic sorcery levelled seriously at his teacher Thomas Allen could now be laughed off, and he had proven that he deserved to be not only ennobled, but respected for his learning. Soon, though, the old anxieties began to creep back in. After news of Kenelm's knighthood spread, the prolific London gossip John Chamberlain wrote to his friend Dudley Carleton, English ambassador to Venice, that 'the King since the Princes return knighted young Sir Everard Digby, sonne to him that was a prime man in the powder treason'. Not only was the treachery of Kenelm's father still all too well remembered, but he could even be mistaken for Everard, and wrongly attributed the same name. The stain would not be forgotten quite as easily as he had hoped.

As it dawned on Kenelm that his own standing remained precarious, he also began to realise just how far Venetia's reputation had fallen in his absence. He was now fully convinced that she had done nothing to deserve the dark swirl of rumours that enveloped her, but it was impossible to ignore. By the time he returned to

England she was commonly described as a 'celebrated Beautie and Courtezane', and it was said that Richard, third Earl of Dorset, not only kept her 'as his Concubine' but even 'had children by her'. She became the butt of malicious jokes, and fodder for crude songs: one night some wit wrote in large letters over the door of her lodgings the words 'Pray Come not neer, for Dame Venetia Stanley lodgeth here', while a ballad sung in drinking houses that invited the city's panders to 'bring fforth your whores by Clusters' also advised 'Gallants, come not neare to brave Venetia Stanley!' Kenelm became painfully aware of the vicious whispers that he and Venetia continued to attract even after his knighthood; then, humiliatingly, the malicious murmurs became open mockery. Kenelm got into an argument with one of the ambassadors to the English court, and the man railed 'bitterly' against him, calling him 'the son of a Traytor & the husband of a whore'. In the long painful silence that followed these words, Kenelm realised with anguish that he remained vulnerable to such insults despite all that he had achieved. His father's crimes might still be placed at his door, and though he and Venetia were not even betrothed, their former intimacy was clearly well known and mocked. He controlled himself, though, and did not rage openly at the man or indignantly draw his sword. Instead, he stepped close to the ambassador, and replied quietly, with an icy calm, that 'he now lookt on him as a publick person and thatt he had nothing to say to him but that when he was himself, he would travel all the world to cutt his throate'. The threat clearly seemed sincere: seeing Kenelm's 'frightfull' countenance, the ambassador 'beg'd K. James to make his peace with him'.

While Kenelm was making the painful discovery that his new-found place in the world of courtly politics was less secure than he hoped, he also came to realise that a series of abrupt and dizzying changes in English life was creating a different set of threats to his standing. Charles and Buckingham had travelled to Madrid with every intention of marrying the Prince to his betrothed, despite her being a deeply pious Spanish princess, and to many of James's Protestant subjects, this was an appalling prospect: they wanted to see England join the holy crusade against the Catholic forces in Europe, not invite one of their number to ascend the nation's throne and send it marching back towards Rome. Kenelm had grown up in a country where he was part of a persecuted minority, viewed as wolves in sheep's clothing: English Catholics like him, it was believed, were sometimes willing to pay lip service to the laws and customs of the land but subtly strove to undermine them while pledging their ultimate allegiance to a foreign Pope, and each was a potential enemy to King and country. During Kenelm's years of travel in Europe, these long-standing fears had been driven to a new and violent pitch by the outbreak of the Thirty Years War in Europe, which began to seem like the apocalyptic struggle with the Roman Antichrist that many English Protestants impatiently awaited, and by the prospect of the Spanish Match. In the autumn of 1623, just before Kenelm returned from Spain in Charles's company, the roof of the French ambassador's chapel in London collapsed while a Jesuit was delivering a sermon: dozens of men, women and children were killed, but this did not stop a widespread outpouring of vicious euphoria among Protestants at this public display of God's displeasure for the way that popery was being allowed to creep back in unopposed. Even before Charles and Buckingham returned to England, though, their minds had changed entirely: they were furious at what they saw as their humiliating and infantilising treatment in the Spanish court, and while they arrived in Madrid intent on a marriage, they left resolved to lead England into a war that would restore their wounded honour and bring the Spaniards down a peg. When Charles returned to England without his Catholic bride, the populace broke out into spontaneous celebration: bonfires were lit, and songs sung of the nation's narrow escape from the Papist yoke. In an astonishing transformation, Charles and Buckingham accepted the new role thrust upon them with gusto, and placed themselves at the head of a belligerent Protestant faction baying for war with Spain.

Among the main obstacles that Charles and Buckingham faced as they adopted their new and unlikely stance was John Digby, the Earl of Bristol. Kenelm's relative had been party to the intimate details of their behaviour in Madrid, and would be able to paint a picture in which the negotiations had collapsed not because of the perfidy and malice of the Spaniards, but thanks to Buckingham's incompetence, tactlessness and naivety. In order to avert this inconvenient possibility, Charles and Buckingham managed to convince the increasingly frail and pliant James to summon Bristol home to England, but to place him under house arrest in London. Buckingham began a programme of character assassination, aiming 'false accusations' and 'the bitterness of his malice' at Bristol until 'his honour . . . was much traduced in most men's opinions'. He claimed that the Earl had become too 'hispaniolated' by his long years in Madrid, and that he had pressured Charles to convert to Catholicism. The problem for the pair was that they could not charge Bristol in any open court for his supposed crimes, because they could not risk allowing him to tell his version of the truth in a public trial – a less flattering version for Buckingham, and one on which his many enemies would have gleefully seized. Neither could they allow him to make his case before parliament, as he requested in a series of plaintive letters. Instead he languished in legal limbo, unable even to attend his mother on her deathbed.

In 1624 Charles and Buckingham convinced James to convene a parliament that would vote to fund the war that they desired. Its sessions rang with violently anti-Spanish and anti-Catholic speeches, and Buckingham took the unprecedented step of delivering a long oration in which he explained and justified his conduct in Madrid, and denounced the Spanish as dishonourable liars. Since James's son-in-law and daughter had been ousted as King and Queen of Bohemia and exiled to the Hague from their rightful dominions in the Palatinate – the events that lit the touchpaper of the Thirty Years War – the hotter kind of English Protestants had urged the King to join the European fray and oppose the evil forces of the Holy Roman Emperor. James had neither the money nor the inclination to send an army overseas, but in the spring of 1624 a cheaper and less risky way of intervening presented itself: a German mercenary named Count von Mansfeld presented himself at court, fresh from victories over the Emperor's armies, and offered to lead an expeditionary force into Europe for a reasonable fee. James, whose sickness was worsening, agreed: Mansfeld recruited 15,000 men in England and left for the Continent in the autumn, planning to form an alliance with Protestant forces from Holland and from Denmark, whose King, Christian IV, was on the verge of entering the war. Charles was pleased by his father's change of heart. He had always shared the desire to restore his sister Elizabeth to the Palatinate, more for the sake of family honour than religious fervour, but he had hoped to do so through the alliance with Spain: now that this had collapsed he could pursue his ambitions for his sister and become a militant Protestant hero. While Mansfeld took the fight to the Austrian Habsburgs in central Europe, he would pursue war with the Spanish Habsburgs, and collectively they would force a settlement that would restore the honour of the nation and confirm its providential destiny; as an added bonus, it would redress the humiliations that he and Buckingham had suffered in Madrid.

On 27 March 1625, a few months after the final session of the bellicose parliament, King James finally breathed his last at Theobald's House with his beloved Buckingham by his bedside. Both the Duke and Charles were genuinely distraught at his loss, but they quickly realised that it left them freer to pursue their own goals. Christian of Denmark entered the war in Europe just before James's death, seeming to swing the pendulum in the direction of the general Protestant crusade that they hoped to join. Aside from these larger goals, Buckingham could now let his deep personal loathing of Bristol have free rein, and following James's death the Earl was banished from London to the family home of Sherborne Castle in Dorset. Even the sound of the word 'Digby' became anathema to Buckingham's ears. The Duke openly told one of Kenelm's distant relations, another member of Bristol's retinue, 'that though he wisht him well, yet he loved him the worse for the name sake which grew odious to him', and when James Howell, who was one of Bristol's protégés, tried to win the Duke's favour and attain a position at court, he found that every window of opportunity was slammed abruptly in his face. He reported to his father that 'some body hath done me ill Offices, by whispering in [Buckingham's] ear, that I was too much *Digbyfied*, and so they told me positively, that I must never expect any employment about him of any trust'.

This was a terrible time to try and make one's way in the world while saddled with the name Digby, and Kenelm was in a particularly vexed position, as he owed allegiance both to Bristol and to Charles. He tried desperately to avoid offending either party, and agreed to act as go-between, trying to alleviate the bitter situation. Bristol, who was enfeebled by an illness brought on by his frustrations and mental suffering, entrusted his young relative with the delicate task of carrying letters to the monarch pleading his right to have a fair hearing, and to make his case in person. Kenelm painted a vivid picture of the Earl's sad plight to the new young King, and reported to Bristol on 27 May 1625 that Charles 'gave me a gratiouse and full audience ... And truely, my Lord, he did receive the newes of your ill state with much tendernes and asked me many particulars how yow were, and bade me hasten to lett your Lordship know he was very sorry for your sickness.' The message that came back from Charles was therefore mixed. He insisted that he knew Bristol to be 'an honest and sufficient man, and one that loved him', and gave assurances that he did not consider the Earl 'to be a delinquent, and to have offended in any matter of honesty'. Nonetheless, he insisted that Bristol had been too passionately in favour of the Spanish marriage; too strong in his criticisms of Buckingham; and that he had a general 'aptness ... to be over confident in the Spaniards'. These were not crimes, and hence did not merit a public trial, but they were faults that required public acknowledgement and contrition, and until these were forthcoming Bristol would continue to languish in Dorset. Kenelm's determination to carry these letters back and forth and to make his relative's case allowed him to stay in close contact with the

King; but it also earned him the Duke of Buckingham's enduring and implacable hatred.

As Kenelm bounced back and forth between his beloved relative and patron and the angry young monarch, the pendulum of political affairs continued to swing alarmingly. Even before James had died, while Charles and Buckingham were enjoying their new-found heroic status at the head of the war party, they realised that the money that Parliament could provide would be insufficient to fund the war against Spain that they craved. It was imperative to find a new bride for Charles, and the options were limited: she needed to be of suitably high rank, and the marriage would have to provide England with financial aid and a useful strategic alliance. The only suitable candidate was Henrietta Maria, the fifteen-year-old sister of the French King Louis XIII, and the daughter of the Queen whose affections Kenelm had eluded at Angers. Even as he was being feted as a Protestant luminary, Buckingham began secretly negotiating Charles's marriage to a Catholic princess, and when the marriage was effected by proxy in May 1625 and made public, the Duke's new and piously Protestant allies rounded on him as a hypocrite. Worst of all, Buckingham had agreed as part of the negotiations with Cardinal Richelieu to lend some English ships to the French. Richelieu was taking a keen interest in the navy, determined to build up a force as strong as the Spanish, but for the time being they lacked a powerful presence on the seas. Buckingham, however, failed to stipulate just what these ships could be used for. Richelieu's most pressing problem was an uprising by the Huguenots, French Protestants, led by the Duc de Soubise;

he added the English ships to his attempt to crush the rebellion, deploying them against the Huguenot stronghold of La Rochelle and its beleaguered population. The English public were devastated and appalled to hear of their co-religionists, an embattled minority in a Catholic country, being attacked using Charles's own navy. Matters grew even worse when Charles's new young wife finally arrived in London, and brought with her a retinue of priests and Capuchin friars, who began publicly to say Mass and hear confession, drawing 'an innumerable multitude of people of both sexes and religions to the Queen's chapel'. The English Catholics, one of her priests crowed, 'looked with joy upon the Capuchins as men sent by heaven . . . and thanked God for having kept them in that religion of which their fathers were genuine professors'. England was still on course for war with Spain, but this was cold comfort when Catholic Mass was openly celebrated in the capital for the first time since the reign of Mary I, three quarters of a century before. Each parliament that the King called resounded with paranoid fury, aimed largely at Buckingham, and stoked by the terrible plague that decimated London in 1625: after the Petition against Recusants was read in the parliament of 1626, a rainstorm washed a dozen coffins out of a churchyard and spilled the gruesome remains of plague victims into the street, while reports claimed that a terrifying ghost had been seen walking atop the floodwaters. At this point, in May 1626, Bristol had finally been permitted to leave Dorset for London and petition the House of Lords for a fair hearing: the case was about to begin when the attempt by the House of Commons to begin impeachment proceedings against Buckingham led Charles swiftly to dissolve Parliament, and Bristol was duly sent to the Tower of London. Before long, events took yet another baffling twist, as Charles fell out with his new young wife and sent most of her retinue back to France. In a repeat of the Madrid fiasco, the King and Buckingham began to suspect that they had been duped by a more experienced and canny politician – Richelieu, who was ascending to supreme power in the French court, and who had no intention of assisting with their anti-Spanish aims. They began to push for open conflict not only with Spain, but with France as well.

Kenelm watched these developments closely, with a mixture of excitement, confusion and trepidation, even as he began to step back from the forefront of political life. He and his family were notorious Catholics, and between 1623 and 1625 the religion that they practised had both been entrenched at the very highest level, and subject to ever more violent and hysterical attacks. England had forged closer connections with the Continent through the new King's marriage, yet seemed to be on course for war with two of Europe's greatest powers, after years spent trying desperately to remain neutral under the old King. With his most powerful relative and patron imprisoned, Kenelm could as yet do nothing to affect the course of events and he felt profoundly lost, all of his efforts to establish himself in the world meaning little amidst such turbulence and uncertainty. There was one thing of which he remained sure despite everything, however, and one part of his life where he could make a decisive change, no matter its risks. Kenelm had decided that he cared nothing for Venetia's bad reputation, and the gossip it had inspired: he still loved her, despite the difficulties of recapturing the first youthful flush of their love following his return from Europe, and this was the firm centre around which all of his disquiet swirled. Venetia's first instinct, after the betrayals she had suffered and the defamation to which she was subjected, had been to retire into a life of pious solitude, but Kenelm, who had learned from his earlier mistake in trying to force his passion on her too abruptly, continued to visit her but in a more tentative and respectful vein. Finally, despite all that had come between them, she realised that she too still loved him above all, and 'of a sudden a most bright and glorious day of joy rose out of the lap of their late dusky and clouded night of sorrow'. In January 1625, just a few months before the King was wed, Kenelm and Venetia were married, joining their hands 'in that sacred knot which had long before knit their affections, and was now equally welcome on both sides'.

For the time being, they kept their nuptials secret; they wanted not only to protect their love from the harsh judgements and insinuations of the courtly world that had already done Venetia so much damage, but also to conceal it from their parents. Mary Digby still disliked the prospect of such an impoverished match for her elder son, and Venetia's father was trying fervently to do right by his daughter and bestow 'some settlement of estate' upon her, which the couple 'feared he would have avoyded if he had knowne she was bestowed' already and could avoid paying a dowry. The secret became ever harder to keep, however, because Venetia fell pregnant almost immediately. As the pregnancy neared its end, Kenelm arranged for her to travel to a place of 'security and secrecy', where she could give birth in private, with all necessary assistance. Their plans were thwarted, however: the day before she was due to depart, Venetia fell from her horse and 'wrenched one of her legges'. The pain of her sprained sinews brought on labour, and she was forced to give birth 'in a place where she could have no assistance', aided by the only servant she could trust, a woman with no experience of childbirth who was 'made yett more uselesse' by her extreme anxiety. Kenelm rushed to be with Venetia, and was humbled by her behaviour throughout 'a most sore and dangerous labor', which she bore with astonishing fortitude. It was unheard of in England for a husband to be in the room while his wife gave birth, but Kenelm knew from his travels 'that it was warranted by the practise of most other countries'. He was determined to stay by her side, and Venetia 'would never permitt me to be absent': thus he was present when on 6 October 1625 their first son, whom they also named Kenelm, was born. Since the infant had endured a fraught and complicated arrival, they rushed to have him baptised, but then they could relax and allow themselves to appreciate their new life as a family, and enjoy the 'extreme tendernesse' that they felt for one another and their son. In two tumultuous years since his return from Spain, Kenelm had become a knight of the realm and a gentleman of the Prince's privy chamber, and had been denounced as a whore's husband and a traitor's son: now, at twenty-two years of age, he was a father himself, but he was no more sure of his place in the world.

II 'The Knowledge of One's Self'

'I need seek no further for arguments to prove what I say, than to entreat you to look a little into yourself, and then you cannot choose but acknowledge how you now scarcely cast an eye upon the studies which, heretofore, you applied yourself unto with much eagerness and no less benefit; that your endeavours to increase upon your master's favour and grace are mainly slackened, which if you had made right use of, in all probability your rank and fortunes might,

by this time, have been ranked with the foremost; and that you do not put yourself forward into great and honourable actions with that zeal and vigour that you have done. All which effects of a weakened and decayed mind, I can attribute to no other cause but your having entertained in your breast a servile affection, which, wheresoever it entereth, is a clog to generous spirits, and freezeth all heroic thoughts in their very births, and overthroweth the worthiest resolutions; and will cause any man to sink in the value of the world.'

These words, with others of like nature, spoken by Aristobulus with much authority and seriousness, through which yet shined much affection, did pierce Theagenes to the very soul . . . But at length, his spirits unfolding themselves out of the net of deep and amazed sorrow, he replied to him in this manner . . . 'I must acknowledge that I have studied so much as to be very well informed that no knowledge is comparable to the knowledge of one's self, and that all learning is vain which teacheth not to better the mind, and that the deepest speculations are but difficult trifles, if they be not employed to guide men's actions on the path of virtue and directed to gain peace and tranquillity to the soul.'

Theagenes then having with incredible diligence got all things in readiness for his voyage, and with equal constancy and magnanimity overcome the many difficulties and oppositions that occurred to him, some of them wrought by a powerful and envious hand, as well as by the malignity of fortune, which most men thought would have disordered and overthrown his designs; and having taken leave of all of his friends, the last whom he visited, as he was going

aboard his ship, was Aristobulus, who then desired him to inform him truly and free from suspense, whether he were married or no; because that, he said, his great familiarity with Stelliana, and her entertaining of it, did make most men believe he was, and yet his not public avowing it did make him doubt it.

Whereupon Theagenes acknowledged ingenuously that he was.

Though his marriage remained a secret, Kenelm's withdrawal from public life in order to attend to his wife and son inevitably caught the attention of his friends, and those who supported him. The Earl of Bristol, who had finally been released from the Tower and permitted to take his seat in the House of Lords since the country was too far down the road to war for his objections to matter to Buckingham, was concerned by his young relative's behaviour: he had identified his talents from a young age and placed great trust in him, and now he heard that Kenelm spent much time in the company of a woman of ill repute. He took it upon himself to offer stern but loving advice, and Kenelm was hurt that the relative whom he revered, and on whose behalf he had petitioned so tirelessly and at such risk to his own reputation, did not have faith in his intentions towards Venetia. He knew, however, that Bristol spoke some truth: Kenelm had abandoned the public realm too entirely, and now, with the new responsibilities of which the Earl was unaware, he needed to return and strive to secure his and his family's future. His experience of ferrying letters and messages between the King and Bristol had earned him the Duke of Buckingham's antipathy but it had also granted him the opportunity to view the strange and repeated shifts of English political life in the mid-1620s; and, with his talent for sharp observation and acute judgement, he learned a great deal from what he witnessed. He now owed it to his wife and son to do something that would guarantee his standing and his reputation, and he gradually began to formulate a grand and unprecedented plan. If Kenelm was still haunted by his father's memory, then during this time he began to notice that the whole nation seemed to be stalked by the ghosts of its past – and especially those of the Virgin Queen, Elizabeth I, and her most illustrious servants. Elizabeth had never been forgotten – every year on 17 November, the bells of London churches whose peals had commemorated the Gunpowder Plot two weeks previously rang again to mark the anniversary of her birth. As English Protestants became increasingly impatient first with King James's determination to pursue peace with Spain, and then with his son's eagerness to marry a Catholic princess, her memory took on a new and critical urgency. Elizabeth's reign began to be gazed back upon through rose-tinted spectacles, as an age when Catholic Europe was viewed with the contempt and belligerence that it deserved, by a Queen and her retinue of magnificent heroes who contrasted dazzlingly with the effete and equivocating leaders of more recent times. As Kenelm trawled the booksellers' stalls around St Paul's Cathedral, eager to add more up-to-date English publications to the library he had augmented in Italy, he became sharply aware of this new tendency. In 1624 the most vociferous Puritan opponent of the Spanish Match, Thomas Scott, anonymously published a work titled *Vox Coeli, or Newes from Heaven*, which consisted of a celestial dialogue between the ghosts of a cluster of deceased English royals, from Henry VIII to Elizabeth herself. Scott had Elizabeth call war with Spain 'farre more safer, and farre more profitable' than peace, and declared that Charles was better married to an English milkmaid than a Spanish princess.

It became clear to Kenelm that the resurgent memory of Elizabeth was closely tied to the belief that, during her reign, England had reigned supreme upon the seas, as proven in 1588 by the providential crushing of the vast Spanish Armada. An MP named Benjamin Rudyerd stood up in the parliament of 1626 and called for a war against Spain to be pursued by private individuals in the West Indies, 'by part of which course, that famous Queen of most gracious memory, had heretofore almost brought him on his knees'. Since he had first delved into English history and litera-ture as a young boy, Kenelm had been fascinated by the legendary figures who had pursued these sea wars, and in 1626 he noted with interest the publication of a volume describing the voyages of one of the greatest of these heroes, with the revealing title, *Sir Francis Drake Revived: Calling upon this Dull or Effeminate Age, to folowe his Noble Steps for Gold and Silver*. Kenelm admired Drake's ambition and military prowess – so much so that he had an obscure treatise written by Drake copied out by hand, and added his own name to the title page: this case for an all-out sea war with the Spanish in the Atlantic was now titled 'A Discourse touching the Annoyinge of the King of Spain written by Sir Kellem Digbie.' While Drake was a fearsomely effective commander, though, he was no scholar, and Kenelm saved his deepest admir-ation for those great Elizabethans who had mingled martial skill with the deepest pursuits of the mind. He felt a particular affinity with Sir Walter Raleigh, whom he considered 'a greate man, very considerable in our state and in his owne eminent talents'. Raleigh had also sailed far and wide, sponsoring and leading privateering voyages against the Spanish, and he had raised himself from humble beginnings to become a consummate courtier; he was not only a fine poet and an omnivorous student of history, but had a keen practical interest in alchemy and chemistry, and was also an enthusiastic amateur cook. His example was, however, sobering as well as exciting: he had been imprisoned for years in the Tower of London after James assumed the throne, his anti-Spanish views having become an embarrassment. It was during his incarceration that he did much of his concocting and his cooking, before he was finally executed in 1618 for treason.

If Raleigh's example showed Kenelm the risks of a life lived between the world of high politics and the realm of ideas, he found a more poignant and unequivocal model in the memory of Sir Philip Sidney, the great poet and paragon of elegant virtue who had died young in 1586, fighting the Spanish in the Netherlands. His memory had been kept alive by his many admirers, and Sidney too returned to particular prominence amidst the anti-Spanish outpourings of the early 1620s. His longest and most ambitious work, a rollocking and fiendishly complex romance titled *Arcadia*, was repeatedly republished: Kenelm, who had been interested in Sidney since he heard tales of him during his student days with Thomas Allen at Oxford, bought one of the new editions and read it with gusto. It convinced him that Sidney was 'the Phoenix of the age he lived in, and the glory of our nation, and the patterne to posterity of a complete, a gallant, and a perfect gentleman'. Sidney's romance combined passages of thinly veiled historical fact and autobiography – he appeared intermittently in the guise of the shepherd Philisides – with fantastical imaginings and far-fetched plots, his characters gallivanting across and around the Mediterranean in a flurry of cross-dressing, mistaken identity, near-death experiences and grand battles. The republication of his work fuelled the surge in patriotism and anti-Spanish feeling that Kenelm encountered upon his return to England, providing another ideal from the recent past which ambitious young patriots might strive heroically to emulate.

Kenelm found the upsurge of nostalgia for these Elizabethan greats and their prowess at sea invigorating, but also unsettling, for at its head stood Buckingham, whose presence Kenelm encountered wherever he turned. Issuing a grand rallying cry in parliament, the Duke proclaimed that 'you that are young men may in these active times gain honour and reputation, which is almost sunk, and gain the ancient glory of our predecessors'. Of the various honours and titles that James had bestowed upon him, the one that Buckingham took by far the most seriously was that of Lord High Admiral. When the Duke began to conduct his duties, it became clear to him that, after James had made peace with Spain in 1604 and removed the main impetus for the upkeep of the navy, it had sunk into a horrendous state of disrepair. Naval officials, from Buckingham's predecessor as the Lord Admiral down to lowly clerks, were guilty of widespread venery and corruption, which a succession of naval commissions tried and failed to remedy. In Thomas Scott's heavenly dialogue, the Catholic Queen Mary acknowledged that at one time 'Englands Navy-Royall could give a Law to the Ocean', but observed that 'now time and negligence hath almost made all these ships unserviceable, who lye rotting at Chatham'. She had a point, but Scott's ghostly Prince Henry replied that 'brave Buckingham hath of late yeares set a new face on that Fleet: and makes it not only his delight, but his glory to re-edifie and reform them'. The financial and practical difficulties that he faced were enormous, however, and

Buckingham's determination to pursue conflict speedily with Spain and France and avenge his injured honour left no time for these long-standing and systemic problems to be remedied. In 1625, while both Charles and Kenelm were busy with their marriage arrangements and as the plague raged in London, Buckingham threw his efforts into organising the first formal offensive against Spain, an assault on the strategically crucial port of Cádiz, which he hoped to capture and hold as an English outpost. Even this plan was an active attempt to recapture 'the ancient glory of our predecessors', for in 1596 another Elizabethan naval hero, the Earl of Essex, had made a triumphant assault on the town, with his troops carrying away rich spoils which included a valuable collection of books. Buckingham originally planned to lead the expedition himself, but the energies he poured into planning it took their toll on his always fragile health, and he had to relinquish command. Ill prepared and under-funded, the expedition was an embarrassing failure. Where Essex had successfully disrupted the silver fleets of 1595 and 1596, Buckingham's men arrived in leaky and badly provisioned ships, made drunken fools of themselves on shore, and slunk home with nothing to show for their troubles. So antiquated were the ships, in fact, that the captain of one vessel, the *St George*, complained that his second suit of sails had been worn against the Armada in 1588: the fleet was a doomed and rotting relic of England's heroic maritime past. After the defeat at Cádiz, a joke reportedly did the rounds in the Spanish-speaking world that 'there were now no more Drakes in England, all were hens'.

Buckingham's failure revealed to Kenelm the risks of seeking to emulate the heroic past, if one fell short of its myths and ideals. Buckingham, increasingly desperate and openly attacked by those who blamed him for all the nation's ills, remained determined to win back his own good name through a grand triumph at sea that would confirm him as an English hero in the Elizabethan model. Following the failure at Cádiz and the breakdown of relations with France, Buckingham turned his attention temporarily away from Spain. No action had done his standing more damage than the use of the ships that he had lent to Richelieu against the Protestant community of La Rochelle, and Buckingham now sought to rectify his earlier wrong and alleviate the plight of the Huguenots. His ambitions had been inflated, not quelled, by the Cádiz disaster: he now proposed personally to lead a fleet carrying nearly 8,000 troops, the largest naval force to sail into foreign waters in English history, and take and hold the Île de Ré, just off the coast by the walled stronghold of La Rochelle, which would prevent the French from blockading the city. The 1626 parliament, which was furious with Buckingham, demanded his impeachment and refused to fund his latest scheme; but Charles, whose loyalty to his closest friend had never wavered since their time in Madrid, dissolved the parliament before they could act and set about raising the requisite funds by extraordinary and controversial means, including a forced loan levied on his subjects.

While these desperate measures were being taken, the course of the war raging in Europe threatened to make matters even worse for England. The Protestant alliance that had inspired such hope in the previous years was destroyed when the armies of Christian of Denmark were routed in August 1626 at the battle of Lutter am Barenberge by the Emperor's troops, a defeat that caused general despair in England; a few weeks later the mercenary force led by Count von Mansfeld that King James had helped to fund meekly dissolved, rather than face the imperial general Albert van Wallenstein in battle. To add to the gloom and embarrassment enveloping the nation, late in 1626 the French seized the entire English wine fleet while it was docked at Bordeaux, damaging a valuable trade and depriving their thirsty nobles at one fell swoop. Protestant hopes were left in ruins and, ominously for England, with the Austrian Habsburgs triumphing there was little need for the Spanish to join a distracting war in central Europe: in March 1627, Spain and France formalised an alliance against the English, with whom both nations were at war, and the Spaniards sent ships to aid the blockade of La Rochelle. The more hopeless matters grew, however, the more determined the Duke of Buckingham became to swing the pendulum back in favour of England and the Protestant cause through a great victory, and his fleet finally departed for the Île de Ré, arriving in July 1627. They besieged the town of Saint Martin and tried to blockade the island, but it became clear that their provisions and equipment were woefully inadequate: the siege ladders they had brought were too short to scale the walls, and Richelieu managed to send small boats through the English lines with supplies for the besieged garrison. Buckingham behaved with genuinely heroic gallantry on the battle-field, personally leading a charge at the walls of Saint Martin – as he lost no opportunity to stress through a concerted public-relations campaign carried out in England – but nothing was gained. This expedition too ended in depressing failure, with thousands of Englishmen losing their lives and nothing of any significance achieved. The Duke's latest attempt to cast himself as a successor to Elizabethan heroes like Raleigh, Essex and Drake had been a catastrophe, as he and the survivors, numbering just 3,000, limped back to England in disarray.

Kenelm kept a low profile following his secret marriage to

Venetia and the arrival of their son, but from 1625 to 1627 he watched this catalogue of disasters unfold with great interest albeit with mixed feelings: like his compatriots he lamented so many pointless English deaths caused by 'these two wars so wretchedly entered into', but he felt a deep sense of affinity with Catholic Europe, where he had undergone such formative experiences, and he could not help enjoying the repeated blows to the pride and reputation of his most powerful enemy, Buckingham. It was another development that caught Kenelm's attention most sharply, however. If the failed assaults on Cádiz and the Île de Ré had revealed the incapacity of the Royal Navy to carry out the large-scale operations of which it had once been capable, Charles and Buckingham had copied Elizabeth's example in another way. They had also permitted a return to the more fragmented and decentralised war at sea under-taken during her reign by privateers – private citizens who were given permission in the form of 'letters of marque' to take ships belonging to the enemy as legitimate prizes.

In practice, the line between state-approved privateering and uncontrolled piracy was difficult to draw, and few had an interest in drawing it: the King started to issue letters of marque with uncontrolled abandon, and hundreds of French and Spanish ships began to be captured by enterprising English captains. The grandest of these privateers were no less driven than Buckingham by a desire to recapture the glories of a heroic past: the most prominent, Robert Rich, second Earl of Warwick, was the nephew of the Earl of Essex who had sacked Cádiz, and his mother had been Sir Philip Sidney's muse. Though in the next decade the pious and puritanical Warwick would have considerable success as a privateer in the Caribbean, during the dark war years of the 1620s he fared no better than Buckingham. His attempted raid on the Portuguese coast in 1627 ended ignominiously: hoping to plunder the incoming silver fleet from Brazil, Warwick's fleet mistakenly blundered into and attacked a much larger flotilla of Spanish vessels, escaping only due to his enemies' confusion and the thick fog, and staggered home to England with the crew squabbling and the officers blaming one another bitterly for the debacle.

Amidst this catalogue of mishaps and spectacular failures, Kenelm glimpsed an opportunity. As a private citizen, he realised, he too might be able to obtain a letter of marque, and set off from England as a privateer. Were he to do so, perhaps he might be able to succeed where Buckingham, Warwick and others had failed so spectacularly. Their misguided adventures had only confirmed their inability to live up to the examples of England's heroic past. But he, a known Catholic and traitor's son, would astound the nation all the more if he could more successfully emulate this pantheon of Protestant heroes. It was a dangerous course of action, for he might fail as resoundingly as they had; but, were he to succeed, he would expunge the memory of his father's treachery once and for all, and render irrelevant his wife's supposed infidelities. Even Buckingham would not be able to diminish him were he to succeed spectacularly enough, whether or not he bore the Digby name that the Duke loathed. He decided 'to employ himself in some generous action that might give testimony to the world' of 'the nobleness of his mind' and 'his active and vigorous spirits', and 'resolved to undertake speedily something that might tend to the King's service, and gain himself honour and experience'.

The failures of Buckingham and Warwick had demonstrated that a privateering voyage of this sort should not be undertaken without considerable forethought. There were various options that seemed plausible in the early months of 1627. Kenelm could patrol the seas around England, France and the Atlantic coast of Spain, like Warwick, but hopefully with better results; he could venture further into the ocean, perhaps even as far as the Caribbean, and see what rich spoils could be found there; or, once he was at sea and answerable to no one, he could sail southwards as far as the Guinea Coast, and investigate the rich trades in gold and slaves of which he had heard tell. As he mulled over these various options, one idea above all began to suggest itself to him with irresistible power. Under Elizabeth, many privateers had sailed into the Mediterranean, hoping to snatch as prizes some of the rich merchant ships that criss-crossed the seas in vast numbers. His own voyage might take him to the same region: it could lead him not into new waters, but back towards the seas that he had experienced, so briefly and so tantalisingly, during his earlier travels. Were he to sail there, he could strive to be much more than just another privateer: he could explore every facet of the world into which he had fleetingly peered, enrich his sense of its peoples and its stories, of the ancient tales and the occult arts that had originated there. He could sail further eastward, to the distant and mysterious realms that so fascinated him. Going far beyond the limits of his previous travels, he could test not only his heroism and military skills, but the limits of his mind, and the person who he was in the process of becoming: he could return having transformed not only his reputation in the eyes of the world, but also his deepest being.

Slowly the plan began to take shape in Kenelm's mind, until he became convinced that it was his only option. He began to make discreet enquiries into the practicalities of such a journey. Kenelm was convinced that he had the necessary mixture of practical and theoretical skills necessary to assume a command. His apprenticeship in mathematics at Oxford had introduced him to more than just the abstractions of geometry: Thomas Allen and the young minds who gathered around him were equally concerned with the practical sciences of geography, cartography and navigation, all of which were debated in his chambers in Gloucester Hall. Kenelm had received the basic training required to oversee a small fleet, and he had augmented it with his own shipboard experiences during his travels, when he carefully observed the proper management of a vessel. If there were gaps in his knowledge, this was no obstacle: the new privateering war had prompted the publication of various practical guides to seamanship, which covered not only the technicalities of navigation and gunnery, but explained how to behave and carry oneself at sea, and detailed all the slang and technical terms that sailors used. As he began to plan his departure in earnest, Kenelm bought one of these recent publications, titled *A Sea Grammar* and written by the explorer John Smith, which was explicitly intended for those 'many young Captaines, and others who desire to be Captaines, who know very little, or nothing at all to any purpose', of life at sea.

With Kenelm assured of his own capacity to undertake such a voyage, the next issue to be considered was finance. His own circumstances had gradually stabilised and improved following his return to England: he still had the £3,000 of annual income that his mother had managed to protect after her husband's execution, and, as he and Venetia gradually realised the inevitability of making their marriage known at least to their families, matters improved

further. Their anxiety about her father's response proved un-
warranted: in fact, Edward Stanley was glad in his old age to have
an energetic and competent young son-in-law to take charge of
his chaotic financial affairs. Kenelm believed that 'the ruines
of a great fortune usually afford a carefull man meanes to gleane
a moderate one out of them', and he was able to salvage the
significant sum of £7,000 from his father-in-law's estate, for his
and Venetia's use as they saw fit. Now that Venetia's father had
provided a dowry of sorts, Kenelm finally broke the news of his
marriage to his mother, and Mary Digby not only reconciled
herself with the turn of events that she had taken such lengths to
avert, but also soon came to love and respect her daughter-in-law.
The money that they possessed, however, was still far too little
for the expedition that he had in mind, and so he began searching
for financial backers.

Kenelm approached three wealthy London merchants named
George Strowde, Nathaniel Wrighte and Abraham Reynerson, all
of whom had extensive knowledge of Mediterranean shipping and
useful contacts in the maritime community. They were impressed
by the confident and physically imposing young man, who spoke
to them with such passion of his former travels, and his determination to return from the Mediterranean with rich spoils of which
they could take a share: they agreed to back him financially, and
helped him to obtain ships. The first was his flagship, a 600-ton
vessel named the *Eagle*; the second, considerably smaller at
250 tons, was named the *Elizabeth and George*. An experienced
seaman named Captain Milborne was given everyday command
of the larger ship, and Kenelm approached a friend named
Sir Edward Stradling, who came from a learned family in
Glamorgan and shared Kenelm's love of both poetry and adventure,

and offered him a position as principal officer of the second vessel, which he accepted.

It still remained for Kenelm to receive the King's official leave to undertake the planned voyage, and to obtain the letters of marque required to formalise his status as a privateer, rather than a mere plunderer. At first, it seemed as if this was going to be a straightforward prospect. Kenelm had seen much less of Charles since he had been crowned, due to the more retired life that he lived following his secret marriage to Venetia, and to the King's immersion in affairs of state and the turbulent beginning of his own wedded life. Kenelm still hoped that the friendship they had struck up in Madrid would stand him in good stead, and when he went to Whitehall in the autumn of 1627 he was allowed an audience. Despite the tensions that had arisen between them while Kenelm was advocating for the Earl of Bristol, Charles was delighted to see his friend from happier days, and more than willing to grant him what he asked. 'The King,' Kenelm noted contentedly, 'promised me a commission under the great seal of England as ample as any had ever granted,' giving him permission to sail where he chose, and take as prizes any ships belonging to the enemies of England.

His wishes seemingly having been granted with astonishing speed, Kenelm turned his mind to the daunting practicalities of undertaking a voyage. Strowde, Wrighte and Reynerson were able to give him the full benefit of their know-how and their connections in the world of seafaring, but there was still an enormous amount to prepare and organise, as Kenelm trudged between the shipyards and warehouses along the Thames. He soon encountered a series of difficulties and frustrating delays: he had commissioned the *Eagle*, shortly before she set out on a trade voyage to Greenland, 'not doubting her return in time for my uses', but, as was often the case with sea voyages, the proposed time frame was little more than an optimistic guess, and the ship was two months delayed in arriving back. To complicate matters further another ship that he had hoped to add to his small fleet, the *Samuel*, was destroyed by fire just as it was finally made ready to sail; the master of his flagship disappeared without explanation; and the replacement master, Brian Harrison, at the very last minute 'married a wife and left the voyage'. These mishaps with his ships and his men were compounded by the same problems with supplies and provisions that had dogged Buckingham's failed expeditions. Because the Duke had bought all available supplies for his ill-fated excursion to Ré a few months before, 'there was but one barrel of gunpowder to be got in London', and Kenelm was forced to send to Amsterdam for 200 barrels, while the shipment of fish being carried from the West Country to feed his men at sea was captured by the Dunkirker pirates who marauded ceaselessly at the mouth of the Thames.

These were typical hiccups, the kind of routine problem that any aspiring commander would need to be able to circumvent or overcome. But the problems piled up during the autumn of 1627, and Kenelm began to suspect that, among the 'many difficulties and oppositions that occurred to him', some were 'wrought by a powerful and envious hand, as well as by the malignity of fortune'. Even after the disastrous defeat that he had suffered at Ré in the summer, Buckingham was determined to return there again and finally win the victory that he craved, and he was travelling frenetically between London and Portsmouth, trying to assemble his own enormous fleet with even scanter stocks of food, weapons and goodwill than before. When he heard of Kenelm's plans, and the commission that the King had granted, he exploded with fury. No man should have been allowed to gather up gunpowder, supplies and able seamen for a voyage of his own when Buckingham needed them so desperately; but that this man should be a Digby, a member of the family he despised above all, was too much to bear. From this point on, Kenelm bitterly observed, 'the Duke's officers . . . caused me many troubles and delays'.

First, Buckingham tried to prevent him from assembling a

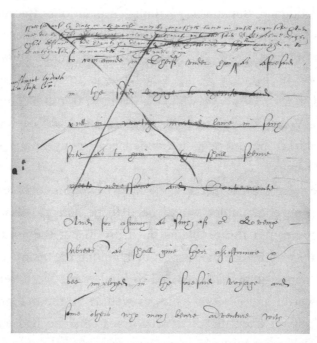

Kenelm's original privateering commission, with deletions and objections by
Buckingham's secretary, Sir Edward Nicholas

crew: naval vessels had first claim to any available sailors and, Kenelm complained, the Duke began 'pressing my men and ships for the King's service' and carrying away so many sailors that 'though I gave great wages yet I could get no good men'. Next Buckingham took aim at Kenelm's royal commission by tasking Sir Edward Nicholas, who was the Duke's secretary and trusted aide, to ensure that Kenelm's expedition would founder. Nicholas demanded to see the document of authorisation Kenelm had been given, and complained that no such commission had ever been granted to a private person: labelling it 'extravagant' and 'unreasonable', he angrily slashed through several offending passages with his pen. He also wrote in darkly threatening terms to Henry Marten, one of the Judges of the Admiralty, warning that 'the Duke . . . will take it as great remissness in those he trusts when he shall hear of such a grant to Sir Kenelm', and that he planned to use all the power of Buckingham's many friends and cronies to dash the commission.

Kenelm was stunned and disheartened by these developments: he had hoped to make his voyage in part to escape from attacks of this sort, based not on who he was but on his family name, but now they threatened to derail him before he had even begun. His first instinct was furiously to challenge Buckingham, denounce him, perhaps even force him to defend his honour in combat, but sensibly he suppressed his anger and formulated a calm and canny response. He realised that, if he could establish precedents for his voyage, then Nicholas's claim that his commission was uniquely extravagant would collapse. Now his long-standing friendships with members of London's scholarly community came in useful. He wrote to the great antiquarian Sir Robert Cotton, with whom he had become acquainted through Thomas Allen, and explained,

'I have spoken to the king to have a commission, and he hath with the fulnesse of his graunt outgone my desire; but referreth me to the finding out of presedentes to draw mine by, assuring me that mine shall be as ample and as full as ever any mans was of my qualitie.' He therefore asked Cotton 'to search over some former patentes given to knightes and gentlemen' and see how they compared to his own. He dashed off another letter to the Masters, Wardens and Assistants of Trinity House, who were the principal naval authority. He enquired after the proper division of any prizes that he might take while at sea, in order 'to determine what shares do belong to mee in my particular, being Command[er] in chiefe, & authorized by Commission', and explained that he aimed to answer the objections of 'many doubting Persons' opposed to his voyage.

As the autumn of 1627 gave way to winter, Kenelm remained stranded in limbo, striving desperately to elude Buckingham's attempts at interference and defend his original commission, and awaiting responses to his enquiries. This was where he found himself, still stranded amidst uncertainty, as 5 November rolled around. He had desperately wanted to be gone from English shores before this wretched anniversary, hoping to avoid the annual reminder of his father's treason and terrible death, but there was nothing to be done. As the manic festivities echoed through the London streets late into the night, Kenelm ceased his pacing and resolved to find better ways to distract himself. He sat and leafed through a pile of volumes that he had collected on his strolls around the booksellers' stalls in St Paul's churchyard, finding in their pages a mixture of solace and inspiration. He dipped into John Smith's *Sea Grammar*, refreshing his memory of the more obscure examples of maritime lingo. He leafed through the newly available collection of Francis Drake's journals, losing himself in the successful escapades of an Elizabethan hero. When he tired of this salty fare, he began to read through an entertaining collection of tales that had just been published about the life of his intellectual hero, Roger Bacon. One of the volumes that he had procured, however, was entirely blank: rather than containing the tales of others, this was the book into which he would put his own story, by keeping a detailed journal of his experiences. As he sat and waited for the grim celebrations to pass, Kenelm decided that he would begin by writing only on the left sheet of each double page, so that when he reached the end of the book he could turn it upside down and continue writing in the opposite direction on the sheets that he had left blank, his words performing their own return journey back to where he had begun.

The combination of these distractions helped Kenelm to make it through an awful night, and in the days and weeks that followed his situation began finally to improve. The enquiries that he had made regarding precedents for his voyage received promising answers: Robert Cotton sent the fruits of his historical labours, and the naval officials also replied. They had determined that Kenelm's was 'noe frequent Case', but they had found one precedent and concluded not only that his commission was valid but that, as the commander of a small fleet, he was entitled to twice the share normally enjoyed by a privateering captain. Armed with these responses, Kenelm triumphantly presented them to Nicholas, who realised that the letters of marque could not be abolished altogether. The Duke's secretary continued to raise

objections, and as the last weeks of November gave way to December
he convinced the King to alter the exact wording and restrict
Kenelm's commission, making it sound less like an official venture
of the Crown. On 13 December 1627, Kenelm was finally granted
a licence by the King 'to take a voyage to sea, tending to the service
of the realm and the increase of his knowledge', and his crew were
commanded 'to yield him all duty, obedience and respect'.

In the next week Kenelm finalised the repair and provisioning
of his two ships and, despite Buckingham's attempt to snatch up
every able-bodied sailor in London, he managed to gather a crew,
since most men preferred the possibility of privateering spoils to
grim naval service, and were happy to elude the Duke's officials
and join Kenelm's adventure instead. There was nothing more
that Buckingham could do: he grudgingly gave his permission,
while making clear that his contempt for Kenelm had only been
increased by these machinations. On 21 December, Kenelm prepared
himself to depart from London for the Kent coast where his ships
waited, but he could scarcely bring himself to believe that the
obstacles facing him had been bypassed. In a final, nervous letter
to Nicholas, he wrote, 'I beseech you remember my Lord Dukes
promise to me that I should not stay at all upon this occasion'.

Kenelm had been so utterly embroiled in these fraught negotiations
that it was only now, as his departure loomed, that he realised that
evading Buckingham's malice would not be the most difficult part
of his departure from England. It would also mean leaving Venetia
behind again, and laying their love open to the same strains and
stresses that it had barely survived during his last prolonged

absence. If this were not difficult enough, he would have to bid
farewell to the infant Kenelm and embark on a dangerous voyage,
just when his son was approaching the age at which Kenelm had
lost his own father. To add to his pain, Venetia had become pregnant again in the spring of 1627. Kenelm had first hoped to leave
during the summer, but as the delays to his voyage dragged on,
he realised that he would have to meet his second-born briefly,
and almost immediately depart. Venetia had responded to Kenelm's
initial announcement of his plans by weeping, and asking, 'What
sin have I committed to alienate me from your affection, or rather,
what have I done not to win and preserve it?' Gradually, however,
she came to accept his plans, and share his hope that his voyage
would finally negate the rumours and threats that might otherwise
deplete the happiness of their shared life, and endanger their
children's future. As Kenelm prepared to leave, Venetia 'wholly
retired and secluded herself from the world', determined to avoid
the courtly insinuations that had done her such damage, and to
find a place where she could give birth to her second child in less
fraught conditions than the first. While he was finalising his
preparations, their second son was born. They named him John:
it was a good, solid family name, shared both by Kenelm's brother
and by his greatest patron, the Earl of Bristol. Kenelm could hardly
bear to leave his newly expanded family, but convinced himself
that it was for their sake as much as his own that he must. As he
held his new son, he decided that the life of nervousness and
secrecy that he and Venetia had been living was at an end. So far,
fearful of the implications of Venetia's reputation for Kenelm's
standing in courtly society, they had informed only their immediate
families of their marriage. He had still not even told Bristol, who
was the closest thing he had ever known to a father; but no longer

would he conceal the full force of his love for his wife and children from the world. Before he left London, Kenelm went to see the Earl again. By now Bristol had heard rumours that Venetia had borne Kenelm a child, and he asked outright whether the pair were married. Kenelm announced unashamedly that they were, that he was a father twice over, and that he wanted all the world to know it. He assured Bristol that he had nothing to fear: Kenelm's love would neither endanger nor stifle his heroic thoughts, but fuel them. By the time he returned from the Mediterranean, he insisted, he would have performed such great feats that they would render any lingering memories of Everard's treason or Venetia's supposed infidelities irrelevant, and he, his wife and his children would have no cause to fear the judgement or malice of the world. On 22 December he departed from the city and made his way on horseback to the port of Deal in Kent where his ships waited, and boarded the *Eagle*, making himself at home in the plush surrounds of his private cabin. Even as he prepared to leave, having eluded Buckingham's attempts at derailment, Kenelm could not entirely banish the deeper anxieties that shadowed his departure. He knew that he risked following in his father's footsteps as he made his own grand plans: he was twenty-four years old, around three years younger than Everard had been when he was swept up into the Gunpowder Plot, and, like his father at that point, Kenelm had two infant sons whom his wild adventures would force him to leave behind. He was a young man in a hurry, hoping speedily to undertake a great feat that would confirm his stature and his difference from his shameful father, both in his own eyes and in the eyes of the world; but he could not entirely banish the fear that he was rushing into this new scheme, much as his father had been swept into the fatal error of his treason.

146

Part II

Time Is
Time Was
Time Is Past

4

December 1627–March 1628
The Bay of Biscay – The Straits of Gibraltar – The Barbary Coast

I 'A Spacious and Pleasant Green Meadow'

From these auspicious beginnings he might have taken to himself the presage of successful proceedings; but the envious arbiter of men's actions, who will suffer one in this life to take nothing pure, did all of a sudden so overwhelm this prosperous entrance with a sea of bitterness, that from the strange difference of estate which twenty days caused in Theagenes' fleet, one might see too evidently how unconstantly she moveth her wheel. For he had been but a while at sea, when with a contrary wind there came among his men such a violent pestilential disease, and raged with such fury, that within a few days he was reduced to such extremity that there were scarce men enough upon any important occasion to trim the sails . . . But that which of all others seemed to cause most compassion, was the furious madness of most of those who were near their end, the sickness then taking their brain; and those were in such great abundance that there were scarce men enough to keep them from running over-board, or from creeping out of the ports, the extreme heat of their disease being such that they desired all refreshings, and their depraved fantasy made them believe the sea to be a spacious and pleasant green meadow. This extremity of evil taught the meanest rank of people what the noblest precepts of philosophy can scarce do to the most elevated minds, that is, a most resupine patience in their sufferance.

Kenelm was determined to make a highly organised and disciplined start to his voyage, and to set a tone that would continue throughout the ensuing months. His departure from England may have been fraught, but now he was liberated: here at sea he could lay down the rules that other men had to follow, instead of being trapped by the opinions and preconceptions of his superiors, and having them dictate the terms of his commission. After arriving at the port of Deal he busied himself in distributing the men and the provisions that he had procured in London. Despite Buckingham's opposition he had managed to enlist nearly 250 crewmen, many of them bearing the physical and mental scars of the expeditions to Cádiz and the Île de Ré, and hoping to accrue some wealth by way of compensation. He placed 150 of them in the *Eagle*, and the remainder in the *Elizabeth and George*. Kenelm also confirmed Sir Edward Stradling's status as vice admiral in command of the smaller of his ships, taking the necessary pre-caution of 'substituting him Commander in chiefe in case of my death'. He named Edward's younger brother, Henry, as second in command on the *Elizabeth and George*, and confirmed the appoint-ment of Mr Milborne as captain of the *Eagle*, to be in charge of its day-to-day operations. He then filled the other vacant positions on both ships according to the experience and status of the remaining crew, naming numerous petty officers, gunners, the pursers who were in charge of disbursing daily provisions, lookouts, and carpenters to patch up the inevitable cracks and leaks.

Having organised his men in this fashion, Kenelm turned his mind to the specifics of the route that he proposed to take. Since his plan was to enter the Mediterranean and pursue any French or Spanish ships that crossed his path, he did not have a firm course to follow, but Kenelm knew that in the likely event that his ships would become separated, they would need a rough itinerary if they were to be successfully reunited. He therefore determined that the vessels should make first for Cape St Vincent, the promontory jutting out from the Algarve into the waters of the Atlantic, and stay thereabouts for fifteen days. If they were not reunited in that time, the ships should enter through the Straits of Gibraltar, sail past Marbella and Malaga, and then spend five days sailing between the Island of Alborán and the North African coast. If they still did not find one another, they should continue 'from thence to the southermost tip of Sardinia', then continue east between Sicily and Malta, and, if necessary, onward to the 'eastward end' of Cyprus. If they traced this route, Kenelm believed, his ships had the best chance of meeting with valuable prizes and, if needs be, with one another.

Having charted this rough course, Kenelm set on paper a series of directions for his principal officers, which he commanded them to relay to the crew, making clear the conduct that he expected of them. He was setting out with just two ships, but had every intention of swelling their number by taking French and Spanish prizes, and the logistics of such plunder needed to be anticipated. Kenelm told his officers exactly what they were to do if they should take another ship as a prize: each of them was to be paid a bonus, but all the goods taken from such a vessel were to be brought to the mainmast and carefully divided between the captain and the crew. They were allowed to pilfer at will from the personal belongings of the crew of any ship that they took as a prize, though they were not to interfere with the chests or private belongings of its captain, principal officers or surgeon. There was to be plenty of plundering, Kenelm assured them, but it should be carefully ordered, honourable and highly proper. He also wrote a series of commands solely for the eyes of his principal officers, explaining the list of directives to be followed in case their ships should lose sight of one another due to bad weather or other mishaps such as a vessel springing a severe leak or suffering a broken mast, and informing them of the specific locations at which they were to rendezvous in such instances. Kenelm outlined a detailed system of cannon shots and lights by which the ships were to communicate with one another at a distance. He sketched several configurations of lanterns and their meanings in the margins of his journal, meticulously tracing their outlines in ink. He had spent the months of frustrated delay in London musing on the precise form of these directives, and now he issued them: every eventuality was anticipated, every aspect of the voyage carefully planned.

Kenelm knew in issuing these instructions that it was essential to exude confidence and know-how at the outset, if he wanted to retain the full trust of his crew. The recent disasters at Cádiz and Ré that had shocked Kenelm and helped inspire his voyage were often blamed on the large number of 'young, needy, and inexperienced gentleman captains', who obtained their position by birth rather than merit or expertise, and who were more concerned with their own honour and prestige than the success of the voyage.

Dec. 1627.

A iournall beginning the 22: day
of December 1627.

The 22. day of December being saterday
and the next after St. Thomas day, j begun
my iourney towardes my shippes, wch lay att
Anchor in the Downes by Deale; where
after my arrivall, contarie windes att south
and southwest kept me ontill the 6. of Jan.
wch day (being sunday and twelfth day)
the winde came in the morning att Northeast,
and about 2 of the clocke afternoone jsett
sayle in the Eagle, and Sr. Edward Stradling
(being my Viceadmirall) in the Elizabeth
and George of London; the rest of the straights
fleete and men of warre being gone 4 houres
before us and then out of sight when wee
sett sayle.
Whiles j remained in the Downes, on new
yeares eve a Hamburg shippe called the
Stanter of about 180. tonnes, came in

Jan: 1627
1628

Such men tended to spend their time at sea either strutting about, or vomiting over the side. Sailors loved to exchange mocking stories of these poltroons, each one 'a brave Signior, a Rhodomantados that shall ruffle it out in his silks and cloth of gold'. These preening types could not abide the pungent realities of life aboard ship: sailors loved to tell the tale of one such man, who 'was sick with the savour of the sea; and his men pumping the ship in their watch, it gave a noisome smell (which notwithstanding is a good sign of a tight ship), whereof this young Neptune in a fume demanding the reason, reply was made that it was the pump. "Why," quoth he, "cast it overboard, for if it stink so, I will have none in my ship!" This was a sweet captain!'

Kenelm was a young gentleman with no prior experience of naval command, and was determined that his intense and unflinching focus on the task at hand would inoculate him against mockery of this sort. During his months of preparation he had plunged into John Smith's *Sea-Grammar* and other guides to maritime lore, learning a language that was nearly as new and as self-contained as the French and Italian that he spoke so fluently. He had memorised a dizzying array of alien words and phrases, like 'spurkit' (the spaces between the timbers along the side of a ship that needed to be kept carefully clean), and taught himself new meanings for everyday terms like 'knee' (crooked pieces of wood used to keep the beams of the deck in place). As his preparations were finalised and he readied himself to leave, Kenelm strode the decks of the *Eagle*, practising his new role and the script that came with it, and barking an unbroken series of commands at his men:

*Let fall your fore-saile. Tally, that is, hale off the Sheats; who is
at the Helme there, coile your Cables in small fakes, hale the Cat, a*

Bitter, belay, loose fast your Anchor with your shank-painter, stow the Boat, set the land, how it beares by the Compasse . . . let fall your maine saile, every man say his private prayer for a boone voyage, out with your spret saile, on with your bonits & Drablers, steare steady & keep your course, so, you go well.

Finally, with the preparations completed and after contrary winds had delayed his departure, on 7 January 1628 Kenelm watched from the deck of the *Eagle* as the English cliffs receded into the distance. A fair wind blowing from the north-east propelled his ships on their way, and that evening Kenelm 'mustered and delivered to their charges all my men, and caused my master to deliver to them such orders as I commanded to be observed in the ship'. The first two days at sea passed quietly, assisted by unusually clement weather for the time of year, and by 9 January the vessels had crossed the English Channel and begun making their way around the French coast. Kenelm remained wary of the dangers that might lurk even in these quieter waters. The Spanish navy were highly active thereabouts, because they were engaged in an ongoing war with the Dutch Republic, but since war had broken out they were attacking English ships as well, as were the pirates known as Dunkirkers who marauded from Ostend and preyed on the vessels of all Protestant nations. Kenelm also knew that a further risk had arisen for English ships, since the feared North African corsairs who had previously limited their activities to the Mediterranean itself had become bolder in recent years and begun to range more widely, even venturing as far as the coasts of Devon, Cornwall and Ireland, and carrying local people away to a life of slavery. The plight of these people, enslaved hundreds of miles from their homeland, was lamented in towns and from pulpits across England, but little had been done to address their plight. For the moment, though, none of these potential threats presented themselves. Kenelm spent these first quiet days of travel proving to his crew, and to himself, that he had the skills and temperament necessary for a successful command.

He began to fill the pages of the journal that he had bought in London. Kenelm's first entries were terse and clipped, documenting the weather and the number of ships that he encountered with economy and precision: 'The 11. day the wind blew strong att east, and in the morning we perceived 5 sailes coming towardes us.' He also threw himself into the rough realities of shipboard life, showing his men that he was eminently willing to dirty his hands amidst routine minor crises. 'That night wee sprung a leake on the starboard bowe in the powder room, so that wee pumped all night, 2,400 strokes a watch.' For the time being, Kenelm had to satisfy himself with these staccato bursts of action, since there were as yet few dealings to be had with other vessels: apart from the five craft glimpsed in the distance, the *Eagle* encountered only a Flemish ship on its way to Rotterdam with a cargo of wine, and a Dutch ship and a Hamburger that managed to flee before they could be apprehended and interrogated.

As he settled into the rhythms of command during this first week, Kenelm's ships made their way rapidly along the French coast and then cut southward into the Bay of Biscay, driven by 'a strong storme of wind . . . and a high sea', and taking advantage of 'a steedie fresh gale' blowing from the north-east. By the middle of the month, it was not France but Spain that he could glimpse in the distance from the port deck. On 16 January Kenelm's lookout 'descryed a saile', and he resolved to intercept it and determine under whose flag it flew. When they were only a league apart, this other ship suddenly 'furled up her maine saile . . . and in warrelike manner fitted herself for fight'. At these close quarters Kenelm could see that his potential quarry was a large Hamburg merchant, the equal of the *Eagle* in sheer heft. Nonetheless, the sight of Kenelm's tall-sided English ship, bristling with artillery, was fearsome. 'In like manner we fitted our selves for fight,' he noted with satisfaction, 'which wee had no sooner done but shee made all the saile shee could to get from us . . . wee chaced her till it was darke, but then perceiving she gott mainely of us wee gave over our chace'. Kenelm was not too perturbed by the merchant ship's successful escape: there would be plenty more where she came from, and at this point he was still learning the realities of his ships' speed and manoeuvrability, rehearsing for greater escapades ahead. The pages of Smith's *Sea Grammar* had warned him that 'in giving chase or chasing, there is required an infinite judgement or experience, for there is no rule for it'. This was simply another skill that he would have to hone, another form of prowess to be developed as he went along.

Kenelm stared out at the coastlines of France and Spain as he passed, catching a distant glimpse of the lands in which he had undergone such formative experiences. His mind took him back first to his encounter with Maria de' Medici and then to the sweltering, exhilarating and vexing months spent in Madrid at the side of the man who was now his King. As the *Eagle* cut its way to the south, these vivid memories were pushed into his mind unbidden by a sweet scent wafting its way from the Spanish coast. As he later recalled, 'I have sailed by sea along those coasts divers times, and I have observed alwayes, that the Mariners know

when they are within thirty or forty leagues of the Continent . . .
and they have this knowledge from the smell of the Rosemary,
which so abounds in the fields of *Spain*; I have smelt it as sensibly,
as if I had had a branch of Rosemary in my hand, and this was
a day or two before we could discover land'. Even far out at
sea, the details of these lands tingled upon his senses. He had
returned from his earlier travels convinced that the world was
bound together by mysterious forces that could act across huge
distances, and now the scent that drifted into his nostrils seemed
to affect him in precisely this way, drawing him onward towards
the seas that he had experienced only fleetingly, and that now
awaited him.

By the morning of 17 January Kenelm found that his ships had
reached the latitude of Cape St Vincent. The calm night-time
weather gave way to 'violent, suddaine and dangerous gustes of
winde' and pouring rain, but his ships were easily strong enough
to withstand such weather. They made their way around the Cape,
and were finally able to turn eastward, and continue towards
Gibraltar and the warmer Mediterranean waters beyond. On the
18th, having emerged unscathed from the storms, Kenelm gave
the order for his ships to wait and take stock before sailing
through the straits, and 'called the Commanders in my Viceadmirall to come aboard me to consult of our future proceedings'. After
a day of discussion with the Stradling brothers, Mr Milborne and
his chief officers, by the morning of the 19th his ships had steered
into a position from which they could survey the coasts of two
continents at once: Spain on one side, and on the other the rocky
outcrops of North Africa, or 'the Barbarie coast' as it was then
known to the English.

Staring at the distant coasts of these continents standing opposite one another, Kenelm spied the Moroccan promontory of Cape Spartel on which was situated Abyla (or Apehill, as he called it), a rock marking the African side of the Pillars of Hercules. For the Ancient Greeks, Kenelm recalled, this point had marked the limits of the known world. To sail beyond the straits was to abandon the familiar comforts of the middle sea and its coasts, to leave behind the limits of humanity itself, and enter the terrifying and formless beyond of the Ocean. Kenelm knew that by entering the Mediterranean, he followed in the footsteps of great sailors from myth and from scripture – Odysseus and Aeneas, Noah and St Paul. This was a place where a person could glimpse surviving fragments of the Bible's central episodes, or step straight into the world of an epic poem: every English traveller believed that Troy was not an elusively mythical site but one that could be visited on these very shores, and even raided for souvenirs. One visitor confidently proclaimed that 'the ruines of olde Troye are yett to bee seene', while another landed at the supposed location and carried off 'a peece of a whyte marble piller, the which I broke with my owne handes, havinge a good hamer'. For such travellers, the books of the ancients served as a map for the contemporary world through which they moved. Kenelm was on the verge of entering a region that he too knew almost exclusively from the reading of ancient stories. His ships paused on the brink of these new waters, 'about 8 leagues from the entrance of the gutt', and bobbed in place on the waves, 'the weather being almost dead calme'. The area was often patrolled by large numbers of Spanish vessels, and Kenelm had no desire to engage in a grand battle before he had managed to take prizes and expand his small fleet. On the night of the 19th, under cover of darkness, the *Eagle* and the *Elizabeth and George* sneaked through the straits 'so to avoide

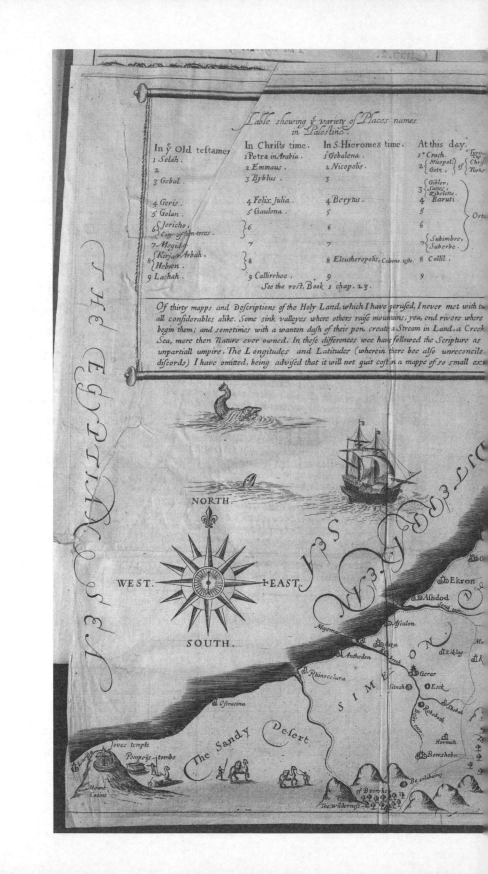

Table shewing ye variety of Places names in Palestine.

In ye Old testament	In Christs time.	In S. Hieromes time.	At this day.	
1 Selah.	1 Petra in Arabia.	1 Gebalena.	1 Crach.	Terra Cap of Christ Turks
2	2 Emmaus.	2 Nicopolis.	2 { Nicopol. Gotz. } of	
3 Gebal.	3 Byblus.	3	3 { Gibler, Saitte, Zibelette. }	
4 Geris.	4 Felix Julia.	4 Berytus.	4 Baruti.	
5 Golan.	5 Gaulona.	5	5	Orte
6 { Jericho, City of palm-trees }	6	6	6	
7 Megido	7	7	7 { Subimbre, Suberbe. }	
8 { Kirjat-Arbah, Hebron. }	8	8 Eleutheropolis, Cedreno. teste.	8 Callil.	
9 Lashah.	9 Callirrhoe.	9	9	

See the rest, Book 1 chap. 23.

Of thirty mapps and Descriptions of the Holy Land, which I have perused, I never met with tw[o] all considerables alike. Some sink valleyes where others raise mountains; yea, end rivers where [they] begin them; and sometimes with a wanton dash of their pen, create a Stream in Land, a Creek [in] Sea, more then Nature ever owned. In these differences wee have followed the Scripture as [an] unpartiall umpire. The Longitudes and Latitudes (wherein there bee also unreconcile[able] discords) I have omitted, being advised that it will not quit cost in a mappe of so small ext[ent]

THE EGYPTIAN SEA

NORTH.

WEST. EAST.

SOUTH.

JUDÆA

Ekron

Alhdod

Ascalon

Magoma

Gura

Antheden

Ziklag

Gerar

Rhinocolura

Sitnah

Eseck

Ostracina

Rehoboth

SIMEON

The Sandy Desert

Hormah

Joves temple

Beersheba

Pompeys tombe

Be erlahairi

of Beersheba

Mount Casius

The Wildernesse

being discovered by the ships at Gibraltar', and Kenelm found himself in the waters of the Mediterranean.

His ships ventured north-east past Apehill, continuing to hug the coast, but with the winds in their favour they made good progress and had passed Marbella and Málaga by the afternoon of 20 January. Over the ensuing days they zigzagged along the southern Spanish coast, where they spied another Hamburg merchant sitting a short way off the shore at Vélez-Málaga, which fired a warning shot at the *Eagle* as it approached: unperturbed, Kenelm commanded three of his cannons to return fire, and one or two of the salvos ripped into the side of the merchant vessel. Immediately, however, the great gun mounted in the castle protecting the port began to hurl its lethal load in Kenelm's direction and, realising that 'there was no fitt proportion betweene the damage I might receive and the good I might gett (for I could have from thence but wine and fruites, and an unfortunate shott among my mastes might hazard the overthrow of my future designes)', Kenelm took his officers' advice and sailed on. The encounter had gained him nothing, but the sound of his cannons,

---

The multiple forms of history and myth simultaneously present in the Mediterranean are captured in this map from Thomas Fuller's 1639 *Historie of the Holy Warre*, a polemically anti-Catholic account of the Crusades. The key explains that it represents four separate moments in historical time, layered within the same space: major landmarks 'In the Old Testament', 'In Christ's Time', 'In Saint Jerome's Time', and 'At this Day', all equally present and accessible. Kenelm wrote a long and caustic note in his copy of this book, which, he stated, 'may peraduenture more properly be stiled, A Poëme in prose of that subiect,' complaining that Fuller writes 'rather like a witty Pedant, then a solide Historian' (BL MS Additional 41846, ff. 106–7)

fired in anger for the first time, still rang satisfyingly in his ears. Before long they had a much friendlier encounter: a group of six sails, all but one of them recognisable as English vessels by the flags that they raised, and soon identified as 'a fleet of merchant men bound homewardes', travelling in a convoy for their collective safety. Kenelm went aboard one of the ships that night and feasted with its commander, one Captain Stephens: discovering that the ships had not made landfall for some months, and were 'in great distresse for water and beere', Kenelm graciously 'supplyed them with what I could spare'. His genuine concern dovetailed nicely with more self-interested motives: given the controversy surrounding the terms of Kenelm's departure, it would not hurt to have a merchant fleet full of grateful sailors returning to England singing his praises, and citing his generosity and compassion for his countrymen.

After they had seen the newly restocked merchants safely on their way, Kenelm's ships 'plyed to and againe along the Spanish shore', and he returned to the business of imperiously checking the cargo of any ships that crossed his path, to see if they belonged to the enemies of the Crown and were therefore fair game as spoils of war: in taking even this degree of care he was being more careful than many privateers, who barely bothered to distinguish friend from foe before attacking and pillaging. One ship, named the *Grey Horse*, was found to have a cargo of Greek salt and silk bound for Holland, and was allowed to depart unharmed; another, the *Little Sapphire*, turned out to be English and homeward bound; a third pair of sails managed to vanish over the horizon before they could be apprehended. At this point a strong easterly wind sprang up, and threatened to carry Kenelm's ships away from the Spanish shore which it had been carefully following. They were blown past the island of Alborán, sitting neatly equidistant between the northern and southern shores of the Mediterranean, and finally came within four leagues of the Barbary Coast. These were potentially treacherous waters: Kenelm knew from his reading that strong winds and 'very fowle weather' were to be expected 'in *Barbaria, Aegypt,* and the most of the Levant'. The effect of the wind was amplified by the infamously powerful currents that propelled ships uncontrollably through these waters. These currents drove eastwards with such force that, throughout the Middle Ages, oarless sailing ships from Northern Europe could enter through the Straits of Gibraltar but not leave, and those who wished to return home were forced to abandon their vessels and travel overland. Kenelm's ships were far stronger than these earlier craft, but they too bounced back and forth between Spain and Barbary at the mercy of the currents, eventually finding a moment of calm by Cabo de Gata, just east of Almería. Propelled onward by vast natural forces, Kenelm veered between Europe and Africa, the opposed edges of the self-contained world into which he now ventured.

As soon as he entered the Mediterranean Kenelm found it to be far more hostile and unforgiving than the place he had envisaged, an arena for triumphant acts of heroism. Before long he discovered that sailing in these waters could bring horrors far worse than the weather. With 150 men packed into a tight space aboard the *Eagle*, and with the source and nature of infectious diseases not yet understood, occasional outbreaks of sickness were to be expected, but when one came it was far worse than Kenelm could have anticipated. One member of his crew began to convulse with the terribly weakening effects of a fever, and then another. On 27 January things rapidly worsened: sixteen men collapsed in the space of an afternoon. Kenelm could only look on, appalled, as the crew that he had desperately assembled in London began to succumb to the 'violent pestilential disease' that erupted with terrible speed in their midst. The disease worsened 'hourly', Kenelm grimly recorded, and took his men 'with great pain in the head, stomach and reins [kidneys], and putrefied the whole mass of the blood, and caused much vomiting, yet they died not suddenly, but lingered on with pain and much weakness'. This was a spectacle of appalling, senseless suffering, from which there was no escape. If his crew 'did but come within distance of each other's breath, or touch any part of their garments, it came to pass that in a very short time almost all were possessed with it, by reason of the great number of men enclosed in a small room'. If a disease could ravage even a great city, it made its way much more swiftly through the crowded and routinely filthy decks of a warship. Kenelm's men tried to flee the intimacy with one another that was an inescapable part of life at sea, abandoning their comrades in arms to the ravages of the disease, which destroyed not only the bodies of those whom it affected but the bonds that bound a crew together. 'Every one strived to avoid those that were sick, whereby they died in much desolation without any help'. The men would not even risk approaching the corpses of those whom the disease had massacred, Kenelm noted in horror, and as a result 'dead bodies lay many days in their cabins and hammocks, nobody daring to go overlook them, and much less to throw the noisome carcasses overboard, until their intolerable stink discovered them'. What terrified him almost as much as the ravages of the disease on the bodies of his men was its dreadful impact upon their minds. The sickness gave rise to a 'furious madness', and men had to stop their deranged shipmates from flinging themselves over the side or through the nearest porthole, since, in their pitiful and deluded state, 'their depraved fantasy made them believe the sea to be a spacious and pleasant green meadow'.

II 'A Much Deeper Sense of his Honour'

But then all the principal officers of the fleet . . . came with one consent to Theagenes, to represent to him how it was impossible for him to keep to the sea and subsist many hours longer . . . therefore they advised and besought him to bear up the helm and return home.

But Theagenes, that had a much deeper sense of his honour than of his life and safety, and yet was so highly compassionate of their great evils that he prayed continually, that all the punishments for his or their sins due unto the divine justice might fall upon his single head, represented to them how in probability the worst counsel they could take would be to return home, since that was now the farthest place of distance that they could go unto . . . Wherefore he told them absolutely, that he would expect with patience the happy hour of a fair gale, and desired them, no longer to persuade him to do what he had set his rest upon that he would not; but to concur with him in prayer to the superior powers to favour their designs as they were honourable and just.

Whether he had been inoculated against the threat of death that stalked the decks of the *Eagle* by his series of childhood illnesses, or whether he simply eluded it as best he could in the relative comfort of the captain's cabin, Kenelm managed to escape the wretched fate that so many among his crew swiftly met. The suffering that he witnessed, and the inhumane and desperate behaviour that it caused, were scored on to his memory. For the time being, though, there was little that he could do but command his men to continue on their bleak way, and try to hold their own against any enemies who crossed their path despite their stricken state. With the sickness worsening – as many as sixty of the one hundred and fifty men who comprised his crew had succumbed by this point, and the rest were 'in generall all drooping' – Kenelm realised that he would have to make for shore before the *Eagle* became a floating tomb. He had not planned to make landfall in this region so soon, and was faced with a dangerous choice. To the north was the coast of Spain, with whom England was at war, and from where belligerent ships might at any moment appear and attack him. To the south was the Barbary Coast, with its hostile outcrops and arid dunes. On 28 January, he crossed paths with an English merchant ship about half the size of the *Eagle*, named the *Patience*, which was bound for Algiers. It was commanded by one Captain Michael, who impressed Kenelm with his unblinking bravery in making for this city without hesitation. When Kenelm, implored by his officers, finally accepted that the extent of the illness made the choice of a port unavoidable, he followed in the footsteps of this bold captain, who sailed on towards his intended destination. 'I resolved,' he wrote, 'by the advice of all my commanders (who deemed it an undispensable necessitie) to putt into Argiers with the first good winde . . . to putt my sicke men ashore in fitting manner to be cured and refreshed', as well as to cleanse his ships from the taint of infection, to buy provisions, and to replace his tainted ballast. Finally, on 6 February, the *Eagle* began to follow an easterly wind towards the Barbary shore, and the city of Algiers itself.

In opting for the African rather than the European coastline Kenelm was setting course for a mysterious and threatening land, which was a source of both fear and fascination to English people; a place Kenelm had never visited but of which he had heard copious stories. Algiers was particularly notorious, and Kenelm knew the remarkable story of its rise to prominence from his extensive reading in the history of the region. What had been a small and fairly unremarkable coastal town was transformed early in the sixteenth century by the arrival of the brothers Aruj and Khair ad-Din, both of whom became known to Europeans, on account of their copper-coloured beards, as 'Barbarossa'. The brothers came from the Greek island of Mytilene, which was part of the Ottoman Empire, and they began as small-scale privateers and traders in the eastern Mediterranean. Their increasingly fervent religious beliefs and desire to ingratiate themselves with the powers that be led them to declare Holy War on the Spaniards and to expand their activities, which they did with enormous success, earning themselves a fearsome reputation. In 1516, the brothers took Algiers: according to the grisly tales that circulated afterwards, Aruj either strangled its ruler, a local lord named Selim ben Tumi, with his own turban, or throttled him in the royal steam bath. This conquest caught the attention of the Spanish, who were becoming unpleasantly aware of the brothers' prowess, and their troops killed Aruj at the siege of nearby Tlemcen in 1518 before carrying his severed head through the streets of the city on a spike. His mantle was ably assumed by his younger brother, however, and Khair ad-Din proved himself not only an able commander and fearsome sea captain, but a brilliantly acute politician. He travelled to Constantinople and offered his services to the Sultan in return for military aid against the Spanish. The arrangement suited both men: the younger Barbarossa would place his conquests under Ottoman rule, adding to the scope and lustre of the Sultan's empire, but Algiers was so far from the Sublime Porte that Khair ad-Din could still enjoy considerable freedom to run the city and its surroundings as he saw fit. In 1525 he began eight remarkably prosperous years as governor of Algiers: he oversaw a massive programme of expansion which led to the building of the great walls and fortresses that Kenelm encountered upon his arrival, and the construction of a fearsome fleet with which he could continue to wreak havoc on the seas.

In the century since the rise of the Barbarossas, however, the nature of sea battles and piracy in the Mediterranean had undergone significant changes. The red-bearded brothers had presented themselves as agents of Holy War, sailing under the banner of Islam against the might of Spain and of Christendom as a whole, and they had done so in an era in which many people shared their polarised vision. With the Ottomans expanding their empire in the east and Spain at its mightiest in the west it was easy to see all minor skirmishes as small components of the larger struggle between two great and opposed forces, representing Good and Evil, Christ and Antichrist, the Cross and the Crescent. The wars driven by this shared Manichean world view culminated in 1573 with the great Battle of Lepanto, at which the united Christian forces of the Holy League, led by Don John of Austria, vanquished the Ottoman navy. Lepanto, though, marked the end of an era of great sea battles. Rather than signalling the beginning of Christian dominance in the Mediterranean, it ushered in a long period of small-scale skirmishes and plunder, of pragmatism and opportunism, in which the lines were blurred between pirate and holy warrior, plunder and trade, friend and foe. A corsair captain, whether a Muslim from Barbary or a Christian from among the Knights of Malta, could still present himself – and even genuinely understand himself – as an agent of Holy War, while continuing to pillage for his own personal gain, or that of his crew or his city.

Algiers had grown into the largest and most feared of the cities that dotted the North African coast, and piracy was the glue that bound its disparate strands together, providing much of its wealth and maintaining the fearsome reputation that kept it safe from invaders. Among the most notorious of the Algerian pirates was a man named Simon Danzer or Dansiker ('the Dancer'). Kenelm had grown up hearing tales of this man, who was often paired in the public imagination with the Englishman John Ward, a convert who led a fleet from Tunis: a few years previously, Kenelm's friend James Howell had written a letter in which he recalled the failed attempt of Emperor Charles V to sack the city in 1541, and observed, 'Algiers is another thing now than she was then, being, I believe, a hundred degrees stronger by land and sea, and for the latter strength we may thank our countryman Ward, and Danskey the butterbag Hollander, which may be said to have been two of the fatalest and most infamous men that ever Christendom bred.' They were loathed not only for their apostasy, but for the expertise that they brought with them and imparted: John Smith angrily claimed that before the two men arrived in Barbary 'the

Moores scarce knew how to saile a ship'. Danziger and Ward inspired ballads and songs lamenting the brutal attacks that they aimed at their former countrymen and co-religionists, and Ward also inspired a play titled *A Christian Turn'd Turk*, which depicted him as utterly depraved, suggested that his conversion was motivated solely by lust for a seductive Turkish woman, and ended with his grisly and unrepentant death. This was, however, a piece of comforting wish-fulfilment. When it was staged in about 1609, Ward was still alive and well, fabulously wealthy and apparently content in his palace in Tunis – 'Ward lived like a Bashaw [*pasha*] in Barbary,' Smith bitterly observed – and he did not in fact die until a few years before Kenelm's visit to Algiers, probably of the plague. His life did not exemplify the wrath and justice of God, as English Christians would have liked reassuringly to see. Instead, it carried a very different message, by showing just how successful a man from a modest background might become by turning Turk and practising piracy. The Ottoman Empire, in contrast to the highly stratified nature of English and European society which was founded on the inheritance of titles and of wealth, was a relative meritocracy. Only the Sultan's own family benefited from hereditary privilege, and when the Ottomans conquered a new nation they would liquidate its old social structure and replace it with their own, in which a person with the proper talents might rise to the loftiest of roles. The transformed lives of these pirates seemed to suggest that here in Algiers, a man might succeed on his own merits, regardless of his background or parentage.

The city, though, seemed to contain the extremes of lavish success and wretched suffering, notorious above all for the tens of thousands of people who were captured and sold in its slave

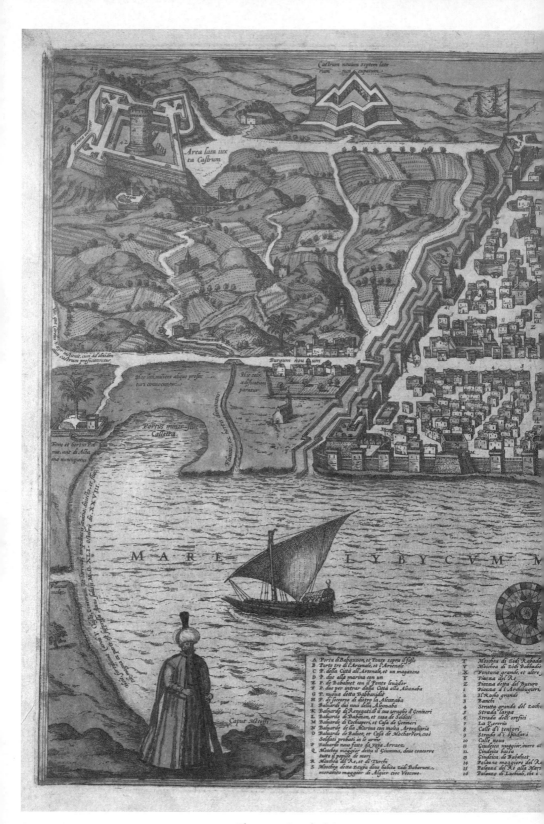

The great city of Algiers

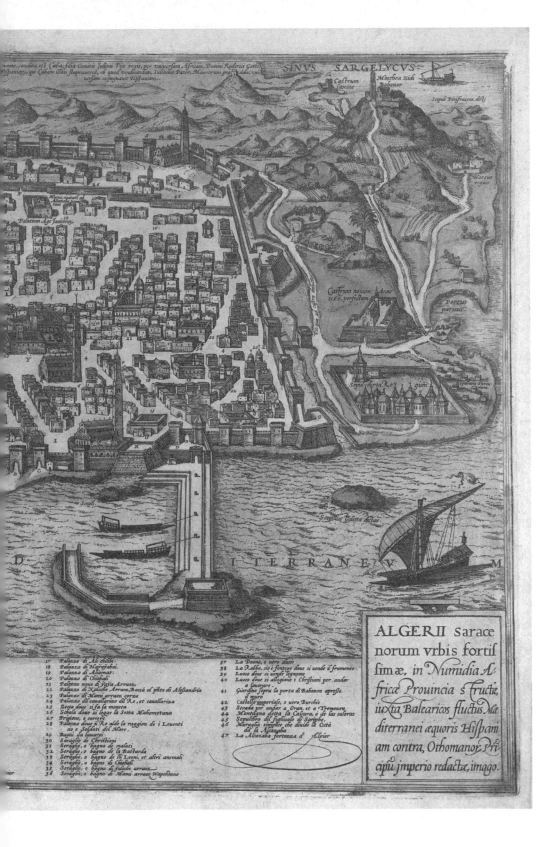

SINVS SARGELYCVS

Castrum Caxine
Moschea zidi Bobonor
Scopuli Binifratres, detti

Hortus regius

Castrum nouum Anno 1569. perfectum

Portus paruus

Sepulchra Regu di Argieri

Scogli

Scopulus Galetta dicta

D I TERRANEV M

ALGERII saracenorum vrbis fortissimæ, in *Numidia Africæ Prouincia* structæ, iuxta *Balearicos* fluctus, *Mediterranei æquoris Hispaniam contra, Othomanor. Principū jmperio redactæ, jmago.

markets in the century before Kenelm's arrival. It was a place
whose very name was likely to provoke fear and loathing: 'the
Throne of Pyracie, the Sinke of Trade and Stinke of Slavery;
the Cage of uncleane Birds of Prey, the Habitation of Sea-Devils',
as the English writer Samuel Purchas colourfully called it. Kenelm
had read tales of the miseries of Algerian slavery before, both true
and imagined: he avidly perused the life story of one Sydenham
Poyntz, who fought as a soldier of fortune in the Thirty Years
War before being taken prisoner by the Turks at Belgrade, 'where
they stripped us of all wee had, Cloathes and all, and shaved our
heads and put us into a slavish habit'. He also knew the details
of life among the city's slaves from the most illustrious of their
number, the great Spanish writer Miguel de Cervantes, who had
spent five years enslaved in the city between 1575 and 1580, making
four unsuccessful escape attempts before his family ransomed him:
he poured his sufferings and his adventures into a series of plays
set in the city and into his masterpiece, *Don Quixote*, a book that
Kenelm knew and loved. In the years leading up to his departure
church pulpits across England had rung with sermons lamenting
the sorry plight of English people taken as slaves, whether snatched
from their own coasts or while traversing the waters of the Mediterranean. These slaves had survived the terrors of capture and
endured the humiliation of being dragged into the market square
in Algiers, inspected and bought like cattle: such was 'the misusage
of poore Captived-Christians, by the barbarous tyranny of savage
Mahumetans', and the victims endured 'multiplyed blowes, fiercely
inflicted . . . by yokes, by manicles and pedicles of iron; by
unwholesome vapours, the cold dampes, and nastiness of Dungeons
in the night; by reproaches, hunger, thirst, nakednes, scorching
heates, labour, and torture in the day'. Huge numbers of

slaves – as many as 600,000 across North Africa in the century preceding Kenelm's arrival – were taken; and in 1628 there were at least 25,000 slaves in Algiers, including several hundred English people. Countless English families petitioned the Crown for assistance in ransoming their captured loved ones, but while the French and Spanish sent members of dedicated religious orders to free their countrymen, there was no parallel in England. Those who had been enslaved relied on the wealth, nous and good fortune of their relatives for their successful release, and the ransom process was slipshod, uneven and inefficient. Slaves who were ransomed – or, much more rarely, managed to escape and make their own way back to England – published gruesome and lurid accounts of their sufferings, in the hope of inspiring compassion for those that they had left behind, and as a means of profiting in some compensatory way for the traumas that they had suffered. Francis Knight, a former slave who was lucky enough to be ransomed, wrote achingly upon his return of 'the Multitude of my poore Country-men, groaning under the mercilesse yoake of Turkish thraldom', and described his own 'misery of 7. yeares slaverie in chaines, and in the Gallies of Argeire', exposed to the supposed threats of sodomy and forced circumcision upon which such accounts luridly focused.

If Algiers was a place in which Kenelm expected to encounter dark-skinned, perfidious idol-worshippers, who harboured nothing but loathing for the decent Christian folk whom they enslaved and tortured, he was also well aware of the attractions that it nonetheless held. From a small fishing town of a few thousand inhabitants, Algiers had mushroomed by the end of the sixteenth century to a huge, densely packed metropolis of more than 100,000, large enough to rival the greatest cities in Europe. The city enjoyed a perfect strategic position, with easy access to the Atlantic, the eastern parts of the Mediterranean, and the European shores to the north, and it had ideal natural environs: perched on the edge of the great trough of the *Mitidja* plain, it was surrounded by lush fields and orchards, which were regularly doused by the hot, heavy rains that would surprise newcomers to the city expecting an arid desert landscape, just as Kenelm had been battered by sudden storms before his arrival. From the days of the younger Barbarossa, Algiers became a city associated with luxury. A succulent array of fruits and meats would pour into it from the surrounding countryside, brought by Berbers and other local tribes: on market days, noted one French visitor, 'an infinite number of people of the Mountaines, Plaines and Vallies' descended on the city, 'which do bring thither all sorts of Fruits, Corne and Foule, of very cheap price'. It was at the harbour, though, that the richest goods arrived. Until around 1570 English ships had largely avoided the Mediterranean, but after this date they flooded in and began to exploit with gusto these new opportunities for trade, to answer the growing demand in England for rich and exotic goods from the East. London shoppers gradually began to take for granted the novelties that these trades brought to the markets of the city: edible treats like artichokes and apricots, splendid new flowers including tulips and damask roses, and finely wrought goods such as ornate china and intricately patterned carpets. Traders from across Europe and beyond were attracted to this new hub of exchange, into which a cornucopia of items flowed to be bought, sold and bartered at the great *souk*, the market that dominated the former Roman road running parallel to the shore. 'This Citie,' noted the same Frenchman, 'is very Merchant-like, for she is situated upon the Sea, and for this cause marveilously peopled, for her bignesse.' Its various inhabitants 'with marveilous gaine exercise the Trade of Merchandise'.

The promise of the city's lavish pleasures and bustling trade convinced Kenelm to acquiesce to his officers' pleading, and sail towards Algiers despite the threats of piracy and slavery that it carried. As his ships made their way towards the city, Kenelm caught sight of two sails. Even with his crew in their sickening state he could not allow the quarry to pass unchallenged. He commanded his men to give chase, and easily caught up with the vessels. The masters of the ships were brought aboard the *Eagle*, and Kenelm discovered that they were Flemish, bound for Amsterdam with a rich cargo of spices and edible luxuries brought from Eastern lands – aniseed, cumin seeds, currants. The Flemings, as they had prepared to repel the English boarders, had got riotously drunk – 'as their manner is upon such an occasion', Kenelm wryly noted – and, once he sent some of his men aboard to investigate, became 'verie unruly and quarrelsome'. He sent forty more men aboard to impose his authority, but this threatened to make things worse, as his own crew were 'disorderly in pillaging their mariners' chestes and clothes'. Kenelm dealt strictly with his own men, ordering that they restore the stolen goods and punishing those responsible. After checking the cargo against the documentation that the Flemings were carrying, and determining that all was in order, he let the two ships depart, their goods intact. Though Kenelm had no good reason for detaining these ships further, he was certain that there was more to them than met the eye. 'In my private opinion,' he wrote, 'I believe they were faulty if I could have proved it.' Their behaviour was decidedly suspicious: while Kenelm's men were inspecting the ships the Flemish crew 'threw many letters overbord' before they could be scrutinised.

When Kenelm himself perused the ships' logs, he saw that on a previous voyage they had carried weapons and 'prohibited commodities' to the Spanish town of Sanlúcar de Barrameda, north of Cádiz, a crucial port for trade with the East Indies from which Columbus and Magellan had begun their voyages. As if this were not enough, 'they all had beades and Catholike primers, which when they saw us they did throw overbord, and wee tooke up floting in the water'. Kenelm strongly suspected that it was only when confronted with a heavily armed warship flying an English flag that the Flemings suddenly sought to conceal their committed Catholicism. Furthermore they had clearly had some sort of business dealings, if not closer affinities, with the Spaniards. He itched to seize their valuable cargo of aromatic spices for himself, but decided, on this occasion, that this was a line he should not risk crossing. Nonetheless, he could not help marvelling at the ambiguities and swift transformations that were possible in the Mediterranean, where a person's identity might be discarded as summarily and as opportunistically as a set of prayer beads cast over the side of the deck and into the sparkling waves.

Having reluctantly seen the suspicious Flemings on their way, Kenelm continued towards Algiers, though it proved a difficult course to follow. The south-easterly gusts propelled his ships along the Barbary coast, past 'a little craggie iland', to a shore that seemed more welcoming, but the powerful Levant wind made it impossible to weigh anchor there. Continuing along the coast at night, Kenelm saw that it was dotted with bonfires, but his men warned him that these were lit by the 'treacherous and false people' living there, who hoped to lure unsuspecting mariners to their doom. By now matters were becoming desperate: the number of sick men equalled those who were still able-bodied, with eighty falling ill by 11 February, and Kenelm's beleaguered ships were battered by another 'furious and cruel storm of wind, with often and violent gusts of rain, snow, and hail'. Realising he was now close to Algiers, Kenelm took the risky decision to haul in the sails and surrender his ships to the storm, fearing that otherwise they might be blown straight past the city that now seemed like his only hope. Finally, on the 15th, the storm passed and fortune seemed to be smiling upon his ships at last, for Kenelm found himself only five leagues from Algiers. At noon the *Eagle* weighed anchor, with the *Elizabeth and George* following close behind, and saluted the fortress with nine cannon blasts.

Algiers from the sea was both a magnificent and an intimidating sight. Jutting out into the waves was the impressive stone bulk of the breakwater known as the Great Mole, which connected a small island to the shore, and which was fronted by a compact fortress and completed with a curved wall, studded with the protruding barrels of large cannons. This unwelcoming promontory was the first sight that struck Kenelm's eye upon arrival at the port: as his eye moved beyond it towards the city itself, this first impression of squat, forbidding strength was both reinforced and altered. The whole city was surrounded by a sturdy stone wall, clamping the buildings within into a neat wedge that sloped sharply away from the sea and towards the hills beyond. The entire wall was punctuated both by a series of gates, and by the barrels of guns that, like those on the mole, pointed menacingly out towards the sea. Its shape was like a great crossbow – the curve at the crest of the hill like the sweep of a bow, the lower walls sharply angled like the weapon's taut string. The comparison was not only apt, but also captured the tense, brutal outline of the heavily guarded city. Within these walls, however, things were very different, as his gaze cast from the ship's deck swiftly discerned. Closest to the sea, the towers of the Great Mosque and the Mosque of the King soared above broad streets and squares. On the hills that rose steeply beyond these grand edifices Kenelm saw a teeming panoply of houses and small buildings, crammed together higgledy-piggledy, vying for space, and all painted a bright white that blindingly reflected the sharp sunlight. If the walls and great buildings suggested power and impressive order, this dense cluster of dwellings gave Kenelm his first glimpse of the ordinary life of Algiers: tight-knit, hectic, busy, squeezed, but alive with activity. A place where lives would have to be lived side by side, in intimate contact with one's neighbours, whoever they might be. Looming over all was the great *ḳaṣba*, the fortress perched at the crest of the hill like a bird of prey, a final reminder of the city's imposing power.

After his ships had weighed anchor a short distance from the Great Mole, Kenelm sent a small boat ashore announcing his arrival to the *pasha*, the viceroy of the city, and waited for a response. At first his frustrating delay continued, and he was told to wait until the following day to be granted safe passage ashore: more bleak hours trapped aboard the sweltering ship with his men falling ever sicker. The reason for the delay, he soon discovered, was not scepticism regarding Kenelm or his motives, but the internal wrangling of Algerian politics: the *divan*, or imperial council, was in the process of replacing the *agha*, the military leader of the city. A visiting Englishman would have to wait until this delicate matter was resolved. Finally, on the afternoon of the 17th, permission to disembark arrived in the form of a pair of letters from the *pasha* and the *divan*. By the evening Kenelm had packed a chest with his belongings, been ferried to the shore, and entered the labyrinth of the city's streets, where he made his way to the house of 'the English Consul', a man named James Frizell. Here at last he could rest and recuperate, safe from the terrors of his infected ship, and reflect upon the city in which he was now enjoying an unplanned sojourn, and the actions that he might undertake while he was there.

5

March 1628
Algiers

I 'Supplies of Many Things'

And within a few hours (God having sufficiently tried their patience and constancy), the unconstant element filled his sails with prosperous breath, and he did put into Rhodes to relieve his men and take in supplies of many things that were wanting.

Kenelm had never intended to visit Algiers, but he had chosen to travel to the Mediterranean in search of new and transformative experiences, and now he found himself in a place that promised to offer them in abundance. He had been empowered by King Charles to undertake any action 'tending to the service of the realm and the increase of his knowledge', and he resolved to investigate how he might fulfil both parts of this broad commission, even in this notorious pirate city. The man at whose house Kenelm found lodgings upon arrival in Algiers, James Frizell, was the ideal guide to the volatile mixture of risks and opportunities that the city presented to a visiting English sea captain. Frizell knew its ins and outs intimately: he was well aware how easily an individual's fortunes might swing here from one extreme to the other, and how precarious life could be in this frontier land.

As mercantile links between England and North Africa bloomed, more and more men drifted towards this region in the hope of making their fortunes. Some found official employment as resident agents of the newly established trading companies that were being founded in England, as merchants banded together and sought to regulate the new Mediterranean markets that were opening up. The Turkey Company received its royal charter in 1581, the Venice Company in 1583 and the short-lived Barbary Company, which hoped to oversee trade in North Africa, in 1585; but all were quickly superseded and swallowed up in the years after 1592, when the more enduringly successful Levant Company was founded. The Levant Company merchants tried – and generally failed – to ensure that all English trading in the Mediterranean took place with their approval: but there were simply too many individuals in the region willing to defy their legal monopoly in pursuit of a quick fortune. There were also many men who were only tenuously associated with these companies, but who involved themselves where and when they could, often boasting of a more official role than they in fact had. Frizell had once been such a man. After an obscure early life he had arrived in Algiers as early as 1613 in pursuit of rich pickings, and in 1620–21 had been involved in King James's doomed attempt to end the threat of Algerian piracy once and for all by attacking and sacking the city. This endeavour was led by an officer named Sir Robert Mansell, who even in an age of widespread venery and ineptitude in naval circles stood out for the depth of both his corruption and his incompetence: as treasurer he stocked the King's ships with rotten provisions and flimsy equipment bought at high price, and pocketed huge kickbacks from suppliers. By the time the fleet arrived at Algiers it was clear that they were ill equipped to launch a direct attack, and so instead they entered into negotiations in the vain hope of bringing piratical attacks to an end: the *pasha* of the city specifically requested that Frizell be sent ashore to speak with him, since he understood the city so well.

The expedition ended embarrassingly and fruitlessly, and the English government wisely concluded that Algiers could not be defeated via a frontal assault: diplomacy rather than war would have to be pursued, and it was proposed to install an official representative there in order to ensure stable relations. An English resident in 1622 suggested that the presence of a consul would transform the previously dangerous city into a refuge for 'ships to retire to in the strayghts, where they may be secured, furnisht and refresht', not to mention working 'for the benefit of trafficke'. The plan was put into action by the English ambassador to the Ottoman court, Sir Thomas Roe, who secured a peace treaty by March 1623. 'I know not any instrument so fitt as Frizell,' Roe later wrote, 'for he is so hardened to patience, and so well beloved, that in all occasions he is able to make a faction, and to defend himself'. Frizell possessed the right mixture of personal charm, subtlety and pure deviousness to make his way through the treacherous terrain of Algiers: he was duly appointed as consul and early in 1624 he returned on an official basis to the city in which he had already made a shady living for a number of years. Not that life there was easy for him – he remained vulnerable to the whims of the *pasha*, and was the first man to be hauled before him when any Englishmen stepped out of line. In 1625, the *pasha* claimed that English ships had broken the treaty by seizing an Algerine man-of-war, and imprisoned Frizell and a number of other English residents, extorting £6,000 worth of property as condition of their release. Fewer than six weeks before Kenelm's arrival, as punishment for the actions of the English ships, Frizell had suffered the horrifying experience of a mock execution, being brought to the great square under threat of being burned alive and only reprieved at the last minute. Learning how to survive these ordeals had made him a seasoned operator, used to the sometimes terrifying vicissitudes of life in Algiers but also a good guide to its back streets and alleys, a man who knew how to chart a course between service and self-interest and whose life and livelihood depended on doing so successfully.

Frizell's ability to ingratiate himself with the upper echelons of Algerine society, and his knowledge of local customs, were of immense use to Kenelm, who received from his host a crash course in the complex structures of the city's politics, its proliferation of officials with their overlapping remits, and the niceties of diplomatic conduct that would be expected of him during the audience that he had been granted the following day. On 18 February, the day after his arrival, Kenelm was summoned before the *pasha*, in his audience chamber in the royal palace. It was an intimidating prospect, facing up to the same volatile ruler who had been harshly imprisoning and fining the English citizens of the city for minor infractions. Fortunately, however, the *pasha* treated Kenelm 'with much courtesie'. Kenelm delivered a speech, via an interpreter, in which he assured the man 'that my example, if I received good usage, would bring many other English thither, and be the cause of a neerer correspondence for the future betweeene the two nationes'. The *pasha* liked the sound of this, and 'assured me of all friendshippe', though he also revealed that he had not yet forgiven the outrages for which Frizell had suffered imprisonment: he explained that 'he hoped the Kinge of England would redresse some injuries done to subjectes of this state by some of his'. With considerable skill, Kenelm trod the fiendishly difficult line that any diplomat was forced to tread, between granting the proper concessions and courtesy to a foreign nation's ruler and upholding the rights of his own. He assured the *pasha* that King Charles would enforce 'exact justice' wherever the treaty had been broken, but also fought Frizell's corner in declaring it a 'great injustice . . . to satisfie private wronges with the goodes and substance' of innocent merchants, simply because they happened to be English. The pasha conceded the point, 'promised that all former errors should be redressed', and swore to uphold the treaty. That afternoon Kenelm was summoned before the *divan*, where he met the military commander of the city, the *agha*, as well as the *qadi*, the chief administrator. They too were well disposed towards him, and happy with the assurances that he had given the *pasha*. 'After due cortesies passed,' Kenelm recorded, 'they assured me not only of all justice but favour, and caused a proclamation to be made much to my advantage, and to secure us from the abuse of the barbarous people, and in every respect made more demonstration than could be expected of their good intentions towards me.'

While Kenelm was conducting these delicate negotiations, he left Mr Milborne and Edward Stradling in charge of cleaning and refitting his ships. Those of his crew who had succumbed to the sickness but still lived were carried off into the city's hospitals with slim hope of recovery, and a good proportion melted away into the port, drinking heavily to distract themselves from their brush with death. Some were already looking for employment on other ships that were soon to sail away, striving to safeguard their livelihoods and unwilling to wait for Kenelm to return to the business of privateering. When Edward Stradling reported this to Kenelm, he realised that before departing he would need not only to repair and replenish his ships, but find new men to fill them.

For the time being, though, he allowed himself to rejoice in his diplomatic triumph, and the next few days passed in a whirlwind of feasting and fraternising with the foremost figures in Algiers. On the 19th Kenelm was visited by the general of the ships and the general of the galleys. On the 20th, he was invited to a grand feast held in his honour, which was attended by the mightiest pirate chieftains in North Africa: it was hosted by a man named Murad *Ra'is*, who was the supreme commander of all the Algerine corsairs, and was also attended by the governor of Salé – the Moroccan port that was scarcely less notorious than Algiers for the viciousness and rapacity of its pirate population – who happened to be visiting the city at this point. On the 21st Kenelm attended another feast, this one thrown by the general of the corsair galleys, and on the 22nd and 23rd he was visited aboard his ship by many of 'the principall men of the town'. The pirate chieftains plied him with the richest delicacies available: he had expanded the range of his palate in Italy, fuelling his desire for new and exotic sensations, but now, just as he had hoped, his voyage gave him the opportunity to indulge his love of foreign food on a new scale altogether.

As he sat in the great banquet hall in the palace of Murad *Ra'is*,

Kenelm marvelled at the vibrantly coloured earthenware dishes and cups of tin-plated copper that the Ottoman elite who ruled over Algiers brought with them from Turkey, designed for hard use rather than elegance, and so different from the lavish silver and golden tableware used at similarly magnificent occasions in England. Even the wealthiest Algerine sat on the floor in the Turkish fashion, and Kenelm sat with them, resting the dishes of food on rush mats and ox-skins, and passing round the narrow towels with which each diner wiped his hands in turn. He sampled couscous, cooked in marinade with fruit and meat, which was the staple food for all Algerians, rich or poor. After this relatively humble beginning came an endless parade of fish, rubbed with pepper and cinnamon and roasted on skewers, and then fowl and game, especially the fat partridges that visitors saw capering about the hills surrounding the city, as well as countless pigeons, doves and rabbits. And, to follow, an abundance of the succulent fruit that the city produced: the famous 'Melons of marveilous good-nesse, and incomparable sweetnesse', which included an even rarer delicacy that Kenelm had never seen before, the watermelon, known locally as *al-battikh*, which Europeans heard as 'pateque'. These melons were eaten 'rawe without Bread or Salt, and hath a taste so delicate and sweete, that it melteth in one's mouth, giving a water as it were sugred, and serve greatly to refresh and digest'. These fruits were not only alluring and sumptuous – Michel de Montaigne considered the eating of melons one of the four great pleasures of life, along with fresh air, wine and one's wife – but troublingly foreign and strange, even hazardous to one's health when eaten in excess, a taste of the danger that came with lingering in Algiers. While these fresh and spiced delights were all quite hearty and unpretentious, they arrived in the hall with dazzling fanfare, carried aloft by servants and placed on low tables that had been magnificently decorated with large and intricate sculptures, carved and spun entirely from sugar, in the shape of animals, buildings, and even a model of a corsair fleet sailing over sweet and rippling waves.

It was highly unusual for a European visitor to be hosted in such lavish fashion and afforded such a welcome: Kenelm proudly observed that 'att Argires I was treated in such a noble and sumptuous manner as they say noe Christian hath bin the like'. The mixture of rustic simplicity and sumptuous theatricality that he encountered delighted and intrigued him: the combination of hunks and collops of meat with exotic spices, from 'Cinnamon and Nutmegs, as much as will please your taste', to sweet dishes sprinkled with sugar that had been 'ambered' – ground together with 'four grains of Ambergreece', the waxy substance that smelled fishy and floral at once and was sometimes washed up on the seashore in huge lumps, a mysterious gift from the deeps. He was equally taken by the theatrics of Algerian dining, his hosts' penchant for culinary trickery and display which could shock or terrify diners as much as delight them, from 'short endes of lute stringes baked in a juicy pye' which 'will att the opening of it moove in such sort, as they who are ignorant of the feate will thinke there are magots in it', to a loaf of freshly baked bread with mercury placed inside which jumped and sprang about as if it too were alive. As Kenelm sat in the banqueting halls of Algiers and delighted in the delicacies on display his imagination was already running ahead of him. The freedom to explore that had been granted to him by the *pasha* after the happy conclusion to their discussion provided a rare and extraordinary opportunity to venture into Algiers with impunity: an opportunity that Kenelm, who was perennially hungry for the new and the unusual, was determined not to miss. The warm welcome that he had received from the city's elite fuelled his hope that during his stay there he could achieve the first great feat of his voyage, one that would see him lauded in England as a hero; but he was also acutely aware that, even given the recent accord between England and the Barbary rulers, feasting in this entrancing fashion with corsair captains and pirate chiefs was dangerous, and unlikely to do much to redeem his reputation at home. He knew, even as he enjoyed them, that the pleasures of the city would have to be held at bay, or presented to the world in a particular light, and he would have to achieve some great and eye-catching feat in Algiers even as he explored it further.

Before he could go in search of these notable experiences and achievements, Kenelm needed to check on the state of his ships and remaining crew. On 26 February, having extricated himself from the hospitality of his Algerian hosts, he returned to the docks to inspect his ships and ensure that they had been 'cleansed fully'. The decks of the *Eagle* and the *Elizabeth and George* were being thoroughly swabbed with strong vinegar, while clusters of garlic and herbs were hung from the overhead beams, the pungent smells designed to drive out any lingering after-traces of the terrible infection. His boatswain informed him that there was still a week's worth of work to be done, and this gave him the time that he required to delve further into the city's streets.

Kenelm's mind was still spinning from having spent time in the company of the foremost pirates of Algiers. What he had en-countered so far was very different from the nefarious 'Turks', barbarous idol-worshippers, whom he had encountered in written accounts of the region. This term, often spat with contempt from Christian mouths, was a cover-all that described not only those born in Ottoman lands, but also those who had transformed themselves by choice: the people like John Ward who had converted to Islam, or 'turned Turk', as it was commonly described in England. Every European account of Algiers noted the preponderance of its inhabitants who had undergone such a transformation, and who were known as 'renegades'. As one former slave observed, 'the Turks are also of two kinds: Turks by nature or by profession', with the latter group having 'turned Turk of their own free will, impiously renouncing and spurning their God and creator'. As European visitors noted, the city contained 'a greate number of Turks' who had once been 'Christians of all nations': not only 'Spanyards, Italians, and other Ilands adjoyninge', but even Russians, Ethiopians and, most remarkably, 'Indians' from Brazil and Mexico. What is more, it was widely agreed that renegade Christians were usually crueller than those who had been born Turks, whether because they felt the need to prove the reality of their conversion, or simply as an expression of the wickedness that had driven them to convert in the first place. Murad *Ra'is*, the corsair commander who had hosted Kenelm in his gorgeous robes amidst local delicacies, was white, and Flemish by birth; his predecessor as leader of the corsair fleet was known as Süleyman *Ra'is*, but he had been born a Dutchman named Ivan Dirkie De Veenboer, and had served under the most notorious of all the Algerine renegades, Simon Dansiker, who became known as Simon *Ra'is* following his conversion.

As he walked the streets of Algiers while he waited for the repair and cleansing of his ships to be completed, Kenelm began to realise that the metamorphoses that these men embodied were not anomalies, but reflections of the city at large. Having experienced the lavish riches that North African piracy made possible, he was now exposed to its human cost. Among the city's 'many stupendous and sumptuous edifices' were a series of forbidding structures that inevitably grabbed his attention – the complexes known as *bagnios* in which the city's slaves, who made up a quarter of its population, were housed. These were open to visitors during the day, and Kenelm wandered into the largest, the *Bagnio Beylic*, which dated from the rule of the Barbarossas, and could house as many as 2,000 slaves. It was a complex of rooms – cells, chambers, offices, a hospital and even a tavern – in which the stringent laws against drinking alcohol that obtained in the rest of the city were relaxed, and slaves who had lost hope of being ransomed could drown their sorrows.

Visiting the *bagnios* brought Kenelm face to face with the stench and squalor of the sufferings of slavery. The horrors inflicted within the confines of these walls appalled him, revealing a side to Algiers so different from the lavish riches he had so far encountered. Nonetheless, the spectacle of slavery was also very different from what he had expected it to be. Kenelm saw people of every skin tone living cheek by jowl, and alongside those who were inured to the scorching sun after years of captivity were terrified, paler faces: just a few months before, Murad *Ra'is* had ventured further into the Atlantic than ever before, and carried away 800 men, women and children from the coast of Iceland to a life of slavery in Algiers. What terrified the Icelanders the most, reported a priest who was among their number, was that their captors looked 'just like other people': the pirates were terrifyingly familiar, not horribly other. The astonishing mixture that existed within the *bagnios* was apparent not only to the eye but to the ear. Kenelm was finely attuned to different languages, and he heard not only the English, French and Italian that he knew well, and snatches of alien tongues like Russian and Icelandic, but the curious hybrid language in which these groups communicated with one another: the so-called *lingua franca*, a linguistic hodgepodge which mixed elements of Italian, Turkish, Arabic, Spanish, French, Greek and other tongues into a strange and ever-evolving medley. Antonio de Sosa, who was captive in Algiers at the same time as Cervantes, called it 'this confused mixture of so many diverse words and speech acts of different Christian kingdoms, provinces, and nations', mangled by 'the bad pronunciation of the Moors and Turks' to produce 'a veritable mumbo-jumbo'. But the *lingua franca* was in many ways the embodiment of the city around it, the shifting fluidity of Algiers made into a soundscape, in which opposites could always blend and bond with one another to form something both strange and fascinatingly novel.

The slaves were as varied as the great city in which they were trapped, not least in the extent to which they were integrated into the world around them. Some stubbornly retained their own clothes as a sign that they had not been totally defeated by their captors, and clung to their European garb, which grew ever shabbier through months and years of hard labour. Others were willing to assume local dress – 'taking the turban', as it was contemptuously known by those who saw it as a slippery slope towards turning Turk – even though they risked being accused, were they ever to return home, of having 'changed thy Habit and Vestmentes, in token, of change in Religion'. The experiences of slaves were also wildly different from one another. For the particularly unfortunate, or those who committed some infraction, it might mean a life chained to the oar-bench of a galley – a death sentence within a few years – or hard labour building and maintaining the walls of the city. Other luckier souls might pass their days in relative comfort as servants of rich citizens, enjoying a degree of domestic ease and even prestige. Even life in the *bagnios* was not without its distractions and moments of respite. In keeping with the wider Ottoman tendency towards toleration of diverse religions, slaves were granted chapels where they might worship, and in which Mass was said as many as three times a week. Like the city that contained them, the *bagnios* became places where the divisions that ripped apart the wider world of Christian Europe suddenly seemed less significant or absolute. Slaves of all religions and nationalities would come together to worship, when elsewhere they might have been at one another's throats.

In this city, with its confluence of goods and people from across the globe, the divisions that tore apart the outside world seemed less stable. Religion, nationality, language: all seemed subject to flux and variation, not fixed absolutely. In a popular play performed in London a few years before Kenelm's departure, and set in a North African city where 'A confluence of all nations/Are met together', one character is asked, 'What's your religion?' He responds, 'I would not be confined/In my belief,' and cheerfully explains, 'Live I in England, Spain, France, Rome, Geneva/I am of that country's faith.' This was the unsettling and riveting promise that Algiers seemed to hold out to Kenelm. English Protestants denounced 'such as are to choose Religion' in Barbary as '*Ambo-dexters, Nulli-fidians*, such Amphibia as can live, both on Land and Water', and to Kenelm's astonishment Algiers was

packed with hybrid figures of this sort, able to drift between identities and repeatedly change the face that they presented. The man
who owned Antonio de Sosa during his years as a slave went by
the name Ka'id Muhammad, but he had been born a Jew before
converting to Islam, then became a Christian during a period of
captivity in Genoa, before again becoming a Muslim when he
returned to Algiers. The Muslim community itself had been transformed by the arrival after 1614 of hundreds of so-called Moriscos,
crypto-Muslims who had practised their faith in a clandestine
fashion, following their brutal mass expulsion from Spain. These
were people who had lived a double life for many years, used to
being one thing in public and another in the quiet and privacy of
their own homes, and they now found themselves displaced from
the land of their birth: small wonder that many became pirates,
happy to use their local knowledge to plan aggressive raids on
the Spanish coast. Kenelm shared the prejudices towards these
groups common among Englishmen of his time – he was happy
to blame the later difficulties of his voyage on 'the perfidiousness
of the Turks and Jews' whom he encountered – but his response
in Algiers was not simply fear or loathing but fascinated ambiva-
lence. These groups, like the whole city, seemed effortlessly to
embody the sorts of thorough self-transformation for which he
yearned.

Kenelm's first foray into the *Bagnio Beylic* allowed him to experience the mixture of peoples, languages and religions first-hand,
but he kept a particularly careful ear out for English voices; after
slipping a few coins to a jailer in return for information, he was
able to ascertain that there were around fifty of his compatriots
who spent their nights within the compound's walls. He had begun
to suspect that this place, which had both intrigued and appalled

him, also offered the best way to make his mark in Algiers, and to perform his first great action.

The disasters at Cádiz and the Île de Ré, and the ongoing disarray in Buckingham's navy, had made the prospect of any organised attempt to rescue English captives all the more remote; only the very wealthiest had any hope of being ransomed, and there was the chance of escape only for the luckiest and hardiest, in tiny numbers. The headway that Kenelm had made with the *pasha* and the other prominent figures in the city gave him hope that he might be able to do something about the plight of the English captives. In addition to its being an act of great human kindness, few achievements would endear him more swiftly to the court and the public, if he could succeed where no other man had even tried. Thanks to his earlier experiences of negotiation in Madrid, and his dealings in the city so far, he knew just what a delicate proposition this would be; he had been just assertive enough to impress that *pasha*, but any more requests would risk undoing his careful diplomatic work. So he resolved to wait, to spend more time investigating the conditions of the English slaves and the likely sums required for their ransom. He had a week before his ships would be ready, and it would be better to delay until just before he left before beginning negotiations. Were he to fail, and enrage the *pasha* with his requests, a swift departure would be preferable; were he to succeed, better to depart post-haste before the *pasha* could change his mind. Now he had a plan, a grand scheme through which he might serve the realm and his own ambitions, but he also had reason to delay; furthermore, this prudent course gave him several days in which to delve beyond the *bagnios*, and discover what else Algiers had to offer.

II 'The Headiness of that Barbarous People'

During his stay he temporised so discreetly with the headiness of that barbarous people, and wrought himself so much into their good opinion and affection, that he not only procured for himself all that he stood in need of, but settled a very good correspondence between the state of Morea and them, which before was upon exceeding bad terms, and yet imported the Moreans much, and redeemed many Morean captives that had lived there in miserable servitude.

Close by the *Bagnio Beylic* was another imposing edifice for which Algiers was famous, but for much more benign reasons: the Baths of Hasan Pasha, named after the son of Khair ad-Din Barbarossa responsible for its erection, which was constructed from a soaring arch of ornately decorated marble. The bathhouses of Algiers were famous institutions and Kenelm was eager to experience them for himself, his appetite whetted by the accounts of Europeans visiting the city who never failed to comment on the 'great number of Bathes', and the profusion and magnificence of the facilities which most of the more affluent residents were in the habit of using every day. Having been granted the freedom of the city by the *pasha*, Kenelm was free not only to marvel at the building's ornamental facade but also to visit its steamy interior. He entered the first of the large chambers in which bathers stripped off their clothes and proceeded to the next hall, which was divided into a number of small rooms with fountains of water pouring from the walls. With the same eye for technological innovation that he had exercised in Spain, he paid close attention to the ingenious system of pipes and furnaces with which the water was heated before it gushed forth into marble basins; bathers queued for these in order to scoop up the water with copper jars and pour it over their heads and bodies. He paid two *aspers*, one of the enormously confusing array of local currencies, to a Moorish servant who bathed and scrubbed his body.

Kenelm revelled in the opportunity to have the filth accumulated on his visits to the *bagnios* scraped from his skin. It was also his first chance to rest and recuperate since he had set foot in Algiers; the terror of the contagion that he was fortunate to have escaped had been succeeded immediately by the pressures of diplomacy, and then by the overwhelming horror and intrigue of the slave quarters. Now, amidst steam and polished marble, he could retreat into his thoughts. The combination of first-hand, worldly experience and bookish learning that had so captivated him in Italy might also be encountered here, he hoped, in far more dangerous and thrilling surroundings. Even as he walked through the steam-filled rooms of the baths, he found food for thought. He observed that just as 'the same liquor is sweete to some mens taste; which to an others appeareth bitter' and 'one man taketh that for a purfume; which to an other, is an offensive smell', 'in the Turkesh bathes (where there are many degrees of heate in divers roomes, through all which the same person useth to passe, and to stay a while in every one of them, both att his entrance and going out, to season his body by degrees, for the contrary excesse he is going unto) that seemeth chilly cold att his returne; which appeared melting hoat att his going in; as I my selfe have often made experience in those countries.' This was what Kenelm experienced as he drifted between and sampled the many halls of the Baths of Hasan Pasha: the same room might feel scorchingly hot at one minute and shockingly cold at the next, depending on the temperature of the chamber from which he had entered it. Words like 'hot' and 'cold', he realised with sudden clarity, did not describe real qualities existing in the world, but were entirely relative to human experience, and had meaning only in relation to its vicissitudes. It was a position that had been articulated and debated in Florence while Kenelm was there, but he had to stroll through the baths of Algiers before he felt its truth against his body, and fully believed it.

As Kenelm bided his time before beginning negotiations for the English slaves' release, he began to venture beyond the *bagnios*, bathhouses and other large structures that clustered near the shore and the marketplace, and to explore the labyrinth of smaller buildings packed on to the steep slopes beyond. He strode past the many 'houses built staire-like one over the other, enjoying a most wholesome ayre and pleasant situation', turning frequently to look back over his shoulder at the sparkling waters of the Mediterranean to which he would soon return, and noting that there was 'scarce any house of the City but hath the prospect of the Sea'. Kenelm peered discreetly down alleys and through doorways when he could, and enlisted the help of the interpreter who accompanied him to converse with any inhabitant who happened to cross his path. He had a particular ambition in mind, though, which had begun as a risky flight of fancy but grown into a solid determination: visitors from across Europe had managed to meet and mix with the men of Algiers, but Kenelm was determined to meet its women. This enterprise was both highly unusual and perilous. Every European visitor reported how jealously Algerian men guarded their wives: the houses were said to be built without windows facing on to the street precisely so that prying eyes could not glimpse the women within, while any man entering a house would cry 'watch out, make way!' so that the women 'could instantly run to hide in their bedrooms, like rabbits to their burrows when they sense a goshawk flying near'. Thomas Dallam, who visited Algiers years before while travelling to Constantinople with an organ sent by Queen Elizabeth to the Sultan, recorded, 'The Turkishe and Morishe weomen do goo all wayes in the streetes with there facis covered, and the common report goethe thare that they beleve, or thinke that the weomen have no souls'. Whether the position of women in Algiers was entirely more restrained and oppressed than in the England that Kenelm had left behind is hard to say – women in the Ottoman Empire retained ownership of their property even after marriage, for example, while Christian women did not – but the women in the city undoubtedly lived a life of enforced invisibility.

Kenelm was not to be deterred. 'When I was att Argiers,' he wrote, 'though it be not easily permitted unto Christians to speake familiarly with Mahometan women; yet the condition I was in there, and the civility of the Bassha gave me the opportunity of full view and discourse with them'. Kenelm had charmed the foremost women of France, of Florence and of Madrid before returning faithfully to Venetia: now in Algiers he somehow managed, thanks to the freedom he had been afforded, to talk his way into the sort of domestic interior that was usually kept so jealously hidden, and to converse with women in a very different setting. It was not enough just to meet them, though: here too Kenelm found material for his ongoing philosophical speculations, when he encountered 'a woman . . . having two thumbes upon the

Muslim women were more typically viewed by Europeans as veiled and inaccessible

left hand'. She was not alone in this peculiarity. 'Foure daughters that she had, did all resemble her in the same accident, and so did a litle child, a girle of her eldest daughters; but none of her sonnes . . . and the old woman told me, that her mother and Grandmother had beene in the same manner.' Even in this most foreign of settings, Kenelm bore witness to the characteristics, both desired and undesired, that parents might pass on to their children. He could barely tear his eyes away from the women whom he had worked so hard to meet: 'Whiles I was there I had a particular curiosity to see them all'.

His encounter with these two-thumbed women inspired Kenelm to return in earnest to 'the increase of his knowledge' stipulated in the commission he had been granted by the King. From the minute that he realised landfall in North Africa had become inevitable, Kenelm had begun to reflect that this was a region associated not only with piracy and commerce, but also with magical and arcane lore. 'In Barbary,' as John Aubrey sensationally reported, 'are Wizards, who do smear their Hands, with some Black Ointment, and then do hold them up to the Sun, and in a short time you shall see Delineated in that black Stuff, the likeness of what you desire to have an answer of. It was desir'd to know, whether a Ship was in safety, or no? There appeared in the Womans Hand the perfect Lineaments of a Ship under Sail'. Kenelm had his own interests in these tales of supernatural apparitions and marvellous abilities: but, as his experience with the Powder of Sympathy had convinced him, there was no need to separate the apparently magical from the thoroughly rational. The arts and sciences into which he had been inducted by Richard Napier and Thomas Allen, and which he had pursued independently in Italy, were all strongly associated with Arabic-speaking lands. Just a few months after Kenelm left England, in June 1628, a young English Puritan named John Winthrop Jr also set sail for the Mediterranean, precisely to develop his alchemical and astrological interests that he pursued later in life, once he had emigrated to the New World and become governor of Connecticut. Not only these arcane arts but also a wide range of human learning were increasingly associated with the Levant and the Middle East: during Kenelm's formative years, while fear and loathing of the Islamic world remained rife, English scholars increasingly came to believe that knowledge of Arabic was necessary for a full appreciation of mathematics and medicine, while other languages such as Syriac and Persian were required for a proper understanding of ancient and sacred texts. 'Bookes of Physicke, Astrologie, Rhetorike' were written in Arabic, Samuel Purchas observed, while the young John Milton claimed in a university oration 'that the Saracens ... enlarged their empire as much by the study of liberal culture as by force of arms'. During these years ambitious young Englishmen were increasingly exposed to Arabic culture. Kenelm's relative and close friend George Digby, the Earl of Bristol's son, had matriculated at Oxford in 1626 and studied some Arabic while he was there, and Kenelm is likely to have done the same during his year as a student with Thomas Allen. He returned to these interests during his time in Tuscany, where he had researched the expressive mysteries of ancient and Eastern languages for his first oration in Siena, and his friend, the Bohemian reformer Samuel Hartlib, reported that Kenelm was 'a great student for the Arabick Language'. These scholarly pursuits were increasingly seeping into the upper echelons of political life, and King Charles himself, his interest in beautiful and exotic objects having been piqued in Spain, later sent a painter whom he trusted into Persia to seek 'any excellent auntient Bookes in ye Persian Arabian or Greeke Language'.

Though a Mediterranean port with a vast and busy marketplace seemed likely to be the perfect place to search for Arabic manuscripts, as Kenelm familiarised himself with the streets and squares of Algiers his optimism began to fade. He had read wonderingly of the Ottoman capital at Constantinople, which was a great city of learning: it boasted a roaring trade in gorgeous and meticulously copied manuscripts, and a range of religious and imperial libraries. Even the men reviled by Europeans as vicious pirates were often learned and somewhat bookish: Khair ad-Din Barbarossa founded a library there, while several Ottoman admirals were renowned for their learning, like Sidi 'Ali *Ra'is*, who wrote poetry as well as mathematical, nautical and navigational treatises. Algiers, however, for all its lavish cosmopolitanism, was not Constantinople. The constant political turbulence in North Africa was hardly conducive to the establishment of learning, and relatively few in its cities could read: boys were often taught the rudiments of Arabic from the Qur'an, but little more. There were none of the libraries and bookstalls of which Kenelm dreamed.

As he began subtly to enquire with his guides and interpreters as to the availability of books in the city, however, new possibilities presented themselves. Books were valuable objects like any other, and a significant number flowed in and out of Algiers along with the countless other forms of booty and contraband that fuelled the local economy. Even some slaves were able to obtain a remarkable range of volumes, and maintain learned and cultured exchanges with one another in the miserable depths of their captivity. Kenelm also knew well that valuable libraries of Arabic books were among the treasures sometimes seized at sea: in 1612, the Spanish Admiral Fajardo had caused a major international incident when he snatched the private collection of the Sultan of Morocco as it was being transported – 'a huge and excellent library' as Kenelm's friend Henry Oldenburg later described it, 'consisting all in manuscripts, mostly Arabia[n], and some Persian and Turkish, bound in Spanish leather, covered with lamés of gold and silver'. These 4,000 volumes, on medicine, philosophy, grammar, law and politics, many lavishly illustrated, were deposited in the convent library of El Escorial, the King of Spain's palace.

Somewhere in the back alleys of Algiers, Kenelm was introduced to a man who had managed to obtain a smaller but scarcely less

gorgeous collection of manuscripts much like these: he seized
upon them greedily, and bought an entire chest-full. He had them
carried back to his ship and sat in his cabin, poring slowly over
their entrancing and alien pages. The volumes that he had obtained
covered many of the areas of learning with which he was already
fascinated, and others that were entirely new. There were seriously
technical works of Arabic science: one was a treatise on the use
of the 'universal astrolabe', a complex device for making mathematical measurements, and others included detailed and knotty
discussions of astronomy. He also procured Arabic volumes on
mathematics, logic, physics and metaphysics. Two of the most
beautiful works, written in the Persian tongue that he could
not understand, were on the nature of language itself: one, an

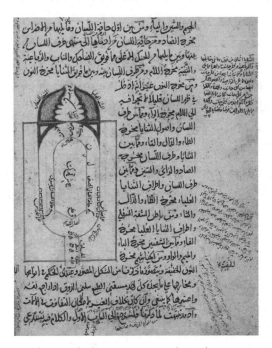

A diagram showing the human tongue, and its role in pronunciation

encyclopedic work on the science of language by the thirteenth-century scholar al-Sakkaki, included vivid diagrams of the tongue and throat, and their role in pronunciation. The other was an enormously heavy and intricately illustrated copy of a rare and sought-after Persian lexicon called the *Qāmūs*. Along with this dazzling array of scholarly wisdom, Kenelm sought to build on his fascination with the place by obtaining its religious books: he bought two richly adorned copies of the Qur'an, one dating back to the fourteenth century, the other of which had been newly copied out only the year before.

Not all the works that he managed to buy were so grandiose and so lavish, however. Some were humbler and rougher, filled with torn leaves and the names of former owners scribbled on their opening pages. They were packed not with arcane wisdom but with incidental and amusing jottings, redolent less of the grandeur of the city in which he had bought them than of the fascinating incidental details that he had encountered in its bathhouses and private homes. One particular manuscript seized his attention: it contained a treatise on the astrolabe, as well as a number of astronomical tables and other technical apparatus; but, scattered in between these learned leaves, Kenelm found a number of pages that spoke to his own eclectic enthusiasms. One page, a vivid reminder of the sweet delicacies that he had sampled in the city, contained a recipe for preparing bananas in syrup, recommended for its aphrodisiac qualities. Below that was a series of short poems, ranging from fragments of practical advice – 'Three things that must not be lent:/A comb, a toothbrush, a slave-girl' – to warnings against excessive indulgence. 'Three things that lead mankind to perdition . . . Always drinking wine and always copulating, and inserting food upon food.' Another poem gave

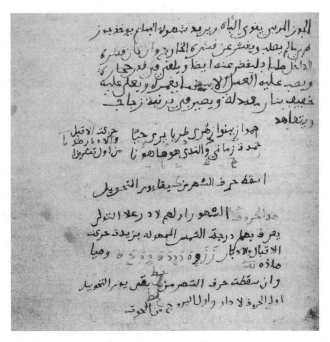

Fragments of Arabic poetry and recipes from one of the manuscripts that Kenelm bought

detailed instructions on how best to trim one's fingernails, beginning with the little finger on the right hand and ending with the ring finger on the left. This unprepossessing volume gathered between its ragged covers both compellingly minute details, and occasions for abstract speculation.

After returning to his ships with his new purchases, Kenelm confirmed that preparations for departure were well under way. His mind returned to the great feat that he had been planning, and he began to consider how best to seek the release of the English slaves. He determined once again to meet face-to-face with the *pasha*, whom he had managed to impress and persuade once before: on 2 March, he was granted an audience. The strategy that he had chosen was extremely risky. He began not by discussing the slaves at all, but by returning to the topic of their previous discussion: the recent skirmishes that had threatened the fragile accord between their two nations, and the treatment of English merchants. He objected in particularly strenuous terms to the way in which Frizell had been punished, and the terrifying mock execution to which he had been subjected. By going on the offensive in this fashion, Kenelm hoped to put the *pasha* on the defensive: to make him fear that the accord that they had delicately agreed was already beginning to fray thanks to these earlier events, and to encourage him to take steps to repair it. It was eminently possible that the *pasha* would not take kindly to Kenelm hectoring him in this fashion and would explode in anger, before subjecting him to the same cruel treatment that Frizell and the other English merchants had endured, or worse. He could only hope that his vociferous words had achieved their effect, as he slid quickly to his main business, 'the hopes that I had of weaving into the treatie the libertie of the English captives there'. Kenelm fell silent when he had finished making his heartfelt appeal, and stood awaiting a response. Finally the governor explained, via an interpreter, that it would be necessary to discuss the request with the *divan* and the other leading figures in Algiers, but that it would have to wait: the city was about to begin the latest in a series of skirmishes with Tunis, a place with which it violently vied for piratical pre-eminence in the Mediterranean, and they were in the midst of preparing to send out a force of 15,000 men against their enemy.

Kenelm returned to the *Eagle*, to endure an anxious wait. He had been banking on an immediate answer that would enable him to depart at once, but now his ships would have to sit, their newly stocked provisions beginning to spoil, while the rulers of Algiers deliberated. As he made his rounds of the ships and spoke to his men, however, the imminent decision on his fortunes was pushed to the back of Kenelm's mind, as he came to realise that something else was afoot. He had been entirely immersed in the sensations of Algiers, in his expanding mind and his emerging plans, and had paid too little heed to how the surviving members of his crew were passing their time in the port. He had tasked his immediate subordinates, Sir Edward Stradling and Captain Milborne, with finding new men to serve under his command; but while they had busied themselves with this task, the men who remained had become restless. At first they were as happy as Kenelm to enjoy the pleasures that the city had to offer, rejoicing in their good luck at having escaped the pestilence that had so terribly massacred their friends and bunkmates, but before long they had begun to get restless. These men had leapt at the chance to serve under Kenelm and avoid being pressed into service in Buckingham's latest madcap expedition to the Île de Ré, but they did so because they expected rich rewards from the prizes they would take. Their commander, however, had wandered off into the city, and since his return seemed more concerned with the chest of moth-eaten and incomprehensible tomes that he had secured than with returning to action on the seas. A sailor named Carveigh gathered together a group of his cronies, and suggested a plan. He had already fallen from grace during the first weeks of the voyage, having begun it as the purser of the *Elizabeth and George* — the officer in charge of provisions and keeping careful accounts — but he had been relieved of his duties for suspected dishonesty. Now he had little to lose. In one of the taverns that surrounded the docks, and served hard liquor in blatant violation of the strict laws against its consumption laid down by the city's Muslim rulers, he had heard a rumour of a ship that had recently docked at Algiers, en route to the Tuscan port of Livorno. It had a valuable cargo aboard, and its damaged sails had just been repaired and rehung, so it lay ready to depart. Carveigh proposed that they seize the vessel and make a break for it, sailing out of the port and searching for another harbour where they could sell the cargo and pocket the proceeds. Like all other ships, Kenelm's were full of loose tongues, and word of what was planned reached his ears. He was furious. He was locked in the midst of delicate negotiations with the leaders of the city; such an attempt would surely be taken to have been carried out with his tacit consent, and he would lose everything for which he had worked and planned. Nonetheless, he knew that he could not entirely alienate his surviving crewmen by doling out harsh punishment to all those involved: instead he had Carveigh 'laid in chains for future punishment, and after a publike reprehension and admonition pardoned the rest'.

With his crew in check, and both his sternness and his magnanimity in evidence, Kenelm continued to bide his time, and on the morning of 12 March a messenger arrived to summon him back before the *pasha*. By now the force that was being prepared had departed for Tunis, and a special meeting of the *Divan* had been called to confirm the accord between Algiers and England and to consider Kenelm's desire to free his enslaved countrymen. Having already met the foremost corsairs, he now had the chance to meet the chief legal and religious authorities of the city – the 'Muftis and Cadies (which are as their Bishoppes and Chiefe Justices)'. Kenelm made his case, via an interpreter, and clearly laid out his aims: he hoped that, in future, if English ships were to take

Algerine prizes at sea, they should 'in a legall manner informe our King of it', rather than take prizes of their own in an endless back-and-forth of retaliation; he requested that English merchant ships and warships alike should be granted the free use of the port as they needed it; and, finally, he asked again that the English captives there should be freed. The governors of the city 'answered that these propositions seemed reasonable to them' but once again they asked for time to consider, the wheels of Ottoman bureaucracy grinding as slowly as ever. Kenelm's hopes hung in the balance, but finally, late in the evening of the 12th, he was summoned back for another audience, and discovered with a surge of exhilarated relief that he had been even more successful than he had allowed himself to hope. Following many 'meetings . . . and private negotiations', the *pasha*, the members of the *divan* and the other officials agreed to his requests: they swore to uphold the treaty with the English Crown, and to repay the large amount of money that the previous *pasha* had extorted from the unfortunate James Frizell; they pledged to restore three prizes lately captured from the Earl of Warwick, and promised to write to King Charles in the event of future disagreements before retaliating.

Finally, and most extraordinarily, they granted Kenelm permission to carry away the fifty English captives for whose release he had petitioned, and to pay for their release no more than the price for which their masters had originally bought them. This was a particular triumph, given that the slaves in question were 'the best and usefulest men they had, gunners, carpenters and pilots', and they would usually have been refused ransom given their value to the upkeep and prowess of the corsair fleet. Even at this price, Kenelm was forced to pay from his own pocket the massive sum of £1,650 – around £150,000 in modern terms – for the captives' release, but he was confident that it would be repaid to him in full upon his triumphant return.

Kenelm was thrilled and carried away with his achievement: before departing he wrote in his journal that he had managed 'to carrie away all the English captives that remained here'. It was the largest successful rescue that any Englishman had achieved up to that point, freeing each of the King's loyal subjects from the most appalling and squalid of circumstances. He had achieved a great good, and wasted no time in making sure that the world knew it. Frizell introduced Kenelm to an English merchant named George Vernon, who was preparing to depart from the port and sail home; the consul assured him that this man could be trusted, and that he had the necessary contacts at court for his voice to be heard. After meeting Vernon, Kenelm was sufficiently impressed by his character and, returning, pressed into his hand a pile of letters that he had rapidly penned, instructing him to take them back to England.

Kenelm made the exceptionally canny decision to write a letter to the English Secretary of State, Edward, Viscount Conway, which was among the sheaf that he entrusted to Vernon. Kenelm explained to Conway that 'an extreme sickenesse raging with much violence in my shippe' had originally led him to take refuge in the port, in case any doubts existed in England as to his motives, and he also explained 'how industrious I have bin to the utmost of my abilities in doing what I conceived might be to the service of my Master and for the good of the Marchantes that trade into these partes, and for his Majesties honor in redeeming his Captive subjectes that remained here in miserable servitude'. He knew the young King well: in Madrid Kenelm had witnessed first-hand Charles's tendency to take politics personally and to respond angrily to perceived slights, and there was nothing that he liked more than acts that burnished his honour. Kenelm had also chosen to stress the selflessness of his actions in Algiers to a particularly suitable addressee. Conway was the Secretary of State with responsibility for foreign affairs (the distant ancestor of the modern Foreign Secretary) but he was also a tough and battle-scarred veteran of the Elizabethan wars, who had been knighted after the 1596 Cádiz expedition. He was now Buckingham's loyal servant, and one of the strongest advocates of a return to the militant glories of Elizabeth's reign, and although he lacked the Duke's elegance – with his blunt personal manner and crabbed, incomprehensible handwriting – he still embodied the age of past heroes that Buckingham, and Kenelm in turn, sought to emulate. Who

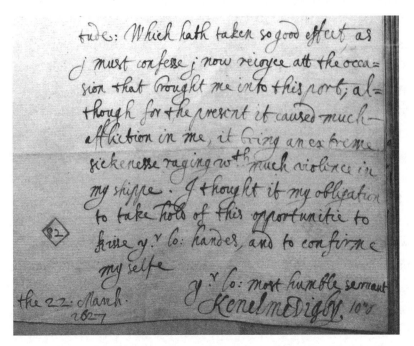

The letter that Kenelm sent from Algiers to Edward, Viscount Conway, Secretary of State

better to receive word of the triumphant condition in which Kenelm departed from Algiers?

On 25 March Vernon departed, carrying Kenelm's letters with him, as well as the letters from the *pasha* and the *divan* to King Charles pledging enduring friendship, and he promised to provide the court with 'a particular account . . . of what had passed there'. The 25th, as Kenelm noted in his journal, was 'our Lady Day', the Feast of the Annunciation, which had traditionally been considered the first day of the new year in England – an appropriate moment for a new start.

George Vernon also agreed to ferry back with him to England the majority of the slaves whose freedom Kenelm had bought, in their pitiable state. A few of the freed men chose instead to join Kenelm's crew and sail onward under his command, whether out of awed gratitude for the man who had freed them, or in the hope of eventually returning to England as wealthy beneficiaries of the voyage's success rather than penurious former slaves. The sometime captives replaced a few of those he had lost, but many more were still required: just as he had instructed them, Stradling and Milborne returned at the right moment with men to flesh out the remainder of the crews that his two vessels required. These sailors, who had been knocking around in Algiers waiting for their next employment, were a seasoned and shrewd bunch, and Kenelm surveyed them with satisfaction and welcomed them aboard. Not only did they possess the know-how and nous that he required, but as he looked them over and listened to their voices as they boarded, he reflected with pleasure on their variety. His new crewmen included 'French, Venetians, Lygornonces, Savoyardes, Greekes, Slavonians, Maltoses and Dutch', among others – a veritable gallimaufry drawn from all the corners of Europe, who brought aboard with them their own languages and customs, and communicated with one another in the improvisatory gabble of the *lingua franca*. Now, he truly felt that his ships belonged in the Mediterranean world as he had imagined it would be. Regardless of the flag under which they flew, vessels routinely gathered together within a tight space an astonishing range of people: one Venetian voyager to Constantinople listed his fellow travellers as 'Catholic Christians, heretics of various sects, Greeks, Armenians, Turks, Persians, Jews, Italians from almost all cities, French, Spanish, Portugese, English, Germans, Flemings, and to conclude in few words, people of almost all regions, and nations of the worlds'. Some Englishmen were appalled by such floating mixtures: Henry Wotton, the former English ambassador to Venice, had once denounced a vessel in the Mediterranean that was supposedly 'English' as in fact 'a ramass of rogues of every nation'. Two days after he had seen George Vernon safely on his way, on 27 March, Kenelm finally bid his own farewell to Algiers, and as he left he reflected with secret pleasure that his own crew now resembled just such a ramass of rogues: it more closely mirrored the glorious, anarchic medley of the city from which he was departing than the stricter divisions of the England he had originally left behind.

Kenelm was exhilarated to be resuming his voyage, but his conversations with merchants who would soon be returning to England had also drawn his own mind homeward. Among the letters that he had entrusted to Vernon were two to Venetia, whom he missed deeply. He told her of the terrible sickness that had decimated his crew, of the urgent flight to Algiers, of the experiences he had undergone there, of his eventual triumph. He also sent his deep affection to her and to their two tiny sons, Kenelm and John. He knew that no letter of hers could reach him on the distant shores of the sea, but he was determined to continue their endless conversations, even if for the time being it meant sending out his own words without any reply – indeed, without even knowing whether she would safely receive them. Nonetheless, Kenelm had resolved to do all that he could to ensure that she should not suffer from fear and false rumours of his death, as she had once before, especially if word of the sickness on his ships had reached England. As he sailed away from the port his mind returned to her again, wondering how she fared, how she was busying herself in his absence, whether she had managed fully to elude the rumours and insinuations that had previously dogged her now that their marriage was public knowledge.

Had Kenelm been able to hear word of Venetia, it would have eased his concerns. The retreat from London life that she had begun during the months when their marriage remained clandestine, and that had culminated in the near total seclusion in which she had given birth to John shortly before Kenelm's departure, had continued in his absence. Venetia had been left reeling and wounded by her experiences in the circles surrounding the court, and the speed with which any word or action might be twisted, turned against her, and used to damage her reputation; she preferred for the time being to shun wider society altogether, in the hope that her faith in other people might be restored. She had 'retired and secluded her selfe from the world' soon after Kenelm had left, and as the months passed she 'never in all that while stirred foote out of her owne dores, nor admitted the visits of any friend whatsoever, though never so neere in blood or estimation'. Apart from two of Kenelm's closest and must trusted associates, whom he had entrusted with his business dealings in his absence and who had 'sometimes occasion to repair unto her . . . and her owne family (which was a very private and frugall one) no man or woman ever saw her all the while'.

Even as Kenelm had ventured out to see the world, Venetia had turned away from it. She had always been religious, and he had admired and respected her for it while they were first falling in love, but now Venetia threw herself into a thoroughly devout life. This was, in part, a response to the rumours that still dogged her, and a way of performing her impeccable morals, but it was increasingly driven by a genuine fervour. 'The greatest part of the day she spent att her prayres, and the rest that was not taken up in ordering domestike business and overlooking her children, she employed in meditating and reading of spiritual bookes'. Like her husband, Venetia's instinctive response to a moment of personal crisis was to read, and rather than passively absorbing these 'bookes of piety and instruction' she 'used to take notes and make collections out of them and sett them downe in her owne hand', copying them into a commonplace book that became a repository for the wisdom that mattered most to her. As the first weeks following Kenelm's departure went by, and the lofty conceptions in Venetia's soul rose ever higher, she reshaped her entire daily routine around her devotions until 'her life was a pattern of mortification, penance and devotion'. She would rise early each day, put on some 'loose clothes', and 'pray and meditate two howres in her oratory', and even on cold January and February mornings after Kenelm had first left 'she would have neither fire kindled nor maid come about her to reach her first garmentes until she had ended her prayers'. She continued meditating throughout the day, whenever the toil of looking after a household and two small children allowed it. She was guided in these excruciating acts of penance by her closest companion in these months, 'a ghostly father; a reverend and holy man', and as he pushed her towards increased fervour Venetia went to extremes and 'often mortifyed herself with disciplining and wearing a shirt of haire; all which she disguised as much as might be'. Despite this punishing regime, and the constant coruscating and irritating of her flesh, Venetia still 'shewed as great cheerfulnesse and livelinesse of spirit as any woman could do', somehow remaining 'excellently well tempered' as she awaited his return.

6

April–June 1628

Majorca – The Italian Coast – The Currant Islands – The Bay of Scanderoon

I 'Singular Examples of Justice'

After which he put to sea again, in prosecution of his former design, which was of a high consequence to the King his master's service, it being to interrupt the great trade of the Athenians in Syria and Egypt for silks and other commodities which those countries yield, that by this means the Moreans might gain it, and make their country the staple for the manufacture and vent of so rich a traffic. And by the way he sailed on, he met with sundry vessels upon the sea, whom he stayed and examined, and with them all shewed singular examples of justice, and particularly with those that were enemies, of humanity and clemency.

'A faire westerly wind' propelled Kenelm's ships away from the steep and crowded hillsides of Algiers, and back out into the waters of the Mediterranean. He had agreed with his vice admiral, Edward Stradling, that if the winds were favourable their ships would strike out towards the Balearic Islands, passing along the easterly side of Majorca and proceeding towards Minorca. Their intended destination was the Isla del Aire, a tiny island off the south-east tip of Minorca. Having restored his two ships to working order in Algiers, Kenelm was determined to swell his fleet by taking a first prize: specifically, he intended 'to seeke for a sattie' – a *saettia*, one of the small and speedy vessels much used in the Mediterranean – 'the want of which I apprehended very much'. He was well acquainted with the many varieties of vessel that swarmed in these seas, and was preparing himself adroitly for what might lie ahead. The *Eagle* was a formidable ship in its own right, extremely large by the standards of the day: rated at 600 tons, it was at least twice as big as the ships which had carried Columbus, Magellan and Vasco da Gama across the oceans in the preceding centuries, and on a par with the larger sort of merchant ship in an age when any vessel of more than 1,000 tons was considered a behemoth. In the previous era, the Mediterranean had been dominated by the fleets of light, speedy and manoeuvrable oared galleys that were employed both by the Ottomans and the various Christian navies, but their pre-eminence had been challenged by the incursion of tubby and tall-masted ships from Northern Europe. These craft lacked the sleek elegance of the galleys, but their stocky strength and large square sails made them durable and able to travel long distances, while they bristled with an unprecedented degree of artillery. Rather than one design simply displacing the other, the two were mingled into potent new combinations. An astounding variety of craft developed over time that mixed the best elements of northern and southern design, and were built for different purposes: from the huge, broad carracks that made it possible to transport vast cargoes, to the tiny, nimble caravels that were perfect for hopping from point to point along a coastline for purposes of trade or exploration. Kenelm sought a *saettia* because he knew that the adventures that lay ahead, whatever they might be, could well require ships that were speedier and more elusive than his lumbering flagship, vessels suited for smash-and-grab raids, not just all-out battles.

On 29 and 30 March Kenelm rounded the south-east shore of Majorca and entered the Bay of Alcúdia, where his ships chanced upon a French vessel that was 'riding att anchor'. It tried to flee, but a volley from the *Eagle*'s cannons tore through its sails: in the heat of the battle, however, Kenelm had failed to notice the *Elizabeth and George* sailing on the other side of the French vessel, 'and one great shott nearly missed Sir Edward Stradling'. Kenelm watched in horror as in their first skirmish he came close to losing his friend and second in command to his own cannons. The Frenchmen responded in kind, sending four cannon shots ripping through the *Eagle*'s lower decks, but the superior size and firepower of Kenelm's ships quickly prevailed. The flagship was able to draw along the starboard side of the French craft before sixty of his men boarded it. The defeated crew tried a final desperate measure, and sought to set fire to the casks of gunpowder on the deck, but 'they would not take', and at last the Frenchmen accepted the inevitable and surrendered.

The vessel, named the *White Lyon*, was one of the Dutch-built *fluyts* or flyboats which had appeared with increasing frequency in the Mediterranean since the late sixteenth century, and set a new standard for speed and efficiency. After Kenelm went aboard and met its captain and masters, he surveyed its cargo and discovered that it was laden with some bales of linen and canvas 'and some other thinges of small value', but it had not yet taken on its intended cargo of Majorcan olive oil, so offered little in the way of valuable booty. Kenelm decided to add the vessel to his small but growing fleet, and renamed it the *Hopewell*. He made the young officer Henry Stradling his rear admiral and gave him the command of the new craft – perhaps by way of an apology for nearly blowing his elder brother to smithereens – and relieved the chief gunner of his duties for his 'great defects in the last fight', putting 'another able man in the place'. After setting his own men in order, Kenelm sent the French crew ashore in a rowing boat, having returned to them 'all their owne clothes that I could gett out of the sailers handes' as well as two days' worth of food and £5 of his own money. This was perfectly decent treatment by the often pitiless standards of marine plunder, and accordingly the French captain 'parted very well satisfyed'.

The search for a *saettia* continued, but when the *Eagle*'s lookout finally glimpsed such a vessel in the distance it fled towards the Majorcan shore. Kenelm swiftly ordered thirty-five of his crew to man two of the ship's shallops – as its large rowing boats were known – and they leapt aboard, arming themselves to the teeth with 'a brasse fauconet and a murderer, and good small shott, swordes and halfe pikes', before they were quickly lowered into the water. They chased the *saettia* as it made for shore, but a hundred armed horsemen appeared at the top of the cliff adjoining the sea and, after a few shots were exchanged, it became clear that this fight was more trouble than it was worth, and they returned, muttering frustrated oaths. Another French ship was glimpsed at around noon on 2 April, but it too managed to flee. That night Kenelm's ships were buffeted by wind and rain, and the choppy sea the following day forced them for the time being to abandon the search for a prize, a quest made less urgent by the unexpected acquisition of the *fluyt*. Instead Kenelm commanded the vessels to strike east, away from the Spanish islands and towards the southern tip of Sardinia.

In the early days of April, Kenelm perused the well-defended shoreline of Sardinia from the deck of his flagship, unable to engage any of the vessels that he saw anchored there. Five ships bobbed temptingly atop the water below the walls of the city of Cagliari, but they were too well protected by the twelve enormous brass cannons whose long barrels protruded forbiddingly from the city's fortress. Loitering close by as he considered how best to proceed, Kenelm's ships stumbled upon a small rowing boat, in which six unfortunate Sardinian fishermen were enjoying a rest from their labours. Understandably panicked by the abrupt appearance of a vast warship, five of the six immediately leapt overboard, 'thinking our men had bin Turkes'. The sixth man was interrogated for any useful knowledge about the surrounding lands before being set ashore — but Kenelm kept hold of the fishing boat, and its tasty cargo of 'mullets and excellent fish'.

Emboldened by this tiny triumph, Kenelm decided to seek further prizes in spite of the fearsome defences of Cagliari. He sent two of his shallops towards the shore, where one sought to tow off a *saettia* from Marseilles, while the other had designs on a frigate carrying as many as twenty tons of wine. As his men pursued their quarries the huge brass guns mounted in the fortress began to send their deadly loads crashing down towards the water. Kenelm was determined to demonstrate his fearlessness, ordering his men to sail straight towards the fort and the terrifying barrage. They weighed anchor scarcely more than the range of a musket-shot from the shore, and returned fire as best they could. As the fight intensified, one of his shallops successfully overwhelmed the *saettia* and took it as a prize, though at some cost – two men were killed and six or seven wounded – and Kenelm ordered the ships to fall back, 'it having bin of all sides a very hott service'. He was both proud of the manner in which his men had acquitted themselves, and relieved that they had escaped relatively unscathed.

Soon afterwards his fleet, augmented by this latest prize, left the dangers of Cagliari behind. They met another ship, though this one yielded immediately, without the need for a chase or a shot fired in anger: it was a Flemish vessel, carrying a cargo of Spanish goods loaded at Naples. Its terrified captain told Kenelm of four even richer ships from Marseilles following in his wake, and so, rather than sailing onward, Kenelm simply ordered the sails of his ships to be taken in, and they bobbed quietly in place while waiting for their victims to arrive. As they loitered he gazed eastwards towards Sicily, where the currents were so strong that the water was said to boil like a cauldron, so different from the moment of calm in which Kenelm found himself. He watched his men scurrying about the *Eagle*, cleaning, making minor repairs and hoisting up large wooden barrels from below with food and drink for their evening repast. He sat with them to enjoy a humble meal of salted beef and hard biscuits as the sun set.

At daybreak on 7 April, the Marsilian ships of which the Flemish captain had spoken sailed into view, but this time fortune was not on Kenelm's side. A sudden dead calm made it impossible for his ships to launch an attack, and so he sent two of his shallops to meet with the Marsilian vessels. Suddenly, though, a strong wind began to whip across the sea, and scattered his ships. The chase had to be abandoned, as the windy day gave way to a stormy night, with waves grown so high that one of the shallops and the men sailing it were lost, along with a brass cannon. The winds continued to batter Kenelm's ships, driving them off course and towards the islands of Marettimo and Favignana at the south-westerly tip of Sicily. It was a grim moment: 'the storme was violent, the sea high, the ground foule and rockie', and so Kenelm cast anchor 'close under the shore, and verie neer to the maine of Sicilie'. The *saettia* that he had taken as a prize was battered so severely that it began to sink. The men aboard her were barely saved, and the forty-ton ship sank into the waves, carrying her 'verie rich' cargo of 'chestes and drie fattes' with her. The storm continued unabated into the ninth day of April, causing Kenelm to reflect 'what a difference of state 2 dayes wrought in us': once again the pendulum of his fortunes had swung with horrible abruptness. His newly taken vessel, carrying enough cargo in itself to have made the voyage worthwhile, had been sunk, and he found his flagship entirely isolated, unaware of the whereabouts of the *Elizabeth and George* and the *Hopewell*, and having neglected to agree on a rendezvous point near Sicily. Kenelm summoned Mr Milborne, a gentleman named Mr Herris, and his other principal officers, and consulted with them as to how best to proceed. They resolved to weather the storm where they lay, before continuing eastward in the hope of finding the vice and rear admirals in the calmer waters near Greece. By 10 April the lashing rains had subsided, although a powerful wind continued to propel the *Eagle* along the Sicilian coast and past Cape Passero, a rocky outcrop pointing out into the sea at the south-easterly tip of the island, and onward towards the waters and islands of the eastern Mediterranean.

At about noon on 11 April, Kenelm's fortunes began to improve. He spied a ship, roughly half the size of the *Eagle*, making its way full pelt towards the Straits of Messina, the narrow strip of water between Sicily and the toe of Italy. Kenelm's men were able to manoeuvre close enough to hail its captain and demand to know his business. The ship's commander claimed to be from Alkmaar in Holland; but, when he refused to show his commission or reveal his cargo, Kenelm brusquely 'warned him that if he did not come I would shoote att him'. This threat, backed up with a warning volley loosed into the waves from his cannons, did the trick, and the thoroughly cowed captain admitted that he was in fact transporting a large cargo of corn to Naples, which was under Spanish dominion. Kenelm gleefully seized the corn for himself, and the captain's rueful response showed that he knew the rules of this unscrupulous game all too well. 'He said he tooke my shippe for a litle one att the first, and meaned to have done by me as I did by him'.

Kenelm unceremoniously dumped the seven 'Spainardes' who had been in command of his new prize on the shore, but kept its skipper aboard as a prisoner, since he could offer useful knowledge of the surrounding waters. He then charted a course for the Ionian Islands, Zakynthos and Cephalonia. These lay just off the west coast of Greece, where he planned to search for the rest of his scattered fleet, and to sell his freshly stolen corn. On the afternoon of the 14th, he spied two sails, which turned out to be the *Elizabeth and George* and the *Hopewell*, who had wandered forlornly across the waves in the days since their separation, slowly running out of food and water. Reunited with his small fleet, Kenelm continued towards the southernmost of the twin islands, Zakynthos, or 'Zante', as it was known to the English. Kenelm was following a well-trodden path for English travellers, and he knew what to expect when he arrived. Since English ships had re-entered the Mediterranean in the last quarter of the sixteenth century, the Ionian islands had been absolutely central to the trade routes that had swiftly been established. As merchants from all lands had been drawn to seek their fortunes on Zante and Cephalonia a distinctive and intermingled culture had been created on the islands, and it was this as much as the possibility of plunder that drew Kenelm there. As the learned English traveller George Sandys, who visited the island, crisply put it in his account of Zante, 'The inhabitants of this Iland are Grecians, the Venetians their soveraignes'.

In the course of the Middle Ages, the tiny, fragile, swampy city-state of Venice had come to exert an extraordinary degree of dominance in the Mediterranean, assisted by their unparalleled expertise in the building and manoeuvring of ships. Never before or since had such a tiny place possessed such an immense reach of power, or exerted such decisive authority over the waves. The spread of its maritime dominions also made Venice the pivotal meeting point between East and West. As the Ottoman Empire rose and spread in all its sprawling magnificence, and even after the Turkish defeat at the Battle of Lepanto, the Venetians realised that, were they to retain any vestiges of their naval might and retain control over the rich flow of exotic goods and necessities that gushed towards the Mediterranean from Asia and Africa, they would have to reach some form of understanding and accord with the Turks. Through a series of ongoing wars and negotiations the rulers of Venice established trading privileges and maintained diplomatic relations with the Sultan, and the islands of Greece were split between Ottoman and Venetian rule. The *Providetori* of Zante and Cephalonia, the Venetian governors of these islands, paid extensive tributes to Constantinople for the privilege of ruling over them unmolested. In the ragged fringe of the Greek islands where Kenelm had arrived, 'a scattered empire' of tenuously held trading posts, the ambiguous and shifting boundaries between Europeans and Ottomans, and between East and West, were constantly in flux. Not only goods but people, ideas, letters, stories and habits of mind could pass back and forth between the Islamic and Christian worlds.

The ships' progress was slowed by two days of calm weather, which Kenelm used to restore a degree of order among his men, for whom the intermittent plundering of the past few weeks had provided opportunities to fill their own pockets. 'I made a generall search through my fleet,' he noted, 'to see what was purloined by the saylors unduely out of the prizes I had taken.' After this business was completed, and Kenelm had extracted an appropriate portion of the booty for himself, he crossed paths with an English ship named the *William and Ralph*, commanded by a man named Captain Trenchfield, who gave him two pieces of news: first, that the prizes that Kenelm had lost in the storm were safely docked at Zante; and second, that Trenchfield himself had recently taken a prize of corn to the same island and sold it. This made it unlikely that Kenelm would get a good price for his own booty, and so he changed course and made instead for Cephalonia, the northern-most of the two islands.

Kenelm's ships weighed anchor off the coast of Cephalonia on the evening of 17 April, within sight of the low and flat-roofed houses, each one decorated on the outside with a pretty round stone, that clustered on the island, and reminded one visitor of the tufted caps worn by old women in the west of England. These squat, humble buildings were a necessity due to the terrifying earthquakes that shook Cephalonia and Zante with remarkable frequency, sometimes as often as ten times in a month. These were thought to be produced by winds trapped in the hollow caves and caverns beneath the islands, and priests would ring the church bells at their onset, encouraging the populace to pray for a swift and harmless end to the awful tremors.

Kenelm was confident that when he came ashore he would be welcomed by the community of English merchants, who had begun to establish trade links with these islands in the latter decades of the sixteenth century, flooding into this ambiguous zone, and seeking to turn a profit. These men were members of the Levant Company, the hard-headed corporation that maintained and jeal-ously guarded a monopoly over trade between England and this part of the world. Cephalonia and Zante were the source of various commodities – wheat, honey, cheese, wool, oil and a particularly valuable scarlet dye – but every English person associ-ated the islands with one item above all others: currants. It is difficult today to appreciate the enthusiasm that these humble berries inspired and the debates they triggered around the time of Kenelm's voyage. Far from being a simple component of buns and puddings, currants were the stuff of which vast fortunes were made and lost, and over which heated political battles were fought, and Zante and Cephalonia were usually known simply as the 'Currant Islands' in England. 'From hence cometh the moste of our Corrance,' wrote Thomas Dallam when he visited the island in 1599, and George Sandys a decade later agreed. 'The chief riches thereof consisteth in currans, which draweth hither much traffick'. The English went wild for currants, stuffing them into every possible dish in lavish quantities, to the bafflement of foreign traders, who liked to observe that only in England were the berries eaten at all: in the rest of Europe, they were treated as a medicine and sold in apothecary shops, or fed to livestock. Some English travellers lamented the excessive fondness of their countrymen for these fruit, and the distorting impact that it had upon foreign trade. Thomas Roe, who was appointed as James I's ambassador to the Ottoman court in 1621, stopped off on Zante on his way to Constantinople, and wrote a letter home in which he complained, 'Here is a barren island or two, that devowres more money, retornes nothing but a trash berry, takes none of our native merchandize, and in conclusion laughs at us.' He estimated that two thirds of the seven-million-ton crop that the islands produced in a year made its way to England, at exorbitant cost. Roe's complaint was echoed by the colourful Scots traveller William Lithgow, who lamented the 'liquorous lips' of the English, 'who forsooth can hardly digest bread, pasties, broth, and . . . Bagge-puddings, without these Currants'. It was a uniquely English vice, he insisted. 'There is no other Nation save this, thus addicted to that miserable Isle'.

English merchants in the Mediterranean had fought fierce battles both over the ownership of the valuable currant trade, and over the Crown's right to tax it. No ingredient prompted fiercer political disputes in Kenelm's lifetime than the humble currant.

Acrimonious disputes concerning the taxation of currants were among the many issues raised in the volatile parliaments of the 1620s as grievances against King Charles and Buckingham. In 1627, the year before Kenelm's departure, the Privy Council resolved strictly to enforce the impositions on currants as a money-making measure, but some Levant Company merchants refused to pay and were controversially jailed. Similar struggles occurred in early 1628 when Kenelm had just departed, and continued while he was at sea: in September 1628, a group of merchants broke into the customs house in London and seized a cargo of currants that had been kept from them because they refused to pay the required tax. The fractious debates between the government and the English public concerning the subjects' right to property and the Crown's right to levy taxes that would even-tually play a role in the road to Civil War were, at their origins, partly a battle over currants. There could hardly have been a more fraught or volatile time for Kenelm to visit the Currant Islands; but, by the same token, there was no more appropriate location for a man whose understanding of the world was so tightly bound up with the inclinations of his palate.

Kenelm spent the evening of 17 April surveying the coast of Cephalonia from his ship; when morning came, he sent a message ashore to the *Proveditore*, a Venetian gentleman named Marin Mudazzo, and swiftly received a friendly response. Kenelm was granted *Pratique* – the right to come ashore, mix with the local inhabitants, and engage in some wheeling and dealing. This was no mean feat: George Sandys, recalling his own visit to these islands, claimed that when an unknown ship arrived 'Prattick . . . will not be granted untill forty dayes after their arrival' and that it was 'death to him that shall come ashore without licence'. The 'extraordinarie courtesy' that he immediately received was, Kenelm rather smugly observed, 'a thing unheard of in these partes'; he met another English ship that had already been waiting a fortnight for a similarly warm welcome, with no end in sight. Kenelm, though, had grandly informed the *Proveditore* of his royal commission; that, and the sight of his large gunship, seemingly made clear that he could not be kept waiting in the manner of a mere merchant.

Kenelm's arrival had in fact caused much greater alarm than he realised, or chose to acknowledge: *Proveditore* Mudazzo wrote a pained letter to the Doge and Senate, the rulers of Venice, to explain what happened when Kenelm arrived. 'He asked me for pratique here, but I absolutely refused, pretending that I could not give it, as he had recently come from Algiers, and I did not know how long [since] he had left those parts.' The extended jaunt that Kenelm had enjoyed in the North African pirate city made his arrival deeply dubious in the eyes of his sceptical con-temporaries. In the end, Mudazzo explained, it was not Kenelm's might nor his reputation that won out, but his cargo of freshly stolen corn. 'The members of the community and all the people came to me in a rage, to get me to grant this pratique and allow the sale of the wheat, representing the scarcity in the island.' Over the past decades, the English craze for currants had led the local inhabitants to dedicate every available patch of land to cultivating the 'trash berry', and they now lacked the ability to grow the most basic staples.

Kenelm, unaware of the reasons for his swift and courteous

welcome, became even more pleased with himself when he managed to sell his corn to some Greek merchants for a better price than Captain Trenchfield had got on Zante. He was not only welcomed by the locals, but entertained by a group of English merchants, 'who had provided and furnished a house for me'. He was shown around the small island, which was roughly triangular in shape: like most English visitors he admired the woods, mountains and 'profitable vallies' that dotted Cephalonia, though it was rather arid and lacking in rivers and fountains. There were local curiosities to be witnessed, especially in the production of the scarlet dye in which English merchants did a small but lucrative trade: this was made from small blisters growing on the leaves of a certain shrub, which, when rubbed, produced a powder that later grew into worms, which were then drowned in wine when they began to move and formed the base of the dye. Being shown the sights of the island and mixing with the English merchants allowed Kenelm to meet the men who lived their lives on the razor's edge of English trade, gaining and losing fortunes by speculating on this lowly berry, and to witness the currants at their source being loaded aboard great Mediterranean vessels by the ton.

With his appetite for delicacies from the region having been fuelled in Algiers, Kenelm was able not only to witness the currant trade in action, but to develop a partiality for the 'trash berry' derided by Thomas Roe that was unusual even by the standards of his greedy compatriots. He learned and tried out new recipes into which great handfuls of currants could be tossed, ranging from the delectable and exotic to the more mundane. He learned a method for preparing 'Currants-Wine' that was poised between the English appetite for these berries and the Continental treatment of them as medicine: 'a pound of the best Currants clean picked' were to be fermented with yeast for three days, then strained 'to leave behind all the exhausted currants', and the resulting wine 'will be exceeding quick and pleasant, and it is admirable good to cool the Liver, and cleanse the blood . . . And you may drink with safety large draughts of it'. Rather less appetisingly, he also prepared 'an excellent and wholesome water-gruel with wood-sorrel and currants', for which one is to boil and then 'press out all the juyce and humidity of the Currants . . . throwing away the insipid husks', before a dash of richness and luxury was infused into the rather pallid-sounding dish with the addition of some Rhenish wine and the yolk of an egg. For Kenelm, currants were not merely ingredients but miniature globules of succulence and power, bursting with healthy potential that could be extracted, the empty skin cast aside.

As he rested in the lodgings that the Levant Merchants had provided for him and expanded his repertoire of currant-based recipes, Kenelm was able to turn his mind from the recent crises and emergencies of his voyage to more practical matters. It was time once again to clean and refurbish the ships that had been scraped and caulked in Algiers, but much battered and storm-tossed since: they now needed to be scrubbed and tallowed, and fitted with new sails and yardarms, and the lost shallop to be replaced. Furthermore, the recently taken prizes presented certain difficulties, since one had a rotten hull and could not possibly survive the return voyage to England; the other was filled with olive oil that would soon spoil. Kenelm made the swift and canny decision to sell them to the merchants who had made him welcome.

While all this business was smoothly being arranged, one of Kenelm's petty officers informed him that 'some ill-disposed persons in my fleet tooke occasion to sowe mutinous discourses', demanding that they immediately be given their shares of the prizes that had been sold. This was not at all in keeping with standard practice, as the spoils of a privateering voyage were always divided at its end; but, Kenelm contemptuously observed, the men 'desired money to supply their present dissolute spending in port', where the taverns and brothels of Cephalonia did a brisk trade with visiting sailors. Calling a general assembly of the crews from all his ships, he insisted on sticking firmly to the letter of his commission and not disbursing the booty any sooner, explaining that he 'flatly refused all they desired', and threatening to report any would-be mutineers to the Court of Admiralty upon their return. The next day, however, after concluding that this short and sharp speech had done the trick, he once again convened his men, and spoke to them in a very different fashion: now, Kenelm 'gave them the strongest assurance I could that I would carrie all thinges evenly and to their best advantage'. Having cowed his men with his stern blast of authority, Kenelm now beguiled them with his charm. He explained to them that, were they to defer their demands for immediate gratification, they would end up with a much larger heap of spoils to divide among themselves. 'Which,' he noted with satisfaction, 'I did in such a manner and was so unexpected to them that it wonne much upon them, so much that then they referred all thinges to me, and in every particular exceeded my desires.'

In dealing with these seditious elements among his men, Kenelm showed himself to be, by the standards of the time, fair and even restrained. There were standard punishments of varying savagery imposed as a matter of course aboard ships in the Royal Navy, ranging from imprisonment in the bilboes – a special kind of naval stocks, made 'more or less heavy and pinching' depending on the severity of the offence – to dreadful whippings, with five lashes inflicted by each member of the crew the standard fate of those discovered stealing from their shipmates. It was possible, but exceedingly rare, for men to be executed at sea, although because privateering vessels tended to attract rowdy crews brazenly seeking personal gain, discipline was often more of a problem and the punishments were accordingly more severe: in the hapless voyage that the Earl of Warwick had undertaken the year before Kenelm's, two men were condemned to death having been moved to 'insolent mutiny' by the outrage of being given 'cheese in lieu of butter with their fish'. In the end they were not executed but given the next harshest punishment – a keel-hauling, which involved being dragged beneath the waves and along the splintery and barnacle-roughened hull of the ship. Kenelm was perfectly capable of inflicting punitive misery of this sort when he felt that the situation called for it: when he discovered that his steward was purloining sugar and rice from the ship's supplies, he had him ducked (violently and repeatedly dunked into the water with a rope around his waist) and then dragged behind each ship in the fleet, 'with a gunne shott off'. This last act was done 'right over [the] head' of a malefactor, 'as well to astonish him the more with the thunder thereof, which much troubles him, as to give warning unto all others'.

Faced with mutinous mutterings on Cephalonia, Kenelm was more diplomatic and forgiving. He had not altogether abandoned the iron fist for the velvet glove, however, and over the next week as his ships were repaired he winkled out the ringleaders of the aborted insurrection: a man called Tillingham, whom Kenelm ordered to be chained in the hold and then shipped back to England as a prisoner aboard a merchant vessel to face justice; and the skipper of the corn ship that he had taken as a prize, who eluded Kenelm's grasp and fled, but not before doing his best to spread the rumour that Kenelm was 'but a pirate having no commission'. This was the first time that Kenelm acknowledged in his journal that this damaging and dangerous accusation might be thrown in his face. Even as he suppressed these threats to his authority, Kenelm began to sense that it was time for him to move on. The warm welcome he had initially received was growing frostier every day: *Proveditore* Mudazzo showed a veneer of friendliness to Kenelm throughout his weeks on the island while dropping increasingly desperate and unsubtle hints that he should leave, acting 'on the pretext of sanitary regulations . . . as his stay here mortifies me exceedingly'. After a little over a month on the island, having successfully sold his corn, sampled the practicalities and delicious delights of the currant trade and restored order among his crew, on 20 May Kenelm finally acquiesced to Mudazzo's desires and bid Cephalonia's shores farewell.

The money that Kenelm had pocketed from the sale of his prize full of corn was a step in the right direction, but it also left him uncertain how best to proceed. He could continue in this fashion, flitting about the seas and grabbing the cargo he encountered in fits and starts; but his achievements in Algiers had given him the taste for grander feats, which would do more for his standing at home than some stolen corn. He had struggled to find a suitable direction for his ambitions on Cephalonia, and so he resolved to make the short hop to nearby Zante, the busier of the Currant Islands, which was a voyage of just six hours. Rather than immediately seeking to dock on Zante as he had on Cephalonia, however, Kenelm chose instead to lurk just off its coast. He had seen a *saettia* coming into port flying a French flag, and this made him wonder whether this might be a good spot in which to prey upon the merchant ships of France as they made their way to and from the eastern Mediterranean. He also harassed several local vessels as they left the island, officiously demanding to check their cargo. This naked and overbearing aggression unsurprisingly meant that Kenelm received a far cooler reception when he finally approached Zante itself. He sent a letter to its Venetian governor, Piero Malipiero, but 'the Proveditore delivered me his answere that he would not graunt me prattike, in respect to the kinges of Spaine and France, whose enemie I professed myselfe to be'. Malipiero was thoroughly sick of 'these English', who were shame-lessly 'plundering the ships which fall into their hands under the pretext of war, and then bringing them to these islands where they try to sell the goods': he had no desire for Zante to turn into a safe haven like Algiers for the spoils of piracy. Furthermore, the officer whom Kenelm sent ashore to explain his desire to dock on the island 'expressed it in a very unseemly manner', and was therefore 'dismissed as his behaviour deserved'. Rather than departing when faced with these rebuffs, Kenelm increased his provocations to the ships coming and going from the island, searching a Venetian ship loaded with Cretan oil and a Dutch vessel with a cargo of silk. Finally, on the evening of 24 May, Kenelm's belligerent ploy worked: Piero Malipiero sent him a message complaining about the damage he was doing to the ship-ping trade, and asking him, 'in a faire and respective manner, to make what hast I could to be gone from thence'. Kenelm agreed to leave if he were sent necessary provisions, and he promised not to inconvenience any ships bound in friendship to Venice. The captain of one vessel, grateful for this clemency, sent him 'a gentile present', but Kenelm haughtily returned it, 'telling them I deemed it very ignoble to receive any guift from such as were under my power'.

Kenelm took advantage of his forced inactivity as he loitered off the coast of Zante. Now, for the first time since Algiers, he had time to sit and put pen to paper, and on 26 May he wrote a long letter to Venetia. He had no idea whether the two letters to her which he had entrusted to the hands of George Vernon had arrived safely – it was impossible to send a letter from anywhere in the seventeenth century, never mind from the furthest shores of the Mediterranean, without the strong possibility of it going

The surviving copy of the letter that Kenelm sent to Venetia from Zante. A later hand, probably in the eighteenth century, has added the words 'A Letter from Sir Kenelm Digby to his Wife giving an ac[coun]t of several piracys committed by him in the Mediterranean 1628'

astray. Kenelm missed Venetia desperately, and longed for news of her and their two tiny sons. 'No newse will be soe pleasing to me as good of you,' he told her. He could not yet allow himself to give full voice to these feelings, however: the unfolding events of the voyage were still too urgent and their outcome too uncertain, and he determined to wait until he had achieved greater things to allow his wife to occupy the forefront of his mind. Reining in the pain that months of separation from his family had caused him, Kenelm focused instead on his various adventures. He told Venetia of his triumph in Algiers, where he had 'redeemed all the English captives that were there'; he described the skirmishes around Majorca and Sardinia, and his reception at Cephalonia. Parts of the letter he copied almost verbatim from his journal, and stressed his valour and bravery. Describing the battery of his ships by the fortress at Sardinia, Kenelm emphasised to Venetia his men's reluctance to enter the dangerous fray: realising 'that all my perswasions & command could not make them goe on upon that adventure; I deemed that nothing but my exampla of like danger would prevaile', and he thus threw himself into the thick of the action, leading by fearless example. Recounting that he had recently averted the threat of mutiny – 'I thinke there never came out of England such a crew of Rascalls,' he commented of his men – he justified his sternness and rigour towards the ringleaders, explaining that since 'there is noe other remidie, I carry thinges with a highe hand with them, and now I see love onely will not serve I alsoe make them feare mee'. Kenelm focused on his achievements in part to control his emotions and defer their expression, but also because, while he certainly hoped that this letter would reach Venetia and assure her of his health, success and well-being, he did not intend it for her eyes only. Unaware of the extent of her seclusion, he meant for her to have it copied and passed from hand to hand so that word of his achievements and his valour could begin circulating in his absence. In an age before printed newspapers, this was one way in which current events were discussed and reputations were made and unmade; Kenelm was sharply aware of the need for his exploits to become known even before his return. He busied himself with his letter while his ships were freshly stocked with 'wine, water, and other necessary provisions' from Zante, and finally on 28 May he sailed south-eastward, leaving the Currant Islands in his wake. As he left he caught a glimpse of the ancient past, a reminder of the mythical region that he was entering, when his ships sailed past the island now called Little Cephalonia by the English and Theaca by its inhabitants. Kenelm, though, was convinced that this was 'the Ile of Ithaca', homeland of Odysseus, the first and greatest of all the Mediterranean's wandering heroes.

II 'Exact Preparations for a Great Fight'

But when he came to Alexandretta, where was the period of his design, he found there a great strength of Athenian vessels, and some Cyprian ones, that did not content themselves with saying that they would defend their companions and friends . . . but also warned him to go immediately out of the port, or otherwise they would sink his ships; so presumptuously confident were they of their formidable vessels, which were made with such admirable force and art, that until this hour no ships durst resist them.

But Theagenes, that thought valiant deeds would be the best answer to their vain words, and that, doubting such entertainment, had made exact preparations for a great fight, as one that deemed caution with valour to be the first step to victory; calling his chief men together, made an oration to them, such a one as the shortness of time permitted, calling to their minds their past victories that they had gloriously obtained together, and how they had been absolute lords of the sea in all places where they came . . . and therefore bade them go on to a certain conquest, praying God that if himself were here to end his life, yet his fleet might return safe home, and he be brought back not in a funeral but in a triumphal pomp.

Which being spoken with notable vigour and alacrity of courage, that was enough to assure the faintest heart, he began the charge with his own admiral ship against that of the enemy's.

Kenelm's sojourn in the waters around the Currant Islands had been a limited success: he had a chest of coin in his cabin from the corn that he had sold, and had undertaken an exciting range of activities on Cephalonia, but he had no clearer a sense of the next grand action that he might undertake following his resounding success at Algiers. Still Kenelm forged eastward, but as June began he was becoming disconcerted by the aimlessness of his own wandering. For the time being he gave himself over to fortune, hoping that as the winds propelled his ships on their way, an occasion would present itself for him to seize. He used the time to survey his flagship's weaponry, and ensure that it was ready for any fight that lay ahead. Kenelm was particularly fascinated by the art of gunnery, which blended action and theory, involving an acute gasp of the practical mathematics of lines, points and angles that could be deployed to devastating effect. Since Kenelm had appointed a new chief gunner following the near-disaster at Majorca, he had been highly impressed with the performance of his men, their bravery at Sardinia, and their rare and remarkable expertise. Now he cast a careful eye over the artillery at his disposal, a fearsome array of guns large and small: cannons, demi-cannons, bastard cannons, culverins, basilisks, serpentines, falcons, robinets – a whole medieval bestiary of death-dealing power.

With Kenelm confident that his ships could win any fight that they chose to enter, the *Eagle* and the *Elizabeth and George* passed Cape Matapan through 'a high popping sea' and proceeded along the coast of Crete (or 'Candia', as it was then known to the English), then sailed on past Rhodes, driven by 'a constant west winde'. On 6 June, he made for a point on the shore at which he had heard that 'a great fresh river disimbogues into the sea', and which was a place for 'excellent watering'. En route, he crossed paths with three Greek vessels, bound for Alexandria, their holds crammed with wood. He let them continue unmolested on their way, but not before they had passed on a most interesting piece of news: they told him of two French ships at a nearby port taking on a cargo of cotton, 'and of many at Scanderone'.

The mention of this place sent a jolt of excitement through Kenelm. This was the port that lay at the easternmost tip of the Mediterranean, the furthest that he could venture into the seas: Iskenderun, known to the English as 'Scanderoon', or by its Greek name, Alexandretta. The mere name of the port was notorious in England. It was not exotic and cloaked in mystery, like Algiers, but straightforwardly terrifying, a place of pestilence and death, of strange creatures and lurking spirits. Every report sent home by an English traveller suggested that even to approach this place was perilous and foolhardy. When Thomas Dallam had arrived at the town en route to Constantinople, he found it surrounded by 'desarte placis, thicke woodes, and boges', and the town itself a ruin, with nothing but 'great peecis of walles wheare goodly housis and monestaris had bene, which in the same is now nothing but boges and pondes'. While Scanderoon had long been sinking into the surrounding swamp in this fashion, it had recently been freshly ruined: a few weeks before Kenelm arrived, another Englishman named Charles Robson passed through and found the place 'full of the carcases of houses, not one house in it. It having beene a litle before sackt by the Turkish Pyrats'. Scanderoon was a place to be vacated as swiftly as possible: Robson dared not loiter for more than two hours, while the Levant Company preacher William Biddulph reported that 'The Aire is very corrupt, and infecteth the bodies, and corrupteth the bloud of such as continue there many dayes ... And it is very dangerous for strangers to come on shore'. The sea thereabouts was said to be the point at which the dregs of the Mediterranean washed up, while the high mountains that surrounded Scanderoon were known to block the sun and its healthful rays.

The terrors of sickness and plague, which Kenelm already knew all too well from his time at sea, were exacerbated by the ferocious and disconcerting creatures that lived in this land, and whose cries echoed through the mountain peaks. Dallam saw various 'wyld beastes' thereabouts, including 'two myghtie greate buffelawes' stuck in the marshy ground, while the ruins of Scanderoon itself were swarming with a 'verrie strainge varmente Runing up and downe at great pace, som of them biger than a great toude, and of the same collore, but they had longe tayles lyk a Ratt'. Picking damsons, he and his men espied 'a great Ader that was in the tre upon the bowes . . . He was even Reddie to leape upon one of us'. For Biddulph, the local predators were more horrifying still, and pursued their human prey even beyond the grave. 'About Scanderone there are many ravenous beasts, about the bignesse of a Foxe, commonly called there Jackalles . . . which in the night make a great crying, and come to the graves, and . . . doe scrape up the earth, and pull up the corps and eat it'. The strange and unfamiliar creatures that scurried around the entire Ottoman world and so fascinated and terrified the English swarmed here with particular malevolence, and the mountains around Scanderoon were 'abounding with wilde beasts, as Lyons, Wylde Boares, Jacalls, Porcupines etc', while the whole region was 'a great Marsh full of boggs, foggs and Froggs'. This was a stinking, sickly, swampy, creeping and crawling landscape, a place where an English body that lingered too long was likely to end up in a shallow grave from which it might well be torn by the jaws of wild creatures.

While English travellers were terrified of Scanderoon, they could not avoid it. In its own right it was a bare and shabby place, but it served a crucial function. Sixty miles inland lay Aleppo — among the world's greatest merchant cities, and the point at which the silks and spices of eastern Asia arrived before being ferried to the markets and the greedy hands and mouths of Europe. Even more than Algiers, Aleppo was a large, sprawling sink into which the whole world seemed to flow, and where the people, the behaviours and the goods of all nations met and mingled: it was 'the chiefe Mart of all the East, frequented by Persians, Indians, Armenians and all Europaeans'. At more than 100,000 inhabitants, Aleppo was smaller only than Istanbul and Cairo among Ottoman cities, and its cosmopolitanism and splendour dazzled English visitors. 'There are here spoken so many severall Languages,'

Biddulph commented after his arrival, 'and here are of most Nations in the World some, who either come here with their Merchandise to sell or buy commodities, or sojourne here as strangers, or else have accesse and recesse to this Citie as Travellers'. Aleppo, though, lay sixty miles from the Mediterranean shore, a logistical problem for the export of its riches to Europe. When Christian traders had first sought goods from Aleppo they had to buy them at faraway Tripoli, but they soon realised that it would be simplest to transport goods illegally by mule or camel through the mountains to the Bay of Scanderoon, and load them there. This was well-established practice by 1590, though not legalised until 1593: as so often in the Mediterranean, laws were made after the fact to justify lucrative and clandestine actions already taking place. The English merchants established a stone warehouse in Scanderoon in 1597 and, apart from a brief interlude between 1609 and 1612 when the Ottoman government shut it down, the port did a busy business as the outlet for goods from Aleppo. European traders in Kenelm's day tried to make the journey to the sea as seldom as possible: the perilous mountain passes were filled with terrifying precipices and supposedly haunted by spirits and populated by devil-worshippers, just more of the horrors with which the riches of Scanderoon were surrounded.

☒

When Kenelm heard of the large number of French merchant ships loading at Scanderoon, he realised immediately that this was where his course must take him. He would now be able to explore the Mediterranean arena to its very limits: he had every chance of amassing huge riches by seizing an entire French merchant fleet in one fell swoop, rather than picking off individual vessels in an onerous and piecemeal fashion, and it would allow him to enter the murkiest and most intimidating of landscapes, the sort of region into which only a hero would venture. He barked immediate orders at his men to hoist the sails and proceed eastward with all possible urgency, and on 8 June his ships raced along the coast of Cyprus. As he passed the easternmost tip of Cyprus, Kenelm recorded in his journal, 'Wee then saw Mount Ararat, whereon Noah's Ark rested.' Sitting in his cabin late that night, he thought better of this confident proclamation and added a marginal note: 'I believe they that informed me so were mistaken, but it is a vulgar opinion among seamen, yet I thinke Mount Ararat is higher within the land and more eastward.' The exact location of this landmark was uncertain, but Kenelm was in no doubt that it existed and could be seen; he was entering a region in which not only the tales of the heroic Greek past but the sacred stories of the Bible had taken place.

The next morning, Kenelm spotted a small boat bobbing atop the waves not far off, and sent a party rowing a dinghy to investigate. 'In it were 2 men that had bin long dead, for their flesh was all rotten.' Repulsed by this sign of the sinister waters that he was entering, Kenelm 'caused her to be left where we found her'. Around four o'clock, even more disconcertingly, Kenelm stumbled across a *saettia*, apparently in good working order but entirely devoid of captain or crew. The mystery of the ghost ship was soon solved. Shortly before nightfall, he met another ship which turned out to be a Maltese man-of-war, a small and nimble vessel of around one hundred tons, but packed with a crew of one hundred and twenty heavily armed men, and bristling with no fewer than eleven cannons. This was a notable encounter, since

The port of Scanderoon, viewed from the sea

Maltese vessels were not to be trifled with in the Mediterranean.
They were manned by the Knights of St John, the most feared
Christian corsairs in these waters. The Knights epitomised the
difficulty of distinguishing religious war from self-interested
plunder in the seas that Kenelm had entered. They understood
themselves to be continuing the Crusades, acting as agents of God
in the apocalyptic struggle between Crescent and Cross; in practice, though, their stark world view allowed them to engage in
some thoroughly unscrupulous behaviour. The Maltese Knights
thought nothing of seizing any cargo that they suspected (or
claimed to suspect) of belonging to Muslim merchants, even if it

were carried in Christian ships, and they were equally content attacking the vessels of Protestant nations. As Kenelm and the Maltese captain scrutinised one another's vessels, however, they both decided against aggression and exchanged greetings rather than cannon-fire. Kenelm's small fleet appeared fearsome enough not to be trifled with, and he had no desire to lock horns with these redoubtable crusaders, who were seasoned and unscrupulous fighters, when an unsuspecting group of French merchant ships lay a day's sailing away. Kenelm came aboard the knights' ship, and its captain explained to him that they had taken the eerily vacant *saettia* as a prize but then cut it loose to ease their own sailing. 'After some courtesies they parted', with the Maltese making their way towards the south of Cyprus in search of easier prey. Kenelm's ships continued east, and as daylight dwindled on 10 June they entered the Bay of Scanderoon. By late evening they had weighed anchor four leagues from the shore, just far enough for their arrival to pass unnoticed. Kenelm waited for the sun to rise and reveal to him what he would find at the port.

As morning broke on 11 June, Kenelm moved his ships towards the swampy, hazy shoreline of Scanderoon. A 'strange thicke viscous dew' had descended on his vessels overnight, no doubt a sign of the unhealthiness of the place, but soon the sun grew 'exceeding hot' and scorched away this damp residue. From the deck of the *Eagle*, Kenelm drew from a fur-lined case one of his most prized possessions: a 'long prospective glass' or telescope that he had bought in Florence. He trained it on the distant town and surveyed the low buildings that lined the shore and sparkled under the relentless rays – the ruined shell of a castle, the ragged stone walls of a mosque, the large Greek Orthodox church whose graveyard contained the remains of several earlier visitors from England. Ahead of him he sent his two shallops, to reconnoitre the port and report what awaited them there. The word that they brought back was promising: the French merchants of which Kenelm had heard tell were still docked at the port. There were four in all, and one carried in its hold 100,000 pieces of eight with which to buy goods in Aleppo, an astoundingly high sum. If Kenelm could descend upon them with sufficient speed, he might snatch this heap of treasure, and all four of the ships.

His scouts informed him that two English merchant vessels had weighed anchor near the port, and they also brought other and less propitious 'intelligence'. 'There was a great force of galliones and galligrosses in the road that might happily oppose me'. These were the renowned and formidable vessels of the Republic of Venice: for several centuries, the Venetian galleys had enjoyed almost unrivalled supremacy in the Mediterranean, and the more recent innovation of the larger and heavily armed 'galligrosses' or galleasses had made them more fearsome still. There were two of these vast ships patrolling the waters near Scanderoon, and Kenelm observed that they 'have betweene 30. or 40. Brasse guns in each of them of incredible bignesse,' and 'carried as many as six or seven hundred men'. The two galleons that were also prowling the bay he estimated at around 800 tons – considerably larger than the *Eagle* – with the galleasses at least half as big again. The latter were ships that had carried all before them for decades. They were brilliant technical innovations, uniquely blending the heavy artillery and ability to sail for long distances that distinguished northern European vessels with the speed, elegance and ramming-power of southern ship design. A triumph of improvisation, the galleasses had allowed the Venetians to increase their firepower enormously, and graft structures specially designed for battle on to the sleek heft of their galleys. In the great Battle of Lepanto at which the Holy League routed the Turks, galleasses had played a decisive role. The Turkish fleet mistook half a dozen galleasses for mere merchant ships and attacked them: unleashing their devastating firepower, the six Venetians sunk no fewer than seventy Turkish vessels. More recently, no less an authority than Galileo Galilei had been asked to employ his mathematical expertise to determine the best way to arrange the decks of a galleass so as to maximise its speed and deadliness. These were the meticulously designed, heavily armed, formidable vessels that stood between Kenelm and his prey. He knew that they were unlikely to attack his ships unprovoked: but as Venice's monopoly over trade with the Ottomans had been eroded over the previous century as the French, the English and more recently the Dutch made incursions into these waters, the Venetians had responded by appointing themselves as peacekeepers, trying to ensure that no squabbles between European powers should be allowed to disrupt the rich trade that was beneficial to all. They would not take kindly to his attempt to bring the war between England and France deep into the Bay of Scanderoon.

Once he learned of the galleasses' presence, Kenelm realised that the question of whether to attack the port would require further thought. He was not deterred altogether, since he suspected that the Venetians were not the naval force that they had once been, and that they avoided conflict largely thanks to their reputation for maritime prowess, not their current strength. The Venetians had a profound sense that the Mediterranean sea was *their* sea, the waters over which they ruled and through which they traded, and which they knew better than anyone. This belief was reinforced every year through a symbolic marriage with the waves, carried out in a magnificent public ceremony: as George Sandys, who witnessed the ritual when he visited Venice, explained, the Doge 'solemnly espouseth the sea; confirmed by a ring thrown therein: the nuptiall pledge, and symbol of subjection'. But Sandys also understood that this state of affairs was changing, drily noting that 'the Pirats here about doe now more than share with them in that Soveraignty'. Their very determination to remain neutral laid the Venetians open to opportunistic incursions from all sides. No nation had suffered more from the free-for-all of Mediterranean trade and plunder than the Venetians, who, in the preceding decades, had endured countless attacks not only from

Mediterranean pirates – both Muslims from the Barbary Coast and Christians like the Uskoks of Senj, who operated from the Dalmatian coast – but especially from English ships. As one Venetian writer complained, the English 'had entered these seas in the guise of brigands, although they brought merchandise too; and they treated every ship they met as an enemy, whether it belonged to friend or foe'. English merchant ships carried unprecedentedly heavy artillery – supposedly to defend themselves against pirates, but it conveniently allowed them to indulge in de facto acts of piracy when they so chose. Venice may have held symbolic sway, but by this point their ships were largely watchmen, with the Mediterranean akin to 'a forest teeming with bandits'. This situation not only had a severely detrimental effect on the trade of Venice and its political standing in the Mediterranean: it was also a direct assault on the Venetians' elevated sense of themselves as a nation, their pride in their prowess as both sailors and merchants.

If the erosion of Venetian dominance in the seas by the depredations of English pirates gave Kenelm hope as he pondered an all-out attack, it also gave him pause. Even if he were to attack the galleasses and to emerge triumphant, he knew that he risked being labelled as a scurrilous pirate himself, the latest in a long line of English villains. Since Roman times, to accuse someone sailing in the Mediterranean of piracy was a deeply serious charge – it was to label him not only as a criminal but as inhuman, the enemy of all mankind and attacking the very glue that bound humanity together. Kenelm had feasted with the chief corsairs in Algiers, but in a sense these were men who, for all the havoc that they wreaked on English ships, were comfortingly easy to categorise. There were comparatively few self-professed pirates of this sort, however, and many more who considered themselves merchants while dabbling in a little piracy on the side; or who indulged in piracy while insisting that it was in fact part of a Holy War; or who, like Kenelm, insisted that they had official commissions and were therefore privateers or soldiers. 'Pirate' was a negative label to be attached to someone whose actions were offensive, as Kenelm first discovered on Cephalonia when the ringleader of the aborted mutiny hurled it at him, and it could be difficult to avoid – as even the great Elizabethen hero whom Kenelm hoped to emulate, Francis Drake, discovered to his fury when he found himself repeatedly denounced as a base pirate by the Spanish for actions that he considered great and just. The difference between a pirate and a mighty conqueror lay not in their respective heroism, but in their success: as the great Church Father Augustine of Hippo memorably observed, 'It was a pertinent and true answer which was made to Alexander the Great by a pirate whom he had seized. When the king asked him what he meant by infesting the sea, the pirate defiantly replied: "The same as you do when you infest the whole world; but because I do it with a little ship I am called a robber, and because you do it with a great fleet, you are an emperor." '

The only solution was to win, and to win so resoundingly that Kenelm's account of his triumph would drown out any insults or outrage that he incurred in the process. He had every faith that he could prevail, since the Venetians were 'presumptuously confident . . . of their formidable vessels, which were made with such admirable force and art, that until this hour no ships durst ever attempt them', but he believed that they might not know how to handle their own formidable guns as effectively as he and his men could wield theirs. The galleasses were large and well armed, but they were no match for the firepower of his English warships. Only relatively recently and belatedly had the Venetians begun trying to match the English in their shipboard artillery, and as yet they were still comparatively unskilled in its deployment. Italian naval experts still assumed that a warship's principal job was ramming and boarding, while Kenelm went along with the English belief which held that, 'Experience teacheth how sea-fights in these days come seldome to boarding ... but are chiefly performed by the great artillery breaking down masts, yards, tearing, raking, and bilging the ships'.

After consulting with his captains, Kenelm resolved to launch an all-out assault on Scanderoon and carry away the French ships and their rich cargos, bringing the fight to the Venetians if needs be: but he would ensure that he did not attack them unprovoked, so that he could not be accused of outright piracy; and, if conflict were to ensue, he would at first order his ships to keep their distance and rely on the force of their artillery. He fully expected to have to do battle, and therefore 'made the exactest preparations I could for a fight, and to fire powerful enemies'. Kenelm realised that success relied on his carefully chosen words as much as his actions: he delivered a stirring speech to his men, and so roused were they by his oration that 'they expressed much desire to adventure in, and gave assurance that they would not faile in performing their duties'. Kenelm then sent the swift and nimble *saettia* ahead 'with letters to the Venetian Generall and the English Captaines, to acquaint them who I was'. This was carefully timed so that the letters arrived just as his ships heaved into view: he thereby ensured that his heavily armed vessels would not be taken for Algerian or Maltese raiders, while also making clear that he possessed the firepower necessary to back up his written demands, whether or not they were granted.

His letter to the Venetian admiral had a veneer of courtesy that barely disguised its brusque and haughty tone. Kenelm announced that he had been 'sent by the King of Great Britain, whom I serve as a gentleman of his Privy Chamber, to attack his enemies', but insisted that he meant no harm to the Venetians, and would leave them unmolested. The Venetian general was a grizzled and experienced commander named Antonio Capello, hardly one to be taken in by Kenelm's profession of honourable intentions. He had been charged simply with protecting the port of Scanderoon, and ensuring that trade there could be allowed to continue uninterrupted, for the benefit of all. The Venetians took no interest in the war between France and England, and simply wanted their money and goods to continue flowing, unimpeded by these distant squabbles. Capello therefore penned a quick note and sent it skipping back across the waves in Kenelm's boat, telling him straightforwardly, 'If you wish to attack the enemies of your king you will have plenty of opportunities away from here.' This answer allowed Kenelm to swell with righteous indignation that his royally sanctioned mission was being impeded, and his response was swift and incendiary. 'Even if I risk sinking here,' he wrote to Capello, 'I shall not fail to carry out the commands of my king and master.' He took the Venetian captain's demand that he leave forthwith as a personal affront to his honour, and immediately challenged him to a duel, since 'it will be more noble for you and more useful for our masters if we two try our strength against each other'. Back went the boat towards the galleasses, conveying Kenelm's challenge and bringing the Venetian's answer. Capello's response was measured, but only provoked Kenelm further. The admiral explained that he could not meet him man to man due to his official responsibilities, 'but if I was free I would certainly give you every satisfaction becoming a gentleman'. The Venetian saw no reason to risk his sword, when he was standing securely aboard one of the most fearsome warships to cut through the waves of the Mediterranean. 'I could injure your ships by a greater demonstration of the strength of these vessels,' he confidently proclaimed, but 'I renounce this because I do not desire to have other than friendly relations with you'.

The personal challenge that Kenelm issued was a tactic designed to needle his adversary, and it worked. The time he had spent pondering his options and the slow exchange of letters, each of which had to be rowed onerously across the bay, had eaten up most of the day: but now, at last, he had provoked Capello into uttering what sounded like a threat of aggression, and that was all he needed. 'The Venetian Generall treated my men ill,' he wrote somewhat disingenuously in his journal, 'and sent me word he would sink my shippes if I went not immediately out of the roade.' Capello had backed his letter up with warning shots from his flagship, and as the first explosions echoed through the air of the Bay of Scanderoon, Kenelm's mind was made up: his opponent had fired first, even if it were meant as discouragement, and now he could respond in kind. His ships hoisted their sails, and drove full pelt towards the Venetians guarding the port, and the French vessels that they were protecting. The time for the weighing of risks and tactics, for delivering speeches and letters, for plotting and negotiating, had passed. As Kenelm recorded with satisfaction in his journal, 'I then fell upon his vessels with all my might'.

To fly directly at the Venetian ships in this fashion was stunningly brave, but Kenelm had the advantage of surprise. He had left it until the last moment to reveal his intentions, sailing ever closer to the shore as he exchanged letters with Antonio Capello. This meant that as soon as he received a threat of aggression backed up by cannon-fire, he was able to unleash the full force of his small but fiercely armed fleet at the Venetians, who still retained the vain hope that he might agree to go meekly on his way. Capello, for all his experience of command, realised far too late what Kenelm was planning, and his ships were horribly unprepared to defend themselves. The two galleons had done their best to get into position, but having loaded a heavy cargo of goods and provisions these vessels had sacrificed their manoeuvrability, and 'were much embarrassed at the time owing to the bags they had taken on board that morning'. Furthermore, they were 'without sails, as is the custom here, as they would suffer harm from the heavy dews in these parts'. Excessive concern for the same sticky condensation which had affected Kenelm's ships overnight meant that the Venetians were sitting ducks, and could not move into properly defensive position as Kenelm's ships hurtled towards them, never mind offer an answering attack of their own. Even the winds were blowing in Kenelm's favour, propelling him towards his quarry and pinning them in place between his vessels and the shore. By the time his ships came within range it was around seven o'clock in the evening, and it was now that Kenelm gave the order to fire, and his ships unleashed a firestorm of cannon and gunshot upon the Venetians.

The full and fearsome array of the *Eagle*'s guns exploded in unison, raining a vicious storm of shot down upon the nearest of the two galleys, and the shrinking distance between the ships was filled with a pungent black smoke. The crack of cannon-fire that echoed through the cloying air of the bay was so thunderous that

the sound brought the inhabitants of the ragged town of Scanderoon racing from their homes to witness the battle for themselves.
The galleons had no choice but to try to flee and keep their distance,
while Kenelm pursued, seeing that the risk of them trying to board
him was slight, and sent volley after volley of vicious iron shot
in their direction. 'We followed them close,' he recalled with grim
pleasure, 'our great guns going off with swiftnesse rather like
Muskets than Peeces of Ordnance.' He also noted with immense
satisfaction that 'our men did exceed beliefe in good performance'.
In the space of a few minutes, 'a scarce credible number of pieces
of ordinance were shott from my fleete' and they raked through
the sails and hull of the galleys and ripped through the bodies of
the Venetian sailors aboard them, adding the sound of splintering
planks, agonised wails and screams of terror to the booms of
cannon-fire echoing about the bay. The sound of this suffering
drifting over the waves brought home to Kenelm the particular
horrors of war at sea, 'the havoc wrought among human limbs
now by iron, now by fire (which is not so terrifying in land battles),
the sight of this man torn to shreds and in the same moment
another burned up, another drowned, another pierced by an
arquebus ball, yet another split into wretched pieces by the
artillery'.

From where Kenelm stood on the deck of the *Eagle*, he saw
with satisfaction that his gamble seemed to be paying off. The
Venetians were unable to offer any meaningful retaliation with
their own guns due to the intensity of his assault, and the response
of their supposedly fearsome sailors was abject cowardice. 'We
laid so well at the Galleons that the men stowed themselves in
their holds, and left their vessels to their owne fortunes without
guidance.' The low oared vessels that had once charged so boldly

over the Mediterranean now floated aimlessly, their sides torn and leaking from the impact of Kenelm's guns. When Antonio Capello saw how meekly these ships had abandoned the fight, he commanded the galleass that was his flagship and its twin vessel to abandon their attempted blockade of the port – where they had been trying to prevent the *Elizabeth and George* reaching the French ships – and sail towards the *Eagle*. By this point, the hapless galleys were offering so little resistance that Kenelm could order his ship to turn its guns towards the galleasses as they arrived, and continue their assault on the larger vessels unabated. Capello's vessels 'received so rude a welcome' that the Venetian quickly realised that his two larger ships were equally unfit to offer any meaningful resistance to the ferocious battery that Kenelm had at his disposal, and risked being damaged or sunk if they brought the fight to him. The vast hulls of the galleasses turned and slunk off, having utterly failed to live up to their formidable reputation or recapture their previous glories, and instead they moved away as quickly as they could and 'sheltered themselves under the English ships that were in the Road', and whose presence Kenelm's scouts had reported. By this point the light was fading, and Kenelm had pursued the Venetians for three hours. The thunderous assault of his cannons had mangled and maimed them with as many as 500 shots. Though certain that his men were capable of sinking these famous adversaries if they continued, Kenelm ordered them to cease fire, to ensure the safety of the English merchants: he was determined to 'be very cautious in that point rather to misse an opportunitie of hurting the Enemie, then to endanger our Countrimen'.

While the heat and the horror of his battle with the Venetian warships was unfolding, Kenelm dispatched his smallest and nimblest vessels, his *saettia* and the *Hopewell*, to slip past the Venetian ships and try to seize the French vessels and their rich cargo. The attempt was led by Henry Stradling, who had command of the *Hopewell*, and his crew of fifty men: but to Kenelm's frustration, when the departure of the galleasses allowed Stradling to enter the port, he discovered that the French had prudently taken advantage of his protracted negotiations and violent engagement with the Venetians. They had ferried to shore the huge quantity of pieces of eight with which they intended to buy goods at Aleppo. When Stradling sent word of this development by boat, Kenelm realised that the promise of the rich prize that had brought him to Scanderoon, and that he so desperately sought, seemed to be receding beyond his grasp. He still knew, however, that a famous victory, a great action that would transform his standing in the eyes of the world, was scarcely less valuable.

By the time that night began to fall, once the galleasses had sailed into the vicinity of the English merchant ships and Kenelm's cannons had ceased their fire, the English consul at Scanderoon, the Levant Company's local representative, felt that he could stand by no longer. He sent his servants rowing out into the bay, weaving their way between splinters of the galleys' masts and the contorted bodies ripped through with cannon-shot that bobbed in the waters. They bore urgent appeals, asking both Kenelm and Antonio Capello to end their conflict. Capello, though embarrassed by his fleet's performance, knew that the French cargo was safe, and therefore considered that he had done his duty in protecting the port. Kenelm had routed the famous Venetian vessels and forced them to flee: he could draw the battle magnanimously to a close and consider himself the victor, thereby showing his mercy and his concern for the prosperity of his fellow countrymen, who 'represented . . . what prejudice it might be to the Merchants of Aleppo' if the fighting continued. The immediate gain for Kenelm was quite meagre: he took the flags from the French ship as a symbol of victory, and some brass fittings for his ship's figurehead, 'besides what our Saylors pillaged', but he considered that he had asserted his supremacy over the seas. As was usually the case, each side had its own inflated opinion of the damage that had been done, and of how honourably each had behaved: Capello wrote a letter back to the rulers of Venice, claiming that eighteen Englishmen had been killed or wounded, their ships pierced, their riggings and masts shredded. As he sat in his cabin that night, Kenelm scribbled in the margins of his journal, adding a series of frenzied notes to the account of the battle that he had originally written: he insisted that 'they killed us never a man but hurt some few (thankes be to God)', while claiming that the damages to his ships were 'in no dangerous places', and that 'by their acknowledgement afterwards we killed them nine and fortie men outright besides a great number hurt'. He also insisted that the Venetians' conduct was shameful, and their acquiescence to him absolute: the request for peace had been made 'in a verie abject manner'. As well as penning this private document, Kenelm began to antici-pate the implications of his victory for other English people in the region who might be held responsible for his actions: he wrote a letter to the Aga of Scanderoon shortly after the battle had ended, expressing 'respect for the ministers of the Sultan' and insisting that the Venetians had been the first to fire a shot in anger.

As midnight approached on 11 June, Kenelm sat in his cabin on the quiet waters and completed the details of the day's events in his journal. He allowed himself to hope that through this great triumph, in the mere space of 'a few hours', he had erased all of the missteps and the damaging perceptions that had dogged his earlier life, and had 'got a glorious victory and gave testimony to the world, that a discreet and stayed valour is not to be resisted in what it undertaketh, although at first sight it may seem to attempt things with much disadvantage'. This was the moment he had been waiting for: the glorious, magnificent act that, he dared to imagine, would render irrelevant the disadvantages of his religion, his lineage and his marriage, and prove his greatness in the eyes of the world.

Even as he reflected with immense satisfaction on the day's events, the perfect execution of his plan and the excellence that he and his crew had displayed when put to the test, Kenelm could not entirely banish the deep anxieties that quickly crept back in. For all that he had achieved, in Algiers and now in the Bay of Scanderoon, Kenelm knew that his work was only half done. His youth, and the vicissitudes of the love that he and Venetia shared, had taught him just how vulnerable a person's actions were to the malicious interpretations and misunderstandings of others. Having undertaken the great feat in search of which he had originally set out, he could not simply assume that it would be viewed favourably, or that he had decisively transformed his standing in the eyes of the world. He would have to do everything in his power to impose his own stamp on what he had done, to ensure that it remained part of the tale that he was spinning out, and was not taken over by the tales of others.

Though he tried to concentrate on the pages of his journal, Kenelm found himself distracted and disconcerted by these anxious thoughts, and gradually he realised why. Still now, hours later, when dark had fallen and the distant howls of jackals could be heard from the mountains that loomed over Scanderoon, the lingering stench of cannon-fire remained thick in the air of the bay, and it filled his nostrils. At first it had been simply the satisfying smell of victory, but now, amidst quieter thoughts, the whiff of black powder took him back much further: to his studies with Thomas Allen, who had taught him that gunpowder was the most mysterious and the most dangerous of all the substances that the alchemist must learn to concoct. Its origins lay with the wisest and most ingenious of men, the great Roger Bacon, who, with a piece 'not bigger than one's Thumb', could make 'Sounds like Thunder, and Coruscations in the Air more dreadful than those made by Nature'. But the stench that enveloped the Bay of Scanderoon led his mind back further still, to the terrible and failed enterprise for which his father, Everard, had died – gunpowder, treason and plot. Even now, at the most distant point of the seas into which he had ventured, and in the aftermath of a great victory, the stain in his blood could not yet be forgotten.

Part III

Time Is
Time Was
Time Is Past

7

June–August 1628

The Coast of Turkey – The Egyptian Coast – Milos

I 'A Discreet and Stayed Valour'

In like manner every one of his fleet took to task an adversary, who did not long hold out, but after the loss of many men, and their vessels being upon terms of sinking, if the fight had continued any longer to keep them from mending their leaks (wherein it appeared what discreet fury could do against men that had more confidence in their floating castles and in their multitude than in their own virtue) the Cyprians sent a humble message to beg a shameful peace; and at the same instant he boarded and took by force the Athenian vessels, so that in a few hours he got a glorious victory and gave testimony to the world, that a discreet and stayed valour is not to be resisted in what it undertaketh, although at the first sight it may seem to attempt things with much disadvantage.

In London on 7 June 1628, just four days before Kenelm fired his cannons at Scanderoon, the House of Commons took a bold and extraordinary step. Its members presented King Charles with a document titled 'the Petition of Right', which formally demanded that every English subject receive the proper protection of 'the good laws and statutes of this realm'. While the King had begun his reign in 1625 in accord with his first parliament, baying for a sea war with the nation's Catholic enemies, this landmark moment in English political and constitutional history confirmed just how violently they now stood at odds with one another. The series of events leading to the Petition was under way even before Kenelm left England, but it gathered pace following his departure as the Duke of Buckingham sought to cobble together another exped-ition to La Rochelle and redeem himself with a great victory, while most of the country blamed him for all their ills and howled for him to be punished. After a succession of parliaments had failed to fund the foolish wars with Spain and France to the extent that Buckingham and Charles desired, the King had responded by raising the money via a 'Forced Loan', a tax imposed without parliamentary approval. Dozens of gentlemen were jailed without trial for refusing to pay it, and five of them sued for their release, in a high-profile case argued during 1627 that focused on the respective rights of a monarch and his subjects. Charles, urged on by Buckingham, had also responded to the financial crisis by declaring martial law across the country, and forcing people to billet soldiers and sailors in their homes, whether they wanted to or not. As even these unprecedented emergency measures failed to raise the required funds, Charles reluctantly called another parliament, which convened in March 1628: it began promis-ingly, granting a large sum for the war effort, but the sessions became increasingly filled with rancour at the recent erosion of the subjects' liberties; criticisms could not be aimed at Charles directly so all the blame was placed at the door of Buckingham, his evil counsellor. The MPs – led by Sir Edward Coke, who had prosecuted Everard Digby with such malice, and a brilliant younger lawyer named John Selden, who had a rising reputation as the greatest Hebraist of his generation – began to draft a document which would enshrine and protect the inalienable rights of English subjects whom the King and the Duke had placed under attack. Buckingham was nowhere mentioned in the Petition, but one specific complaint – that 'great companies of soldiers and mariners have been dispersed into divers counties of the realm, and the inhabitants against their wills have been compelled to receive them into their houses . . . against the laws and customs of this realm, and to the great grievance and vexation of the people' – was clearly aimed at the Duke, and the desperate measures he had taken to pursue war at all cost. The implication was clear: Buckingham was not only foolhardy and incompetent as a military leader, but also represented a profound threat to treasured English liberties.

The Petition was ready to be presented to Charles by the end of May. The King sent word that he would reluctantly accept it, since it appeared to be the only way to protect his closest friend, for whose blood the MPs were baying: he instructed the Speaker of the House to interrupt any member who disparaged any great Minister of State, especially Buckingham. These instructions were ignored: Coke and Selden publicly inveighed against the Duke and demanded his removal, but Charles's financial straits were so dire that he capitulated nonetheless. The Petition was presented to him on 2 June and he approved it in parliament on the 7th, insisting, 'The King willeth that right be done according to the laws and customs of the realm'.

The King's apparent capitulation was a euphoric moment for Parliament and for the nation at large, their endangered rights having been publicly asserted, and bonfires were lit across the land in celebration. Its long-term implications, however, were deeply unclear. The debates surrounding the Petition had revealed a deep and widening gulf between the King's belief that his subjects should grant him unquestioned trust and obedience, and the MPs' determination to safeguard individual rights. Buckingham remained in place for the time being, the King having done nothing to suppress the swell of criticism aimed in his direction: as soon as the Petition was passed and further funding for the war had been promised, the Duke raced to Portsmouth to continue frantic preparations for his expedition to France. Parliament was suspended for the time being but not dissolved, and as its members left they remained divided as to how far they could and should go in pursuing their agenda without the King choosing to dismiss them, perhaps for good. The deep fractures in the sovereign's relationship with his people had been lightly plastered over, not fully healed, and they seemed doomed to reappear before long.

As the sun rose over the Bay of Scanderoon on 12 June, burning away the sticky dew that had again settled overnight as the last of the acrid smoke dissipated, Kenelm sat and did nothing. His victory seemed to be confirmed that morning, when the *Hopewell* sailed threateningly close to one of the injured galleasses, but the cowed Venetian vessel offered only salutations, 'in evidence how much they had lost of their former pride'. Kenelm might have been crowing in his moment of triumph and rallying his crew, but instead he locked himself in his cabin, paralysed by the anxieties that had crept in upon him during the night, unsure what to do now that the moment towards which he had striven had arrived. 'The English are staying here,' Antonio Capello wrote glumly back to his superiors in Venice, misreading Kenelm's inaction as a brilliant tactic, a sign of the English captain's implacable confidence in his continued superiority. In fact, now that his ambitions had seemingly been fulfilled and he had allowed himself to stop rather than forging compulsively onwards, Kenelm had been overwhelmed for the first time by a combination of deep homesickness, and uncertainty as to the reception he would receive upon his return. He yearned for Venetia and their sons, but could not altogether banish the panicked thought that prolonged absence would prove to have damaged their love once again; he dreamed of a triumphant homecoming, but feared the malicious plots that the Duke of Buckingham might spin in his absence to dislodge him once and for all from the King's favour. Three tense and uneventful days passed in the Bay of Scanderoon as the Venetian sailors, Kenelm's own men, and the English merchants who made their living in the town awaited his next move.

Kenelm's funk was interrupted by the arrival on the 14th of a visitor who had been rowed out from the shore to speak with him: the English vice consul at Scanderoon, who represented the Levant Company merchants in the town and reported to the consul in Aleppo. The vice consul began by flattering Kenelm, and telling him that he had never witnessed such a valiant attack, or encountered such fearsome firepower: Kenelm learned that 'the report of our gunnes, had, during all the time of the fight, shaken the drinking glasses that stood upon shelves in his house; and had splitte the paper windowes all about; and had spoyled and cracked all the egges that his pigeons were then sitting upon'. The consul then moved deftly from compliment into complaint, and began to explain just how difficult Kenelm's actions had made life for the Levant merchants in the area: word of the battle had been carried to Aleppo by carrier pigeon soon after it had ended and, despite Kenelm's letter to the Aga of Scanderoon, 'all our marchants were putt in prison' following an official complaint by the Venetian consul. This man, Alvise da Pesaro, was too experienced an observer of Ottoman politics to believe that the *pasha* of Aleppo had imprisoned his English counterpart out of any true sympathy for the Venetians' grievances: he acted rather 'with the firm resolve to profit from this affair so that he should no longer be short of money', but the result for English traders was still dire. As soon as a returning pigeon had brought word of their plight to the vice consul at Scanderoon, he had dashed into the bay to meet with Kenelm. He did not dare issue a demand, merely reporting what had taken place and leaving it hanging in the air between them, but the implied message was clear: please leave, and quickly.

The vice consul's visit snapped Kenelm out of his torpor. He had other reasons to take action, since his crew had begun to grumble about the deleterious effects of the climate. 'The weather was extreme hott' and the 'exceedingly unwholesome' atmosphere and resulting 'corruption and stinkes' took their toll. 'Our men were verie sensible of the badnesse of the aire,' Kenelm noted, 'and generally all broke out in their bodies to a sharpe itch,' so he resolved to move his ships away from the sickly shadows of the mountains looming over Scanderoon. He was not yet ready to depart altogether, however. Kenelm had begun to wonder whether his lingering dissatisfaction in the aftermath of his victory arose in part from an excessive focus on the active side of his voyage; he had enjoyed his triumphant stay in Algiers so much precisely because he had managed not only to undertake the grand action of freeing the English slaves, but to combine this feat with opportunities for novel experience and philosophical contemplation. He resolved not to leave the vicinity until he had sought out similar occasions.

On 17 June, the *Eagle* set sail but did not go far; the crew weighed anchor in a sandy bay around seven leagues from Scanderoon, and Kenelm set foot in Ottoman Turkey itself for the first time. He sought out the inhabitants of the place, who promised to furnish him with fresh provisions. Word of their hospitality got out, and a message arrived from Scanderoon threatening the locals not to provide food, on pain of death; whether charmed by Kenelm's words or by his coin, they ignored the command, and 'came down in troopes on horse back to our men', bringing valuable sustenance with them. Though a short sail from the sickly surrounds of Scanderoon, the land in which Kenelm now found himself was much fairer and finer, a 'verie frutifull' valley replete with 'groves of figges, mirtle, laurell, and trees that give aromatike gummes, and of wild vines'. Kenelm continued to pass his days there 'in much recreation', punctuated only by the need to suppress another conflict within his crew – this time preventing a duel between Edward Stradling and a gentleman named Mr Herris. He mollified the pair with well-chosen words and restored 'love and quietnesse' among his men.

Though Kenelm enjoyed the pleasures of the landscape, he reluctantly returned to practical matters: the attempt from

Scanderoon to deny him provisions was a troubling sign that his victory might have done his reputation less good than he had hoped. Still concerned about the plight of the imprisoned English merchants, Kenelm sat and wrote letters to two of the men who were likely to be directly affected by his actions. The first, which he wrote on 23 June, was to Peter Wyche, the newly installed English ambassador at Constantinople. Wyche was likely to bear the brunt of any anger that Kenelm's actions inspired at the Sultan's court, and it was imperative to send him some justification. Kenelm insisted that he was the innocent and wounded party, and was utterly shocked to be met with Venetian aggression, 'for I was not conscious of givinge any occasion of disgust'. He claimed that his adversaries had acted recklessly in firing willy-nilly towards the shore, while he was much more careful, and also maintained that he had consented mercifully to cease fire 'even when the wind was freshed much to my advantage'. Far from the English deserving censure, he told Wyche, it was the French and Venetians who had 'behaved themselves so, as they deserve well to have an Havania passed uppon them' — an *avania* being a tax forcibly imposed by the Sultan. The following day, Kenelm wrote a second letter to another diplomat whom he had reason to placate — Sir Isaac Wake, who had been English ambassador to Venice since 1624. To him Kenelm wrote briefly but more assertively, painting himself as a national champion and stressing that an affront to his command was an insult to their monarch: the galleasses, he insisted, 'shott at my flagg, the King of Englands colours', and he demanded of Wake that 'in his Majesties name you may of the State aske reason for the Captaines insolency'. He also wrote a third document, a longer and more detailed account of the battle; this was not addressed to any particular person, but was designed to trumpet his victory in England; he hoped that if he could find an English merchant to carry it homeward then his friend James Howell, who was well connected to the world of London booksellers, might be able to have it printed and published in his absence.

Two weeks had now passed since Kenelm's victory, but the English merchants still languished in prison in Aleppo as punishment for his actions. On 25 and 26 June the English vice consul at Scanderoon twice made the journey out to where the *Eagle* lay at anchor 'with letters from the consul and all the marchantes att Aleppo, expressing their hard condition in verie pittifull manner, and earnestly desiring me to depart from this coast'. Still Kenelm lingered, deaf to their pleas. He accepted further provisions from the locals, who confirmed the large number of Venetians killed in the battle. On 3 July, still apparently very much at home, Kenelm went ashore again, 'invited by the countrie people to hunt the wilde boare'. He ventured three or four miles inland during the chase, and could not help remembering the youthful hunt through the very different landscape around Gayhurst, where he and Venetia had snatched their first kiss. Returning at last to the seashore, he discovered that the wind was too strong to return to the *Eagle* in his boat. He decided instead to settle down for the night with the local people, sharing their food and their fire, and he was plied with 'goates, sheepe, hens, milke, egges, mellons, and bread baked as thinne as strong paper'. As he munched on this humble fare and felt the foreign bread crinkle between his teeth, Kenelm delighted in another opportunity to sample local delicacies, in an atmosphere much more rustic and cheerfully intimate than the banqueting halls of Algiers. For the first time on his voyage, he allowed himself to experience total rest and repose, untroubled momentarily by the anxieties that had inspired his journey and the new challenges that he now faced. 'Wee made great fires in a grove by the sea side, and rosted the flesh upon the endes of pikes, and passed the night verie well.'

The pleasure of hunting and eating with these ordinary Turks broke the spell which had kept Kenelm frozen in place since his victory. When he returned to the *Eagle* he was met by the English vice consul, who had returned for a fourth time to implore him respectfully to leave for pastures new. Kenelm was finally ready to listen. 'We sayled all that night with an easterly wind.' He had turned his back on Scanderoon, and forged westward: his return journey had begun, and his immediate plan was to retrace his steps, returning to the vicinity of the Currant Islands where he could rely on a large and sympathetic English community to help with the repairs and provisions that he required. By the afternoon of the 9th his ship passed the easternmost point of Cyprus. Kenelm could glimpse the Syrian coast in the distance, where he was afforded another tantalising glimpse of the region's lost and ancient past, 'the relikes of a brave great and stately cittie'.

Soon afterwards he crossed paths with the Greek ship that had brought provisions to the defeated galleasses, and he learned to his fury of the 'scandalous rumors' that the Venetians had been spreading since his departure. The worst fears that Kenelm had harboured before the attack had been realised: the Venetians might have fallen from their position of naval dominance, but they still boasted an unparalleled web of merchants and officials who constantly exchanged letters and new gossip, and now damning accounts of Kenelm's conduct were spreading across the

Mediterranean at terrifying speed. Alvise da Pesaro, the consul at Aleppo, wrote that 'I believe this man is nothing but a thief and a pirate, who wrongfully uses his Majesty's name', and claimed that when Kenelm's ships arrived 'they sent a letter to the Captain of the Galeasses, openly declaring themselves to be pirates'. Before long letters were flying between the scattered outposts of the Venetian Empire, calling Kenelm 'a very audacious and impertinent fellow', 'a pirate, who had sold all his property for the sake of robbing', 'this pirate . . . named Kenelm Digby, knight', 'this audacious pirate', 'the pirate Digby'.

Kenelm fully expected rumours of this sort to be spread by the Venetians, his new-found enemies, but he could not rely upon his own compatriots in the Mediterranean to be any more sympathetic. Just days before the fight at Scanderoon, Thomas Roe had departed from Constantinople after seven eventful and often terrifying years as ambassador to the Sultan's court, to be replaced by Peter Wyche. When his ship, the *Sampson*, docked at the cosmopolitan Black Sea port of Smyrna, Roe heard tell of Kenelm's victory: he immediately fired off a series of letters, protesting that 'the great license taken by our ships, will leave us no friend, nor place to relieve with a drop of water . . . At Scanderoon the roade hath been scandalized by Kenelme Digbye, who hath done bravely . . . but our poor merchants suffer'. Writing to the Levant Company merchant Edward Stringer, Roe complained, 'Whatsoeuer Sir Kenelm Digbyes commission be, Scandaron was no fitt place wherein to execute it, to disturbe the quiet trade of merchants . . . and to give attention to the greedy and needy Turke to prey upon us.' Roe was offended not only as a diplomat, but as a staunch and severe Protestant. 'For myne owne part,' he wrote, 'I doe not like the libertye and trust given to any of that religion.' As he saw it, Catholics tended to 'have other and vaster dessignes then only punishing the foolish French'. 'In queen Elisabeth's time,' he wistfully concluded, 'no papist in England could prevayle for a letter of mart'. Kenelm hoped that his actions would elevate him to the level of the great Elizabethan heroes; instead, all of his escapades were still being reduced to the inescapable fact of his religion, and his triumphs were suspiciously viewed as the sort of wicked plot for which his father had died.

As he gradually became aware of the damaging accounts that circulated in the aftermath of his great triumph, Kenelm realised that he would have to take action to prevent himself being seen by the wider world in the least flattering of lights. He resolved to seek a place where he would be able to reflect upon his anxieties and his prospects at greater leisure, but he was unsure for the moment as to where this might plausibly be. He was keen to retain the loyalty of his crew by soliciting and respecting their advice, and so he convened a Council of War to debate the best course to take. He explained to his officers that he preferred to sail directly westwards and meet any potential retribution from France or Venice head on, 'telling them that it would be a great dishonour unto us to forsake our best road for fear of the enemy'; but Edward Stradling pointed out that, while the shots fired by the Venetian galleasses had failed to kill any of Kenelm's men, they had left his fleet 'in some disorder', damaging the hulls and sails in numerous places, and he could not risk further conflict before repairs had been made. The officers thus urged Kenelm to sail south before cutting west, into the much quieter waters off the coasts of Egypt and Libya. Kenelm was deeply reluctant to do so: he knew of these lands from the writings of the ancients, and while he found their mysteries alluring, he also feared them. There was 'nought else but moving sands' to be found there – the same sands that had, according to the Greek historian Herodotus, 'buried at one glut the puissant Army of King Cambyses', the Persian tyrant, as they were taking their midday meal – and in the absence of humidity there would be no winds to propel his ships on their way. But Kenelm was loath to overrule his men having solicited their counsel, and to risk being 'justly accused of rashnesse or wilfulnesse, if I should prefer my own advice before that of all the rest'.

So deeply was Kenelm immersed with these deliberations, and with navigating the tricky waters and heavily guarded bays of the Cypriot coast, that the landmark of his twenty-fifth birthday, which fell on 11 July, passed unremarked in his journal. Already leaning towards the diplomatic acceptance of his officers' advice, despite his reservations, Kenelm's hand was forced by powers beyond his control when a great wind propelled his ships first south-west and then directly south towards the North African coast, until on 19 July they 'came within 20 leagues of the Coast of Ægipt, all along which we saw store of flying fishes'. Once they arrived in these waters, however, Kenelm's direst predictions came to pass and 'our Land-briezes failed us'. For five sweltering days his ships bobbed aimlessly, as 'adverse winds . . . hindered my design' of sailing north towards Greece. It was a potentially dire moment, but by now Kenelm had seen enough during his voyage to resist immediate panic. A confidence was growing in him that he could overcome such periods of adversity, and he chose to see the forced inactivity as an opportunity to read and to reflect.

Kenelm sheltered from the hottest part of the day in his cabin, catching up on the entries in his journal, leafing through the opaque pages of the manuscripts that he had bought in Algiers, and perusing some volumes from the chest of books carried with him from England, which as yet he had found little time to read. Some of his crewmen, who had sailed along this coast before and were well versed in its lore, told him fearfully that they risked being stuck there, 'unlesse some extraordinary wind happen . . . from the bottom of *Æthiopia*, where the mountains of the Moon are'. Hearing of this exotic possibility inspired Kenelm to pluck a particular volume from his trunk of books and lose himself in its pages: this was the sprawling romance written by the Greek writer Heliodorus, which bore the title *Æthiopica* and told the tale of two lovers named Theagenes and Chariclea who criss-crossed the Mediterranean before finding their way to the distant African land of its title. Kenelm had long meant to read this ancient work, which had become a wildly popular sensation since its rediscovery almost exactly a century before: it had been translated into many languages, and seeped into popular culture to the extent that one writer could ask, 'What school-boy, what apprentice, knows not Heliodorus?' It was lauded and emulated by countless great writers, notably the Elizabethan soldier-poet Sir Philip Sidney. The *Æthiopica* related the adventures of the heroic Theagenes and his love for Chariclea, a beautiful and pure woman who was found abandoned as a baby, and raised as a priestess at Delphi, ignorant of her origins. The pair flee together to avoid her forced marriage, and they zigzag across the Mediterranean, being battered by storms, captured by pirates, imprisoned, wounded and flogged, before being conveyed to Ethiopia, where they are to be burned as a sacrifice. At the moment of their apparent doom, Chariclea leaps on to the flames but survives unscathed; at the last she is recognised by the tokens she has carried with her since birth as the daughter of the King and Queen of Ethiopia. The Queen, it transpires, had stared intently at a painting of the light-skinned Andromeda at the moment of conception, and her imagination had conferred upon her daughter similarly white skin. The mystery solved, Chariclea and Theagenes are triumphantly married. Kenelm was gripped by this intricately told tale of lost children who wander across the Mediterranean, lurching between the familiarity of Europe and distant African lands.

In the evenings, when the air cooled, Kenelm tore himself away from the pages of Heliodorus' work and went out on deck to gaze at the dry and forbidding coastline, which he scoured for wonders and novelties. This was the closest that he had come to the Eastern lands that so fascinated him, the places from which the secret of the Powder of Sympathy and the spirit-conjuring Brahman had emerged, and he was determined to miss no opportunity to scrutinise the shoreline. He caught sight in the distance of a series of bumps and ridges that rose above the flat expanse of the desert: one of the Slavonian sailors who had joined his crew at Algiers, and who had sailed along this coast before, explained to Kenelm that it was the remnants of a town that had been turned suddenly to stone amidst the sands, all of its houses and their inhabitants frozen for ever in place. As Kenelm stared at the remote outlines of this unsettling curiosity, he caught the whiff of a sweet smell drifting from the shore, like the scent of rosemary that had tickled his nostrils as he rounded Spain: an 'odoriferous, wholsom and pleasing' wind that blew 'from *Arabia Felix*, which produceth Spices, Perfumes, and Gummes of sweet savour', and finally dislodged the lingering stench of gunpowder. For a fleeting moment, it seemed to Kenelm that the winds blowing through the Mediterranean bound the disparate corners of the world together, carrying 'small bodies or Atoms' from place to place, and allowing him the passing scent of a distant and mythical land that he would never see for himself.

In the last days of July strong winds from the north began once again to blow Kenelm's ships towards the Barbary coast, bringing him on the 25th no further than three leagues from the shore. The situation threatened to become grim, as supplies on board grew low and the drinking water began to emit an acrid stink. There were other, deadlier dangers afoot in the seas at this point. The French had decided that Kenelm's attack on their merchants at Scanderoon should not pass unavenged; on 28 July, the Puritan traveller John Winthrop Jr wrote to his father from the Tuscan port of Livorno and reported the rumour that 'from Marseiles the Duke de Guise is come to sea with 4 gallioones and 12 sailes of gallies, it is supposed to meete with Sir Chillam Digby, who hath taken 3 or 4 frenchmen, hath beene at Algiers, and redeemed some 20 or 30 Christian slaves'. If this proved to be true, it was no small matter: Charles de Lorraine, Fourth Duc de Guise, was governor of Provence and admiral of the French fleet in the Levant, and commanded a fearsome force. It would be prudent to find a safe port where the prowling French navy could be avoided.

Finally, as July gave way to the scorching days of early August, a strong wind from the south drove his ships up in the direction of the islands that clustered at the south of the Greek archipelago.

By the morning of the 5th he could survey the southern coast of Crete from deck. This chance to survey the island so closely also allowed Kenelm to realise that the 'booke of mappes' which he had taken with him to guide his travels was far from flawless. 'Our English plottes,' he noted, 'are verie ill made, and the land wrong drawne where we have litle trade, (as there), which troubled us much in our accounting, but where we have frequent trade all is most exactly described.' He was acutely aware that such maps emerged gradually, haphazardly: the limits of the known world were often the limits of commerce.

Kenelm's men began to look out for further opportunities to seize merchant ships flying the French flag, but as they rounded Crete the *Eagle* was once again pounded by 'a long and violent storm which took me between Rhodes and Candia and separated me from all the vessels of my fleet', and which broke his flagship's cables and split its topsail. When Kenelm commanded the anchor to be wound in, he saw that it too had broken badly on wrenching a huge branch of coral from the depths of the sea. Even in the midst of the tempest he took a moment to scrutinise this strange substance, hovering between animal and vegetable, that many naturalists could only understand as Nature herself playing a witty joke. The brutal battering of wind and rain made it essential to find a safe harbour in which to 'mend the defects of a leaky ship' and escape 'the relics of the tempest's fury', especially since 'we were now in great want of water'. As the supplies ran out, Kenelm's ships ricocheted between the Greek islands, unable to make safe entry into any of the ports that they glimpsed. At last, with the crew reduced to half-rations of brackish water and beginning to despair, on 14 August new hope arrived, when Kenelm sighted to the north-east the island of Milos.

II 'The Mists and Clouds of Various and Inconstant Passions'

Nature, without other tutor, teacheth us how all agents work for some precise end, and to obtain that, do contribute all their endeavours and make use of all the means that are within the reach of their power. But, herein, natural agents that are guided by an original necessity, have one great advantage over those that have liberty of election of the ends and means: for they are levelled by a certain and never failing rule which was given to all things when their first being was given them, and from the which they cannot depart nor swerve without the immediate and express intersessing of him that was their lawgiver, who governs them with infinite justice, wisdom, and goodness. But these being composed of such differing parts, that one may well say they bear about within them a perpetual civil war — the rational part striving to preserve her dignity and the superiority due to her, as being the nobler substance; and the inferior part, wherein reign the mists and clouds of various and inconstant passions, aspiring to overshadow and dim her brightness, and to range at liberty without any curb —, they are always in great and almost inevitable hazard of miscarrying, as well in the proposing to themselves the worthiest end as in the election of the true and sincere means to attain unto it.

Which hath made me many times retire my looser thoughts within their own centre, and with serious meditation fix them upon this subject, through the desire I have to direct this my journey in the right way.

As the storm-tossed *Eagle* limped towards Milos it passed a small island that was named on Kenelm's map as Anania, 'but the Greekes I had in my shippe named it *L'Isola de Diavoli*, because they say no men inhabite there, but is infested with divels'. One of the Greek sailors who had joined him at Algiers had moored on the island once before with a Florentine crew, 'and in the night they heard a loud voice out of the sea that bad them quickly rowe away, and cry'd "*Hala! Hala!*" ' The place itself was said to have emerged suddenly from the sea decades before, 'with great thundering noises like shooting pieces of artillerie': these tales of sinister islands and chilling cries reminded Kenelm that he had entered a region haunted by strange presences and voices, one that might possess terrors as well as possibilities. As he approached Milos itself, though, these stormy and sinister waters gave way to something more cheery. This was an outpost of the Ottoman Empire, an island described in the English adventurer Thomas Sherley's account of the place as 'one of the delicatest . . . that ever I sawe, full of fruictefull vallys and pleasant hilles', its 'brave & exellent harboures' thronged with 'curteous & kinde' inhabitants. Kenelm was not disappointed, as he too found it to be 'a brave port . . . able to containe a vast number of shippes', and a friendly cohort of locals 'immediately came abord me'. He explained that he was a knight of England with a commission from his King, upon which a man from the welcome party, 'one that is consull there for strangers', sent for the Ottoman governor of the island and 'assured me of all fair correspondence with him, and supplye with all necessities'.

Over the ensuing days, Kenelm was free to explore Milos: he admired its landscape and the rich bounty that it produced, noting that 'we had excellent fruites, and very good other provisions, but especially abundance of partridges, and as cheape as larkes in England'. As well as admiring these natural beauties, he also took the time to learn something of its political and religious organisation, and, as he did so, he began to realise just how thoroughly his own convictions had been unsettled during his time at sea. Many English travellers, like the learned George Sandys, believed that the Greek Church was 'in a great part desolate' and that the Christian inhabitants of this region 'groneth under Turkish thraldom'. English Protestants were deeply concerned with the plight of the Greek Orthodox, whom they saw as natural allies, trapped between the contempt and oppression of the Roman Catholics and the Turks. On Milos, though, Kenelm encountered something quite different. 'This Iland liveth freer than any other of the Turkes dominions,' he wrote, 'and hath indeed nothing of the name of servitude, for they pay a reasonable tribute, and are no further molested, nor have Turkes come to oppress them'. The Ottomans chose to rule the outer fringes of their empire with a light touch, allowing local ways of life to continue relatively untroubled.

Until he experienced mingled worlds of this sort for himself, Kenelm had never truly questioned the religious mentalities amidst which he had grown up. The Earl of Bristol had once pointed out to Kenelm that it was merely 'fortune that hath given you your education in a religion that is contrary to what now reigneth', and since Kenelm was a Roman Catholic only because his father, his mother and all of his early tutors had been, he had never truly probed the basis of his beliefs. His realisation went deeper still: he had never questioned the apocalyptic assumption, shared by Catholics and Protestants alike, that their opponents were absolutely and purely evil and false. This was the same sort of polarised,

Manichean world view that threatened to rip the whole continent apart in the terrible religious wars that were already in their tenth year. As soon as he had set out on his voyage, however, Kenelm discovered that life at sea was very different. He had initially been worried that his crew would resent serving under a Catholic, since English sailors had earned a reputation for anti-Spanish and anti-papist militancy since the days of Queen Elizabeth: just a few years before Kenelm's voyage a 'great disorder and miscarriage' was reported among the ships of the Royal Navy due to 'the popish insolent gentlemen, in so grievous a manner interrupting prayers'. He soon discovered that his fears were groundless: a ship in motion was a world unto itself, a self-contained commonwealth that ran according to its own rules. Differences of belief seemed to matter far less than they did on land, and could not be allowed to endanger the success of the voyage. Life at sea lent itself to pragmatism and flexibility: one writer, describing the religion of the sailor, insisted, 'A fore wind is the substance of his creed; and fresh water the burden of his prayers . . . he can pray, but tis by rote, not faith'. This cheerful matter-of-factness became all the more pronounced when Kenelm took on his new polyglot crew at Algiers, and he was surrounded by men divided by nation, language and creed, but united in the pursuit of fortune and success.

The sort of pragmatic coexistence to be found aboard ship, he now discovered, extended also to the mingled societies of places like Milos. Decades of routine proximity in these Mediterranean islands allowed different religions not only to flourish side by side, but also to assume curiously mixed forms. Whereas debates about the nature of the Eucharist had threatened to tear Europe asunder during the religious wars of the Reformation, one monk described the highly unusual manner in which it was celebrated in this region:

The Latins hold a procession with the unleavened bread which they consecrate and call the Holy Gift. In front walk the Jews, then the Greeks, and after them the Latins — all of them together dressed up in their holy vestments; they sing together and all become one . . . The Greeks read the epistle first, and then the Latins, and the same thing happens with the Gospel. As for the people, both nations stand mixed up together in front of the two altars, praying together and singing together.

It was not only Greeks, Jews and Catholics who lived these sorts of mixed lives: when Thomas Dallam travelled through these islands, his party was guided by a man whom he repeatedly referred to as 'our Turke', and he only belatedly thought to mention that in fact this person 'was an Inglishe man, born in Chorlaye in Lancashier; his name Finche. He was also in religion a perfit Turke, but he was our trustie frende'.

Following his explorations of the island, Kenelm received a courteous invitation from 'a person of quality of that place' who offered him lodgings and warm hospitality. Mulling over the chain of events that had led him to Milos and the continued challenges to his beliefs that he had encountered, Kenelm gratefully accepted, eager for somewhere that 'I might somewhat refresh myself, who was then much distempered in body and suffered great affliction in my mind'. Though he had the relative privacy of his captain's cabin aboard the *Eagle*, the past few months at sea living cheek by jowl with his crew had provided Kenelm with little opportunity to be truly alone; now on Milos, 'I passed my time there with much solitude, and my best entertainment was with my own thoughts'. This contemplative behaviour was misconstrued as melancholy brooding by Kenelm's host, who 'was much troubled at my retirement, and omitted nothing that might avail to divert me from it; and among other things, made me a liberal offer to interest me in the good graces of several of the most noted beauties of that place'. Kenelm had barely seen a woman since the two-thumbed family he had interviewed at Algiers, but he declined the offer as politely as he could, 'which might peradventure have been welcomely accepted by another that had like me youth, strength, and a long time of being at sea to excuse him if he had yielded to such a temptation'. Venetia's face floated into his mind, and Kenelm 'had fresh in my soul the idea of so divine and virtuous a beauty' that, even when faced with this enticing offer, he 'thought it no mastery to overcome it'. Nonetheless, he 'was in some perplexity how to refuse my friend's courtesy, without seeming uncivil. In the end, after some debate with myself, I concluded that the best way for me would be to pretend some serious business, which of necessity did call upon me to write many dispatches and into several places; and thus, without his offence or suspicion, I might enjoy solitude and liberty'.

Kenelm sat in the chamber where he had been lodged and tried to think, but the sound of his host and the assembled guests carousing in the hall below was too distracting – the feasting of the Turks here was 'verie barbarous and bestial in respect of others that I have seen', he noted in his journal, recalling the more elegant banquets of Algiers and the simple fare shared around the camp fire near Scanderoon. He thought instead that he would read, but discovered to his chagrin that 'my books, which use to be my faithful and never failing companions', had been 'all left aboard through the negligence, or rather mistake of my servant, who thought I would not have stayed longer than one night ashore'. In the absence of his beloved tomes, instead Kenelm snatched up a quill and some 'loose sheets of borrowed paper', and started to write.

He began spontaneously, 'writing my wandering fantasies as they presented themselves to me', but could not bring himself to stop: 'one's thoughts and mind may outwork themselves', he discovered, racing uncontrollably from one idea to the next. He started to muse on the recent past, on the chain of events that had led him to this candlelit chamber on this distant island, and once he started 'to please myself in looking back upon my past and sweet errors', the floodgates of his recollections opened. As he thought back over the events of his own life, they began to mingle and blend with the books and stories in which he had lost himself from an early age. 'Many times the memory of some passages which afforded me great delight stole unexpectedly upon me'. He was surprising himself as he wrote, giving himself over to the process of composition and allowing memories, figures and events from his past, scattered impressions and snatches of conversation, to leap unbidden into his head and be given a new shape and order as they made their way on to the page. For most of a frenzied week, Kenelm remained cloistered in his lodgings, scribbling frantically as the heap of borrowed sheets at his elbow grew, pausing only to sleep and to eat the simple meals which his rather bemused host had sent to this reclusive guest.

The idea not simply to retell his life but to reshape it as a romance had taken root in Kenelm's mind as his ships had bobbed impotently off the arid coast of North Africa, and he had lost himself in the pages of Heliodorus' *Æthiopica*, following the adventures and the love story of its protagonists, Theagenes and Chariclea. Another admirer of Heliodorus who had traversed the Mediterranean – Miguel de Cervantes – had created in the figure of Don Quixote a man who loved romances so much and 'plunged himself so deeply in his reading of these bookes', that 'he dryed up his braines in such sort as he lost wholly his judgement. His fantasie was filled with those things that he read, of enchantments, quarrels, battels, challenges, wounds, wooings, loves, tempests and other impossible follies', and he resolved to 'goe throughout the world, with his horse and armour to seeke adventures, and practise in person all that he had read was used by Knights of yore'. While Quixote's attempts proved hilariously hapless, for Kenelm there was nothing absurd about following in the footsteps of such heroes, and bringing romance to life. He realised on Milos that he could recreate himself as a romance hero because, since he had set out from England, he had been living like one.

As he retold his own tale, Kenelm renamed himself Theagenes, in direct emulation of Heliodorus' protagonist; mindful of his own dubious ancestry, Kenelm took the name of a heroic character of impeccable birth, who 'traces his lineage back to Achilles, and I think he may well be right, if his stature and looks are anything to go by . . . except that Theagenes has none of his conceit or arrogance'. As he wrote, however, Kenelm's concern with his own parentage began to fade into the background, and it was the story of his own love for Venetia that returned to the forefront of his mind. Sidney had admired the *Æthiopica* above all for its central love story, the 'sugared invention of that picture of love in Theagenes and Chariclea', and it was their ability to survive shipwreck, pirate attacks, dark sorcery, attempted seduction and threatened execution, before triumphantly marrying one another, that held the divergent threads of the *Æthiopica* together. Until this point Kenelm had forced himself to banish thoughts of Venetia that might distract him from his endeavours and tempt him homewards, but now, in his hard-won moment of solitude and with his achievements at Algiers and Scanderoon behind him, he allowed his memories and fantasies of her to take a newly vivid shape in his mind.

As Kenelm returned obsessively to the vicissitudes of the love that he shared with Venetia, he increasingly found himself ruminating upon the nature of love itself. As their relationship had deepened, even after they had children, Kenelm had never entirely lost the fear that an all-consuming passion of this sort would ultimately cost him the worldly advantages that he so craved. He recalled his youthful conviction that 'the relations that follow marriage are such a clog to an active mind' that they limit the potential of a man who enters into them; by contrast, to one who 'remaineth free and single, the world seemeth to be at his command in choosing what course is like to succeed best to him, and in the process of which he is then like to have least difficulties'. He also looked back on a series of conversations in which he had been forced to resist 'the dissuasions of some of his friends' who, fearful of Venetia's ill repute, sought to convince him that his devotion could only drag him down. Robert Digby, the Earl of Bristol's brother, had once well-meaningly criticised Kenelm 'for his too much indulgency in his passions', and sought 'to put you in mind of your honour, entreating you not to let it suffer shipwreck in the ruinous ocean of sense and pleasure . . . Consider how love is the weakest of all passions, and whereas some good resulteth out of all others, the least evils of this, is to abastardise the mind, to make it effeminate, unfit for any worldly action, and so wholly and anxiously employed in low desires that it can think of nothing else, as long as it is possessed with this fever'. Even Bristol himself, the man who had helped Kenelm the most and on whom he looked as a father, had warned him that love would distract him from the heroic actions that he sought, 'begetting, if not contempt, at least a mean esteem'.

When Kenelm had first heard these words, spoken 'with much authority and seriousness, through which yet shined much affection', they pierced him 'to the very soul'; he had been able to do little but brood on them, with a mixture of resentment and fear that they might be true. Now, on Milos, he was able to answer them at last, and give Theagenes the voice that he lacked. By sailing into the Mediterranean in search of magnificent feats that would secure his place in the world as well as Venetia's, he had proven that love could be a spur to great triumphs, not an obstacle. He realised as he wrote that his love for Venetia was not just part of who he was: it bound together the disparate strands of his being, the competing inclinations that he had sometimes struggled to reconcile. He wanted both to change the world, and to understand it, just as he wanted both to transform and to understand himself; yet during the preceding years it had sometimes seemed to him that he would have to choose between an active and a contemplative life. Now, as he wrote, he realised jubilantly that this was not so. He gave full expression to his love for Venetia and their children, and reinforced his belief that it would deepen further still. 'Our mutual desires will make each other happy, and our fervent loves will reflect strongly upon those that shall come of us, adding that increase to natural affection, and consequently to our joys in them'. But as he gave voice to his thoughts through Theagenes he also developed, for the first time, a philosophy of love that went beyond his particular attachment to his family; he realised that he need not fly from his passions and desires in order to explore the loftiest and most obscure of questions. Love, he exclaimed, belonged not only to humans but to God, the 'infinite and eternal Essence', whose deepest being is 'continually taken up entirely in loving and being beloved'. God 'made our souls his lively images', and gave us understanding, through which we reach knowledge and contemplation, and a free will, by which each person achieves 'an excellent love of what he understandeth'. The highest and most divine activity of which a person is capable, Kenelm insisted, 'is to employ our understanding about the objects of greatest perfection that it is capable of, and the will in loving such'. Once he had achieved this insight, Kenelm could pronounce for the first time, and with total confidence, 'The love of a virtuous soul, dwelling in a fair and perfect body, is the noblest and worthiest action that a man is master of; it exerciseth in due manner that superior talent that God and nature hath given him; and by choosing a perfecter object than himself to love, it exalteth and refineth those seeds of goodness that are in him.' He realised that his love for Venetia, as he gave it new and forceful shape on Milos, in no way weakened or demeaned him, or impeded 'the prosecution of heroic and virtuous actions, since the nature of it is to raise it up to the perfectest notions, and inciteth any generous heart to do worthy things'.

As he pursued these lofty conclusions, Kenelm allowed his mind to wander back over the specific course of his love for Venetia, from their earliest years together through the separation and estrangement that they had suffered and overcome, to their eventual reunion and marriage. The more he thought of her as he wrote, and yearned for her presence, her touch and her voice, he transformed her increasingly into something perfect and flawless in his mind, the quirks of her features and of her personality that had first led him to fall in love with her clouded by the idea of her perfection, which seemed to shine ever more purely. 'In beauty, modesty, sweetnesse and gentlenesse,' it seemed to him, 'she was the perfectest of her sexe; and in transcendent goodness, piety, vertue and charity, she was an Angell'. Her physical features took on a new shape, refracted through the lens of his reading. He had always admired her nose, which was 'carried down from her forehead with an even and straight line, onely bowing gently in such places as might give it greatest grace; such a one as in auntient times . . . was held the most lovely and accounted as a signe of magnanimity and courage; the nostrils large, and most exactly proportioned'; in exactly the same way, 'in Heliodorus the valour and generousnesse of Theagenes collected (among other markes) out of the largenesse of his nosethrilles and an even and well shaped nose'.

In his imagination, even Venetia's exhalations as she woke from a night's sleep became subtly perfumed: 'From between her coral lips came out a gentle breath, which not smelling of any thing, was yet more fragrant than the morning air'. The rumours that dogged her and threatened to ruin her reputation became in his mind not simply the product of malicious people; they also took on a life of their own and grew into a vicious monster named 'Fame', 'begot of some fiend in hell', which 'feedeth itself upon the infected breaths of the base multitude', and possessed 'a fantastic aerial body that admitteth no hold to be taken of it, nor can be traced to the ground or author thereof'. Kenelm allowed himself to be swept up into the romance that he was writing, where he could render Venetia as simply pure and virtuous as her foes were hellishly wicked.

Try as he could, however, Kenelm could not comfortingly simplify his wife in this way. As he made her into Stelliana and turned her into a character, he also found, for the first time, that he was seeing himself and the world through her eyes. Until this point, he had lamented when he thought he had lost her; he had fulminated when he heard rumours of her infidelities; he had violently threatened those who impugned her good name once he became convinced of her loyalty to him. But until he sat down and wrote on Milos, and told a tale that was as much hers as it was his, Kenelm had never truly thought through what these experiences had been like for her. Only now did he imagine Venetia's 'agony of distracted thoughts' as she lurched from one threat and near-disaster to the next, and the 'extreme grief' that constantly threatened to 'oppress her spirits'. He had raged petulantly when he had heard of her supposed infidelity during his time in Florence, but only now did he truly inhabit 'the stormy violence of the first impression of grief' that she felt at the false news of his death, and the lonely plight in which it left her, 'solitary lamenting by herself'. He formed a new-found respect for the strength with which she had roused herself from this torpor and protected herself from betrayal, when 'a generous disdain enflamed her heart' and made her 'resolve to sequester herself from the conversation of men'. He even found himself recalling, and better understanding, her words to him during their period of estrangement, when he had told her histrionically that without her love he 'would wander like a lost man through the rest of the world'; she had responded by smiling wryly, and asking, 'Is absence, then, the most expedient means to increase or confirm affections? or peradventure is it, that you are so well acquainted with foreign parts, that all places are alike to you to afford you content, and those best liked of you, where you shall not be in danger to have my true zeal to check your loose delights, and tax you of inconstancy and gratitude?' She had seemed to realise, even before he himself understood, that his grandest gestures and his ceaseless wanderings – including the journey that he was now undertaking – were also a pretext for the pursuit of delight in all of its forms.

that shee onely sought to gett a further right vnderstan-
ding of her inclinations that shee might follow them and
fortifie her in them: wch shee did so effectually that in
conclusion they remained of accord that the next day Seriana should send for *Theagenes* to come by ye pri-
uate way to ~~that~~ her lodginges; & that ~~
~~ should then come thither to enioy those embrases
wch shee so much longed for not doubting but that shee
should finde him as forward as shee could wish him; as
one that had reason to thinke his starres had blessed him
much in making him to be so highly fauoured by so great
a Lady, that was so neere to the Queene, and so much valued by her
~~
~~ Accordingly the next day a messenger
came to *Theagenes* in *Serianas* name, and conducted
him by the backe way into her chamber wch was next to ~~
~~ where *Seriana* sate expecting him, and after
more courteous salutation then vsuall, shee first went to
shutt the dore fast and to see all about that none, else were
wth in hearing, and then in this manner addressed her selfe

A page from *Loose Fantasies*, in which Theagenes is described to the Queen of Attica by her maid, containing Kenelm's last minute alterations and additions

It was a scintillating but draining week that Kenelm spent cloistered on Milos as he filled sheet after sheet of paper with these memories, thoughts and imaginings. Finally, on 21 August, he allowed his pen to cease its hurtling motion. Before he gave thanks to his gracious host and prepared to return to the *Eagle*, Kenelm read back one final time over the pages that he had produced, and realised that here, at last, was the outcome of the self-reckoning that he had desired since he first set out for the Mediterranean, no less heroic and spectacular an achievement than his feats at Algiers and Scanderoon. Here was a document through which he could lay claim to the meaning of his actions, and shape not only his reputation but his very identity. Arranging the loose leaves into a tidy pile, he added two words on the front in large, looping letters: 'Loose Fantasies'. He placed the sheets carefully into his trunk, and left the calm and shaded interior of his chambers for the bright light of the outside world.

8

September 1628–February 1629
Delos – Zante – Patras – The Atlantic – London

II 'A Man of Vigorous Spirits and of a Clear Understanding'

To end this long, and I fear tedious, discourse of mine, let me put you in mind, how some ancient and much esteemed philosophers were of opinion, that a man of vigorous spirits and of a clear under-standing might not only love, but without blame use the liberty of his own election and inclinations, and ought to oppose the original rules of nature against vulgar laws and customs; and that limited and artificial ordinances are only for weak minds, who are not able to judge of things truly as they are by the dim light of their own feeble nature.

On 22 August, as he prepared to leave Milos behind, Kenelm was dragged back from the realms of romance and into reality by a recurrence of the 'disorders on shore' which flared up with depressing predictability among his men whenever his ships made landfall: a drunken argument had erupted between Henry Stradling and one of the crew under his command, the master of the *Hopewell*, to which Kenelm responded by demoting the insubordinate man but restoring him to his role 'upon his humble submission'. Having re-established order, he prepared his ships to depart. His head still buzzed with the words that he had passed a delirious week setting down on paper, and he felt settled and confident for the first time in his voyage, the doubting voices that had chattered in his head ever since his victory at Scanderoon finally silenced.

Kenelm resolved to spend the last of his time in the Mediterranean fulfilling both parts of his commission, by pursuing both rich prizes and new knowledge. In January 1627, just as he was beginning to prepare for his voyage, a huge shipment of several hundred ancient statues had arrived in London, sent to the Earl of Arundel by his agent in the Levant, William Petty. Kenelm saw some of the marbles for himself, and was overwhelmed by the beauty and poise of these pieces, whose 'lively presence is able to persuade a man, that he now seeth two thousand yeares ago'. Along with the ancient statues arrived a handwritten document, which was copied and passed from hand to hand at court, in which Petty gave clear instructions concerning the kinds of object for which an aspiring treasure seeker might search, and where they might be found. 'Statues clothed & naked' are to be sought, Petty wrote, 'but the naked ones are of greatest value, Heads of all sorts that can be found, marbles carved with halfe round figures . . . or pedestalls with any kinde of carved work on them.' He also noted that 'if a statue have an inscription on the pedestall or Bases, it is more rare'. 'The places in greece where these things are to be found are infinite,' Petty continued, but he particularly singled out 'the island of Delos' which 'was the mart of all Greece where yett remaineth the ruine of Apolloes temple; neare unto which by digging, many Statues of the best ancient sculptours may bee had'. Thomas Roe, the ambassador at Constantinople who assisted Petty, concurred, and told Arundel, 'Concerning antiquities in marbles, there are many in divers parts, but especially at Delos, unesteemed here; and, I doubt not, easy to be procured for the charge of digging and fetching'. Kenelm had arrived on Milos by accident, storm-tossed and in dire need of water; but once he was there, he realised that he was only a few day's sailing from Delos, the island where the foremost experts agreed that further treasures waited to be unearthed.

The large shipment that Petty sent back to England was the latest manifestation of the ever-increasing craze for ancient statues and inscriptions among the luminaries of the English court. The mighty and austere Earl of Arundel was the greatest connoisseur and collector of the age: he had obtained some ancient works on his travels through Italy, then began to send agents into Greece and the Levant specifically to procure him more pieces with which he could adorn his house on the Strand in London. After Charles and Buckingham returned from Madrid with their own artistic tastes newly formed – Charles having bought three busts of ancient marble in Spain for himself – the pair sought to emulate Arundel's collection: as one observer wonderingly wrote, the Earl sought 'to transplant old Greece into England', while the King 'amply testifies a Royall liking of ancient statues'. Arundel had asked

Thomas Roe to search for antiquities when he set out on his diplomatic mission to Constantinople, but soon Buckingham made the same request, and the ambassador found himself torn between his loyalty to two patrons who were fierce rivals. To increase his chances of obtaining the finest works for himself, in 1625 Arundel sent Petty – who, though a clergyman, was utterly unscrupulous – to scour the region for fine pieces. After seeing Petty in action Roe wrote to Arundel, with a mixture of wonder and horror, 'Ther was never man so fitted to an imployment, that encounters all accident with so unwearied patience, eates with Greekes on their worst dayes; lyes with fishermen on plancks, at the best; is all things to all men, that he may obteyne his ends, which are your Lordships service'. While Roe was no connoisseur – 'My skill is not great,' he wrote to Arundel, 'I judge only by the eye' – Petty knew just what he was looking for, and would stop at nothing to get it. He cooked up a plot to have some of the greatest public artworks in Constantinople dismantled and shipped back to the Earl, and thought nothing of stealing works from under the noses of rival collectors. When Petty suffered shipwreck and lost a rich trove of statues that he had recently acquired, and dragged himself to shore only to be arrested for lack of identifying papers, he negotiated his freedom, returned apparently undaunted 'to the place where he left his boate to fish for the marbles', and, astonishingly, recovered them from the depths of the seabed.

Kenelm shared Roe's conviction that ancient works 'carry in them a shadow of eternitye, and kindle an emulation of glorye, by seeing dead men kept long among the living by their famous deedes'; from that point on, he yearned to see for himself the ancient lands from which these works emerged. He was no less struck by the various reasons for which they were valued. Buckingham, who had no pretensions to learning and was drawn to ancient works only for their surface beauty, as status objects, warned Roe against sending him anything too battered or worn. 'Neither am I so fond of antiquitye,' he wrote, 'to court it in a deformed or misshapen stone.' He was interested only 'where yow shall meete beautye with antiquitye together in a statue'. Arundel, by contrast, numbered some of the foremost scholars in the land among his clients – some of whom Kenelm knew personally, like Robert Cotton, who had helped find precedents for his royal commission – and he was interested both in nubile marble forms and in crumbling inscriptions; likewise King Charles himself professed interest both in 'Antique statuaes [sic]' and 'any Antique Coins or gravings'.

Kenelm's ships left Milos on 24 August, and wound their way north-east towards Delos, 'in search of antiquities'. His ships stopped briefly on the way to pick up a large quantity of wine at Mykonos, 'where it is verie good and exceeding cheape', and he bought as many barrels as he could fit into the hold of the *Elizabeth and George*, reserving space in the *Eagle* for the ancient marbles he hoped to procure. On Mykonos he discovered delightedly that these islands rang with happy reports of his victory at Scanderoon, due to 'the disaffection they generally bear here to the Venetians and the extraordinarinesse of the action'. The warmth with which the local population once again received him emboldened Kenelm, and informed the approach that he took to his search for statues. Petty advised any Englishman in search of buried treasure on these islands 'to weare poor apparell, for by that meanes the Turkes will imagine the things he seeks for to be of no great estimation'. He also thought it wisest and most practical to 'saw them asunder with Iron Sawes' and drag the pieces on to carts with 'tackles & pullies', being sure to gather 'all the smallest bits & fragments', before loading them aboard ship in boxes. Kenelm, though, was the hero of Scanderoon; he would not skulk about on the islands, or disguise himself as a poor man in the hope of avoiding detection, and he would not smash his treasures into easily portable smithereens. He arrived still full of the swagger of victory, and was determined to snatch what ancient pieces he could find, in all their gorgeous entirety.

On 28 August the ships arrived at Delos. Over the next three days Kenelm 'spent my time in taking in some marble stones and statues'. It was, he observed, 'a desert island': Delos had flourished under the Greek and Roman empires, but devastating piratical assaults and changes to trading routes in the first century CE led to its eventual desertion. In the absence of reluctant local inhabitants, who might have sought to prevent him stealing their ancient treasures or demanded that he pay a high fee for them, Kenelm was able to 'avayle myselfe of the conveniencie of carrying away some antiquities there'. Many of these were fragments taken from the imposing temple dedicated to Apollo that had once stood on the island, marking its significance as the mythical birthplace of the god and his sister, Artemis.

The eerie emptiness of the place was also useful to Kenelm because it denied his men further opportunity for 'idlenesse' and indulging their 'untoward fancies', as they had done in the taverns and brothels of the ports which he had previously visited. He kept the men preoccupied with the hard and bracing labour of purloining ancient treasures. 'I busied them in rolling of stones down to the sea side, which they did with such eagernesse as though it had been the earnesyt businesse that they came out for, and they mastered prodigious massie weights.' Carrying away some of the larger pieces, however, proved a daunting challenge: 'one stone, the greatest and fairest of all, containing 4 statues,' would not shift even after the entire crew of 300 men, drawn from the *Eagle*, the *Elizabeth and George* and the *Hopewell*, had assailed it. Kenelm rose to the challenge of this technical difficulty, and managed to contrive a mechanism using the 'mastes of ships' as a lever and one vessel, riding in the water as close to the beach as it could safely sail, as a counterweight. By this ingenious means his men managed to hoist the vast hunk of marble aboard 'with much ease and speede' – a masterwork of maritime engineering and improvisational flair.

As Kenelm loaded these ancient objects, large and small, aboard his ships, he initially focused exclusively on the practical challenges that they presented, and imagined the rapturous reception that they would receive from scholars and connoisseurs alike upon his return. As he wandered about the ruins of Delos, however, and ran his eyes and his fingers over the 'brave marble stones heaped up' in the ruins of Apollo's temple, these worldly concerns melted away. Even the most damaged and weather-beaten of the imposing forms radiated a precision of execution and a beauty; somehow, these vast slabs of cold stone managed to convey the contours and the fleshly vulnerability of the human body. To encounter a statue of this sort was to confront the ancient past distilled into an intensely physical form, as a gorgeously crafted marble work which seemed, despite its impassive nature, to pulse with life. One piece in particular captivated Kenelm, and for nearly an hour he stood before it, silently contemplating this 'huge statue, broken in two pieces about the wast, which the Greekes told me was Apollos. It weigheth att least 30 tonnes, and time hath worn out much the softness and gentilenesses of the worke, yet all the proportions remain perfect and in grosse; the yieldings of the flesh and the musculous parts are visible, so that it is still a brave noble piece.' Kenelm marvelled at the monumental figure of the Greek god, so compelling even in its shattered state that it seemed as if it might return to life and ripple its marble muscles once more. He knew that this was one great fragment of the ancient world that he could not take with him: the statue 'hath by divers bin attempted to be carried away, but they have all failed in it'. Not even Kenelm could construct an array of pulleys and levers ingenious enough to shift this magnificent behemoth.

Close by this immovable object, though, Kenelm stumbled across another piece that, while less immediately captivating, was still intriguing, and much more portable. It was a stubby marble pillar, a little over two feet high. Many of the other objects that he had encountered had partial inscriptions and fragments of Greek writing on them, but this one was remarkable for its completeness, and the legibility of the words that were inscribed upon it. Though Kenelm had studied Greek, not least for his orations in Siena, it was not his strongest language; nonetheless he was just about able to make out the sense of the words. The small monument, the inscription explained, had been erected in the honour of a man named Theophrastus Heraclitus, who had governed the place in ancient times: it praised his piety and his probity, and extolled his virtuous treatment, not only of the island's inhabitants, but of the many travellers who passed through,

A drawing of the inscribed monument that Kenelm brought back from Delos,
in a book by his friend John Selden

strangers from centuries past who found their way to Delos on their wanderings.

On 30 August, the newly purloined marbles clattering in their holds, Kenelm's ships left Milos and began making their way back around Greece and towards the Currant Islands, where he planned

to stop again for provisions before continuing homeward. The first half of the month passed uneventfully, bar some minor matters of shipboard discipline, as tempers among his crew frayed beneath the glare of the summer sun. Kenelm took advantage of the quiet days to retire to his cabin and continue the reading that he had pursued so avidly since Scanderoon. His appetite having been whetted by Heliodorus, he plucked from his trunk of books another long and rambling romance, but this one much more recent, and English; the vast sprawling poem titled *The Faerie Queene*, by Edmund Spenser, that he had purchased shortly before departing. Like Philip Sidney, Spenser was an Elizabethan poet who had returned to prominence in the years before Kenelm's voyage as part of the upsurge in nostalgia for a heroic earlier age: his poem told tales of knights, dragons, wizards and monsters, but it was shot through with philosophical ambition and militantly Protestant fervour. Kenelm was immediately enraptured by the 'majesty and sweetnes of verse' throughout *The Faerie Queene*, but one of its many nine-line stanzas stood out to him for its density and obscurity, and as his ships rounded Greece he spent many hours puzzling over it. The lines in question described a castle that represented the human body: its shape, Spenser enigmatically wrote, is 'partly circulare,/And part triangulare', part masculine and part feminine, built in the proportions of seven and nine. At first, these words seemed to Kenelm like 'an indissoluble riddle', but gradually their meaning became clear to him. He grew convinced that Spenser was not simply a poet but 'thoroughly verst in the Mathematicall Sciences, in Philosophy, and in Divinity'. The circle and the square, he decided, represented the human body and soul; the triangle was a reference to the arcane mysteries of alchemy, since the human body contains the three fundamental chemical elements – salt, sulphur and mercury. The numbers seven and nine he understood as an astrological allusion – a reference to 'the influences of the superior substances', specifically 'the seven Planets' and 'the Angels divided into nine Hierarchies or Orders'. Contemplating these nine dense lines of poetry allowed Kenelm to return to the ecstatic mood in which he had composed *Loose Fantasies*, where he had found himself elevating the love that he shared with Venetia to the level of a divine principle: now he felt that reading Spenser's opaque verses opened a window on to a rapturous and mystical form of union with God, in which his senses would be 'drowned in eternall delight'. Kenelm wrote down his thoughts on these lines in a letter to his vice admiral, Edward Stradling, who came from a Welsh family known for supporting poets and scholars; he was the only other man in the fleet likely to understand or be interested in such arcane musings. Kenelm found himself blotting the paper repeatedly as he wrote, the smooth flow of his thoughts interrupted by the rocking and keeling of the *Eagle*.

By the middle of September Kenelm's ships came once again into the vicinity of the Currant Islands, and made landfall at Zante, where he hoped to procure provisions – 'hoopes, tallow, tarre, pitch, wine, bread' – as well as adding some more English sailors to his crew and procuring good-quality English powder for his guns. He heard news from the merchants there of developments at Aleppo since he had left Scanderoon: the persecution of English traders following his victory, they told Kenelm, 'proceeded from the consuls feare and weakeness', but the situation had been resolved once the proper bribes were paid to the Ottoman officials, and the Venetians were now publicly blamed for firing on him first. Reassured for the time being by this account, Kenelm decided to scour Zante for all the natural wonders that were to be found, so that he might take them back to England where he and his philosopher friends could peruse them for the lessons that they held. He obtained seeds and cuttings for a range of exotic plants – Mediterranean garlic, Algerian apricot, musk melon, nectarine – and stowed them in his hold to carry homeward.

As well as availing himself of the flora of the region, Kenelm also attended closely to its fauna. He had not encountered the exotic beasts of which many English travellers into the Mediterranean told wondrous tales – elephants that danced and played with balls; camels, giraffes and hippopotamuses – but what caught his eye instead was the unfamiliar behaviour of a much more familiar creature. 'The marchantes at the Isles of Zante and of Cephalonia' told him, 'It was the custome of our English doggs (who were habituated unto a colder clyme) to runne into the sea in the heate of summer, and lye there most part of the day, with only their noses out of the water, that they might draw breath, and would sleepe there with their heads layed upon some stone, which raysed them up, whiles their bodies were covered with the sea'. Kenelm could well understand the respite that these poor dogs sought when they could not handle the heat, and the impressively creative action that they took to escape it: as he approached Zante he found it 'so hott' that it was impossible to sleep at night. Leaving the stifling interior of his cabin, he climbed a rope ladder down the side of the *Eagle* and lowered himself into the inky waves, where he 'found the water warmer than att any time in England'. He allowed himself a moment of repose, bobbing in the mercifully cooling waves of the seas over which he usually prowled.

Having spent the second half of September observing and collecting these natural phenomena, Kenelm left Zante behind at the end of the month and continued to Patras, a port tucked into a large bay on the Greek mainland. Here the local Ottoman governors, hearing that he had 'taken rich prizes' at Scanderoon, demanded 'great presents' before they would provide him with provisions. When Kenelm finally walked ashore on 9 October following some negotiation, it was straight into a trap. 'As soone as I was come into the consuls house,' he recorded, several servants rushed in and tried to lead him forcibly away, 'and did beate severall of my followers in outragious maner, and carried them away prisoners.' The locals were convinced that Kenelm had vast riches at his disposal, and were determined to hold him and his men for ransom in order to extort payment from the men who remained aboard his ships. Kenelm, however, 'subtilely gott out of their handes', and used 'industrious negotiation' and carefully selected 'presentes' to win over 'a strong faction in the place' and secure the release of his men without paying the hefty bribes.

Having deftly resolved this minor crisis, Kenelm knew that he needed to do everything he could to obtain provisions in this place for his return voyage, since he was reluctant to stop at Tunis or return to Algiers, and all Venetian ports were now effectively closed to him. Over the ensuing days in Patras he managed to load his ships with the necessary victuals, and sell a *saettia* that he had taken as a prize to a man named Signior Bego, a local dignitary. Towards the end of October Kenelm left Patras behind and sailed round the nearby coast. He commented on the richness of the lands there, replete with silk and valuable mines, and allowed himself to fantasise that it might one day be re-conquered from the Ottomans: the Sultan's forces were spread thin by the wars raging with the Christian forces to the west and the Persians to the east, and 'could not assist it if it was invaded', while 'the Greekes of the countrie would infallibly take part with a Christian invader'. Kenelm also took time to note a particularly important crop grown in this region – 'excellent tobacco' which, he noted, could be sold at home at twenty times the price paid in the region. He imagined sending 'one out of England that knew how to cure it and make it up very well'. He was keeping a sharp eye out for new commercial ventures, reports of which would ensure him an even warmer welcome on his return.

As October drew to a close Kenelm directed his ships to loop back once again towards Zante and Cephalonia, in the hope of securing provisions for his fleet. His need had become severe, since his emergency rations, the English beef that had been hastily pickled and packed in the hold before his departure, turned out to be rancid. Near the islands Kenelm's vessels fell in with the fleet that was waiting offshore to transport the latest vast crop of currants back to England. He saw a *saettia* nearby that he first took to be a prize of the English ships, before realising that it was in fact a French vessel: he attacked it, took its captain prisoner, and seized 'severall bagges of money' that he found hidden in the ship's ballast. With this booty in hand he took the opportunity to speak with the vessel's captain, who was the first to convey to Kenelm a stunning piece of news.

II 'My Happiness and Content'

And while it remaineth in controversy what is best for a man to do, let him in the mean time at least do what pleaseth him most: and for my part, I can never deem those humours very vain that are very pleasing ... nor guide my actions by other men's censures, which hurt not at all when they are neglected or patiently endured; nor be afflicted when they condemn me. And thus I shall be free from the servitude that most men live in, who are more troubled by the opinions of evils than by their real essence; and then the world shall see that my happiness and content is not proportioned to the estimation that they make of it, which will soon be forgotten and vanish away; but to what I truly enjoy and feel in myself, which will remain with me forever.

On the morning of 23 August, just as Kenelm was preparing to leave Milos after completing *Loose Fantasies*, the Duke of Buckingham had left his quarters in the Greyhound Inn in Portsmouth, hundreds of miles away on the south coast of England. Buckingham had been finalising the preparations for the English fleet with which he intended to make a renewed assault on Île de Ré, the Protestant stronghold that the French navy sought to besiege. He had rushed to the town in June, after Charles had accepted the Petition of Right from Parliament and the MPs had voted to fund the war in exchange; it was the Duke's last desperate throw of the dice, his final chance to redeem his reputation and silence his army of detractors through a resounding victory. He had become ever more horribly aware of just how deep and ubiquitous the hatred for him had become: a week after the Petition was granted, on 13 June, Buckingham's personal astrologer, an aged man named John Lambe, was kicked to death in the London streets after a visit to the theatre, with the crowd calling him 'the Duke's devil' as they beat and mutilated his frail body. This horrible scene boded ill for the Duke himself: 'the example is very perilous', noted the Venetian ambassador fearfully, and one of the many poems chanted and covertly passed around in taverns across the country proclaimed, 'Let Charles and George do what they can/ The Duke shall die like Doctor Lambe'. Still Buckingham had forged ahead with his preparations, and on the 23rd he proceeded downstairs to the hall of the inn, intending to spend the day over-seeing the continued stocking and arming of the fleet. The entrance was, as ever, thronged with people – the various sycophants, petitioners and hangers-on who followed in the Duke's wake wherever he went. Among them was a man called John Felton. He had seen the naval failures of the past few years from close quarters, having served both in the debacle of the 1625 Cádiz expedition and in the Duke's first disastrous expedition to Ré the year before, where he had been badly wounded in his hand, and left unable to work for his living. Felton had joined the multitude of impoverished former sailors who roamed in belligerent gangs through London, and he shared their resentment towards Buckingham for the dire struggles that they had endured, and their lack of pay. Unlike the majority of these men Felton was also 'a melancholy man and much given to reading'. He spent his spare time perusing works of political theory, and closely followed the attacks that Members of Parliament levelled at the Duke, all of which reinforced his growing conviction that Buckingham was entirely to blame for his and the country's malaise. Having waited quietly in the packed hallway of the Greyhound Inn until he saw the tall and elegant figure of the Duke stride by, Felton darted from the crowd and, before anyone present realised what was happening, plunged his dagger into Buckingham's chest just below the heart, killing him instantly.

There was bedlam in the hall, and amidst the chaos Felton slipped away, though he later turned himself in, openly proclaiming the rightness of his action. The Duke's few defenders excoriated the assassin as a madman and a fanatic, though Felton insisted at his trial that he had clear and rational motives: Buckingham's weakening of English military might, and his conspiring with European Catholics. Ultimately, the baffled Henry Wotton declared, 'Whatsoever were the true motive . . . none can determine, but the prince of darkness it self'. So hated was the Duke that he was mourned only by his wife, who collapsed into 'shrikings and distraction' at the news of his death, and by the King, who had stuck by his closest friend even when it cost him a great deal to do so, and who now retired into his private chamber for three days of solitary grieving. The rest of the country was overcome with 'extraordinarie Joy' at Buckingham's demise, and when Felton was brought into London for his trial the streets were lined with 'multitudes of people' crying out, 'Lord comfort thee' and 'God bless thee!' as he passed. During Felton's trial the knife that he had used was placed before him, the Duke's blood still congealed upon it; he pleaded guilty and was hanged, after which his body was carted back to Portsmouth and strung up in chains at the entrance to the town.

When Kenelm heard tell of this news from the captain of the French *saettia*, he was dumbstruck. During the decade in which

George Villiers had stood astride the world of English politics he had survived countless plots to discredit, displace and topple him; now he had been laid low by an ordinary man armed only with a dagger. Kenelm had admired the Duke before circumstances had driven a wedge between them; he once saw in Buckingham an image of what he aspired to be – a man who had risen to the pinnacle of English life thanks almost entirely to his personal charm and talent – and he rued the speed and indignity of his death. At the same time, Kenelm could not suppress a shiver of relief at the thought that, with a single stab of Felton's blade, perhaps his greatest obstacle to worldly success had been removed.

Since Scanderoon Kenelm had allowed himself to meander, to explore his own past and the world around him without great urgency, as he wrote *Loose Fantasies*, collected ancient works and scientific specimens, and mused on the significance of his voyage; when he heard news of Buckingham's death he knew that he must return home with all possible speed. He still longed to see Venetia and their sons; but now, with the Duke gone, he could not fully anticipate the situation into which he would be returning. Buckingham had wielded more power, and accrued a longer string of titles, than any other royal favourite before him. He had achieved the nearly impossible, by retaining his immense influence when a new King ascended to the throne. This also meant that his death was likely to produce changes more seismic than those that had followed the demise of King James himself. There was bound to be upheaval and jostling for preference at court, since this followed the death of any prominent figure: but with the assassination of Buckingham, it seemed likely that the entire shape of English political life would be transformed.

Before Kenelm could return and see these changes for himself, some final practical concerns needed to be addressed. After seizing the French *saettia* near the Currant Islands he proceeded again to Cephalonia, where he hoped that the *Providetore* would permit him to take on water. He was kept waiting on a variety of pretexts until he realised that the delays were a result of 'the Venetians subtle and false dealing', so he decided to return once again to Zante, where he had been more warmly received despite his actions at Scanderoon, to see if he would fare any better. The early days of November, though, brought dire weather, 'the greatest storme of raine that ever I saw'. With this latest squall came terrible spectacles, including a huge whirlwind which lifted the sea by Kenelm's ship 'and carried it almost as high as the mountains', much like Charybdis, the terrifying whirlpool that menaced Odysseus in these waters. Kenelm realised that it was best not to linger in these seas during the winter months, and so he resolved to accelerate his departure as much as possible. Fortunately at this point Signior Bego, the man with whom Kenelm had done business at Patras, sent supplies of wine and bread by boat to the *Eagle*, the final portion of payment for the vessel that he had bought. Kenelm eased tensions by returning the French *saettia* that he had taken as a prize and giving its crew sixty pieces of eight and a month's worth of bread, though he kept the bulk of the money he had taken. His ships then proceeded once again to the waters around Zante, still looping between the islands but with Kenelm's mind increasingly turning to home. On 10 November he kept a careful eye on another French *saettia* that arrived near the port, since he had caught wind of a rumour that the French hoped to torch his fleet while they were anchored thereabouts. Now, though, the *Providetore* of this island also denied him the chance to take on provisions, angrily dismissing Kenelm's request and forbidding any English merchant from supplying him, and 'att every word called the King of Englandes shippes of warre *ladroni e corsari,*' thieves and pirates. Kenelm had had enough: at this point, he wrote, 'I shaped my course homeward'.

As November progressed Kenelm's ships drove westward through the seas, passing Sicily and Malta as they did so. He saw the volcano of Mount Etna, which he called Mont Gibello, 'casting out much smoake', and also set eyes on the Isle of Lampedusa. It was now entirely deserted, its inhabitants having abandoned their homes after suffering the ravages of pirates from the nearby Tunisian coast, but it still exuded a strangely compelling power. 'The Turkes,' Kenelm observed, 'beare great reverence to this place, and allwayes leave oyle or bread or something behind them (through devotion) though they know not for whom.' Soon after, he crossed paths with a Dutch ship sailing from Amsterdam to Venice with a cargo of Irish pilchards; since it flew the flag of a neutral nation Kenelm let the vessel pass unmolested, but not before he had grilled its captain in order to confirm the truth of Buckingham's death, and had the grisly tale corroborated. Chasing the occasional ship that crossed his path and weathering small storms and squalls barely detained him as November gave way to December and Kenelm re-entered the Bay of Cagliari. Near Sardinia, remaining opportunistic even as he made his swift departure from the seas, Kenelm took a small French ship loaded with salt but behaved with ostentatious gallantry, sending one of his French captives and one of the crewmen whom he had liberated from Algiers ashore with forty crowns and some letters to 'the Vicequeene of Sardinia' and 'some other ladyes' whom he knew there, missing no opportunity to charm as he went on his way.

On 5 December, Kenelm's lookout spotted two vessels bobbing nearby. Because the *Eagle* was lagging slightly behind the rest of the fleet and all of its shallops were being stored aboard the *Elizabeth and George* to make room for the bulky cargo of ancient marbles, he sent one of the smaller boats under his command ahead of the flagship to approach these vessels and cry, 'Amaine for the King of England!', demanding that they lower their topsail ('amain') as a sign of yielding. In response the captain of one of the unknown vessels 'spoke words of high disrespect to the King' and fired his guns at Kenelm's craft, cutting down its mizzen mast and shredding its rigging. In response to this aggression, Kenelm ordered his men to sail the *Eagle* close to these hostile ships, but to keep their sails furled 'and never putt out gunne till she was within pistole shott', so that they might be mistaken for a merchant vessel; when they were close, the mainsail and the flag of England were unfurled with a flourish, and the flagship's deadly array of cannons were revealed and trained on Kenelm's adversaries 'with great soddaineness, and with as much dexterity'. The master of the *Eagle*, Captain Milborne, repeated the demand that these ships humbly honour the King of England, but their foolhardy captain still 'answered in a muttering manner', and sent his men to prepare their guns for another sally. A swift broadside from Kenelm's guns, and two raking volleys of small-shot that ripped through the enemy's topsails, made clear just how foolish this was, and the two vessels quickly submitted to Kenelm's superior power. He sent a shallop loaded with his crewmen to board the vessel and investigate their cargo, and summoned men from both ships whom he interrogated himself. On 11 December, 'after examining the principall parties', Kenelm discovered that the larger of the two was a sizeable and formidable merchant ship from Hamburg, which had been carrying prohibited goods to Sardinia and Spain, and was loaded with a cargo of wool from Granada. The other vessel, which he estimated at 400 tons, was from Ragusa and 'continually traded with corne to Naples', so it too was fair game under the terms of his commission. Kenelm added both prizes to his fleet, and was sufficiently impressed by the larger of the two that he renamed it the *Jonas*, and put Sir Edward Stradling in charge of it as his vice admiral. He demoted the *Elizabeth and George* to be his third ranking ship, and placed new commanders in his smaller vessels.

This shuffling of his forces was partly in response to new and unsettling rumours that Kenelm heard from the Hamburg captain, 'of great preparations to be made in Spaine to fight with me about the Streightes mouth'. The prospect was sufficiently daunting that the Greeks and Italians who had joined Kenelm's crew at Algiers came to him and asked for permission to leave the voyage behind and make their way to the nearest shore. Since he planned to make a quick and quiet exit from the Mediterranean, Kenelm had little reason to deny their request; he gave them what he considered a generous estimate of their share of the spoils, and let them go on their way. In fact, Kenelm and his men need not have worried. Though word of it had not yet reached them, just a few weeks before a fleet of ships from the Dutch West India Company had achieved an astonishing coup by seizing the Spanish silver fleet carrying a priceless cargo from Mexico. The Dutch commander, Piet Heyn, managed to trap the lavishly laden Spanish vessels at Matanzas

Bay in Cuba, and as Kenelm's ships left the Mediterranean word of his feat was echoing through Europe, to general astonishment. The Dutch had confirmed their status as the ascendant power on the seas; the Spanish were devoting all their efforts to restoring their prestige on the waves through attacks against this tiny upstart nation; and the waters through which Kenelm sailed as he approached the straits were uncommonly quiet.

By 20 December Kenelm's men had finished redistributing the cargo from the Hamburger and the Ragusan ship between the holds of the fleet, and his reduced crew continued their way westwards. Christmas Day passed unremarked in his journal; the rumour of the patrolling Spaniards required such constant vigilance that it left no time for festivities at sea. On 28 December Kenelm glimpsed Algiers in the distance, but could barely pause to recall the splendours of his earlier sojourn since the newly acquired *Jonas*, though 'a rich shippe esteemed worth above two hundred thousand crowns', had sprung a severe leak, which required every available hand to patch it up for the remaining voyage through the rough Atlantic waters. Once the repairs were complete the wind continued to propel Kenelm homewards, but the limping *Jonas* slowed their collective movement, and an attempt to chase down four vessels proved fruitless. Appropriately enough, it was on the first day of the new year that Kenelm passed back through the Straits of Gibraltar, leaving the Mediterranean behind along with 1628 itself, which he had passed largely amidst its shores and waters. The 'leakinesse and ill sailing' of the *Jonas* continued to slow his progress, but by 3 January Kenelm caught

a fine view of Lisbon from the sea, the city perched atop its steep hills and the Castle of St Julian forbiddingly guarding the river-mouth. There was little shipping thereabouts, Kenelm noted, because of the preponderance of raiders from Barbary: he saw two pirate sails that rushed swiftly away, and met an English captain who reported seeing forty Turkish sails in a single day.

The crew of this other English ship, Kenelm noted, was rowdy and disorganised, and this prompted him to reflect on the better order that he had maintained among his own men – the occasional and forgivable disorders on shore aside – and 'the happinesse and quiet that I had by the good discipline in my fleete'. So pleased was he as he reflected on their brave and orderly conduct that Kenelm chose this moment to cast the chests of gold that he had taken from the French captain publicly on to the decks, to allow his men to view the spoils that they would soon divide among themselves. He estimated the total to be 5,800 pieces of eight, a sizeable sum. The English captain also warned him of Dunkirk pirates raiding in the English Channel, the final threat that he would have to face before returning, but Kenelm proudly proclaimed his faith in his 'very good strength of 5 good shippes and above 120 good peeces of ordinance; but the maine thing that I relyed upon,' he exclaimed in a fit of pride, 'was the courage and expertnesse of my men.'

The next few days were quiet, and the only threat that materialised arose from further storms and the much colder weather and heavier seas of the Atlantic, which led many of his crew to fall sick: Kenelm quietly cursed the *Proveditore* of Zante, who had refused him the chance to purchase new and warmer clothing. The men remained healthy enough, though, to continue guiding the ships smoothly back towards England, and Kenelm was able to keep an eye on his surroundings: he noted on the night of 19 January that 'over against the moone, there appeared part of a circle exactly like unto a rainbow', and he observed the inaccuracy of the ship's compasses, which, he believed, were caused by the large iron guns affecting the magnet. He also confirmed the course that the ships were taking by dropping hollow lead weights packed with tallow to the seabed, and carefully scrutinising the quality of the sand that stuck to the soft fatty substance as they were brought back up: 'broune sand, somewhat great, and two or 3 litle shels in it' at one point, 'grosse sands somewhat reddish' at another. As Kenelm prepared to leave behind the watery world that he had occupied for the past year he was able to run the textured grains of the seabed through his fingers and sniff its salty tang.

Finally, on the morning of 26 January, Kenelm stood on the deck of the *Eagle* as it approached the distant shores of England, watching the cliffs of the Isle of Wight as he passed them by. He glimpsed a Dunkirker and gave chase but soon decided not to delay his return any further; staying on course, his flagship passed the tall cliff at Beachy Head in Sussex by eight o'clock that evening. Soon the *Jonas* and *Elizabeth and George* caught up with him, the ships still being battered by harsh winter storms as they made their way towards the mouth of the Thames. On the last day of the month, still enduring the 'foul and rainie weather', Kenelm's fleet came to anchor near Gravesend. On 2 February they proceeded upriver, and arrived at Woolwich docks.

As the *Eagle* weighed anchor for the final time on its voyage,

Kenelm gazed down over the deck-rail towards the dock and saw that it was thronged with friends and relatives, notified of his triumphant return by messengers riding from the Kentish coast. The gangplank was lowered on to the wooden pier, and Kenelm strode down it towards the waiting gaggle. At its head was the Earl of Bristol, staring impassively, and as Kenelm grew near he could not help recalling the stern words that his illustrious relative had spoken to him in the months leading up to his departure, the doubts the Earl had expressed about his character and his choices; but, as Kenelm approached, Bristol's face relaxed into a broad grin and he threw his arms wide, welcoming into a firm embrace the young man whom he had come to view as another son. Behind the Earl stood the gaggle of energetic young men whom Kenelm had first befriended in Madrid, and who took it in turns to clap him on the back and comment laughingly on the drawn features and deep suntan that he had acquired at sea. George Digby, Bristol's son, had taken a break from his studies at Oxford to greet his returning cousin. Now sixteen years old, he had acquired a new seriousness and a patchy red beard while Kenelm had been away; George's new passion was for astrology, and he was desperate to impress his dashing relative, who had studied the art so extensively, with his new-found knowledge. James Howell, his hand having fully recovered with the aid of Kenelm's sympathetic powder, had remained an inveterate letter-writer during the past year; his correspondents had sent him rumours of Kenelm's triumphs at Algiers and Scanderoon, and he was desperate to hear the details for himself. Wat Montague, the Earl of Manchester's son, increasingly spent his days lost in dense theological tomes, and found himself filled with questions and doubts; he was eager to hear of the religions that Kenelm had encountered across the seas, and what he made of them. And Lewis Dyve, with a roguish grin, wanted to know whether the ladies whom Kenelm had met in those far-off lands could hold a candle to the beauties of Spain.

Kenelm enjoyed this 'happy welcome from all my frendes' and 'much other company' and answered their barrage of jests and questions as best he could, but he also tried to interject some of his own; he was desperate for further details of Buckingham's death, of the progress of the wars with France and Spain, and of the changes that were under way in the court and the wider world. Above all, he waited for a quiet moment to ask each man if he had heard any word of Venetia or his boys; but none had. She had told him that she intended to retire from society while he was away, and she had seemingly been as good as her word. Every fibre in Kenelm's body wanted to cut these conversations short, leap on to a horse and ride through the night to Buckinghamshire where he could see them, but he could not do so just yet. Bristol had come to the docks not only to welcome Kenelm, but also to bring him news that both thrilled and troubled him: the King had summoned him for an audience.

The company rode to the Palace of Whitehall, where Kenelm made his way through the series of guarded and richly decorated rooms that led to the main audience chamber, and there he found the King waiting. He was shocked by the changes that had taken place over the past year in the monarch who greeted him. Kenelm could not help lamenting the disappearance of the young man whom he had befriended in Madrid, the naive adventurer enjoying his first taste of freedom from the role into which he had been born, and who thought nothing of riding through France wearing a false beard, or leaping over a high wall to pursue the woman he loved. Even in the years before Kenelm departed, as Charles struggled to impose his will as a newly crowned King, there was an undeniable fire in his belly that led him to pursue his ill-advised wars and defend his friend Buckingham to the bitter end. But the man whom Kenelm encountered upon his return in February 1629 seemed exhausted, broken; he asked polite questions about the voyage, and laughed thinly when Kenelm told and embellished tales of his victories and of the narrow escapes and indignities suffered at sea, but he did not lean forward in his chair to savour every thrilling detail or pester the teller for more, as the old Charles would have done. In Spain, Kenelm had seen just how impressed Charles had been by the dignified and reserved style of the Spanish King, who maintained power over his subjects by remaining mysterious to them and appearing in public as seldom as possible. He had sought to replicate this way of doing things when his own reign began, observing 'a rule of great decorum' that contrasted with the messy jumble of his father's court. Now, though, he seemed to have retreated further from the world and into himself.

As Kenelm stood before Charles and told his tales, he realised that it was not just the King who had changed so much, but the tableau of which he was a part. Never before had Kenelm had an audience with his monarch that had not featured the Duke of Buckingham standing at the King's shoulder, sneering or interjecting with cutting and witty comments, while Charles glanced in his direction in admiration, and for approval when he himself spoke. Now it was not the Duke at the King's side but Henrietta Maria, his young French Queen. She was still only eighteen years old, and when Kenelm had left she and Charles had barely been on speaking terms, following a series of fallings-out concerning her large entourage of servants whom he sent packing back to France, and her refusal to be crowned by a Protestant bishop. Now, Kenelm could tell just by watching them, matters stood very differently. The Queen still spoke little English but she understood it well enough and was sufficiently confident in her role to ask questions of her own in French, while Kenelm answered smoothly in the same tongue; Charles smiled at her approvingly as she did so, and the glances and words that they exchanged confirmed the ease and intimacy that they shared.

As the audience drew to a close, Kenelm began to tell Charles of the antiquities he had brought back from Delos, and that he wished to present as a gift, if the King would be so gracious as to accept them. He expected Charles to respond enthusiastically, but instead the King gave a watery smile and replied that it remained to be seen if the gifts that he had brought back were indeed his to give. Then he dismissed Kenelm swiftly from his presence. Concerned by this gnomic response, Kenelm went in search of James Howell and the other court rumour-mongers who could fill him in on what had happened in his absence, and what Charles might have meant. He quickly learned that his assessment of the King's state of mind had not been wrong; Charles had emerged only gradually from his devastation following Buckingham's murder, and found solace with Henrietta Maria, but with the Duke gone the direction of events changed with remarkable rapidity. Even before John Felton's violent intervention at Portsmouth, the wider appetite for the wars with France and Spain had been waning. When the wars had begun, France and Spain had temporarily been at peace with one another, and England would have needed to raise an impossibly large force to pursue conflict with them both; but in January 1628, soon after Kenelm had left for the Mediterranean, a struggle had erupted surrounding the disputed succession in Mantua, a small province in Northern Italy that had assumed hugely inflated strategic significance in the first decade of the Thirty Years War. Spain and France ended the alliance against England that they had established early in 1627 and resumed hostilities with one another for control of the region: it seemed to most English people that they could withdraw from two wars that could not be won and sit back while their great Catholic enemies gouged at one another. In October, when Buckingham's final attempt to rally a fleet died with him, La Rochelle fell to the French Crown and the central reason for England's war with France evaporated. The mood of general belligerence amidst which Kenelm had left was dissipating; only Buckingham's desperation had kept it alive and after his death, the slide towards peace seemed inevitable. Charles had little appetite to stand at the head of a religious crusade or surf a wave of Elizabethan nostalgia without the Duke by his side; he was more interested in the astonishing collection of artworks, ancient and modern, that the Dukes of Mantua possessed, and even in the midst of political crisis he sought to take advantage of the chaos enveloping the province and purchase it for himself. As he retreated further from the world, Charles found solace only in his art collection and the first sparks of love for the young woman he had married three years before as an act of political expedience.

As he refamiliarised himself with these courtly circles, Kenelm also began to understand the cool reception that he had received from the King. After word of the fight at Scanderoon had reached

England in October, he was told, the Venetian ambassador to the court, Alvise Contarini, had begun to petition Charles vociferously; he claimed that Kenelm's was the scurrilous conduct of a mere pirate, and 'insisted on punishment, as an example to others'. Charles gave a vaguely sympathetic reply, assuring the ambassador that Kenelm had never been given permission to attack the republic's subjects, or even enemies of England who were using their harbours, as he had done at Scanderoon; but mostly the King resented having to pay attention to the issue at all. After hearing reports of Contarini's insistent appeals at court Kenelm travelled into the City of London, where he met with the three merchants who had helped finance his voyage, George Strowde, Nathaniel Wrighte and Abraham Reynerson, in order to give them an account of his success and of the share of the spoils that they would soon receive. The three men told him that in October they had been summoned before the Privy Council, the King's most eminent and trusted advisors, who had received a petition from the Levant Company merchants at Aleppo, demanding compensation for the harsh fines levied upon them in retaliation for Kenelm's actions. The council did not explicitly pass judgement on his behaviour, but they sought to ensure the 'prevencion of further disturbance of Trade in the Turkes Dominions for the tyme to come' by ruling that no letters of marque should be issued to English ships authorising acts of reprisal east of Sicily, and later they issued a declaration forbidding hostilities within the Mediterranean altogether.

In choosing to undertake his voyage Kenelm was striving to seize a particular historical moment, and he grasped the opportunities that it afforded with an astuteness that no other Englishman of his age could match. Now that he had returned, though, this moment seemed on the verge of disappearing. He needed quickly to reassess the achievements of his voyage, to determine the best light in which they could be presented, given the new and changing situation. Even before he had decided how to proceed, however, one thing had become painfully clear. Kenelm had hoped that he might present *Loose Fantasies* to the King himself, as the triumphant culmination of his voyage and of his life to date; but now there seemed to be no more opportunities for Mediterranean voyages, no room for poet-adventurers who might spin their grand actions into tales of heroism. Rather than placing it before the eyes of the world, Kenelm kept *Loose Fantasies* with his own collection of treasured books, to be read and reread only in private moments.

As he came to this difficult realisation, Kenelm determined to leave London; he could wait no longer. He had planned to send letters from the capital to forewarn Venetia of his arrival, but he felt so different from the man who had set out a year before that he scarcely knew what to write. Rather than request a carriage, he made the long journey on horseback, racing through the narrow roads until the familiar hills and woods in which he had passed his childhood began to appear. Arriving at last at the house of her guardians, the Fortescues, where Venetia had cloistered herself away, Kenelm left the servants to stable his horse and hurried towards the private inner chambers before he could be announced. There Venetia sat with their sons Kenelm and John, now three and one years of age. Seeing them filled him both with joy, and with an aching recollection of the dark shadows under which he had passed his own childhood. He could not even recall his father, Everard, and knew him only from overblown tales of his magnificence, his foolish naivety and his dreadful death; now, having been away for a year, Kenelm resolved never to abandon his own sons again. When Venetia saw him in the doorway she rose in pale shock. Where before she had been 'wonderfull slender in her waist', he saw that, following her second pregnancy and a sedentary year of near seclusion, 'she grew fatt'; but, he realised, 'it disgraced nothing of her shape; and if it tooke off any thing of the verdant beauty of her face, it recompenced it with giving her majesty in her lookes'. She had grown into a new person in the past year as much as he had. From the cloak-bag that was slung over his shoulder Kenelm pulled his journal, and the creased bundle of sheets that he had written on Milos: in their pages, Venetia could read what, in the past year, he had made of himself.

9

March 1629–May 1633
London

I 'The Weaving of this Loose Web'

If these loose papers should have the fortune to fall into any man's hands, to the which they were never designed, I desire that this last scrawl may beg pardon for the rest; all which I am so far from justifying, that I know the only way to preserve me from censure, is the not owning of them. But since the remembrance of the original cause that hath drawn these lines from me, is so sweet, that I cannot choose but nourish whatsoever refresheth it in me, which appeared in that I had not the power to sacrifice these trifles in the fire, whereunto my judgement had condemned them; and that if ever they come to be seen by any, their author and scope cannot choose but be known (my follies being therein so lively expressed, that no hand but my own could have traced them so exactly), I will ingenuously confess how I came to spend any time upon so vain a subject, hoping that I may in some measure be excused when it shall be known that in the weaving of this loose web, which was done without any art or care, I employed only the few empty spaces of tedious hours, which would have been in danger to be worse filled if I had not taken hold of this occasion of diversion, which my continual thoughts administered me.

K enelm lingered with his wife and children in Buckinghamshire for as long as he could, recuperating and telling tales of his adventures. He also made the day's ride to Gayhurst where he saw his mother, Mary, who was still living her own life of pious seclusion. Soon after that he visited Richard Napier at Great Linford, who was intrigued by Kenelm's accounts of his Mediterranean experiences, especially the sickness that had driven him to Algiers and the remarkable phenomena he had encountered there. Before long, though, news brought from London convinced him that he would soon have to return. In January, just as the *Eagle* had been making its way towards the English coast, Charles had reconvened for its final session the parliament that had gathered in the summer of 1628 and formulated the Petition of Right. The King had grown thoroughly sick of the constant wrangling with the House of Commons that he had endured during the first years of his reign, but he could not avoid convening them once more. He relied for a significant portion of his income on the customary grant of tonnage and poundage, which guaranteed the monarch a series of duties and levies on all exports and imports passing across the country's borders; but the turbulent series of sessions that ensued after 1625, as a series of parliaments took aim at Buckingham and were summarily dissolved, meant that they had not voted him the customary grant for life. Now, with peace imminent and the Duke gone, Charles hoped that the Commons might be more tractable and efficient: but he had badly miscalculated. In the past six months royal agents had continued to seize goods whenever they felt that they had the right to do so – including huge cargoes of currants from Zante – and had clashed with merchants who defended their own property as sacrosanct; it seemed that the Petition of Right had done little to circumscribe the King's sense of his own absolute sovereignty and right to snatch from his subjects what he desired.

Furthermore, with Buckingham gone, the Commons found another focus for their collective ire. Charles's father James had made it a point carefully to balance the differing factions that vied for supremacy within the English Church and fought for its soul; neither those who leaned towards Puritan sparseness and simplicity, nor those who preferred the grand theatre of sacraments and ceremonies, were allowed to dominate, and James maintained his own supremacy by playing the two sides off against one another. This precarious equilibrium ended when Charles assumed the throne: informed in no small part by his experiences in Madrid, where he witnessed the majesty of ceremonial religion and defended his Protestantism publicly for the first time, the new King threw in his lot firmly with the High Church party. He had a much more elevated sense of his own dignity and majesty than his father, and saw no reason to moderate for tactical purposes what he believed: the fact that he was King, and believed it, should be enough.

Soon, a group of churchmen who shared these core beliefs began rapidly climbing the ladder of the ecclesiastical hierarchy: their foes called them 'Arminians', after the Dutch theologian, Jacobus Arminius, whom they loosely followed. The Arminians were less pessimistic than many English Protestants about the state

334

of the human soul, and placed greater emphasis on the value of worldly deeds; they insisted on the irreplaceable dignity of priests and bishops, on the need for churches to be splendid places that reflected the majesty of God, and on the value of sacraments and rituals for ordinary believers. To those who bitterly opposed them, this was nothing but rank popery creeping in through the back door; but it was even more terrifying than outright popery, for its exponents claimed to be the true representatives of the reformed English Church.

Charles was wholly uninterested in such critical opinions, which he saw both as hysterical and as unwelcome commentary on his royal commands, which should have been accepted unquestioningly. The rise of the Arminians was confirmed when William Laud, their most powerful member, was named in 1627 as the new Bishop of London. In the summer of 1628, just weeks after Charles accepted the Petition of Right, the King named Richard Montagu, whose theological works had proven the most controversial of all the Arminian writings in the preceding years, as Bishop of Chichester, seemingly giving royal approval to the views that terrified so many.

When parliament reconvened in 1629, far from the pacific assembly for which Charles hoped, it met in a mood of fury and fear at these new ecclesiastical appointments, which threatened to send the country back into the jaws of Rome. In a series of impassioned speeches, members denounced the religious changes under way with a new degree of fury and directness. At the end of January one spoke apocalyptically of 'Popery and Arminianism, joining hand in hand', while another sought to invoke memories of the 'miraculous deliveries' from the Armada and the Gunpowder Plot during the previous reigns as a warning not to let this new

'Trojan horse' of crypto-Catholicism creep in. Charles repeatedly sent warnings to the parliament not to venture opinions on controversial matters of religion or impinge on his royal prerogative, but once the floodgates had opened there was no closing them. By the end of February, there was talk that Charles would dissolve Parliament once again, but instead he suspended it for a week in the hope of reaching an agreement. When they gathered again on 2 March, Sir John Eliot, the MP who had led much of the opposition to Arminianism and implicitly to the King, stood and proclaimed that he wanted to read a declaration, and flung the paper he had prepared down upon the floor. The Speaker of the House, Sir John Finch, refused his demand and tried to rise from his chair, an act that would have brought the session to an end; but, in a radically unprecedented move that provoked a bedlam of encouraging and protesting cries, two of Eliot's accomplices held him down in his chair and prevented him from doing so. Dozens of MPs made for the exit but discovered it had been locked by Eliot's men. The King's serjeant thumped on the outside of the door demanding entry, as the restrained Speaker broke down in tears, protesting that he could not serve two masters at once. Amidst the chaos Eliot read his declaration, which denounced innovations in religion, the rise of Arminianism and popish conspiracy, and non-parliamentary taxation. By the end of the day Eliot was a prisoner in the Tower and the Parliament had at last been dissolved; Charles vowed not to call another for as long as he lived.

When he heard tell of this astonishing piece of political theatre, in which all of the latent tensions of the preceding years erupted,

Kenelm raced back to London. It was clear, with Parliament disbanded and the King mulling over alternative means by which to rule, that new opportunities would arise, and Kenelm was determined to make the most of his achievements at sea and to seize them. After arriving in the city he met with Edward Stradling, his erstwhile vice admiral, whom he had left in charge of the various spoils that they had brought back from the Mediterranean. Before he could begin considering his future prospects, Kenelm needed to deal with the more pressing threat of the enraged Venetian ambassador; Alvise Contarini was still petitioning the King for compensation, and for all those responsible to be punished. He had shifted his focus from the fight with the galleasses at Scanderoon to Kenelm's seizure of the *Jonas* near Sardinia on his return voyage; since the ship was bound for Venice, he insisted, it should have been deemed under their protection and left unmolested. Despite the ambassador's ever-shriller denunciations of his conduct, Kenelm was confident that he knew just how to prevail. What Contarini wanted from Charles, above all else, was a fair trial and a legal judgement; but this was what the King was reluctant to give. As Kenelm was all too aware, maritime law was enormously convoluted and disputed, an intractable mess of competing jurisdictions and legal systems; if he could avoid a firm decision being taken against him, then possession became nine tenths of the law and he was likely to be able to retain the vast majority of what he had snatched. The best thing that he could do was to frustrate the ambassador with further delays, while winning as many influential members of the court to his side as he could.

In a warehouse near Woolwich, Kenelm and Edward Stradling directed a team of men as they heaped up the goods that they had extracted from the holds of the fleet: the bales of wool from the *Jonas*, the crates of wine from Mykonos, the shining stacks of ancient marbles from Delos, the smaller boxes containing the Arabic manuscripts from Algiers and the specimens culled from Zante. Kenelm faced up ruefully to the prospect of parting with the most compelling of these objects, which he had enjoyed contemplating during quieter moments at sea, but he knew that they would have to serve their purpose. First, and most importantly, he requested another audience with the King, and invited him to come and see for himself the ancient marbles brought from Delos. Kenelm rightly judged that, despite his initial show of indifference, this was an offer that Charles could not resist, the only thing likely to rouse him from his torpor; the King was still awaiting the arrival of the vast collection from Mantua, for which he had agreed to pay the astonishing sum of £15,000 at a time when the royal coffers were troublingly empty, and he was eager for a sneak preview of the ancient treasures that awaited him. Charles examined the pieces with gusto, some of his old energy returning as he fired off questions about their origins and asked how the larger ones had been spirited away; after answering, Kenelm humbly presented the King with the cream of the collection, including the large statue that his men had taken aboard with such difficulty, and the low pillar with its intriguing inscription. As the pieces began to be transported back to the King's palace at Whitehall, word of their arrival echoed around the court and many came to watch them being installed.

With Charles's delighted acceptance of this gift the tide began to turn in Kenelm's favour, and he wasted no time building on his advantage by sending smaller gifts to other luminaries of the court. He ingratiated himself with everyone that he could – from

the red-nosed nobles whom he surprised with bottles of Greek
wine, to the King's gardener, John Tradescant, to whom he gave
the seeds and cuttings that he had collected on Zante as well as
a Moor's costume that he had been given in Algiers, complete
with cap, Barbary shoes and spurs, for Tradescant's growing
collection of exotic rarities. Soon word of Kenelm's largesse was
on everyone's lips: Henry Peacham marvelled at the King's
augmented collection, noting that 'some of the Old greeke
marble-bases, columnes, and altars were brought from the ruines
of Apollo's Temple at Delos, by that noble and absolutely compleat
Gentleman Sir Kenhelme Digby Knight'. Contarini, meanwhile,
wrote furious missives to his masters in Venice.

> *Digby is working with all his might to keep this plunder, as it forms
> the chief part of his profit. He has brought presents for all the chief
> lords of the government. For the king, a stone carved in low relief,
> brought from Greece, which is said to have belonged to the temple at
> Delphi, with some ancient statues, according to his majesty's taste.
> He distributed a variety of delicacies among the ministers, some
> receiving wine from Crete, and some other things.*

Kenelm's strategy was a brilliant success: the King continued to
make sympathetic noises to Contarini while doing nothing. The
Privy Council appointed Sir Henry Marten, judge of the High
Court of the Admiralty, to investigate the matter: but, as the
ambassador observed, the fact that the Crown received ten per
cent of all gains from privateering meant that they had a vested
interest in Kenelm maximising his spoils, 'not to speak of the
presents that he continues to make in large quantities'. With
the slide towards peace in the aftermath of Buckingham's death

continuing, the government was increasingly preoccupied by negotiations with France, and the end of hostilities was confirmed with the Treaty of Susa in April. At the same time, it seemed as if the vicious religious wars consuming Central Europe might grind to a halt: following the defeat of the Protestant alliance, the ragged and starving remainder of the troops who had left England with Count von Mansfelt in 1626 surrendered in April 1628, effectively ending English involvement in these struggles. In May 1629 the Holy Roman Emperor agreed a fragile peace on harsh terms. With these grander events playing out, the dispute over Kenelm's prizes received little attention, and the weeks and months passed with nothing being resolved. In August Contarini was replaced as ambassador by Girolamo Soranzo, but he fared no better, and by early October he wrote dolefully to the Senate, 'There is nothing left for me to do about the ships plundered by Digby'.

Kenelm worked to establish himself at court as the dispute with the Venetians fizzled out, disbursing gifts and circulating copies of his Mediterranean journal that he had copied at considerable expense. He was able to meet and impress a wide array of the people who had risen to prominence at court in his absence, and to familiarise himself with the changes that were taking place. It became clear that there was no single figure who would wield anything like the degree of power with which the Duke of Buckingham had been invested: instead Charles was trying to begin an overhaul of the workings of his government that would allow it to function without the need for quarrelsome and meddling parliaments, and he was dividing its responsibilities between a range of figures. A man named Richard Weston, a competent bureaucrat with strong Catholic and Spanish sympathies, was made Lord Treasurer, and charged with rectifying the dire mess of the royal finances; and as Bishop of London, William Laud was encouraged to begin imposing on the nation at large the kind of austere and splendid religion in which he and Charles believed.

Kenelm delighted in the growing conviction that his voyage had been a resounding success. Before leaving he had felt his position in the world to be precarious and in constant need of justification; now, for the first time, he was the sort of man whom people sought out and wanted to know. He still enjoyed spending time with his circle of contemporaries – Howell, Montague, Dyve, George Digby – and other young bucks who looked up to his achievements and his worldliness; but Kenelm also found himself forging new friendships with much older men. Venetia remained in Buckinghamshire, but he began to make plans to rent a house in London so that she and their sons could join him there. He also started to forge new intentions for his future, as he built up an acute understanding of the changed society emerging in the wake of Buckingham's death. The heroic and nostalgic impulses that had animated the King and the Duke before his departure might have dissipated, but Kenelm saw that the King and his circle were still captivated by poetry and art; now, though, it was not great martial endeavours that were to be celebrated, but the court's own elegance and sophistication. Charles no longer saw himself as the hero in an adventurous romance, as he had since he rode to fetch the Infanta from Madrid, but as the protagonist of a domestic romance with his new Queen. Kenelm realised that the passion for reading and writing that he had developed during his voyage could still productively be pursued in this changing milieu, by inserting himself into these newly self-confident artistic circles.

As spring turned to summer, an opportunity presented itself when James Howell came to Kenelm with a suggestion. Howell was living in Westminster at the time, where his next-door neighbour was the foremost poet and playwright in the land, Ben Jonson. Howell often dined with this illustrious figure who, though plagued by money problems and growing corpulent and irascible in his old age, still hosted many a 'solemn supper', where 'there was good company, excellent cheer, choice wines and jovial welcome'. Knowing Kenelm's proclivities for all of these things, Howell suggested that his friend join him at the next of these gatherings. Jonson liked to surround himself with brilliant young men who wove wit and learning together, and Kenelm took his place effortlessly among their number, and began to join the regular gatherings at the Mermaid Tavern of the 'Sons of Ben', as they were known. Moving in these circles allowed Kenelm to display the cosmopolitan ease that he had developed during his year away, and his new writer friends also offered new ways of promoting his achievements to the wider world. Jonson in particular delighted in the younger man's tales of the Mediterranean and his quick-tongued humour and grew to love and to trust him, as well as relying on him for financial help and patronage. He wrote a poem extolling Kenelm as 'prudent, valiant, just, and temperate', while also marvelling at his physical gifts, the large body 'built like some imperial room' and his breast 'a broad street/ Where all heroic ample thoughts do meet'. As evidence for Kenelm's greatness, Jonson proclaimed, 'Witness his action done at Scanderoon'. In November 1629 James Howell repeated the feat in a letter designed for public consumption, congratulating

Kenelm for 'your happy return from the Levant, and the great honour you have acquired by your gallant comportment in Algiers in re-escating [sic] so many English slaves,' and 'by bearing up so bravely against the Venetian fleet in the bay of Scanderoon'. 'I do not remember to have read or heard that those huge galleasses of Saint Mark were beaten before', Howell commented.

Kenelm enjoyed the word-games and one-upmanship in which the Sons of Ben indulged, and he was thrilled to see his great triumphs trumpeted in public in this fashion. Here he could develop the love of poetry he had pursued at sea, and Jonson surrounded himself not only with wits but with serious scholars and thinkers, allowing Kenelm to forge further into the learned circles to which he aspired. He was introduced to the brilliant and unorthodox philosopher Thomas Hobbes, and John Selden, a formidable lawyer who knew more than any English person alive about Hebrew, Arabic and the learning of the ancient world, and was particularly keen to hear of the pieces bought from Delos. The more he and Selden talked, the more they discovered their shared interests – not least in astrology, and in the arcane learning of Roger Bacon – and eventually Kenelm gifted his new friend one of the treasures from his travels that he had intended to keep for himself, the heavy and intricately illustrated Persian lexicon known as the *Qāmūs* that he had procured in Algiers. Selden was the man most likely to make good use of it, and on the first page he gratefully wrote in Latin that it was a present from 'that greatest of men, Kenelm Digby'.

Moving in these lively and learned circles allowed Kenelm to establish himself in just the manner he had hoped, displaying his credentials both as a hero and as a man of learning. But as his status became increasingly secure and the immediate threat of the

343

Venetian ambassador's fury receded, he began also to search for ways to continue ruminating upon the variety of religions that he had encountered in the Mediterranean, and the impact that they had upon his own beliefs. The opportunity to do so came when he was introduced by John Selden to William Laud, initially on the basis of their shared scholarly interests. Laud was deeply interested in the Levant, and eager to hear more of the plight of Greek Christians, and of Kenelm's exposure to Arabic and other Eastern writings that might offer insights into how the heathens could eventually be converted; he was in the process of endowing the first professorship in Arabic at Oxford, and had instructed every Levant Company ship returning from the East to bring back an Arabic or Persian book. When Kenelm realised the depth of Laud's interests, he decided, with a heavy heart, to give the manuscripts that he had collected in Algiers as a gift to the Bishop, who was delighted to have them, scribbling out Kenelm's signature in each book and adding his own.

Initially Kenelm had expected this to be just another bribe, a way to further his worldly advancement; but as he got to know Laud he formed a deep liking and respect for the older man. Slowly but surely, they began to discuss religion at length, and as their friendship deepened Kenelm described to the Bishop the fascinatingly mixed religious worlds that he had encountered in the Levant, the way in which faiths and nationalities seemed able to mingle or to exist side by side, in a manner so different from the harsh divisions that still obtained in the England to which he had returned, and which the anarchic and virulently anti-Catholic end to the 1629 parliament had confirmed. He also admitted to Laud the doubts that had crept in as he had pondered his father's treacherous legacy: his voyage, and the writing of the *Loose Fantasies*,

344

Kenelm gave this Persian manuscript to his friend, Archbishop William Laud: Kenelm's signature has been scribbled out and replaced with Laud's

had convinced Kenelm so deeply of the importance of the free and loving human will that he felt anxious belonging to a religion simply because he had been born into it, and more uncomfortable still because his parents' faith seemed to place ultimate worldly authority not in the individual believer but in the Pope. All of this was excellent news for Laud: constantly attacked by his enemies as a thinly veiled papist, the Bishop knew all too well that the conversion of a prominent young Catholic from a notorious family would be an excellent piece of propaganda. He subtly stoked Kenelm's doubts, and strove to convince him that the Church which he was in the process of building would provide him with an ideal home. Laud's mantra was 'the beauty of holiness', and

345

under his watch English worship would retain much of the majesty and ceremonial splendour that appealed so strongly to Kenelm's body and senses; but it would be non-dogmatic, eschewing the extremes of Puritan and Catholic fanaticism and pursuing a moderate middle way that would give considerable latitude to learned and pious men like Kenelm. Ultimately, Laud strove to convince him, England might grow into a world as vibrantly open as the Mediterranean coastlines that Kenelm had seen for himself.

Once Kenelm had re-established himself at court, he sent for Venetia and his sons to join him in London; she could continue to pursure her pious life there, but in light of his triumphs there was no need for her to fear the rumours that had formerly been so threatening. He rented a house for them in Charterhouse Yard in Clerkenwell, and once he had successfully managed to elude the challenges of the Venetian ambassador and sell the valuable cargoes of wool and wine, he devoted the majority of the remaining profits from selling the spoils of his voyage to building a new house 'in Holbourne between Kings-street and Southampton street', the first home that would be entirely his and his family's. It would have room not only for them but for his vast and growing book collection, and Kenelm intended 'a gallery for a library to be built' at the side of the house. He was exceedingly busy with machinations at court and his new social appointments, as well as overseeing this building work, but he spent all the time he could with Venetia and their children. He had talked to her at length of his experiences in the Mediterranean, and she had told him how she had spent her time while he was at sea. As they reacquainted themselves with one another, Kenelm continued to marvel at the complexities of her personality, her effortless ability to combine and keep in check the sorts of seemingly incompatible trait that he felt bubbling unstably within himself, and her ability to adapt herself to changing circumstances. Her piety remained intense. 'And yet with all this devotion and meditations of mortifying objects and abstracting her thoughtes, she no sooner came into company but she shewed as great cheerfulnesse and livelinesse of spirit as any woman could do; a rare temper that could bind and unloose itself so easily'. They re-established their former intimacy with ease, and by the summer Venetia was pregnant again; at the end of 1629 she gave birth to another son, whom they decided to name Everard. Having spent the preceding years wrestling with his father's legacy, Kenelm decided boldly to reclaim the name that until this point had reminded him only of the past that he strove to escape. Kenelm gazed wonderingly at this latest arrival, 'who was the fairest, largest and the finest childe that ever yet I saw'; yet as he held the baby in his arms it began to droop and grow pale, and within a few hours, this new and tiny life came to an end. Kenelm tried to conceal the devastating fact of their son's death from Venetia, who was lying in bed, still weakened by the struggles of labour, 'least such a surcharge of grief upon her indisposition might have overborne her'. He could not keep it from her, though: 'she read in my face the sorrow of my heart', and in fact it was Kenelm who collapsed in anguished sobs as Venetia comforted him 'with an unmoved constancy', insisting that their son had been 'taken into heaven . . . while we remained in our wearisome pilgrimage in this miserable world'.

Kenelm and Venetia endured the awful loss of their son together, trying as best they could to assuage one another's grief and offer some consolation. Together in their new home with their two sons, trying to establish a stable life as a family after years during which they had endured repeated separation, they hoped at first that they could mourn as one. Soon, though, their different responses to this bereavement threatened to drive them apart. Venetia, who had managed to oscillate between pious seclusion and sociability, now once more retreated from the world altogether: even in 'such places as company resorted most unto for ayre and pleasure', like Hyde Park, 'where the chief delight is the meeting of the company and the going many together to increase the entertainment by conversation and mirth, yett her desire was to still to have us two goe alone together and avoid the company what we might'. At first Kenelm delighted in this closeness, finding that 'we that were so much together could never have time to say as much as we would say', yet he found that he could not shut out the wider world as fully as Venetia seemed to desire; he was too swept up with Jonson and the Sons of Ben, in lofty debates with Hobbes and Selden, in ruminative conference with Laud. Increasingly Venetia stayed in the house in Clerkenwell while Kenelm roamed London trying to recapture the thrills of his voyage. Soon, for the first time, his fidelity to her wavered, and he 'scattered else where what was onely her due'. As a younger man Kenelm had raged indignantly when he heard rumours of Venetia's unfaithfulness and convinced himself they could not be true, but now he was guilty of the worst sins that he had once attributed to her; no sooner had he 'committed any scape' with another woman than he 'had presently horror in it and resolved never to do the like again', and he 'wondered what Divell rained in my blood that I should ever be false to her'. He could not conceal his dalliances from her for long, but when Venetia heard of them she responded with high-minded advice rather than rage, and 'her faire discourses, counsailes, and wise-dome detained me from many evils that otherwise I would have incurred', bringing Kenelm back to himself when he was 'plunged in all voluptuousness'.

By the beginning of 1630 the last remnants of the voyage had been sold or given away, the final barrels of wine and marble fragments from Delos carted off into London. In the spring Kenelm entered into negotiation for the sale of the *Eagle* with a group of Puritans headed by John Winthrop, whose son and namesake had been travelling in the Mediterranean at the same time. Having witnessed the ease with which commercial arrangements could transcend religious disagreements, Kenelm agreed on £750 as the sale price. On 29 March the ship, having been renamed the *Arbella*, departed for the New World packed with Puritan colonists, one of many boatloads driven out of England by the rise of Laud and his followers. By the summer the damage to Kenelm's marriage had tenuously been repaired and his reputation in courtly and learned circles was rapidly rising. He had managed to achieve stability and deftly sidestep the threats that faced him upon returning from the Mediterranean, but he had not yet resolved upon a particular vocation or path for his future. There were rumours that he would be granted an official role, but the ghosts of his past had not been entirely forgotten: Ambassador Soranzo reported back to Venice 'that Sir Kenelm Digby . . . will very soon be added to the Council of State, notwithstanding that his father was a convicted criminal, beheaded for his share in the gunpowder plot against this king's father'.

This gossip came to nothing, but one of the new contacts he had made at court blossomed into a close friendship that promised to influence Kenelm's next steps. Like his other new intimates, Jonson and Laud, Sir John Coke was a much older man, aged sixty-seven. As the Secretary of State with principal responsibility for foreign affairs he was an important figure: he had spent much of his life attempting to remedy the decay, corruption and incompetence that had grown rife in the Royal Navy under James I, and had been one of Buckingham's chief instruments in the Duke's energetic attempts at naval reform. They had differing temperaments, since the Lord Secretary was not only the quintessential dusty and pedantic bureaucrat, but a stern figure with puritanical leanings, but Coke recognised Kenelm's talents and sought to harness them. It had already become clear that, although the war with Spain was winding down, the King was determined to possess a powerful navy and to take an active hand in its running; Coke would need able and trustworthy men to help make Charles's desires a reality. In October 1630, Kenelm was called away from the library to the hall of his house where he met one of Coke's servants, who handed him a message. Reading it, he was astonished to discover that, at Coke's suggestion, the King was naming him as one of the Principal Officers of the navy, the body for overseeing its proper and honest running. Coke wrote to the other Principal Officers, urging them to 'reform all abuses and disorders as have crept into any part of the service', and explaining that he had sent 'Sir Kenelm Digby, a gentleman of worth and well acquainted with the seas', to assist.

Kenelm had never allowed himself to hope that he would receive this degree of preferment so soon, nor that it would proceed so directly from the expertise he had gained in the Mediterranean.

The honour also presented him with a deep quandary, however. In order to accept an official position in the government, Kenelm would have to publicly recite the Oaths of Supremacy and Allegiance, which acknowledged the King as the supreme head of the Church and were anathema to Catholics. Even as his stock was on the rise Kenelm had continued his discussions with Laud and the soul-searching that they provoked, and now his new appointment tipped the balance. His innermost thoughts and his ambitions led him in the same direction, away from the religion for which his father had died and in which his wife, his mother and his brother still lived. In November 1630, the Treaty of Madrid officially ended the war with Spain, and England found itself at peace with all the world. A month later, Kenelm 'received the sacrament at Whitehall, and professed the Protestant Religion'. As Ambassador Soranzo contemptuously put it in a letter, updating his masters in Venice on Kenelm's behaviour, 'moved by ambition he has recently abandoned the Catholic faith and become a Protestant'.

II 'Sad Messengers of this Doleful News'

It is too high a task for my rude pen to draw any counterfeit of the deep sorrow which then took possession of her heart; which was of such a heavy nature that, at the first, it locked up all her senses in a dull lethargy; to that, with too deep a sense, she became insensible of grief. But after a while, when she seemed to wake out of a dream by the heart's dispersing abroad of the spirits to be the sad messengers of this doleful news to the other faculties of the soul, that they

*might bear their part in due mourning, then did her tongue frame
such lamentable complaints as, to have heard them, would have
converted the most savage heart into a flood of tears; and yet sorrow
sat so sweetly enthroned within her mournful eyes, as would have
made the lightest heart in love with those blessed tears, that seemed
like the morning dews sprinkled upon Aurora's face.*

Kenelm found himself, like the nation at large, at peace. He and
Venetia had found a way to live together despite the divergence
in their religious convictions, and he pursued his new professional
responsibilities with gusto. The violent political clashes and religious disagreements of the preceding five years began to seem
like a distant memory to many people in the learned and courtly
circles in which Kenelm moved, and the immediacy of his own
struggles also began to fade as he devoted himself to the happy
rhythms of professional and private life. England in these years
seemed like 'the garden of the world', enjoying 'a longer peace,
a greater plenty, and in fuller security, than had been in any former
age'. The irenic mood seemed all the more pronounced, because
although the vicious religious wars had resumed in Europe, this
simply meant 'that every other kingdom, every other province,
were engaged, many entangled, and some almost destroyed, by
the rage and fury of arms'. Just as King Charles withdrew increasingly from his own people, England withdrew from the rest of
Europe into splendid isolation.

The damaging and costly wars with France and Spain having
ended, Charles and his advisors also hoped that peace would be
more lucrative: they were now the most powerful neutral nation
in Europe. It was a practical necessity for the King to have a
formidable navy at his disposal: having resolved to rule without

the traditional aid of parliamentary grants, the King sought to promote trade that would lead to increased taxes flowing into the exchequer, but in order to do so he would need a fleet that could prowl the waters and protect English and foreign merchants from pirates, rogue Catholics, and the newly established and ascendant power on the seas, the Dutch. But it was also a matter of personal honour: Charles wanted the nation to retreat into its shell, but he also wanted it to be the most splendid and the best protected shell in Christendom. The King began to concern himself with the smallest naval details, visiting the docks and entering 'almost into every room in every ship', while lecturing master shipwrights on the best way to design a hull. Kenelm took a while to find his feet with his new duties, and struggled to reconcile himself to a life spent pushing paper – 'I do nothing here, but please myself with looking over a few books,' he wrote to Coke from his office at Deptford – but soon he was accompanying the King as he inspected new-built ships in Portsmouth, and putting the skills he had gained in the Mediterranean to good use in helping to improve the navy, advising on the design, manning and provisioning of the fleet. The outcome of these endeavours was propitious. 'Trade increased to that degree, that we were the Exchange of Christendom . . . all foreign merchants looking upon nothing as their own but what they laid up in the warehouses of this kingdom; the royal navy, in number and equipage much above former times, very formidable at sea, and the reputation of the greatness and power of the King much more with foreign princes than any of his progenitors'.

Kenelm worked hard in his new role throughout 1631 and into 1632, contributing to the improvement of England's navy following the disasters of the previous decade, but he managed to maintain his other activities as well. He rekindled old connections, riding out as often as he could to see his mother at Gayhurst and then continuing to Great Linford to talk alchemy and astrology with Richard Napier. On occasion he would continue on to Oxford to resume his 'great friendship' with Thomas Allen, now in his early nineties but still poring over ancient manuscripts as his eyesight faded. He still dined and spoke often with Jonson, Laud and Coke, and formed a new and particularly close friendship with the painter Anthony van Dyck, who had recently arrived in England for his second visit, and who found in Kenelm a kindred spirit. As the artist's first biographer wrote, 'As this gentleman was praised among the foremost subjects of the realm for his worthy qualities and learning, van Dyck entrusted all his fortunes to him, in a mutual relationship of sympathy and good will'. The King's taste for sophisticated European art was ever increasing, further fuelled by the belated arrival of the vast collection from Mantua early in 1630, and van Dyck brought a skill and subtlety in portraiture never before seen in the English court: he painted magnificent new depictions of the King and Queen, radiating heroism and domestic bliss, and other court connoisseurs like the Earl of Arundel. Kenelm therefore commissioned his new friend to paint a portrait of his family as a happy household, and a striking portrayal of Venetia as an allegorical figure of Prudence, the polar opposite of licentiousness and decadence; van Dyck portrayed her staring implacably into the middle distance, her lower body cloaked in gorgeous folds of ruddy silk, the light catching their lustrous texture, as if the viewer could reach out and crinkle them softly.

The remainder of 1632 brought a mixture of joy and sadness for Kenelm. Venetia had become pregnant again the previous year, but history had horribly repeated itself and 'she miscarried of a twinne of two sonnes about two monethes before she expected delivery'. Kenelm never had a chance to hold these boys in his arms as he had with Everard, and since they had not survived until birth 'they could not be baptised', yet he allowed himself a silent prayer 'that God hath some meanes unknowne to us to bring them into his kingdom'. Soon Venetia was pregnant again, and, while each day seemed precarious after three such dreadful losses, all seemed to be going well. In the spring Kenelm's brother, John, returned at last from his long years of travel and education in Europe. Despite his early disinclination to study he too had become well versed in theology and philosophy and, while less dashing than Kenelm, he had earned a reputation for remarkable strength and prowess with a blade – 'the best swordsman of his time', some said. Kenelm was thrilled to rekindle their childhood closeness, and they were able to speak at length of their youthful memories and experiences of foreign travel. Before long, though, John was sent off as part of a large embassy into Europe that planned to meander between the courts of France, Savoy, Venice and Florence. Kenelm regretted that his brother had been forced to depart so soon after returning, but looked forward to enjoying their restored intimacy following the embassy's return. In September, news arrived from Oxford that Thomas Allen had died – a loss that saddened Kenelm, even as he reflected that his teacher had lived longer than most men dared to dream. Soon he received word that Allen had left him the vast majority of the magnificent collection of medieval manuscripts that Kenelm had spent so many hours perusing; he was deeply touched by this bequest but, in the interest of further gratifying his learned friends and since the house he was having built in Holborn would scarcely hold the collection he already owned, he gave most of them to

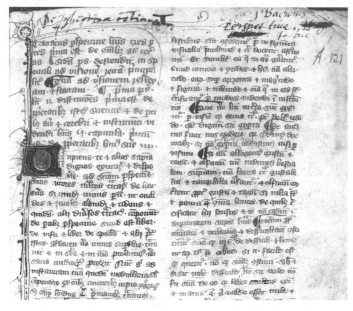

The manuscript of Roger Bacon's *Perspectiva*, owned by Kenelm's teacher
Thomas Allen. He obtained it from the Elizabethan magus John Dee,
whose signature is visible at the top right

the new Bodleian Library at Oxford, which Allen had helped to
found. This won Kenelm praise and respect, and a mathematical work was dedicated to him on the basis of his 'excellent
accomplishment . . . both of vertue, and learning, and particularly
in the Mathematical Sciences'.

The improvement in Kenelm's worldly standing was completed
when, at the start of 1633, Venetia successfully gave birth to another
son, whom they named George: he seemed a happy and robust
baby, likely to escape the tragedies that had befallen three of his
brothers. It was a frenetic but a happy time, and in early 1633, as
he enjoyed his newly expanded family, Kenelm felt settled and
self-confident. 'My reputation, I am persuaded, standeth fair with
the world', he could write with satisfaction. The nation at large

seemed to share in his confidence. 'England was generally thought secure, with the advantages of its own climate; the Court in great plenty . . . the country rich, and, which is more, fully enjoying the pleasure of its own wealth'. As one prescient observer of this seeming tranquillity observed, however, 'The land was then att peace . . . if that quiettnesse may be call'd a peace which was rather like the calme and smooth surface of the sea, whose darke womb is already impregnated of a horrid tempest'.

On the morning of 1 May 1633, Kenelm was sitting in the study of his house in Clerkenwell while his friend, the Catholic poet Thomas Hawkins, 'was reading to me some ingenious compositions of a friend of his'. Suddenly the quiet of the house was shattered by 'a shrill and baleful voice', and one of the servants dashed into the room with a look of blank panic on her face. She explained that she had been unable to rouse her mistress from her bed. Kenelm raced through the house to Venetia's chamber; she was reclining on her pillow as though sleeping, her face serene. There was no sign of struggle or suffering. 'No part of the very linen or clothes were disordered or untucked about her, but lay close to her bodie and thrust under her as her maid had putt them; even her hand . . . lay just as she left it; no bodie would have thought other than that she had bin fast asleep'. But she did not respond to Kenelm's rising cries or to his touch. He had to press his fingers repeatedly against his wife's cold flesh before he could convince himself that the life had left her body. 'Untill I putt my lippes to hers, and my cheekes to hers, I thought she had bin but asleep. But then (alas) cold death spoke from thence, and bad me never to hope to heare her speake againe.' As the realisation of what he had lost dawned on him, Kenelm's mind was seized with 'various and suddaine raptures', and 'in an instant . . . ranne over more space than is betweene heaven and earth'. He sank to his knees and clasped her hand, 'and with words as broken as my thoughts, could not choose but pray'.

The memories of the beginnings of their love flooded back into his mind, of the moments when it had wavered but ultimately survived separation, slander and misunderstanding; of the weeks and months that he had spent at sea, sustaining himself with the thought of finally returning to her. He would not believe that she was gone, that their perpetual conversations had come to an end, that the body of which he knew every inch would soon begin to fade and decay. He had found her, still and white, like one of the statues he had brought back from Delos, and now in a frenzy he allowed himself to believe that he could keep her that way, frozen in time, for ever. He seized a lock of her fine brown hair – 'so gentle and soft', he had often noticed with amusement, 'that it would not continue curled one quarter of an houre; the very moisture of the air would undoe it' – and cut it from her head, resolving to 'keepe it whiles I live as a holy relike of her'. He sent two servants running out into the London morning: one to Blackfriars to fetch van Dyck from his house on the water, specially built with a pier so that the King could visit him by boat; the other to Westminster, to command Ben Jonson to make his slow and ponderous way through the London streets to Clerkenwell. While he waited, still unable to tear his eyes from Venetia's body, he sent another servant into the scullery to mix up a batch of plaster of Paris; when it arrived he tentatively took first her feet, then her hands and, finally, her face, and pressed them into the plaster so that her shape would not be lost. When van Dyck and Jonson arrived, Kenelm told them softly through his tears that his wife was dead but not gone; they were the finest painter and poet that he knew, and they must help him to ensure she was never forgotten. Jonson left to tell the Sons of Ben to gather and sharpen their quills; but van Dyck set up his easel by Venetia's bedside and began to paint her there and then. As he captured her in the soft glow of his oils, Kenelm's friend painted Venetia not in death, but as she would have looked at the peaceful and oblivious moment just before death arrived.

During the weeks that followed Kenelm ate almost nothing, subsisting on 'a litle miserable pittance that may keepe soule and bodie together to endure a longer time of torture', and became delirious with grieving memories and self-deprivation, compulsively recalling 'particular passages betweene my wife and me so strongly that me thinkes they are even then present with me; I see her and I talke with her'. Even when Venetia had lain in her deathbed for two days, even when his friend Theodore Mayerne and others among 'the most eminent doctors and surgeons of London' came to fetch the body and perform an autopsy, Kenelm could not tear himself away and demanded to be there 'att the opening of the bodie'. He watched with grim fascination as they sliced into the flesh of his beloved wife, finding only some gall-bladder stones, and 'her other vitall partes . . . admirably strong and sound and perfect'. But, as Kenelm endured the screech of the bone-saw against Venetia's cranium, all present recoiled in horror to discover 'the braine much putrifyed and corrupted; all the cerebellum was rotten, and retained not the form of braine but was meere pus and corrupted matter'. Kenelm was appalled by the rotten interior of his wife's exquisite head, which he had

always believed 'was made of so even and uncornered a dimen-
sion, and of so just a quantity as it was a fitt lodging for the noble
braine that it enclosed'. The doctors assured him that it must have
been a hereditary condition that ended her life, and 'the disease
was original from her birth and conception'. The interior of
Venetia's body made an awful spectacle, one that he could not
banish from his mind.

   Kenelm's hopes lay in ruins. The home that he was building
for his family was still unfinished, and the future he had imagined
for them was torn away. He sent his three sons to his mother at
Gayhurst, their very sight reminding him only of Venetia and
his own inadequacies, and he roamed the house restlessly, his
footsteps echoing around its empty rooms: 'Here where I have
had so much company, so many entertainments and so much jollity,
now raigneth desolation, lonelinesse and silence'. He tried to
read but after a few lines would 'in a kinde of fury starte up and
throw away my booke', and he believed that having 'ever been
delighted with reading and in studie . . . henceforward bookes will
savour no better to me', so he should 'sell that library which with
so much cost and labor I have raked together'. His collection
of paintings, including the magnificent religious scenes that van
Dyck had also created for him, lay 'confusedly scattered upon
the ground with their heeles and wrong sides upwardes, all dusty
and foule'. He was haunted by the thought that he should have
seen Venetia's death coming, prepared himself for it even if he
could not prevent it: it seemed so obvious in retrospect that the
fervent piety and retreat from the world of her final years was not
just a 'continuall meditation upon death' but a rehearsal for it, and
'she used to talke of dying as familiarly as an other would of going
abroad to take the ayre'. He tortured himself with memories of

his infidelities, of the time spent away from her for his naval work and with his friends, when he assumed that they had so many more years together.

Kenelm was convinced that Venetia's loss had destroyed any possibility of earthly happiness for him. The whole world seemed to be hardening and splintering around him, the divisions that he had dreamed of bridging widening into chasms. On 22 June 1633, less than two months after Venetia's death, Galileo Galilei, who had been deemed 'vehemently suspect of heresy', appeared before the Roman Inquisition in the white robes of a penitent. Under threat of torture he publicly recanted his ungodly belief that the Earth was just one planet among others, and was sentenced to perpetual house arrest: his condemnation prompted free-thinking Catholics across Europe fearfully to limit the expression of their ideas, and battered the hopes of those, like Kenelm, who believed that emerging and novel ideas could be reconciled with the ancient authority of their Church. Soon afterwards in England, it was confirmed that William Laud would be named Archbishop of Canterbury, and placed at the head of the English Church. With Laud's power now confirmed there was no need for him to pursue the capacious and broad-minded policies that had impressed Kenelm, and the Archbishop began to impose the vision of beautiful, austere, ceremonious, priestly Protestantism that he shared with the King on to every parish in the land, with aggressive disregard for the feelings of local communities.

It seemed to Kenelm that the only response to these signs of harsh authoritarianism in the wider world, and the best way to honour Venetia's memory, was to retire, as she had, into seclusion. As he passed his thirtieth birthday, his very appearance was changing, and he increasingly sported 'a long mourning cloake, a high crowned hatt, look't like a Hermite, his beard unshorne, as signes of sorrowe for his beloved Wife'. Twice his friend van Dyck painted him that way, his face sunken and his hair thinning from grief and self-denial, the very embodiment of loss: in one portrait a navigational instrument known as an armillary sphere lay broken at Kenelm's side, a relic of his Mediterranean adventures now lying in ruins. He wrote to Coke that he was retiring from the navy. 'My time of hoping to performe any part upon the stage of this world, other than of a continuall mourner, is now worne out'. He could not bear to be with his sons at Gayhurst, nor in the house in Clerkenwell that echoed with memories, nor in the unbuilt house at Holborn; instead he found new lodgings in Gresham College, which had been founded in 1597 in Bishopsgate in order to make learned ideas available to a wider public. Kenelm was drawn to Gresham by his 'distaste of worldly things', convinced that 'nothing but solitarinesse is tolerable to me', but soon, despite himself, he began to find distractions, as he 'diverted himself with his Chymistry, and the Professors' good conversation'.

The frenetic life that he had lived since returning from the Mediterranean had left Kenelm little time for his alchemical pursuits, but now he threw himself into them with renewed gusto. Having been given a large suite of six rooms he devoted four of them to fitting out a cutting-edge laboratory, with multiple ovens and furnaces – including a 'New Oven to bake pies in' – and he employed a learned Hungarian Protestant named Johannes Bánfi Hunyades to be his assistant. But even in this secluded setting, further dark rumours reached Kenelm's ears. As the grisly accounts of Venetia's autopsy and Kenelm's mourning became public knowledge, prurient observers took his extravagant behaviour as a sign of guilt, and his retirement as an attempt 'to avoyd envy and scandall'. 'Some suspected that she was poysoned. When her head was opened, there was found but little braine, which her husband imputed, to the drinking of viper-wine. But spitefull woemen would say, that 'twas a viper-husband who was jealous of her that she would steale a Leape'. By now, however, Kenelm was too deeply immersed in his work to care for such rumours. He turned to alchemy not to distract himself from Venetia's death, but to understand and come to terms with it. Having first been appalled by the putrefying interior of her skull, now Kenelm formed the firm belief that 'the spagyrike art', alchemy, could provide some consolation. His studies of this arcane science had convinced him that no earthly being could be entirely destroyed, and that nothing, not even 'a contemptible nettle out of a ditch', was too lowly to be refined to perfection through the alchemist's endeavours. He retained a desperate hope that a person could change utterly, even if it seemed to involve pain or loss, and still emerge purified. It was necessary for his wife to putrefy, to decay into 'the most corrupt and foetide masse', because only then was it possible to isolate her essence, the core of her identity, consisting of a 'little substance which virtually containeth in it all the partes of the whole'. This was the unchanging core of a person, existing beyond alteration, in which Kenelm desperately wanted to believe. 'And when our body dyeth, yet that remaineth untouched, still the same; and no length of time, nor violence or variety . . . can alter or corrupt that or extinguish the power it hath to make up a bodie againe, the same that as before.' Sweating over his furnaces

in his black cloak, singeing the tips of his fingers and his beard as
he laboured late into the night, Kenelm believed that somewhere,
in the depths of a glass funnel or limbeck, he would glimpse the
secret of his lost love.

⊠

As Kenelm passed his days with these alchemical investigations
of Venetia's immortal being, he began slowly to emerge from his
abyss of despair. Van Dyck wrote to tell him that the painting of
Venetia was finished, and Jonson sent a copy of a volume in which
he and many of the Sons of Ben – including Kenelm's cousin,
George – had written heartfelt and extravagant accounts of his
wife's virtue and their pain at her loss. Jonson was engaged in
writing a magnificent series of poems in her memory, renaming
Venetia 'Eupheme' or 'fair fame', in which he lamented her devastating loss and imagined her eventual resurrection at the Day of
Judgement. As he read through these verses Kenelm began to
believe that he too should put pen to paper in the forlorn hope of
giving some shape to his grief.

Now, for the first time since Milos, he poured his innermost
thoughts on to paper in a series of soul-searching letters – to Sir
John Coke, to his brother John, who had returned from the
Continent just before Venetia died, and to his three young sons.
They would now grow up, as he had, scarcely recalling one of their
parents, but he was determined that they would have more by which
to remember their mother than the sort of vicious gossip and rumour
amidst which he had spent his own childhood. For their benefit he
detailed the delightful and difficult course of their love, every inch
of Venetia's body and character, and every pang of pain that he had

felt since her death. He was grateful to the friends who sought to capture her in poetry or paint, but remained convinced that only he had known her well enough to do her justice: the complex features of her face simply 'could not be captured upon a flatt board or cloth', and so he determined to produce 'some draught of them, the best I can with this pencill that is fitter to shadow out her mind than her shape'. He strove through his words not only to freeze Venetia in time for his sons' sake but, once again, to see the world from her perspective even as she left the world behind: he wanted to experience death in her company, to be with her as her soul separated from her body and made its way to heaven, to look through her eyes as she gazed at 'the starres under her feete; and our earth, that dazeleth so many with the lustre and glory of it, appeareth to her scarce as a point, an inconsiderable atome'.

Venetia's death marked a decisive break in Kenelm's life: rather than turning him away from the world, however, it threw him back towards the strength of character and the habits of mind that he had first developed in the Mediterranean. It was the need to make sense of his devastating loss that inspired Kenelm to begin writing again, as well as surrounding himself with the beautiful words and artefacts created by his friends; in doing so he managed, through the impassioned exercise of his imagination, to continue by other means the magnificent project that he had begun on Milos, but suppressed following his return. Venetia's death brought the most important stage in Kenelm's life to a decisive and traumatic close: but it was also a new kind of beginning, which wrenched him from the distractions of his everyday pursuits. Since returning from the Mediterranean, Kenelm had tried, but ultimately failed, to live the sort of life that he had managed to pursue at sea: a life in which bold and decisive action was seamlessly interwoven with opportunities for reflection and self-transformation. The urgent need to defend himself from charges of piracy, and the overwhelming minutiae of his naval work, left Kenelm little time for contemplation amidst hectic action. Kenelm coped with Venetia's death by striving once again to attain the right kind of position in relation to the world: close enough to understand and relish its fine details and idiosyncrasies, but removed enough from the frenetic activity around him to seek an understanding of it. The writings that he produced in his remaining decades would be studded with recollections of his Mediterranean voyage – the steam baths at Algiers, the pigeon eggs shattered by the sound of his cannons at Scanderoon, the scents wafting from the coastlines of Spain and North Africa. These were the memories to which he incessantly returned; but, beyond such delightful details, it was the ability that he had formed during his voyage, the ability to reflect upon his life even while he was in the midst of living it, that Kenelm never relinquished.

EPILOGUE

11 October 2015
London

O n a blowy autumn afternoon, I stood in the midst of
wandering shoppers and looked up at the buildings lining
the north side of Covent Garden Square, where, 350 years ago,
Kenelm Digby breathed his last. He had set out on that early June
morning in 1665 eager to return to the friends, the laboratory and
the vast library that he had left behind in Paris, but desperate
above all to keep moving, to forge ever onwards, until the very
end. Kenelm's last journey was beyond his failing strength, and
his carriage made it only as far as Sittingbourne in Kent before
he succumbed to a raging fever and had to return to his rooms in
the heart of London. Summoning a final desperate energy, he
added a handwritten coda to his will; he knew that his 'owne
proper debts' would force his executors to sell most of the beautiful objects to which he had clung, leaving him with 'so broken,
encumbred and scanty an estate', but he was determined to do
what he could for his 'worthy frendes'. He left the large burning-glass

that he had inherited from Thomas Allen to his cousin George; bequests to the poor near Gayhurst; 'and all my wearing clothes and linen' to his servants George and Anne Hangmaster. To his surviving son, John, he left nothing but a single book. This was no ordinary volume, however, but 'a great book as big as the biggest Church Bible . . . and the richliest bound, bossed with Silver', its enormously heavy pages made 'of curious velame', which had cost him the vast sum of a thousand pounds. This tome contained 'the History of the Family of the Digbyes', and Kenelm had paid to have copied into it 'all that was to be found any where relating to them', from extensive family trees to drawings of tombstones and inscriptions. Having fought to escape his own father's treacherous legacy, Kenelm could at least bequeath to his son a richer sense of the family's past. On 11 June, the anniversary of his victory at Scanderoon, Kenelm died.

I tried to look at Covent Garden through Kenelm's weakening eyes as he was carried from his carriage and up the stairs to his chambers for the final time. None of the original buildings on its north side remain, but the modern replacements, with their plain flat fronts and covered arcades beneath, still had something of the flavour of the square that I'd sampled from seventeenth-century pictures. I had originally assumed that Kenelm had chosen to live here when he returned to England in 1660 because it was a fashionable district, but learning more about the history of the area led me to other conclusions. Covent Garden Square was conceived and built in the 1630s, not long after Kenelm returned from the Mediterranean; it was designed by Inigo Jones, the Master of the King's Works, with significant input from Charles himself. Jones had travelled extensively in Italy with the Earl of Arundel, the great connoisseur of European art, and the whole square was a

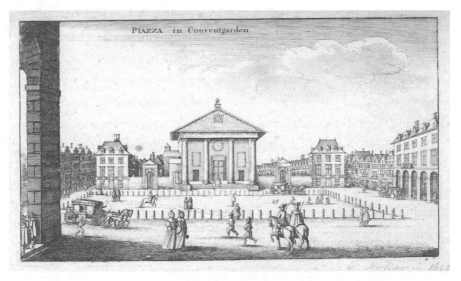

Covent Garden Square in the seventeenth century

slice of deliberate foreignness in the heart of the city, its architecture resembling recent designs in Tuscany, Paris and Rome more than any other space in London. As James Howell noted, the sudden introduction of Continental style was 'distastfull at first, as all innovations are' to parochial English sensibilities, but their 'firmnesse, and beauty' gradually won wide popularity, and it became known, aptly and simply, as 'the Piazza'. I imagined Kenelm looking out of his window as he faded in his final days, and finding a flash of consolatory pleasure in the sight of St Paul's Church on the west side of the square. Inigo Jones had designed it to look like a primitive Tuscan temple, and even if Kenelm's last attempt to travel had been cut painfully short, he could allow the view to take him back to his earliest peregrinations through

Europe. It was this lifelong restlessness, both geographical and intellectual, that initially drew me to Kenelm. When I first began to take notice of his name, it was because it only ever cropped up fleetingly, in a dazzling variety of contexts: whether I was reading about the history of literature, of science, of philosophy, of religion, of magic, of cookery, there Kenelm was, talking, arguing, writing, developing his own idiosyncratic ideas in contact with the greatest minds of his day, but always introduced as a part of someone else's story, never allowed to tell his own. Had his name not been so distinctive, I might have assumed that these were the activities of a whole host of different men, not woven together within the confines of a single life.

In the years that I have spent following in Kenelm's wake, trying to trace the lineaments of his experiences and to comprehend the contours of his mind, I have come to see him as very much like the place in which he died: both English and not English, at once rooted within the country of his birth and entirely foreign to it; and, in a parallel fashion, both intimately familiar to me and insuperably alien, receding ever more speedily from my grasp the more I raced to catch him. I began to relish those moments when it felt as if I knew Kenelm intimately, could vault over the centuries that separated us, could imagine us sitting and talking amiably over a gritty, bitter mug in one of Covent Garden's famous coffeehouses; but I came as well to value the pleasures of inscrutability and distance, the feeling that I would never fully know or understand him, or the world through which he moved. It seems to me now that we should care about the past not because it is entirely and comfortably familiar or absolutely alien, but precisely for those unsettling and provocative moments in which it is both at once.

Were Kenelm and I to meet for that imagined coffee near Covent

Garden, we would doubtless argue a great deal. If I were to admit to him that, despite valiant efforts by recent historians to rescue the reputation of Charles I, I still found it difficult to muster anything but contempt and irritation for the executed King, he would probably hurl the table between us to one side and demand immediate satisfaction. Nonetheless, the years I have spent trying, however impossibly, to reconstruct Kenelm in my mind have also been a humbling exercise in the value of trying to do so with an individual for whose political beliefs I do not have immediate and instinctive sympathy. Like all the people from the past who fascinate me the most, Kenelm has increasingly seemed to me to be at odds with himself, a civil war raging between his personal convictions scarcely less furious than the one that tore England asunder during his lifetime. He strained to reconcile his own deeply idiosyncratic habits of mind and belief in individual freedom with his unthinking Royalism and desire to believe himself, at least, to be an orthodox Catholic; he struggled to integrate his reverence for the distant past with a commitment to the present, venturing scientific explanations for phenomena that many would have swiftly dismissed as magic or superstition; he seemed both to crave the hurly-burly of worldly involvement, and to want above all to flee it for good. The more I sought to understand him, I came increasingly to realise that, while he remained utterly unique, he nonetheless distilled within himself, perhaps more than any other single figure, the unreconciled tensions of the period in which he lived.

Ending my own pursuit of Kenelm in the place where his own life had ended was, at first, a melancholy experience. As I recalled the course of his later life, Venetia's untimely death seemed like just the first in a series of tragedies: first Kenelm's brother John, and then his eldest son, were killed fighting for the King in the Civil Wars. Mere months after the death of his heir and namesake, Kenelm's youngest son, George, died of an illness while away at school: in the most poignant of his letters, full of exhausted grief, Kenelm told the Italian scholar and collector Cassiano Dal Pozzo that he had fathered six sons and outlived all but one. This life of disappointment and mourning, lived in flight from the wider world, seemed to represent the extinguishing of all the hopes and plans that Kenelm had fostered during his year in the Mediterranean, and his voyage began to seem to me, in retrospect, to have been crammed with possibilities that ultimately remained unfulfilled.

As I thought back over the years that separated Venetia's demise from Kenelm's own, however, this came to seem like a partial and unduly gloomy appraisal of the life he had lived. Even after his wife's death Kenelm's retreat into seclusion was never total. Within two years he had become a Catholic again, his change of heart prompted both by Venetia's pious memory and by the dawning realisation that he would find no true freedom of conscience as a Protestant. He relocated to Paris, where he could sometimes be seen wandering the streets 'like an Anchorite in a long gray coat . . . and his beard down to his middle', leading about a large mastiff on a leash. But he was more than just a perpetual mourner in these years. While in Paris in the 1630s he continued to practise alchemy and involved himself deeply in religious and philosophical debates, while continuing to travel back and forth between England and France and advising Sir John Coke on the management of the splendid navy that King Charles was building up to defend the nation's honour. To live a life flitting between nations in this fashion, as Kenelm had long wished, seemed increasingly plausible: Henrietta Maria's influence at court continued to grow, and her circle contained many who were Roman Catholics or whose sympathies lay in that direction, and who helped establish strong bonds between England and the Continent. Kenelm found many kindred spirits who shared his love of art and his religious views, and he was involved in a number of prominent conversions to Catholicism. He became increasingly close with the Queen herself, with whom he shared a love of cooking, and she taught him how to make white marmalade and baste roasting meat with egg yolks. During the mid-1630s Kenelm drifted contentedly between Henrietta Maria's palace at Greenwich and the salons and bookstalls of Paris, falling in with a group of likeminded Englishmen headed by an unorthodox philosopher-priest named Thomas White; this man, known by the alias 'Blacklo', became Kenelm's closest friend and mentor, convincing him that he could be a pious Catholic whose principal allegiances were nonetheless to his intellect and his country of birth, not to the Pope. Kenelm flourished in these circles, passing his time by publishing his first theological works, and with procuring beautifully bound books not only for friends in England but for Cardinal Richelieu, the most powerful man in France.

A life divided between London and Paris, and between the confines of his library and laboratory and the wider world of the court, would have suited Kenelm well, and been a fitting culmination to the range of interests pursued and developed in the Mediterranean. But this too proved impossible to sustain: King Charles could only maintain the glittering self-satisfaction of his reign by ignoring the fury that it provoked among much of the nation at large, who, in the absence of a parliament, lacked any outlet for their grievances. Many of his subjects believed that there was a Catholic plot under way to convert the King and lead the country back to Rome, and it was the presence at court of men like Kenelm that seemed to confirm their worst fears. Eventually, in 1637, Charles and Laud pushed their preference for stately and ceremonial religion too far when they tried to impose a new prayer-book and church service in Scotland; this provoked a rebellion, and the invasion of England by a Scots army. Charles and his Queen were desperate to avoid calling another parliament to fund the defence of the northern border, and Henrietta Maria suggested an alternative scheme to raise money from loyal English Catholics. When the King gave his approval, Kenelm was one of the men she placed in charge of collecting the funds. Very little money was forthcoming, however, and Charles was forced to summon Parliament after all, for the first time in eleven years; when the Long Parliament convened in November 1640, instead of granting the King the assistance he required, it burst forth with a decade of pent-up resentment. The deep divisions that had simmered silently since Buckingham's death, regarding the limits of the King's power, the nature of the subject's rights, and the proper form of English religion, came bubbling violently to the surface: the country began to move towards civil war. Because of Kenelm's involvement in the Queen's money-raising scheme, he was thrust against his will back into the forefront of English political life, and became the public face of devious court Catholicism: he was detained by Parliament, repeatedly questioned, and publicly named and denounced as a ringleader of 'the Popish faction, that labour lustily for the advancement of Popery'.

Even captivity could not still Kenelm's mind, or keep him from the pursuits to which he was devoted. Imprisoned in Winchester Palace on the South Bank of the Thames, he managed to get access to a small laboratory in which 'he practiced Chymistry' and 'made there artificiall pretious stones, e.g. Rubies, Emeralds etc: out of Flints', as well as distilling medicines, including 'tincture of strawberries' for the treatment of kidney stones, which had begun to trouble him. He also threw himself into writing his most ambitious philosophical work, setting out to produce 'a totall Survey of the whole science of Bodyes', and before he knew it he had filled up 'neere two hundred sheets of paper'. He crammed these pages not only with his ideas regarding the nature of substance, a unique blend of up-to-date materialism and atomism with the ancient wisdom of Aristotle, but with his memories: his mind took him back to the steam baths and the two-thumbed women of Algiers, to the pigeon eggs shattered by the sound of his cannons at Scanderoon and the dogs sheltering from the hot sun in the seas around Zante, and he mined these rich recollections for their philosophical significance.

Finally released by Parliament on condition that he return to Paris, Kenelm was appointed Chancellor of Henrietta Maria's court in exile, and with civil war having broken out he devoted himself to aiding the Royalist war effort from afar. The Queen sent him repeatedly to Rome in the late 1640s to petition Pope Innocent X for aid, but despite Kenelm's best diplomatic efforts this mission failed: finally, brimming with frustration, Kenelm 'grew high, and Hectored with his Holiness', denouncing the Pope at length in a performance of undiplomatic and unprecedented daring. Some at least were impressed by this display, with one courtier writing to the Grand Duke of Tuscany and calling Kenelm '*Cavaliere ripieno di quelle virtu, che lo anno reso famoso per tutta Europa*' – 'a gentleman full of virtues, that have made him famous through all Europe'. He returned to Paris at the start of 1648: within a year two of his sons had died, and at the start of 1649 Charles I himself was executed as a tyrant.

These events would seem to have left Kenelm's personal and political hopes in ruins, but still his mind could not be repressed, nor could his restless desire to travel and to forge new and unexpected connections be extinguished. Along with Thomas 'Blacklo' White and his associates, Kenelm became involved in a scheme to win toleration from the Protectorate of Oliver Cromwell, the new figurehead of the English Republic, for the nation's Catholics: if they pledged loyalty to the regime and became just one religious sect among others, they might be afforded freedom of conscience. In the end this scheme came to nothing, but for a time, as Kenelm travelled back to England in the 1650s to try and salvage some of his sequestered possessions, he struck up a close and highly unlikely friendship with the arch-republican and Puritan, Lord Protector Cromwell himself. They often dined together in private and, writing a letter to John Winthrop Jr in 1656, Kenelm stated, 'My restitution to my country and estate, I owe wholy to my lord Protectors goodnesse and justice'. Kenelm's friendship with Winthrop, by then Governor of Connecticut, blossomed at the same time: at the high point of his Roman Catholic piety, Kenelm bonded with this fervent Puritan over their shared love of alchemy, and he went so far as to donate two batches of theological books to the newly founded library at Harvard.

After once again travelling to France from England, Kenelm did not simply malinger in Paris like so many exiled Royalists: he set off on yet more new travels, journeying through northern

Europe, spending an extended period in Frankfurt, and then venturing even further, into Scandinavia, where he began a correspondence with Norwegian and Danish alchemists. Moving irrepressibly between worlds in these years, he was able to connect people who might otherwise have remained impossibly distant, divided by nation and religion: he helped the foremost English mathematician, John Wallis, enter into a correspondence with his French Catholic counterpart, the great Pierre de Fermat. When Kenelm returned to England five years before his death, he was among the earliest fellows elected to the newly founded Royal Society not only because of his learning, but because he could boast wisdom gleaned from the full range of his reading, his array of friends and contacts, and his wide-ranging travels.

Kenelm's later life seemed, as I surveyed it from the place where it ended, almost impossibly rich and varied, a sequence of startling and abrupt transformations. I remained convinced, however, that it was the experience of his Mediterranean voyage that enabled him to bind these disparate strands together, to become a resplendent whole containing within himself the extremes of the times through which he lived. It was during his time at sea that he developed his talent for improvisation and adaptation, his willingness and ability to interact meaningfully with people whose lives and beliefs differed vastly from his own, and his gift for taking the scattered parts of himself and weaving them into a single, coherent story. This man who passionately pursued alchemy, who believed that the stars can influence human lives and that wounds can be cured by treating the weapons that have inflicted them, would seem on the surface to belong to a distant and benighted past; but, I realised, the person he became during his voyage, determined to move nimbly between worlds and to combine many selves into one, would not have felt entirely out of place in the Covent Garden in which I stood.

After poking around the piazza, I walked south with my family to the Strand, and then cut eastwards. Because it was a chilly Sunday, the streets grew strangely quiet as we approached the City of London and the dome of St Paul's began to loom ahead of us. This hulking landmark was not our destination, however. As we rounded the north side of the cathedral we cut off sharply to the left, up an alley that led to Newgate Street. There, on the opposite side of the road, stood a neatly laid out garden, beds of carefully tended plants and paved paths running between them, framed by three ruined walls and with a tower pointing skywards. Once this had been the site of Christ Church, Greyfriars, where Venetia Digby was buried following her death in 1633. Kenelm had a monument constructed in her memory, an imposing tomb built of polished marble, as black as the robes that he resolved to wear from that day forth. It was enlivened with bright copper panelling and topped with two shining cherubs and, rising above them, a bust of Venetia herself, her beauty and dignity publicly preserved for prosperity. On the tomb, Kenelm had inscribed the Latin phrase '*Uxorem vivem amare, voluptas est, defunctam religio*' – 'it is a delight to love one's wife when she is alive; a sacred duty to do so when she is dead'. After his own death in June 1665, in keeping with the wishes stated in his will, Kenelm's body was brought to the same church along the route that we had just walked, and interred along with his wife. Words had poured unstoppably from him during his sixty-two years of life, but now he had nothing to add, and insisted that no further inscription be added to mark his memory. Having striven throughout his life to ensure that he be remembered, he was happy at the last to be a part of his monument to her. At last, despite all the losses that he had suffered throughout his life, he had managed to erect a tribute to their love that, he hoped, would stand for centuries to come.

On 2 September 1666, just over a year after Kenelm was interred in his final resting place, a fire broke out in a bakery on Pudding Lane, about a mile east of where the monument to Venetia stood. Soon it was raging uncontrollably, and over the next four days the Great Fire of London consumed the majority of the densely sprawling city. On Tuesday 4 September the flames reached the area around St Paul's Cathedral, which was drawn into the inferno. Christ Church Greyfriars was one of the eighty-seven parish churches that were destroyed utterly in the blaze. Kenelm's friend John Evelyn, who rode as far as he could into the city that day to witness the fire's progress, reported, 'It was now gotten as far as the Inner Temple, all Fleetestreete, old baily, Ludgate Hill, Warwick Lane, Newgate, Paules Chaine, Wattling-streete now flaming & most of it reduc'd to ashes, the stones of Paules flew like granados, the Lead mealting down the streetes in a streame, & the very pavements of them glowing with a fiery rednesse'. The flames obliterated the monument that Kenelm had designed, its inky marble and copper trappings adding to the hellscape of exploding stones and the river of molten metal.

As well as the more famous cathedral a stone's throw away, Sir Christopher Wren — whom Kenelm also knew, from their days together in the early Royal Society — took charge of designing a new church to occupy the site where Christ Church Greyfriars had once stood. Wren's church remained there until the end of December 1940, when a firebomb dropped by a German plane ripped through its roof during one of the worst nights of the Blitz. Since then the pieces that survived the blast have been repeatedly tweaked and adapted, parts of it demolished and rebuilt or given over to corporate sponsors and private residents, before arriving at the pleasant and finely manicured garden that fills the space today. Visiting it on an autumn afternoon, a final act of homage to Kenelm, was at first a disappointment. There was no plaque to commemorate him or Venetia, no trace of the memorial that he had hoped to leave behind. The destruction of the monument in the Great Fire seemed to trigger the descent into relative oblivion that had begun soon after Kenelm's death: he was lauded in his epitaph as 'The Age's wonder for his Noble Parts/Skilled in six tongues and learned in all the arts'; praised by his friend Robert Boyle, the greatest scientist of the age, as 'our deservedly famous Countryman Kenelm Digby'; and grouped with Descartes as one of the greatest modern philosophers. His works, especially the *Two Treatises* and the discourse on the Powder of Sympathy, were translated into Latin, German and numerous other tongues, and widely read and debated across Europe and New England. Gradually, though, his writings fell from fashion, and the very mixtures of ancient and modern, or of the soberly rational and the imaginatively exuberant, that had so impressed Kenelm's contemporaries saw him discredited, then mocked, then forgotten. It is perhaps the worst fate that could be imagined for him; the only thing worse than being remembered only as the son of a traitor would be not being remembered at all.

As I walked for the last time around the carefully choreographed ruins of Christ Church Greyfriars, however, my mood began to

The garden and ruined church that stands today on the site of Christ
Church on Newgate, where Kenelm and Venetia were interred

lift. The monument might not still stand, but Kenelm was never
entirely forgotten. Ten years after the Great Fire, John Aubrey
claimed that 'as I was walking through Newgate street, I sawe
Dame Venetia's Bust standing at a Stalle'. He rushed back to
buy it, but found it was already gone. Perhaps the pinnacle of her
monument really did survive the blaze; perhaps it was not melted
down, as Aubrey was told, and will one day re-emerge from some
dusty corner. But it seems apt that this is largely how the Digbys

have survived, in fleeting glimpses and whispered possibilities. Given that Kenelm told his own story so insistently, in numerous and sometimes contradictory forms – and given that he was so gripped by fragments and snippets of the ancient past – it feels appropriate that he should survive in this splintered, inchoate manner, and not through a single great statue or commemorative inscription. The more time I spent in Greyfriars Gardens, the more I noticed not the artfully arrayed flower beds or the meticulously preserved ruins but other, discordant notes; a stone with writing scratched into it, too high and too spidery to read clearly; three low stairs that led nowhere. There was a story here all right, as slickly and compellingly told as a rollicking romance; and I knew by now to look for Kenelm amidst these minutiae, the curiosities and quirks that transformed the larger picture by not fitting into it, and that seemed to form a fitting monument of their own.

BIBLIOGRAPHY

A note on referencing

In the notes, all printed works by Kenelm are referred to by short title, as listed below, and page number. All other works are referenced by author only (and date where there is more than one work by an author of that name), with the exception of the other abbreviations listed below.

Abbreviations

Works by Kenelm

A Relation   Digby, Kenelm. *Articles of Agreement made betweene the French King and those of Rochell (the 28 day of October, 1628), upon the Rendition of the Towne the 30. of October last 1628* . . .

	Also a Relation of a . . . Sea-Fight, made by Sr K. Digby (on the Bay of Scandarone the 16. of June last past), with certaine Galegasses and Galeasses, belonging to the States of Venice (London, 1628)
Conference	*A Conference with a Lady about Choice of Religion* (Paris, 1638)
Honour	*Sr. Kenelme Digbyes honour maintained. By a most couragious combat which he fought with the Lord Mount le Ros, who by base and slanderous words reviled our King* (London, 1641)
Observations, 1643a	*Observations on the 22. stanza in the 9th canto of the 2d book of Spencers Faery queen, full of excellent notions concerning the frame of man, and his rationall soul* (London, 1643)
Observations, 1643b	*Observations upon Religio Medici occasionally written by Sir Kenelme Digby, Knight* (London, 1643)
Two Treatises	*Two Treatises in the one of which the nature of bodies, in the other, the nature of mans soule is looked into in way of discovery of the immortality of reasonable soules* (Paris, 1644)
Letters	*Letters Between The Lord George Digby and Sir Kenelm Digby, Kt, concerning Religion* (London, 1651)
A discourse, 1652	*A discourse concerning infallibility in religion written by Sir Kenelme Digby to the Lord George Digby, eldest sonne of the Earle of Bristol* (London, 1652)
A Treatise	*A Treatise of Adhering to God; written by Albert*

	the Great, Bishop of Ratisbon. Put into English by Sir Kenelme Digby, Kt (London, 1653)
A late discourse	*A late discourse made in a solemne assembly of nobles and learned men at Montpellier in France touching the cure of wounds by the powder of sympathy*, trans. R. White (London, 1658)
A discourse, 1661	*A discourse concerning the vegetation of plants: Spoken by Sir Kenelme Digby at Gresham College, on the 23. of January, 1660. At a meeting of the Society for promoting philosophical knowledge by experiments* (London, 1661)
Receipts	*Choice and experimented receipts in physick and chirurgery, as also cordial and distilled waters and spirits, perfumes and other curiosities, collected by the honourable and truly learned Sir Kenelm Digby, Kt., Chancellour to Her Majesty the Queen Mother* (London, 1668)
Bibliotheca Digbeiana	*Bibliotheca Digbeiana, sive Catalogus Librorum* (London, 1680)
Journal	*Journal of a Voyage into the Mediterranean*, ed. John Bruce (London: Camden Society, 1868)
'Letter-Book'	'A New Digby Letter-Book: "In Praise of Venetia," ' ed. Vittorio Gabrieli, *National Library of Wales Journal* 9 (1955–6), pp. 113–48, 440–62; 10 (1957–8), pp. 81–106
Loose Fantasies	*Loose Fantasies*, ed. Vittorio Gabrieli. (Rome: Edizioni di Storia e Letteratura, 1968)
Closet	*The Closet of Sir Kenelm Digby Opened*, ed. Jane Stevenson and Peter Davidson (London: Prospect Books, 1997)

Other Abbreviations used in Notes

BL   The British Library, London

CSPD   *Calendar of state papers preserved in the State
                Paper Department of Her Majesty's Public Record
                Office, Domestic series: Charles I*, 22 vols (London:
                Longman, Roberts & Green, 1858–93)

CSPV   *Calendar of state papers and manuscripts, relating
                to English affairs, existing in the archives and
                collections of Venice, and in other libraries of
                northern Italy*, 40 vols (London: Longman,
                Roberts & Green, 1864–1940)

HMC   Historical Manuscripts Commission

SP   State Papers

TNA   The National Archives, Kew

General Bibliography

Abulafia, David. *The Great Sea: A Human History of the Mediterranean* (London: Penguin, 2011)

Abun-Nasr, Jamil M. *A History of the Maghrib in the Islamic Period* (Cambridge: CUP, 1987)

Adams, S. L. 'The Road to La Rochelle: English Foreign Policy and the Huguenots, 1610–1629', *Proceedings of the Huguenot Society of London* 22 (1975), pp. 414–29

Adamson, J. S. A. 'Chivalry and Political Culture in Caroline England', in *Culture and Politics in Early Stuart England*, ed. Kevin Sharpe and Peter Lake (London: Macmillan, 1994), pp. 161–95

Albion, Gordon. *Charles I and the Court of Rome* (Louvain: Bureaux du Recueil, Bibliotheque de l'Université, 1935)

Alexander, Gavin. 'Fulke Greville and the Afterlife', *Huntington Library Quarterly* 62.3/4 (1999), pp. 203–31

—*Writing After Sidney: The Literary Response to Sir Philip Sidney, 1586–1640* (Oxford: OUP, 2006)

Allen, P. S. 'Books Brought from Spain in 1596', *The English Historical Review* 31 (1916), pp. 606–10

Ames-Lewis, Francis (ed.) *Sir Thomas Gresham and Gresham College: Studies in the Intellectual History of London in the Sixteenth and Seventeenth Centuries* (Aldershot: Ashgate, 1999)

Anderson, Adam. *An Historical and Chronological Deduction of the Origin of Commerce*, 4 vols (London: J. White et al, 1801)

Andrews, Charles M. *The Colonial Period of American History I: The Settlements* (New Haven: Yale University Press, 1934)

Andrews, Kenneth. *Elizabethan Privateering: English Privateering during the Spanish War 1585–1603* (Cambridge: CUP, 1964)

—'Sir Robert Cecil and Mediterranean Plunder', *The English Historical Review* 87 (1972), pp. 512–32

—*Ships, Money and Politics: Seafaring and Naval Enterprise in the Reign of Charles I* (Cambridge: CUP, 1991)

Anon. *Ward and Danseker two notorious pyrates, Ward an Englishman, and Danseker a Dutchman. With a true relation of all or the most piracies by them committed* (London, 1609)

Anon. *The Famous Historie of Fryer Bacon, Containing the wonderfull things that he did in his life: also the manner of his death; with the lives and deaths of the two conjurors, Bungye and Vandermast. Very pleasant and delightfull to be read* (London, 1627)

Anon. *A Short Discoverie of the Coasts and Continents of America* (London, 1642)

Anselment, Raymond A. 'Clarendon and the Caroline Myth of Peace', *Journal of British Studies* 23.2 (1984), pp. 37–54

Appleby, John. 'An Association for the West Indies? English Plans for a West India Company 1621–29', *Journal of Imperial and Commonwealth History* 15.3 (1987), pp. 213–41

Appleby, John H. 'Arthur Dee and Johannes Bánfi Hunyades: Further Information on their Alchemical and Professional Activities', *Ambix* 24.2 (1977), pp. 96–109

Arbel, Benjamin. *Trading Nations: Jews and Venetians in the Early Modern Eastern Mediterranean* (Leiden: Brill, 1995)

Armitage, David. *The Ideological Origins of the British Empire* (Cambridge: CUP, 2000)

Ascham, Roger. *The Scholemaster* (London, 1570)

Astengo, Corradino. 'The Renaissance Chart Tradition in the Mediterranean', in *The History of Cartography, Volume Three: Cartography in the Renaissance*, ed. David Woodward (Chicago: University of Chicago Press, 2007), pp. 174–237

Aubrey, John. *Three Prose Works*, ed. John Buchanan-Brown (Fontwell: Centaur Press, 1972)

—*Brief Lives: With an Apparatus for the Lives of our English Mathematical Writers*, ed. Kate Bennett, 2 vols (Oxford: OUP, 2015)

Augustine of Hippo. *The City of God Against the Pagans*, trans. R. W. Dyson (Cambridge: CUP, 1998)

Aylmer, G. E. *The King's Servants: The Civil Service of Charles I* (London: Routledge & Kegan Paul, 1961)

Bacon, Francis. *Sylva Sylvarum: or, a Naturall Historie* (London, 1627)

—*Baconiana, or Certain Genuine Remains of Sir Francis Bacon* (London, 1679)

Baetens, R. 'The Organisation and Effects of Flemish Privateering in the Seventeenth Century', *Acta Historiae Neerlandicae* 9 (1976), pp. 48–75

Baldini, Ugo. 'The Roman Inquisition's Condemnation of Astrology: Antecedents, Reasons and Consequences', in *Church, Censorship and Culture in Early Modern Italy*, ed. Gigliola Fragnito, trans. Adrian Belton (Cambridge: CUP, 2001), pp. 79–110

Bamforth, Stephen. 'Melons and Wine: Montaigne and *joie de vivre* in Renaissance France', in *Joie de Vivre in French Literature and Culture: Essays in Honour of Michael Freeman*, ed. Susan Harrow and Timothy Unwin (Amsterdam: Rodopi, 2009), pp. 99–128

Bard, Nelson (ed.) 'The Earl of Warwick's Voyage of 1627', in *The Naval Miscellany* vol. 5, ed. N. A. M. Rodger (1984), pp. 15–93

—' "Might and Would Not": The Earl of Warwick's Privateering Voyage of 1627', *American Neptune* 55 (1995), pp. 5–18

Barkan, Leonard. *Unearthing the Past: Archaeology and Aesthetics in the Making of Renaissance Culture* (New Haven: Yale University Press, 1999)

Barlow, Thomas. *The gunpowder-treason: with a discourse of the manner of its discovery . . . And by way of appendix, several papers or letters of Sir Everard Digby* (London, 1679)

Barnes, Susan. 'Van Dyck and George Gage', in *Art and Patronage at the Early Stuart Court*, ed. David Howarth (Cambridge: CUP, 1993), pp. 1–11

Bayle, Pierre. *A general dictionary, historical and critical: in which a new and accurate translation of that of the celebrated Mr. Bayle, with the corrections and observations printed in the late editions at Paris, is included; and interspersed with several thousand lives never before published*, 10 vols (London, 1734–41)

Beer, Anna R. *Sir Walter Ralegh and his Readers in the Seventeenth Century* (Basingstoke: Macmillan, 1997)

Bellany, Alastair. 'The Murder of John Lambe: Crowd Violence, Court Scandal and Popular Politics in Early Seventeenth-Century England', *Past & Present* 200 (2008), pp. 37–76

Bellori, Giovan Pietro. *The Lives of the Modern Painters, Sculptors and Architects*, trans. Alice Sedgwick Wohl (Cambridge: CUP, 2005)

Benton, Lauren. 'Legal Spaces of Empire: Piracy and the Origins of Ocean Regionalism', *Comparative Studies in Society and History* 47.4 (2005), pp. 700–24

Bergeron, David. *King James and Letters of Homoerotic Desire* (Iowa City: University of Iowa Press, 1999)

Biagioli, Mario. *Galileo, Courtier: The Practice of Science in the Culture of Absolutism* (Chicago: University of Chicago Press, 1993)

Bidwell, William B. and Maija Jansson (eds.) *Proceedings in Parliament, 1626*, 4 vols (New Haven: Yale University Press, 1992)

Birch, Thomas. *The History of the Royal Society*, 4 vols (London, 1756–7)

—*The Court and Times of James I*, 2 vols (London: Henry Colburn, 1848)

Bligh, E. W. *Sir Kenelm Digby and His Venetia* (London: Samson Low, 1932)

Blom, F. J. M. 'Lucas Holstenius (1596–1661) and England', in *Studies in Seventeenth-Century English Literature, History and Bibliography*, ed. G. A. M. Janssens and F. G. A. M. Aarts (Amsterdam: Rodopi, 1984), pp. 25–39

Boas, Marie. 'An Early Version of Boyle's *Sceptical Chymist*', *Isis* 45.2 (1954), pp. 153–68

Boccaccio, Giovanni. *L'amorosa Fiammetta . . . di nuovo ristampata, e . . . ricorretta* (Venice, 1557)

—*The Decameron*, trans. G. H. McWilliam (London: Penguin, 1972)

Boeckhius, Augustus (ed.) *Corpus Inscriptionum Graecarum*, vol. 2 (Berlin: G. Reimeri, 1843)

Bonet, Juan Pablo. *Reduction de las Letras, y Arte para Enseñar a Ablar los Mudos* (Madrid, 1620)

Bossy, John. 'Rome and the Elizabethan Catholics: A Question of Geography', *Historical Journal* 7.1 (1964), pp. 135–42

Bourdieu, Pierre. *The Algerians*, trans. Alan C. M. Ross (Boston: Beacon Press, 1962)

Boyle, Robert. *The Works of Robert Boyle*, ed. Michael Hunter and Edward B. Davis, 14 vols (London: Pickering & Chatto, 2000)

—*The Correspondence of Robert Boyle*, ed. Michael Hunter, Antonio Clericuzio and Lawrence Principe, 6 vols (London: Pickering & Chatto, 2001)

Bracewell, Catherine Wendy. *The Uskoks of Senj: Piracy, Banditry, and Holy War in the Sixteenth-Century Adriatic* (Ithaca, NY: Cornell University Press, 1992)

Braudel, Fernand. *The Mediterranean and the Mediterranean World in the Age of Philip II*, trans. Siân Reynolds, 2 vols (New York: Collins, 1972)

—*Civilisation and Capitalism 15th–18th Century, Volume III: The Perspective of the World*, trans. Siân Reynolds (London: Phoenix Press, 2002)

Brenner, Robert. *Merchants and Revolution: Commercial Change, Political Conflict and London's Overseas Traders* (London: Verso, 2003)

Brockliss, Lawrence and Colin Jones. *The Medical World of Early Modern France* (Oxford: Clarendon, 1997)

Brotton, Jerry. 'Buying the Renaissance: Prince Charles's Art Purchases in Madrid, 1623', in *The Spanish Match: Prince Charles's Journey to Madrid, 1623*, ed. Alexander Samson (Aldershot: Ashgate, 2006), pp. 9–26

Brown, Alison. *The Return of Lucretius to Renaissance Florence* (Cambridge, MA: Harvard University Press, 2010)

Brown, Christopher. *Van Dyck* (Oxford: Phaidon, 1982)

Brown, Christopher and Hans Vlieghe (eds.) *Van Dyck, 1599–1641* (London: Royal Academy of Arts, 1999)

Browne, John. *The Confession of John Browne a Jesuite* (London, 1641)

Bruce, Philip. *Economic History of Virginia in the Seventeenth Century* (New York: Macmillan, 1896)

Brugman, J. 'Arabic Scholarship', in *Leiden University in the Seventeenth Century: An Exchange of Learning*, ed. Th. H. Lunsingh Scheurleer and G. H. M. Posthumus Meyjes (Leiden: Brill, 1975), pp. 203–15

Brummett, Palmira. 'Visions of the Mediterranean: A Classification', *Journal of Medieval and Early Modern Studies* 37.1 (2007), pp. 9–55

Buchanan, Brenda J. ' "The Art and Mystery of Making Gunpowder": The English Experience in the Seventeenth and Eighteenth Centuries', in *The Heirs of Archimedes: Science and the Art of War through the Age of Enlightenment*, ed. Brett D. Steele and Tamera Dorland (Cambridge, MA: MIT Press, 2005), pp. 233–74

Bulgarini, Belisario. *Riprove delle Particelle poetiche sopra Dante disputate dal Sig. Ieronimo Zoppio* (Siena, 1602)

Burch, Brian. 'Sir Kenelm Digby and Christchurch, Newgate Street', *The Guildhall Miscellany* 2.6 (1964), pp. 248–56

Burke, Peter. 'Early Modern Venice as a Centre of Information and Communication', in *Venice Reconsidered: The History and Civilization of an Italian City-State, 1297–1797*, ed. John Martin and Dennis Romano (Baltimore: the Johns Hopkins University Press, 2002), pp. 389–419

Butler, Samuel. *Hudibras*, ed. John Wilders (Oxford: Clarendon, 1967)

Bynum, William F. 'The Weapon-Salve in Seventeenth-Century English Drama', *Journal of the History of Medicine* 21 (1966), pp. 8–23

Camerota, Michele. 'Galileo, Lucrezio e l'Atomismo', in *Lucrezio, la Natura e la Scienza*, ed. Marco Beretta and Francesco Citti (Florence: Olschki, 2008), pp. 141–75

Capatti, Alberto and Massimo Montanari. *Italian Cuisine: A Cultural History*, trans. Áine O'Healy (New York: Columbia University Press, 2003)

Carleton, George. *A Thankefull Remembrance of Gods Mercy, in an Historical Collection of the great and mercifull Deliverances of the Church and State of England* (London, 1627)

Carmody, Francis J. *Arabic Astronomical and Astrological Sciences in Latin Translation: A Critical Bibliography* (Berkeley: University of California Press, 1956)

Cervantes, Miguel de. *The History of Don-Quichote: The First Part*, trans. Thomas Shelton (London, 1612)

—*Exemplary Stories*, trans. Leslie Lipson (Oxford: OUP, 1998)

Chambers, David S. 'The Earlier "Academies" in Italy', in *Italian Academies of the Sixteenth Century*, ed. D. S. Chambers and F. Quiviger (London: The Warburg Institute, 1995), pp. 1–14

Chaney, Edward. *The Grand Tour and the Great Rebellion: Richard Lassels and 'The Voyage of Italy' in the Seventeenth Century* (Geneva: Slatkine, 1985)

—Review of *The Late King's Goods*, ed. Macgregor, *The English Historical Review* 108 (1993), pp. 719–21

—'*Quo Vadis?* Travel as Education and the Impact of Italy in the Sixteenth Century', in *The Evolution of the Grand Tour: Anglo-Italian Cultural Relations since the Renaissance* (London: Frank Cass, 1998), pp. 58–101

Chapman, Allan. 'Astrological Medicine', in *Health, Medicine and Mortality in the Sixteenth Century*, ed. Charles Webster (Cambridge: CUP, 1979), pp. 275–300

Charmasson, Thérèse. *Recherches sur une Technique Divinatoire: La Géomancie dans l'Occident Médiéval* (Geneva: Librairie Droz, 1980)

Chew, Samuel C. *The Crescent and the Rose: Islam and England During the Renaissance* (Oxford: OUP, 1937)

Christianson, Paul. 'Two Proposals for Raising Money by Extra-ordinary Means, *c.*1627', *The English Historical Review* 117 (2002), pp. 356–73

Cipolla, Carlo M. *Guns and Sails in the Early Phase of European Expansion 1400–1700* (London: Collins, 1965)

Clarendon, Edward Hyde, Earl of. *The History of the Rebellion and Civil Wars in England*, ed. W. Dunn Macray, 6 vols (Oxford: Clarendon, 1888)

—*The History of the Rebellion: A New Selection*, ed. Paul Seaward (Oxford: OUP, 2009)

Clark, Stuart. 'Inversion, Misrule and the Meaning of Witchcraft', *Past & Present* 87 (1980), pp. 98–127

Clericuzio, Antonio. 'Chemical Medicine and Paracelsianism in Italy, 1550–1650', in *The Practice of Reform in Health, Medicine, and Science, 1500–2000: Essays for Charles Webster*, ed. Margaret Pelling and Scott Mandelbrote (Aldershot: Ashgate, 2005), pp. 59–79

Clericuzio, Antonio and Silvia da Renzi. 'Medicine, Alchemy and Natural Philosophy in the Early Accademia dei Lincei', in *Italian Academies of the Sixteenth Century*, ed. D. S. Chambers and F. Quiviger (London: The Warburg Institute, 1995), pp. 175–94

Clissold, Stephen. 'The Ransom Business: Christian Slaves and Moslem Masters in North Africa from the Twelfth to the Nineteenth Centuries', *History Today* (1 December 1976), pp. 779–87

Clucas, Stephen. 'Corpuscular Matter Theory in the Northumberland Circle', in *Late Medieval and Early Modern Corpuscular Matter Theories*, ed. Christoph Lüthy, John E. Murdoch and William R. Newman (Leiden: Brill, 2001), pp. 181–207

Cobbett, William (ed.) *Cobbett's Complete Collection of State Trials and Proceedings for High Treason and Other Crimes and Misdemeanours*, 34 vols (London, 1809)

Cochrane, Eric W. *Tradition and Enlightenment in the Tuscan Academies 1690–1800* (Rome: Edizioni di Storia e Letteratura, 1961)

Cogswell, Thomas. 'Foreign Policy and Parliament: The Case of La Rochelle, 1625–1626', *English Historical Review* 99 (1984), pp. 241–54

—'Prelude to Ré: The Anglo-French Struggle over La Rochelle, 1624–1627', *History* 71 (1986), pp. 1–21

—'England and the Spanish Match', in *Conflict in Early Stuart England*, ed. Richard Cust and Ann Hughes (London: Longman, 1989), pp. 106–32

—*The Blessed Revolution: English Politics and the Coming of War, 1621–1624* (Cambridge: CUP, 1989)

—' "Published by Authoritie": Newsbooks and the Duke of Buckingham's Expedition to the Île de Ré', *Huntington Library Quarterly*, 67.1 (2004), pp. 1–25

—'John Felton, Popular Political Culture, and the Assassination of the Duke of Buckingham', *The Historical Journal* 49.2 (2006), pp. 357–85

Colley, Linda. *Captives: Britain, Empire and the World, 1600–1850* (London: Pimlico, 2002)

Collins, Jeffrey. 'Thomas Hobbes and the Blackloist Conspiracy of 1649', *Historical Journal* 45.2 (2002), pp. 305–31

Cormack, Lesley B. *Charting an Empire: Geography at the English Universities, 1580–1620* (Chicago: University of Chicago Press, 1997)

Craven, W. Frank. 'The Earl of Warwick, A Speculator in Piracy', *The Hispanic American Historical Review* 10.4 (1930), pp. 457–79

Cressy, David. *Bonfires and Bells: National Memory and the Protestant Calendar in Elizabethan and Early Stuart England* (London: Weidenfeld & Nicolson, 1989)

Crinó, Anna Maria. 'Inediti su alcuni contatti tosco-britannici nel Seicento', *English Miscellany* 12 (1961), pp. 147–209

Curry, Patrick. *Prophecy and Power: Astrology in Early Modern England* (Princeton: Princeton University Press, 1989)

Curtis, Mark. *Oxford and Cambridge in Transition, 1558–1642: An Essay on Changing Relations between the English Universities and English Society* (Oxford: Clarendon, 1959)

Cust, Lionel. *Anthony van Dyck* (London: Hodder & Stoughton, 1911)

Cust, Richard. 'News and Politics in Early Seventeenth-Century England', *Past & Present* 112 (1986), pp. 60–90

—*The Forced Loan and English Politics 1626-1628* (Oxford: Clarendon, 1987)

—*Charles I: A Political Life* (Harlow: Longman, 2007)

Dallam, Thomas. 'Dallam's Travels with an Organ to the Grand Signieur', in *Early Voyages and Travels to the Levant*, ed. J. Theodore Bent (London: Hakluyt Society, 1893)

Dallington, Robert. *The Survey of the Great Dukes State of Tuscany* (London, 1605)

Dati, Carlo Roberto (ed.) *Prose Fiorentine Raccolte dallo Smarrito Accademico della Crusca*, 17 vols (Florence, 1716–45)

Davis, Ralph. 'England and the Mediterranean, 1570–1670', in *Essays in the Economic and Social History of Tudor and Stuart England in Honour of R. H. Tawney*, ed. F. J. Fisher (Cambridge: CUP, 1961), pp. 117–37

Davis, Robert C. 'Counting European Slaves on the Barbary Coast', *Past & Present* 172 (2001), pp. 87–124

—*Christian Slaves, Muslim Masters: White Slavery in the Mediterranean, the Barbary Coast, and Italy, 1500–1800* (Basingstoke: Macmillan, 2003)

de Castries, Henri (ed.) *Sources Inédites de l'Historie du Maroc*, 22 vols (Paris: E. Leroux, 1905–61)

de Divitiis, Gigliola Pagano. *English Merchants in Seventeenth-Century Italy*, trans. Stephen Parkin (Cambridge: CUP, 1990)

de Gaetano, Armand L. *Giambattista Gelli and the Florentine Academy: The Rebellion Against Latin* (Florence: Leo S. Olschki Editore, 1976)

Debus, Allen G. 'Robert Fludd and the Use of Gilbert's *De Magnete* in the Weapon-Salve Controversy', *Journal of the History of Medicine* 19 (1964), pp. 389–417

Dekker, Thomas. *A Rod for Run-awayes. Gods Tokens, of His*

Feareful Iudgements, Sundry Wayes Pronounced Vpon this City, and on Seuerall Persons, Both Flying from It, and Staying in It (London, 1625)

Delisle, Leopold. 'Sir Kenelm Digby and the Ancient Relations between the Libraries of France and England', *The Library* 5 (1893), pp. 1–15

Descartes, René. *Oeuvres de Descartes*, ed. Charles Adam and Paul Tannery, 12 vols (Paris: Léopold Cerf, 1908)

D'Ewes, Simonds. *The Journal of Sir Simonds D'Ewes From the Beginning of the Long Parliament to the Opening of the Trial of the Earl of Strafford*, ed. Wallace Notestein (New Haven: Yale University Press, 1923)

Digges, Thomas. *Of the Great Art of Artillery* (London, 1624)

Dobbs, Betty Jo. 'Studies in the Natural Philosophy of Kenelm Digby: Digby and Alchemy', *Ambix* 20 (1973), pp. 143–63

Dobranski, Stephen B. *Readers and Authorship in Early Modern England* (Cambridge: CUP, 2005)

Donagan, Barbara. 'A Courtier's Progress: Greed and Consistency in the Life of the Earl of Holland', *Historical Journal* 19.2 (1976), pp. 317–53

Donaldson, Ian. *Ben Jonson: A Life* (Oxford: OUP, 2011)

Drake, Francis. *Sir Francis Drake Revived: Calling upon this Dull or Effeminate Age, to folowe his Noble Steps for Gold and Silver* (London, 1626)

Dubois, Elfriede. 'Conversions a la Cour de la Reine Henriette-Marie', in *La Conversion au XVIIe Siecle: Actes du XIIe Colloque de Marseille* (Marseille: CMR, 1983), pp. 201–8

Dubost, J. F. 'Between Mignons and Principal Ministers: Concini, 1610–1617', in *The World of the Favourite*, ed. J. H. Elliott and L. W. B. Brockliss (New Haven: Yale University Press, 1999), pp. 71–8

Duggan, Dianne. ' "London the Ring, Covent Garden the Jewell of that Ring": New Light on Covent Garden', *Architectural History* 43 (2000), pp. 140–61

Dursteler, Eric R. *Venetians in Constantinople: Nation, Identity and Coexistence in the Early Modern Mediterranean* (Baltimore: Johns Hopkins University Press, 2006)

Eamon, William. *Science and the Secrets of Nature: Books of Secrets in Medieval and Early Modern Culture* (Princeton: Princeton University Press, 1994)

Earle, Peter. *Corsairs of Malta and Barbary* (London: Sidgwick & Jackson, 1970)

Edgerton, Samuel Y. Jr. 'Galileo, Florentine "Disegno," and the "Strange Spottednesse" of the Moon', *Art Journal* 44.3 (1984), pp. 225–32

Edwards, Francis (ed.) *The Gunpowder Plot: The Narrative of Oswald Tesimond alias Greenway* (London: Folio Society, 1973)

Elliott, J. H. 'El Greco's Mediterranean: The Encounter of Civilisations', in *Spain, Europe and the Wider World 1500–1800* (New Haven: Yale University Press, 2009), pp. 233–53

Engels, Marie-Christine. *Merchants, Interlopers and Corsairs: The 'Flemish' Community in Livorno and Genoa (1615–35)* (Hilversum: Verloren, 1997)

Epstein, Mortimer. *The Early History of the Levant Company* (London: George Routledge & Sons, 1908)

Ernst, Germana. 'Astrology, Religion and Politics in Counter-Reformation Rome', in *Science, Culture and Popular Belief in Renaissance Europe*, ed. Stephen Pumfrey, Paolo L. Rossi and

Maurice Slawinski (Manchester: Manchester University Press, 1991), pp. 249–73

Evans, Robert C. 'Jonson, Weston and the Digbys: Patronage Relations in Some Later Poems', *Renaissance and Reformation* 28.1 (1992), pp. 5–37

Evelyn, John. *The Diary of John Evelyn*, ed. E. S. de Beer, 6 vols (Oxford: Clarendon, 2000)

Fairholt, Frederick W. (ed.) *Poems and Songs relating to George Villiers, Duke of Buckingham, and his Assassination by John Felton, August 23, 1628* (London: Percy Society, 1850)

Farmer, Norman Jr. 'Fulke Greville and Sir John Coke: An Exchange of Letters on a History Lecture and Certain Latin Verses on Sir Philip Sidney', *Huntington Library Quarterly* 33.3 (1970), pp. 217–36

Faroqhi, Suraiya. *Subjects of the Sultan: Culture and Daily Life in the Ottoman Empire* (London: I. B. Tauris, 2000)

Fehl, Philipp. 'Access to the Ancients: Junius, Rubens, and van Dyck', in *Franciscus Junius F. F. and His Circle*, ed. Rolf H. Bremmer Jr (Amsterdam: Rodopi, 1998), pp. 35–70

Feingold, Mordechai. *The Mathematicians' Apprenticeship: Science, Universities and Society in England, 1560–1640* (Cambridge: CUP, 1984)

—'John Selden and the Nature of Seventeenth-Century Science', in *In the Presence of the Past: Essays in Honour of Frank Manuel* (Dordrecht: Kluwer, 1991), pp. 55–78

—'Decline and Fall: Arabic Science in Seventeenth-Century England', in *Tradition, Transmission, Transformation*, ed. F. Jamil Ragep and Sally P. Ragep (Leiden: Brill, 1996), pp. 441–69

Ferrell, Lori Anne. *Government by Polemic: James I, the King's*

Preachers, and the Rhetorics of Conformity, 1603–25 (Stanford: Stanford University Press, 1998)

Ferrier, R. W. 'Charles I and the Antiquities of Persia: The Mission of Nicholas Wilford', *Iran* 8 (1970), pp. 51–6

Finch, John. 'The Diary of John Finch', *Report on the Manuscripts of Allan George Finch Esq., of Burley-on-the-Hill, Rutland* (London: HMSO, 1913)

Fincham Kenneth and Peter Lake. 'The Ecclesiastical Policy of King James I', *Journal of British Studies* 24.2 (1985), pp. 169–207

Findlen, Paula. 'Jokes of Nature and Jokes of Knowledge: The Playfulness of Scientific Discourse in Early Modern Europe', *Renaissance Quarterly* 43.2 (1990), pp. 292–331

—*Possessing Nature: Museums, Collecting, and Scientific Culture in Early Modern Italy* (Berkeley: University of California Press, 1994)

Finocchiaro, Maurice A. *The Galileo Affair: A Documentary History* (Berkeley: University of California Press, 1989)

Fisher, Godfrey. *Barbary Legend: War, Trade and Piracy in North Africa 1415–1830* (Oxford: Clarendon, 1957)

Foley, Henry (ed.) *Records of the English Province of the Society of Jesus: Historic Facts Illustrative of the Labours and Sufferings of its Members in the Sixteenth and Seventeenth Centuries*, 7 vols (London: Burns & Oates, 1875–83)

Forcione, Alban K. *Cervantes, Aristotle and the Persiles* (Princeton: Princeton University Press, 1970)

Ford, Mr. 'A Seventeenth-Century Letter of Marque', *Proceedings of the Massachusetts Historical Society* 59 (1925–6), pp. 3–25

Foster, Michael. 'Walter Montague, Courtier, Diplomat and Abbot, 1603–77 – I', *The Downside Review* 96 (1978), pp. 85–102

—'Thomas Allen (1540–1632), Gloucester Hall and the Survival of Catholicism in post-Reformation Oxford', *Oxoniensia* 46 (1981), pp. 99–128

—*Major-General Sir John Digby, 'Peerlesse champion and mirrour of perfect chivalrie'* (London: Royal Stuart Society, 1982)

—'Thomas Allen, Gloucester Hall, and the Bodleian Library', *Downside Review* 100 (1982), pp. 116–37

—'Sir Kenelm Digby (1603–65) as Man of Religion and Thinker I: Intellectual Formation', *Downside Review* 106 (1988), pp. 35–58

—'Digby, Sir Kenelm (1603–1665)', *Oxford Dictionary of National Biography* (Oxford University Press, 2004; online edition, Jan 2009)

Fowler, Alastair. *Spenser and the Numbers of Time* (London: Routledge, 1964)

Fraser, Antonia. *The Gunpowder Plot: Terror and Faith in 1605* (London: Weidenfeld & Nicolson, 1996)

Freedberg, David. *The Eye of the Lynx: Galileo, His Friends, and the Beginnings of Modern Natural History* (Chicago: University of Chicago Press, 2002)

Friedman, Ellen G. *Spanish Captives in North Africa in the Early Modern Age* (Madison: The University of Wisconsin Press, 1983)

Fuchs, Barbara. *Mimesis and Empire: The New World, Islam, and European Identities* (Cambridge: CUP, 2001)

Fuller, Thomas. *The Historie of the Holy Warre* (Cambridge, 1639)

Fulton, Thomas Wemyss. *The Sovereignty of the Sea* (Edinburgh: W. Blackwood & Sons, 1911)

Fury, Cheryl A. 'Health and Health Care at Sea', in *The Social*

History of English Seamen, 1485–1649, ed. Cheryl A. Fury (Woodbridge: Boydell, 2012), pp. 193–227

Fusaro, Maria. *Uva Passa: Una Guerra Commerciale tra Venezia e l'Inghilterra (1540–1640)* (Venice: Il Cardo, 1996)

Gabbey Alan and Robert E. Hall. 'The Melon and the Dictionary: Reflections on Descartes's Dreams', *Journal of the History of Ideas* 59.4 (1998), pp. 651–68

Gabrieli, Vittorio (ed.) 'La Misione di Digby alla Corte de Innocenzo X', *The English Miscellany* 5 (1954): pp. 247–88

—*Sir Kenelm Digby: Un Inglese Italianato Nell'eta Della Controriforma* (Rome: Edizioni di Storia e Letteratura, 1957)

Galileo Galilei. *Discoveries and Opinions of Galileo*, ed. and trans. Stillman Drake (Garden City, NY: Doubleday Anchor, 1957)

Garcés, María Antonia. *Cervantes in Algiers: A Captive's Tale* (Nashville: Vanderbilt University Press, 2002)

—(ed.) *An Early Modern Dialogue With Islam: Antonio de Sosa's Topography of Algiers (1612)*, trans. Diana de Armas Wilson (Notre Dame, IN: University of Notre Dame Press, 2011)

García-Arenal, Mercedes. 'Religious Dissent and Minorities: The Morisco Age', *Journal of Modern History* 81.4 (2009), pp. 888–920

García-Arenal, Mercedes and Miguel Ángel de Bunes. *Los Españoles y el Norte de Africa, Siglos XV–XVIII* (Madrid: MAPFRE, 1992)

García-Arenal, Mercedes and Gerard Wiegers. *A Man of Three Worlds: Samuel Pallache, a Moroccan Jew in Catholic and Protestant Europe*, trans. Martin Beagles (Baltimore: Johns Hopkins University Press, 1999)

Gardiner, Samuel Rawson. *The Earl of Bristol's Defence of His Negotiations in Spain* (London: Camden Society, 1871)

—(ed.) *The Constitutional Documents of the Puritan Revolution 1625–1660* (Oxford: Clarendon, 1889)

Godfrey, Eleanor S. *The Development of English Glassmaking 1560–1640* (Oxford: Clarendon Press, 1975)

Golius, Jacobus. *Catalogus Rarorum Librorum quos ex Oriente nuper advexit* (Paris, 1630)

Graves, Robert and Raphael Patai. *Hebrew Myths: The Book of Genesis* (London: Cassell, 1963)

Grayson, Cecil. *A Renaissance Controversy: Latin or Italian?* (Oxford: Clarendon, 1960)

Greene, Molly. *Catholic Pirates and Greek Merchants: A Maritime History of the Mediterranean* (Princeton: 2010)

Grogan, Jane. *The Persian Empire in English Renaissance writing, 1549–1622* (Basingstoke: Palgrave Macmillan, 2014)

Grosart, Alexander B. (ed.) *The Voyage to Cadiz in 1625, being a Journal, written by John Glanville* (London: Camden Society, 1883)

Guilmartin, John Francis Jr. *Gunpowder and Galleys: Changing Technology and Mediterranean Warfare at Sea in the Sixteenth Century* (Cambridge: CUP, 1974)

Guy, J. A. 'The Origins of the Petition of Right Reconsidered', *The Historical Journal* 25.2 (1982), pp. 289–312

Hakluyt, Richard. *The Principal Navigations, Voyages, Traffiques and Discoveries of the English Nation, Volume 5* (Cambridge: CUP, 1908)

Hale, J. R. 'Men and Weapons: The Fighting Potential of Sixteenth-Century Venetian Galleys', in *Renaissance War Studies* (London: The Hambledon Press, 1983), pp. 309–31

—'Gunpowder and the Renaissance: An Essay in the History of Ideas', in *Renaissance War Studies*, pp. 389–420

Hales, John W. and Frederick J. Furnivall. *Bishop Percy's Folio Manuscript: Loose and Humorous Songs* (London: N. Trübner & Co., 1867)

Hall, A. R. *Ballistics in the Seventeenth Century: A Study in the Relations of Art and War with Reference Principally to England* (Cambridge: CUP, 1952)

Hall, Joseph. 'The Honour of the Married Clergy', in *The Works of the Right Reverend Father in God Joseph Hall*, ed. Josiah Pratt, 10 vols (London, 1808), vol. 9, pp. 77–213

—'Quo Vadis? A Just Censure of Travel, as it is Commonly Undertaken by the Gentlemen of our Nation' [1617], in *The Works of Joseph Hall*, 12 vols (Oxford: D. A. Talboys, 1837–9), vol. 12, pp.101–132

Hall, Kim F. 'Culinary Spaces, Colonial Spaces: The Gendering of Sugar in the Seventeenth Century', in *Feminist Readings of Early Modern Culture: Emerging Subjects*, ed. Valerie Traub, M. Lindsay Kaplan and Dympna Callaghan (Cambridge: CUP, 1996), pp. 168–190

Hamilton, Alastair. *William Bedwell the Arabist 1563–1632* (Leiden: Brill, 1985)

Hammer, Paul E. J. 'Myth-Making: Politics, Propaganda and the Capture of Cadiz in 1596', *Historical Journal* 40.3 (1997), pp. 621–42

Hankins, James. 'The Myth of the Platonic Academy of Florence', *Renaissance Quarterly* 44.3 (1991), pp. 429–75

Hardie, Philip. *Rumour and Renown: Representations of Fama in Western Literature* (Cambridge: CUP, 2012)

Hardwicke, Philip Yorke, Earl of (ed.) *Miscellaneous State Papers from 1501 to 1726*, 2 vols (London, 1778)

Harris, Enriqueta. 'Velazquez and Charles I: Antique Busts

and Modern Paintings from Spain for the Royal Collection', *Journal of the Warburg and Courtauld Institutes* 30 (1967), pp. 414–20

Harvey, L. P. *Muslims in Spain, 1500–1614* (Chicago: University of Chicago Press, 2005)

Haskell, Francis. *Painters and Patrons: A Study in the Relations between Italian Art and Society in the Age of the Baroque* (London: Chatto & Windus, 1963)

Haskins, Charles Homer. *Studies in the History of Mediaeval Science* (New York: Frederick Ungar, 1955)

Haynes, D. E. L. *The Arundel Marbles* (Oxford: Ashmolean Museum, 1975)

Haywood, John A. *Arabic Lexicography: Its History, and Its Place in the General History of Lexicography* (Leiden: Brill, 1960)

Hebb, David Delison. *Piracy and the English Government 1616–1642* (Aldershot: Scolar, 1994)

Hedrick, Elizabeth. 'Romancing the Salve: Sir Kenelm Digby and the Powder of Sympathy', *British Journal for the History of Science* 41.2 (2008), pp. 161–85

Hegel, G. W. F. *Reason in History*, trans. Robert S. Hartman (Indianapolis: Bobst-Merrill, 1953)

Helgason, Thorsteinn. 'Historical Narrative as Collective Therapy: The Case of the Turkish Raid in Iceland', *Scandinavian Journal of History* 22 (1997), pp. 275–89

Heliodorus. *An Ethiopian Story*, trans. J. R. Morgan, in *Collected Ancient Greek Novels*, ed. B. P. Reardon (Berkeley: University of California Press, 1989)

Heller-Roazen, Daniel. *The Enemy of All: Pirates and the Law of Nations* (New York: Zone, 2009)

Henninger-Voss, Mary J. 'How the "New Science" of Cannons

Shook up the Aristotelian Cosmos', *Journal of the History of Ideas* 63.3 (2002), pp. 371–97

Herodotus. *The Histories*, trans. Aubrey de Sélincourt (Harmondsworth: Penguin, 1954)

Hess, Andrew. 'The Battle of Lepanto and Its Place in Mediterranean History', *Past & Present* 57 (1972), pp. 53–73

—*The Forgotten Frontier: A History of the Sixteenth-Century Ibero-African Frontier* (Chicago: University of Chicago Press, 1978)

—'The Mediterranean and Shakespeare's Geopolitical Imagination', in *"The Tempest" and Its Travels*, ed. Peter Hulme and William H. Sherman (London: Reaktion, 2000), pp. 121–30

Heylyn, Peter. *Cosmographie in four bookes: containing the chorographie and historie of the whole world, and all the principall kingdomes, provinces, seas and isles thereof* (London, 1652)

Hibbard, Caroline. 'The Contribution of 1639: Court and Country Catholicism', *Recusant History* 16.1 (1982), pp. 42–60

—*Charles I and the Popish Plot* (Chapel Hill, NC: University of North Carolina Press, 1983)

Hill, Christopher. *The Intellectual Origins of the English Revolution* (Oxford: Clarendon, 1965)

Hodges, H. W. and E. A. Hughes (eds.) *Select Naval Documents* (Cambridge: CUP, 1936)

Hodgkins, Christopher. 'Stooping to Conquer: Heathen Idolatry and Protestant Humility in the Imperial Legend of Sir Francis Drake', *Studies in Philology* 94.4 (1997), pp. 428–64

Holstun, James. ' "God Bless Thee, Little David!": John Felton and his Allies', *English Literary History* 59. 3 (1992), pp. 513–52

Holt, P. M. 'The Study of Arabic Historians in Seventeenth-Century England: The Background to the Work of Edward Pococke', in *Studies in the History of the Near East* (London: Cass, 1973), pp. 27–49

Horden, Peregrine and Nicholas Purcell. *The Corrupting Sea: A Study of Mediterranean History* (Oxford: Blackwell, 2000)

Horniker, Arthur Leon. 'Anglo-French Rivalry in the Levant from 1583 to 1612', *Journal of Modern History* 18.4 (1946), pp. 289–305

Howard, Deborah. *Venice and the East: The Impact of the Islamic World on Venetian Architecture 1100–1500* (New Haven: Yale University Press, 2000)

Howarth, David. *Lord Arundel and his Circle* (New Haven: Yale University Press, 1985)

—'Charles I, Sculpture and Sculptors', in *The Late King's Goods: Collections, Possessions and Patronage of Charles I in the Light of the Commonwealth Sale Inventories* (Oxford: OUP, 1989), pp. 73–113

Howell, James. *Instructions for Forreine Travell* (London, 1642)

—*Epistolae Ho-Elianae: Familiar Letters Domestic and Forren, divided into sundry sections, partly historicall, politicall, philosophicall, upon emergent occasions* (London, 1650)

Hudson, Hoyt H. 'Penelope Devereux as Sidney's Stella', *The Huntington Library Bulletin* 7 (1935), pp. 89–129

Hughes, Philip. 'The Conversion of Charles I', *The Clergy Review* 8 (1934), pp. 113–25

Hutchinson, Lucy. *Memoirs of the Life of Colonel Hutchinson*, ed. James Sutherland (London: OUP, 1973)

Hutton, Ronald. *Stations of the Sun: A History of the Ritual Year in Britain* (Oxford: OUP, 1996)

Huxley, Gervas. *Endymion Porter: The Life of a Courtier 1587–1649* (London: Chatto & Windus, 1959)

Israel, Jonathan I. *The Dutch Republic and the Hispanic World 1606–1661* (Oxford: Clarendon, 1982)

James, Alan. *The Navy and Government in Early Modern France 1572–1661* (Woodbridge: The Boydell Press for the Royal Historical Society, 2004)

Janacek, Bruce. 'Catholic Natural Philosophy: Alchemy and the Revivification of Sir Kenelm Digby', in *Rethinking the Scientific Revolution*, ed. Margaret J. Osler (Cambridge: CUP, 2000), pp. 89–118

Jardine, Lisa and Alan Stewart. *Hostage to Fortune: The Troubled Life of Francis Bacon* (New York: Hill and Wang, 1998)

Jonson, Ben. 'The Underwood', ed. Colin Burrow, in *The Cambridge Edition of the Works of Ben Jonson, Volume 7*, ed. David Bevington, Martin Butler and Ian Donaldson (Cambridge: CUP, 2012)

Justel Calabozo, Braulio. *La Real Biblioteca de El Escorial y sus Manuscritos Árabes: Sinopsis Histórico-Descriptiva* (Madrid: Instituto Hispano-Árabe de Cultura, 1978)

Kahane, Henry, Renée Kahane and Andreas Tietze. *The Lingua Franca in the Levant: Turkish Nautical Terms of Italian and Greek Origin* (Urbana: University of Illinois Press, 1958)

Kamil, Neil. *Fortress of the Soul: Violence, Metaphysics, and Material Life in the Huguenots' New World, 1517–1751* (Baltimore: Johns Hopkins University Press, 2005)

Kassell, Lauren. *Medicine and Magic in Elizabethan London. Simon Forman: Astrologer, Alchemist and Physician* (Oxford: OUP, 2005)

Keevil, J. J. *Medicine and the Navy, Volume I: 1200–1649* (Edinburgh: E. & S. Livingstone, 1957)

Keller, Eve. 'Embryonic Individuals: The Rhetoric of

Seventeenth-Century Embryology and the Construction of Early Modern Identity', *Eighteenth-Century Studies* 33.3 (2000), pp. 321–48

Kellett, Edward. *Returne from Argier: A Sermon Preached at Minhead in the Country of Somerset the 16 of March 1627 at the Re-admission of a Relapsed Christian into the our Church* (London, 1628)

Kelsey, Harry. *Sir Francis Drake: The Queen's Pirate* (New Haven: Yale University Press, 1998)

Kennedy, D. E. 'The Crown and the Common Seaman in Early Stuart England', *Historical Studies: Australia and New Zealand* 11 (1964), pp. 170–77

Kepler, J. S. 'The Value of Ships Gained and Lost by the English Shipping Industry During the Wars with Spain and France, 1624–1630', *Mariner's Mirror* 59 (1923), pp. 218–21

King, Henry. *A Sermon of Deliverance Preached at the Spittle on Easter Monday, 1626* (London, 1626)

Kishlansky, Mark. *A Monarchy Transformed: Britain 1603–1714* (London: Penguin, 1996)

—'Tyranny Denied: Charles I, Attorney General Heath, and the Five Knights' Case', *The Historical Journal* 42.1 (1999), pp. 53–83

—'Charles I: A Case of Mistaken Identity', *Past & Present* 189 (2005), pp. 41–80

Kissling, Hans J. 'Venezia come centro di informazioni sui Turchi', in *Venezia, Centro di Mediazione tra Oriente e Occidente, secoli XV–XVI: Aspetti e Problemi*, ed. Hans-Georg Beck, Manoussos Manoussacas and Agostino Pertusi, 2 vols (Florence: L. S. Olschki, 1977), vol. 1, pp. 97–109

Knight, Francis. *A Relation of Seven Yeares Slaverie Under the Turkes of Argeire* (London, 1640)

Knoppers, Laura Lunger. 'Opening the Queen's Closet: Henrietta Maria, Elizabeth Cromwell, and the Politics of Cookery', *Renaissance Quarterly* 60.2 (2007), pp. 464–99

Kuin, Roger (ed.) *The Correspondence of Sir Philip Sidney* (Oxford: OUP, 2012)

Lake, Peter. 'Constitutional Consensus and Puritan Opposition in the 1620s: Thomas Scott and the Spanish Match', *The Historical Journal* 25.4 (1982), pp. 805–25

—'Calvinism and the English Church, 1570–1635', *Past & Present* 114 (1987), pp. 32–76

—'Anti-Popery: The Structure of a Prejudice', in *Conflict in Early Stuart England: Studies in Religion and Politics, 1603–1642*, ed. Richard Cust and Ann Hughes (London: Longman, 1989), pp. 72–106

—'The Laudian Style: Order, Uniformity and the Pursuit of the Beauty of Holiness in the 1630s', in *The Early Stuart Church, 1603–1642*, ed. Kenneth Fincham (Basingstoke: Macmillan, 1993), pp. 161–85

Lando, Ortensio. *Commentario delle piu notabili e mostruose cose d'Italia ed altri luoghi*, ed. G. P. Salvatori (Bologna: Edizioni Pendragon, 2002)

Lane, Frederic C. 'Tonnages, Medieval and Modern', *Economic History Review* 17.2 (1964), pp. 213–33

—*Venice: A Maritime Republic* (Baltimore: the Johns Hopkins University Press, 1973)

Laud, William. *The History of the Troubles and Tryal of the Most Reverend Father in God, and blessed martyr, William Laud . . . and some other things relating to the history* (London, 1695)

Le Febvre, Nicolas. *A Discourse on Sr Walter Rawleigh's Great Cordial* (London, 1664)

Leroquais, Victor. *Les Livres d'Heures Manuscrits de la Bibliothèque Nationale*, 4 vols (Paris: Mâcon, 1927–43)

Lewis, Archibald R. 'Northern European Sea Power and the Straits of Gibraltar, 1031–1350 A. D.', in *Order and Innovation in the Middle Ages: Essays in Honour of Joseph R. Strayer*, ed. William C. Jordan, Bruce McNab and Teofilo F. Ruiz (Princeton: Princeton University Press, 1976), pp. 139–64

Lewis, Bernard. 'Corsairs in Iceland', *Revue de L'Occident Musulman et de la Méditeranée* 15–16 (1973), pp. 139–44

Leyland, John. 'Another Seventeenth-Century Sailor', *The Mariner's Mirror* 2 (1912), pp. 153–5

Lightbown, Ronald. 'Bernini's Busts of English Patrons', in *Art the Ape of Nature: Studies in Honour of H. W. Janson*, ed. Moshe Barasch and Lucy Freedman Sandler (New York: Harry N. Abrams, 1981), pp. 439-76

—'Charles I and the Tradition of European Princely Collecting', in *The Late King's Goods: Collections, Possessions and Patronage of Charles I in the Light of the Commonwealth Sale Inventories* (Oxford: OUP, 1989), pp. 53–72

Lilly, William. 'Mr Lilly's History of his Life and Times', in *The Lives of those Eminent Antiquaries Elias Ashmole, Esquire, and Mr William Lilly, Written by Themselves* (London, 1774)

Lister, Susan Madocks. ' "Trumperies Brought From Rome": Barberini Gifts to the Stuart Court in 1635', in *The Diplomacy of Art: Artistic Creation and Politics in Seicento Italy*, ed. Elizabeth Cropper (Milan: Nuova Alfa Editoriale, 1998), pp. 151–75

Lithgow, William. *The Totall Discourse, of the Rare Adventures, and painefull Peregrinations of long nineteen yeares Travailes* (London, 1640)

Lloyd, David. *Memoires of the lives, actions, sufferings & deaths of those noble, reverend and excellent personages that suffered by death, sequestration, decimation, or otherwise, for the Protestant religion and the great principle thereof, allegiance to their soveraigne, in our late intestine wars* (London, 1668)

Lockyer, Roger. *Buckingham: The Life and Political Career of George Villiers, first Duke of Buckingham, 1592–1628* (London: Longman, 1981)

London, April. '*Musæum Tradescantianum* and the Benefactors to the Tradescants' Museum', in *Tradescant's Rarities*, ed. Arthur MacGregor (Oxford: Clarendon, 1983), pp. 24–39

Lüthy, Christoph, John E. Murdoch and William R. Newman (ed.) *Late Medieval and Early Modern Corpuscular Matter Theories* (Leiden: Brill, 2001)

Mabbe, James. *The Spanish Bawd*, ed. José María Pérez Fernández (London: The Modern Humanities Research Association, 2013)

Macdonald, Michael. *Mystical Bedlam: Madness, Anxiety and Healing in Seventeenth-Century England* (Cambridge: CUP, 1981)

—'The Career of Astrological Medicine in England', in *Religio Medici: Medicine and Religion in Seventeenth-Century England*, ed. Ole Peter Grell and Andrew Cunningham (Aldershot: Scolar, 1996), pp. 62–90

MacGregor, Arthur (ed.) *Tradescant's Rarities* (Oxford: Clarendon, 1983)

Maclean, Gerald. *Looking East: English Writing and the Ottoman Empire before 1700* (Basingstoke: Macmillan, 2007)

Maclean, Gerald and Nabil Matar. *Britain and the Islamic World, 1558–1713* (Oxford: OUP, 2011)

Malcolm, Noel (ed.) *The Correspondence of Thomas Hobbes*, 2 vols (Oxford: Clarendon, 1994)

Malettke, Klaus. 'The Crown, *Minésteriat*, and Nobility at the Court of Louis XIII', in *Princes, Patronage and the Nobility: The Court at the Beginning of the Modern Age* c.*1450–1650*, ed. Ronald G. Asch and Adolf M. Birke (Oxford: OUP, 1991), pp. 415–39

Mann, Nicholas. *Petrarch Manuscripts in the British Isles* (Padova: Editrice Antenore, 1975)

Markham, Clements R. (ed.) *The Voyages of Sir James Lancaster, Kt., to the East Indies* (London: Hakluyt Society, 1877)

Marsden, R. G. 'Early Prize Jurisdiction and Prize Law in England', *English Historical Review* 25 (1910), pp. 243–63

—(Ed.) *Documents Relating to Law and Custom of the Sea*, 2 vols (London: Navy Records Society, 1915)

Martin, John and Dennis Romano. 'Reconsidering Venice', in *Venice Reconsidered: The History and Civilization of an Italian City-State, 1297–1797*, ed. John Martin and Dennis Romano (Baltimore: the Johns Hopkins University Press, 2002), pp. 1–35

Marvell, Andrew. *The Poems of Andrew Marvell*, ed. Nigel Smith (Harlow: Longman, 2007)

Massinger, Philip. *The Renegado*, ed. Michael Neill (London: Methuen, 2010)

Masters, Bruce. 'Trading Diasporas and "Nations": The Genesis of National Identities in Ottoman Aleppo', *The International History Review* 9.3 (1987), pp. 345–67

—'Aleppo: The Ottoman Empire's Caravan City', in *The Ottoman City Between East and West: Aleppo, Izmir, and Istanbul*, ed. Edhem Eldem, Daniel Goffman and Bruce Masters (Cambridge: CUP, 1999), pp. 17–78

Matar, Nabil. *Islam in Britain 1558–1685* (Cambridge: CUP, 1998)

—'English Accounts of Captivity in North Africa and the Middle East: 1577–1625', *Renaissance Quarterly* 54.2 (2001)

Mather, James. *Pashas: Traders and Travellers in the Islamic World* (New Haven: Yale University Press, 2009)

Maylender, Michele. *Storia delle Accademie d'Italia*, 5 vols (Bologna: A. Forni, 1926–30)

McClure, Norman E. (ed.) *The Letters of John Chamberlain*, 2 vols (Philadelphia: American Philosophical Society, 1939)

Mendoza, Ilenia Colón. *The Cristos Yacentes of Gregorio Fernández: Polychrome Sculptures of the Supine Christ in Seventeenth-Century Spain* (Farnham: Ashgate, 2015)

Mercer, Christa. 'The Vitality and Importance of Renaissance Aristotelianism', in *The Rise of Modern Philosophy: The Tension Between the New and Traditional Philosophies from Machiavelli to Leibniz*, ed. Tom Sorrell (Oxford: Clarendon, 1993), pp. 33–67

Mercer, Eric. *English Art, 1553–1625* (Oxford: Clarendon, 1962)

Miller, Peter N. 'Peiresc, the Levant and the Mediterranean', in *The Republic of Letters and the Levant*, ed. Alastair Hamilton, Maurits H. van den Boogert and Bart Westerweel (Leiden: Brill, 2005), pp. 103–22

Milton, Anthony. *Catholic and Reformed: The Roman and Protestant Churches in English Protestant Thought, 1600–1640* (Cambridge: CUP, 1995)

Milton, John. *Complete Prose Works of John Milton*, ed. Don M. Wolfe et al, 8 vols (New Haven: Yale University Press, 1953–82)

Mintz, Sidney W. *Sweetness and Power: The Place of Sugar in Modern History* (London: Penguin, 1985)

Molland, A. G. 'Roger Bacon as Magician', *Traditio* 30 (1974), pp. 445–60

Monson, William. 'The Office of a Gunner', in *The Naval Tracts of Sir William Monson*, ed. M. Oppenheim, 5 vols (London: The Naval Record Society, 1913), vol. 4, pp. 36–42

Montaigne, Michel de. *The Complete Essays of Montaigne*, trans. Donald M. Frame (Stanford: Stanford University Press, 1943)

Morris, John (ed.) *The Condition of Catholics under James I: Father Gerard's Narrative of the Gunpowder Plot* (London: Longmans, Green & Co., 1871)

Morrissey, Mary. *Politics and the Paul's Cross Sermons, 1558–1642* (Oxford: OUP, 2011)

Mortimer, Cromwell. Dedication to *The Philosophical Transactions of the Royal Society* 50 (1741)

Moshenska, Joe. ' "Spencerus isthic conditur": Kenelm Digby's Transcription of William Alabaster', *Spenser Studies* 27 (2012), pp. 315–28

Muir, Edward. 'The Marriage of the Sea', in *Civic Ritual in Renaissance Venice* (Princeton: Princeton University Press, 1981), pp. 119–34

Muldoon, James. 'Who Owns the Sea?', in *Fictions of the Sea: Critical Perspectives on the Ocean in British Literature and Culture*, ed. Bernhard Klein (Aldershot: Ashgate, 2002), pp. 13–27

Mundy, Peter. *The Travels of Peter Mundy, in Europe and Asia, 1608–1667, Vol.1: Travels in Europe, 1608–1628*, ed. Richard Carnac Temple (Cambridge: the Hakluyt Society, 1907)

Murphey, Rhoads. 'Merchants, Nations and Free-Agency: An Attempt at a Qualitative Characterization of Trade in the Eastern Mediterranean, 1620–1640', in *Friends and Rivals in the East: Studies in Anglo-Dutch Relations in the Levant from the Seventeenth to the Early Nineteenth Century*, ed. Alastair

Hamilton, Alexander H. de Groot and Maurits H. van den Boogert (Leiden: Brill, 2000), pp. 25–58

Nardo, Anna K. 'Academic Interludes in Paradise Lost', *Milton Studies* 27 (1992), pp. 209–41

Nashe, Thomas. *The Unfortunate Traveller and Other Works*, ed. J. B. Steane (London: Penguin, 1985)

Newman, William R. 'The Philosopher's Egg: Theory and Practice in the Alchemy of Roger Bacon', *Micrologus* 3 (1995), pp. 75–101

Newman, William R. and Anthony Grafton. 'Introduction: The Problematic Status of Astrology and Alchemy in Early Modern Europe', in *Secrets of Nature: Astrology and Alchemy in Early Modern Europe*, ed. William R. Newman and Anthony Grafton (Cambridge, MA: MIT Press, 2001), pp. 1–37

Nicholls, Mark. *Investigating Gunpowder Plot* (Manchester: Manchester University Press, 1991)

Norbrook, David. *Poetry and Politics in the English Renaissance*, revised edition (Oxford: OUP, 2002)

Oppenheim, M. *A History of the Administration of the Royal Navy* (Aldershot: Temple Smith, 1988)

Oughtred, William. *The circles of proportion and the horizontall instrument. Both invented, and the uses of both written in Latine by Mr. W. O. Translated into English: and set forth for the publique benefit by William Forster* (London, 1632)

Panofsky, Erwin. *Studies in Iconology: Humanistic Themes in the Art of the Renaissance* (New York: Icon Editions, 1972)

Parker, Geoffrey. *The Thirty Years War* (New York: Military Heritage Press, 1987)

—*The Military Revolution: Military Innovation and the Rise of the West, 1500–1800* (Cambridge: CUP, 1988)

Parker, Patricia. 'Preposterous Conversions: Turning Turk, and its "Pauline" Rerighting', *Journal for Early Modern Cultural Studies* 2.1 (2002), pp. 1–34

Parry, J. H. *The Age of Reconnaissance: Discovery, Exploration and Settlement 1450–1650* (London: Weidenfeld & Nicolson, 1963)

Partington, J. R. *A History of Greek Fire and Gunpowder* (Cambridge: Heffer, 1960)

Passannante, Gerard. *The Lucretian Renaissance: Philology and the Afterlife of Tradition* (Chicago: University of Chicago Press, 2011)

Patterson, Annabel. *Censorship and Interpretation: The Conditions of Writing and Reading in Early Modern England* (Madison: University of Wisconsin Press, 1984)

Patterson, W. B. *King James VI and I and the Reunion of Christendom* (Cambridge: CUP, 1997)

Peacham, Henry. *The Compleat Gentleman: Fashioning him absolute in the most necessary and commendable qualities concerning minde or body, that may be required in a noble gentleman* (London, 1637)

Peacock, John. *The Look of van Dyck: The Self-Portrait with a Sunflower and the Vision of the Painter* (Aldershot: Ashgate, 2006)

Pearsall Smith, Logan (ed.) *The Life and Letters of Sir Henry Wotton*, 2 vols (Oxford: Clarendon, 1907)

Peck, Linda Levy. *Court Patronage and Corruption in Early Stuart England* (London: Routledge, 1990)

—*Consuming Splendor: Society and Culture in Seventeenth-Century England* (Cambridge: CUP, 2005)

Pepys, Samuel. *The Diary of Samuel Pepys*, ed. Robert Latham and William Matthews, 11 vols (Berkeley: University of California Press, 1995)

Pérez Fernández, José María. 'Translation, Diplomacy, and Espionage: New Insights into James Mabbe's Career', in *Translation and Literature* 23.1 (2014), pp. 1–22

Pérotin-Dumon, Anne. 'The Pirate and the Emperor: Power and the Law on the Seas', in *The Political Economy of Merchant Empires*, ed. James D. Tracy (Cambridge: CUP, 1991), pp. 196–227

Petersson, R. T. *Sir Kenelm Digby: The Ornament of England.* (Cambridge, MA: Harvard University Press, 1956)

[Petty, William?]. 'Of Statues & Antiquities', in *The Works of John Milton*, ed. Frank Patterson (New York: Columbia University Press, 1931–8), vol. 18, pp. 258–61

Pevsner, Nikolaus and Elizabeth Williamson, with Geoffrey K. Brandwood. *The Buildings of England: Buckinghamshire* (London: Penguin, 1994)

Philip, Ian. *The Bodleian Library in the Seventeenth and Eighteenth Centuries* (Oxford: Clarendon, 1983)

Pinke, William. *The Triall of a Christians Sincere Love Unto Christ* (Oxford, 1636)

Pistolfilo, Bonaventura. *Oplomachia . . . nella quale con dottrina . . . e col mezzo delle figure si tratta . . . del maneggio, e dell'vso delle armi Distinta in tre discorsi di picca, d'alabarda, e di moschetto* (Siena, 1621)

Plot, Robert. *The Natural History of Oxford-shire, Being an Essay towards the Natural History of England* (London, 1705)

Plutarch. *Lives*, ed. and trans. Bernadette Perrin, 11 vols (Cambridge, MA: Harvard University Press, 1967)

Pons, Jacques. *Traite' des Melons, ou, il est Parle', de leur nature, de leur culture, de leurs vertus, & de leur usage* (Lyon, 1680)

Power, Amanda. 'A Mirror for Every Age: The Reputation of

Roger Bacon', *English Historical Review* 121 (2006), pp. 657–92

Principe, Lawrence M. 'Newly Discovered Boyle Documents in the Royal Society Archive: Alchemical Tracts and His Student Notebook', *Notes and Records of the Royal Society of London* 49.1 (1995), pp. 57–70

—'Sir Kenelm Digby and His Alchemical Circle in 1650s Paris: Newly Discovered Manuscripts', *Ambix* 60.1 (2013), pp. 3–24

Privy Council. *Acts of the Privy Council of England 1628 July–1629 April* (London: Her Majesty's Stationer's Office, 1958)

Pryor, John H. *Geography, Technology and War: Studies in the Maritime History of the Mediterranean, 649–1571* (Cambridge: CUP, 1988)

Purchas, Samuel. *Hakluytus Posthumus or Purchas His Pilgrimes*, 20 vols (Glasgow: James MacLehose and Sons, 1905–7)

Questier, Michael. 'Arminianism, Catholicism and Puritanism in England during the 1630s', *Historical Journal* 49.1 (2006), 53–78

Quinn, David Beers (ed.) *The Voyages and Colonising Enterprises of Sir Humphrey Gilbert*, 2 vols (London: Hakluyt Society, 1940)

Quintrell, B. W. 'Charles I and his Navy in the 1630s', *The Seventeenth Century* 3.2 (1988), pp. 159–79

Quiviger, François. 'A Spartan Academic Banquet in Siena', *Journal of the Warburg and Courtauld Institutes* 54 (1991), pp. 206–25

Raylor, Timothy. *Cavaliers, Clubs, and Literary Culture: Sir John Mennes, James Smith, and the Order of the Fancy* (Newark: University of Delaware Press, 1994)

Read, Sophie. 'Ambergris and Early Modern Languages of Scent', *The Seventeenth Century* 28.2 (2013), pp. 221–37

Redondi, Pietro. *Galileo: Heretic*, trans. Raymond Rosenthal (London: Allen Lane, 1987)

Redworth Glyn and Fernando Checa. 'The Kingdoms of Spain: The Courts of the Spanish Habsburgs 1500–1700', in *The Princely Courts of Europe 1500–1700*, ed. John Adamson (London: Weidenfeld & Nicolson, 1999), pp. 43–65

Reeve, L. J. 'The Legal Status of the Petition of Right', *Historical Journal* 29.2 (1986), 257–77

—*Charles I and the Road to Personal Rule* (Cambridge: CUP, 1989)

Revill, Philippa and Francis W. Steer. 'George Gage I and George Gage II', *Bulletin of the Institute of Historical Research* 31 (1958), pp. 141–58

Richards, Judith. ' "His Nowe Majestie" and the English Monarchy: The Kingship of Charles I before 1640', *Past and Present* 113 (1986), pp. 70–96

Rietbergen, Pieter. *Power and Religion in Baroque Rome: Barberini Cultural Policies* (Leiden: Brill, 2006)

Rhodes, Dennis E. 'Sir Kenelm Digby and Siena', *British Museum Quarterly* 21.3 (1958), pp. 61–3

Roberts, Julian and Andrew G. Watson (eds.) *John Dee's Library Catalogue* (London: The Bibliographical Society, 1990)

Roberts, Michael. 'The Political Objectives of Gustavus Adolphus in Germany, 1630–32', in *Essays in Swedish History* (London: Weidenfeld & Nicolson, 1967), pp. 82–110

Roberts, R. S. 'The Early History of the Import of Drugs into Britain', in *The Evolution of Pharmacy in Britain*, ed. F. N. L. Poynter (London: Pitman Medical Company Ltd., 1965), pp. 165–85

Robinson, Benedict. 'The "Turks", Caroline Politics, and Philip Massinger's *The Renegado*', in *Localizing Caroline Drama: Politics and Economics of the Early Modern Stage, 1625–1642*, ed. Adam Zucker and Alan B. Farmer (Basingstoke: Macmillan, 2006), pp. 213–37

Robson, Charles. *Newes from Aleppo: A letter written to T. V. B. of D. vicar of Cockfield in Southsex* (London, 1628)

Rodger, N. A. M. *The Safeguard of the Sea: A Naval History of Britain, 660–1649* (London: Penguin, 1997)

—'Queen Elizabeth and the Myth of Sea-Power in English History', *Transactions of the Royal Historical Society*, Sixth Series, 14 (2004), pp. 153–74

Roe, Thomas. *The Negotiations of Sir Thomas Roe, in his Embassy to the Ottoman Porte, from the year 1621 to 1628 Inclusive* (London, 1740)

Romm, James S. *The Edges of the Earth in Ancient Thought: Geography, Exploration and Fiction* (Princeton: Princeton University Press, 1992)

Rose, Susan. 'Mathematics and the Art of Navigation: The Advance of Scientific Seamanship in Elizabethan England', *Transactions of the Royal Historical Society*, Sixth Series, 14 (2004), pp. 175–84

Rushworth, John. *Historical collections of private passages of state, weighty matters in law, remarkable proceedings in five Parliaments* (London, 1682)

Russell, Alexander. *The Natural History of Aleppo and Parts Adjacent* (London, 1756)

Russell, Conrad. *Parliaments and English Politics 1621–1629* (Oxford: Clarendon, 1979)

Salvini, Anton Maria. *Discorsi Accademici di Anton Maria Salvini . . .*

Sopra Alcuni Dubbi Proposti nell'Accademia degli Apatisti, 3 vols (Florence, 1735)

Samuels, Richard S. 'Benedetto Varchi, the *Accademia degli Infiammati*, and the Origins of the Italian Academic Movement', *Renaissance Quarterly* 29.4 (1976), pp. 599–634

Sanders, Julie and Ian Atherton. 'Introducing the 1630s: Questions of Parliaments, Peace and Pressure Points', in *The 1630s: Interdisciplinary Essays on Culture and Politics in the Caroline Era* (Manchester: Manchester University Press, 2006), pp. 1–27

Sandys, George. *A Relation of a Journey begun An. Dom. 1610: foure bookes, containing a description of the Turkish Empire, of Aegypt, of the Holy Land, of the remote parts of Italy, and ilands adjoining* (London, 1627)

Savage-Smith, Emilie et al. *A Descriptive Catalogue of Oriental Manuscripts at St John's College Oxford* (Oxford: OUP, 2005)

Scappi, Bartolomeo. *The Opera of Bartolomeo Scappi (1570): L'arte et prudenza d'un maestro Cuoco*, trans. Terence Scully (Toronto: University of Toronto Press, 2008)

Scarisbrick, Diana. *Portrait Jewels: Opulence and Intimacy from the Medici to the Romanovs* (London: Thames and Hudson, 2011)

Schuchardt, Hugo. 'The Lingua Franca', in *Pidgin and Creole Languages: Selected Essays by Hugo Schuchardt*, ed. and trans. Glenn G. Gilbert (Cambridge: CUP, 1980), pp. 65–88

[Scott, Thomas?]. *Vox Coeli, or Newes from Heaven* ('Printed in Elesium', 1624)

—*Essex his Ghost Sent from Elizian* ('Printed in Paradise', 1624)

—*Sir Walter Rawleighs Ghost, or Englands Forewarner* (Utrecht, 1626)

Scott-Elliott, A. H. 'The Statues from Mantua in the Collection of King Charles I', *Burlington Magazine* 101 (1959), pp. 218–27

Selden, John. *Marmora Arundelliana* (London, 1628)

—*De Synedriis & Praefecturis Iuridicis veterum Ebraeorum Liber Secundus* (London, 1653)

—*The Table Talk of John Selden*, ed. Samuel Harvey Reynolds (Oxford: Clarendon, 1892)

Sells, A. Lytton. *The Paradise of Travellers: The Italian Influence on Englishmen in the 17ᵗʰ Century* (London: George Allen & Unwin, 1964)

Sharpe, Kevin. 'The Earl of Arundel, his Circle, and Opposition to the Duke of Buckingham, 1618–1628', in *Faction and Parliament: Essays on Early Stuart History*, ed. Kevin Sharpe (Oxford: Clarendon, 1978), pp. 209–44

—*The Personal Rule of Charles I* (New Haven: Yale University Press, 1992)

—'Van Dyck, the Royal Image and the Caroline Court', in *Van Dyck and Britain*, ed. Karen Hearn (London: Tate Publishing, 2009), pp. 14–23

Sherley, Thomas. *Discours of the Turkes by Sr. Thomas Sherley*, ed. E. Denison Ross (London: Camden Society, 1936)

Sherman, William. *John Dee: The Politics of Reading and Writing in the English Renaissance* (Amherst: University of Massachusetts Press, 1995)

Shirley, John William. 'The Scientific Experiments of Sir Walter Ralegh, The Wizard Earl, and the Three Magi in the Tower, 1603–17', *Ambix* 4 (1949), pp. 52–66

Shumaker, Wayne (ed.) *John Dee on Astronomy* (Berkeley: University of California Press, 1978)

Shuttleworth, J. M. (ed.) *The Life of Edward, First Lord Herbert of Cherbury, written by himself* (London: OUP, 1976)

Sidney, Philip. *An Apology for Poetry*, ed. Geoffrey Shepherd (Manchester: Manchester University Press, 1973)

—*The Countess of Pembroke's Arcadia*, ed. Victor Skretkowicz (Oxford: Clarendon, 1987)

Skretkowicz, Victor. 'Sidney and Amyot: Heliodorus in the Structure and Ethos of the *New Arcadia*', *The Review of English Studies* 27 (1976), pp. 170–74

—*European Erotic Romance: Philhellene Protestantism, Renaissance Translation and English Literary Politics* (Manchester: Manchester University Press, 2010)

Smith, Daniel Starza. ' "*La conquest du sang real*": Edward, Second Viscount Conway's Quest for Books', in *From Compositors to Collectors: Essays on the Book Trade*, ed. Matthew Day and John Hinks (London: The British Library, 2012), pp. 199–216

Smith, David L. 'Digby, John, First Earl of Bristol (1580–1653)', *Oxford Dictionary of National Biography* (OUP, 2004; online edition, May 2015)

Smith, John. *A Sea Grammar, with the Plaine Exposition of Smiths Accidence for Young Sea-men, Enlarged* (London, 1627)

—*The True Travels, Adventures and Observations* (London, 1630)

Smith, Nigel. 'Windmills Over Oxford: Quixotic and Other Subversive Narratives in England, 1606–1654', *The Journal of Medieval and Early Modern Studies* 39.1 (2009), pp. 95–117

—*Andrew Marvell: The Chameleon* (New Haven: Yale University Press, 2010)

Smith, Thomas. *Certain Additions to the Booke of Gunnery, with a Supply of Fire-Workes* (London, 1627)

Smuts, R. Malcolm. *Court Culture and the Origins of a Royalist*

Tradition in Early Stuart England (Philadelphia: University of Pennsylvania Press, 1987)

Southgate, B. C. *'Covetous of Truth': The Life and Work of Thomas White, 1593–1676* (Dordrecht: Kluwer, 1993)

Sparke, Michael. *Crumms of Comfort, the Valley of Teares, and the Hill of Joy: with the thankefull Remembrance, 1588 by water. The wonderfull Deliverance, 1605 by fire. And the Miracle of Mercy, 1625 by earth* (London, 1627)

Spencer, T. J. B. 'Turks and Trojans in the Renaissance', *The Modern Language Review* 47.3 (1952), pp. 330–33

—'Robert Wood and the Problem of Troy in the Eighteenth Century', *Journal of the Warburg and Courtauld Institutes* 20.1–2 (1957), pp. 75–105

Spenser, Edmund. *The Faerie Queene*, ed. A. C. Hamilton (London: Longman, 2001)

Spiller, Elizabeth. *Reading and the History of Race in the Renaissance* (Cambridge: CUP, 2011)

Spinka, Matthew. 'Acquisition of the Codex Alexandrinus by England', *Journal of Religion* 16.1 (1936), pp. 10–29

Starr, G. A. 'Escape from Barbary: A Seventeenth-Century Genre', *Huntington Library Quarterly* 29.1 (1965), pp. 35–52

Stedall, Jacqueline A. 'Catching Proteus: The Collaborations of Wallis and Brouncker II: Number Problems', *Notes and Records of the Royal Society of London* 54.3 (2000), pp. 317–31

Steensgaard, Niels. 'Consuls and Nations in the Levant from 1570 to 1650', *Scandinavian Economic History Review* 15 (1967), pp. 13–55

Stewart, Richard. 'Arms and Expeditions: The Ordnance Office and the Assaults on Cadiz (1625) and the Isle of Rhé (1627)', in *War and Government in Britain, 1598–1650*, ed. Mark Charles

Fissell (Manchester: Manchester University Press, 1991), pp. 112–32

Stoye, John. *English Travellers Abroad 1604–1667*, revised edition (New Haven: Yale University Press, 1989)

Strachan, Michael. '*Sampson*'s Fight with the Maltese Galleys, 1628', *The Mariner's Mirror* 55 (1969), pp. 281–9

—*Sir Thomas Roe, 1581–1644: A Life* (Salisbury: Michael Russell, 1989)

Strong, Roy. *Van Dyck: Charles I on Horseback* (London: Allen Lane, 1972)

—*Henry Prince of Wales and England's Lost Renaissance* (London: Thames and Hudson, 1986)

Summerson, John. 'Inigo Jones', *Proceedings of the British Academy* 50 (1964), pp. 167–92

—'Inigo Jones: Covent Garden and the Restoration of St Paul's Cathedral', in *The Unromantic Castle and Other Essays* (London: Thames and Hudson, 1990), pp. 41–62

Sumner, Ann. 'The Political Career of Lord George Digby until the End of the First Civil War', Unpublished PhD Thesis, University of Cambridge, 1986

—(ed.) *Death, Passion and Politics: van Dyck's Portraits of Venetia Stanley and George Digby* (London: Dulwich Picture Gallery, 1995)

Swaen, A. E. H. 'Robert Daborne's Plays', *Anglia* 20 (1898), pp. 153–256

Tenenti, Alberto. *Piracy and the Decline of Venice*, trans. Janet and Brian Pullan (London: Longman, Greens & Co., 1967)

—'The Sense of Space and Time in the Venetian World of the Fifteenth and Sixteenth Centuries', in *Renaissance Venice*, ed. J. R. Hale (London: Faber and Faber, 1973), pp. 17–46

Thrush, Andrew Derek. 'The Navy Under Charles I, 1625–40', Unpublished PhD Thesis, University College London (1991)

Tibbutt, H. G. 'The Life and Letters of Sir Lewis Dyve, 1599–1669', *Publications of the Bedfordshire Historical Record Society* 27 (1958), pp. 1–156

Todd, Margaret. *Christian Humanism and the Social Order* (Cambridge: CUP, 1987)

Toner, Jerry. *Homer's Turk: How Classics Shaped Ideas of the East* (Cambridge, MA: Harvard University Press, 2013)

Toomer, G. J. *Eastern Wisedome and Learning: The Study of Arabic in Seventeenth-Century England* (Oxford: Clarendon, 1996)

—*John Selden: A Life in Scholarship*, 2 vols (Oxford: OUP, 2009)

Tradescant, John. *Musæum Tradescantianum: or, A collection of rarities. Preserved at South-Lambeth neer London* (London, 1656)

Trevor-Roper, Hugh. 'A Case of Co-Existence: Christendom and the Turks', in *Historical Essays* (London: Macmillan, 1957), pp. 173–8

—*Archbishop Laud, 1573–1645* (London: Macmillan, 1962)

—'The Church of England and the Greek Church in the time of Charles I', in *Religious Motivation: Biographical and Sociological Problems for the Church Historian*, ed. Derek Baker (Oxford: Basil Blackwell, 1978), pp. 213–40

—*Europe's Physician: The Various Life of Theodore de Mayerne* (New Haven: Yale University Press, 2006)

Tucci, Ugo. 'The Psychology of the Venetian Merchant in the Sixteenth Century', in *Renaissance Venice*, ed. J. R. Hale (London: Faber and Faber, 1973), pp. 346–78

Tutino, Stefania. *Thomas White and the Blackloists: Between Politics and Theology during the English Civil War* (Aldershot: Ashgate, 2008)

Tyacke, Nicholas. *Anti-Calvinists: The Rise of English Arminianism,* c.*1590–1640* (Oxford: Clarendon, 1987)

van Eerde, Katherine S. 'The Spanish Match through an English Protestant's Eyes', *Huntington Library Quarterly* 32.1 (1968), pp. 59–75

Vérane, Léon (ed.) *Oeuvres Poétiques de Saint-Amant* (Paris: Librairie Garnier Frères, 1930)

Vitkus, Daniel (ed.) *Three Turk Plays from Early Modern England: Selimus, A Christian Turned Turk, and The Renegado* (New York: Columbia University Press, 2000)

—*Turning Turk: English Theatre and the Multicultural Mediterranean* (Basingstoke: Macmillan, 2003)

Waddell, Mark A. 'The Perversion of Nature: Johannes Baptista van Helmont, the Society of Jesus, and the Magnetic Cure of Wounds', *Canadian Journal of History* 38 (2003), pp. 179–97

Wadkins, Timothy. 'The Percy–"Fisher" Controversies and the Ecclesiastical Politics of Jacobean Anti-Catholicism, 1622–1625', *Church History* 57 (1988), pp. 153–69

Wakefield, Colin. 'Arabic Manuscripts in the Bodleian Library: The Seventeenth-Century Collections', in *The 'Arabick' Interest of the Natural Philosophers in Seventeenth-Century England,* ed. G. A. Russell (Leiden: Brill, 1995), pp. 128–46

Wall, Cynthia. *The Literary and Cultural Spaces of Restoration London* (Cambridge: CUP, 1998)

Wallis, John. *The Correspondence of John Wallis, Vol. 1,* ed. Philip Beeley and Christoph Scriba (Oxford: OUP, 2002)

Walsham, Alexandra. ' "The Fatall Vesper": Providentialism and Anti-Popery in Late Jacobean London', *Past & Present* 144 (1994), pp. 36–87

[Walsingham, E.?]. 'Life of Sir John Digby, 1605–1645', ed. G. Bernard, *Camden Miscellany* 12 (1910), pp. 67–114

Walter, John. ' "Affronts & Insolencies": The Voices of Radwinter and Popular Opposition to Laudianism', *The English Historical Review* 122 (2007), pp. 35–60

Ware, Timothy. *Eustratios Argenti: A Study of the Greek Church Under Turkish Rule* (Oxford: Clarendon, 1964)

Warneke, Sarah. *Images of the Educational Traveller in Early Modern England* (Leiden: Brill, 1998)

Waters, David W. *The Art of Navigation in England in Elizabethan and Early Stuart Times*, 2 vols (Greenwich: Trustees of the National Maritime Museum, 1978)

Watson, Andrew G. 'Thomas Allen of Oxford and his Manuscripts', in *Medieval Scribes, Manuscripts and Libraries: Essays Presented to N. R. Ker*, ed. M. B. Parkes and Andrew G. Watson (London: Scolar, 1978), pp. 279–314

Watson, Katharine J. 'Sugar Sculpture for Grand Ducal Weddings from the Giambologna Workshop', *Connoisseur* 199 (1978), pp. 20–26

Weiss, R. 'The Sienese Philologists of the *Cinquecento* – A Bibliographical Introduction', *Italian Studies* 3 (1946), pp. 34–49

Wheaton, Barbara Ketcham. *Savouring the Past: The French Kitchen & Table from 1300 to 1789* (London: Chatto & Windus, 1983)

Whitaker, Lucy. 'L'Accoglienza della Collezione Gonzaga in Inghilterra', in *Gonzaga: La Celeste Galeria*, ed. Raffaella Morselli (Milan: Skira Editore, 2002), pp. 233–49

White, Christopher. *Anthony van Dyck: Thomas Howard, Earl of Arundel* (Malibu: The J. Paul Getty Museum, 1995)

Whitmarsh, Tim. 'The Birth of a Prodigy: Heliodorus and the

Genealogy of Hellenism', in *Studies in Heliodorus*, ed. Richard Hunter (Cambridge: Cambridge Philological Society, 1998), pp. 93–124

Wiener, Carol Z. 'The Beleaguered Isle: A Study of Elizabethan and Early Jacobean Anti-Catholicism', *Past & Present* 51 (1971), pp. 27–62

Wilkins, Ernest Hatch. *Life of Petrarch* (Chicago: University of Chicago Press, 1961)

Williams, Glanmor. 'The Stradling Family', in *The Story of St Donat's Castle and Atlantic College*, ed. Roy Denning (Cowbridge: D. Brown & Sons, 1983), pp. 17–53

Williams, Michael E. *St Alban's College, Valladolid: Four Centuries of English Catholic Presence in Spain* (London: Hurst, 1986)

Winthrop, John. *The Journal of John Winthrop, 1630–1649: Abridged Edition*, ed. Richard S. Dunn and Laetitia Yeandle (Cambridge, MA: Harvard University Press, 1996)

Winthrop Jr, John. 'The Winthrop Papers', *Collections of the Massachusetts Historical Society*, third series, vol. 10 (Boston, 1849), 1-126.

—*The Winthrop Papers volume I: 1498–1628* (Boston: The Massachusetts Historical Society, 1929)

—*The Winthrop Papers Volume 4: 1638–1644* (Boston: The Massachusetts Historical Society, 1944)

Winthrop, Robert C. (ed.) *Life and Letters of John Winthrop* (Boston: Tickner and Fields, 1864)

Wolf, John B. *The Barbary Coast: Algiers Under the Turks, 1500 to 1830* (New York: Norton, 1979)

Wolfert, Paula. *Mediterranean Grains and Greens* (London: Kyle Cathie, 1999)

Wood, Alfred C. *A History of the Levant Company* (Oxford: OUP, 1935)

Wood, Anthony à. *Athenae Oxoniensies*, ed. Philip Bliss, 4 vols (London, 1817)

Wood, Jeremy. 'Van Dyck: A Catholic Artist in Protestant England, and the Notes on Painting Compiled by Francis Russell, 4th Earl of Bedford', in *van Dyck, 1599–1999: Conjectures and Refutations*, ed. Hans Vlieghe (Turnhout: Brepols, 2001), pp. 167–98

Woodward, Walter W. *Prospero's America: John Winthrop, Jr., Alchemy, and the Creation of New England Culture, 1606–1676* (Chapel Hill: University of North Carolina Press, 2010)

Woolf, Daniel R. 'Two Elizabeths? James I and the Late Queen's Famous Memory', *Canadian Journal of History* 20.2 (1985), pp. 167–91

—'Constance, Constancy and Ambition in the Career and Writings of James Howell', in *Public Duty and Private Conscience in Seventeenth-Century England: Essays Presented to G. E. Aylmer* (Oxford: Clarendon, 1993), pp. 243–78

Wootton, David. *Galileo: Watcher of the Skies* (New Haven: Yale University Press, 2010)

Worden, Blair. 'Toleration and the Cromwellian Protectorate', in *Persecution and Toleration*, ed. W. J. Shiels (Oxford: Blackwell, 1984), pp. 199–233

Wotton, Henry. 'The Life and Death of George Villiers, Late Duke of Buckingham', in *Reliquiae Wottonianae* (London, 1654)

Wright, Thomas Goddard. *Literary Culture in Early New England 1620–1730* (New Haven: Yale University Press, 1920)

Wynn, Richard. 'Sir Richard Wynn's Account of the Journey of Prince Charles's Servants into Spain in the Year 1623', appended to *Historia vitæ et regni Ricardi II Angliæ Regis* (Oxford, 1729), pp. 299–341

Yates, Frances. *The Rosicrucian Enlightenment* (London: Routledge, 1972)

Young, Michael B. *Servility and Service: The Life and Work of Sir John Coke* (Woodbridge: Boydell, 1985)

Young, Patrick (ed.) *Clementis ad Corinthios epistola prior* (Oxford, 1633)

NOTES

Prologue

1   '. . . his body was failing . . .' With his extensive medical knowledge,
     Kenelm knew that these pains were caused by gout and kidney stones.
     These maladies were common among the well-to-do of the time, but
     the attempted cures were either useless, or more dangerous and painful
     than the condition itself, and he had no wish to go under the knife at
     his advanced age. Just surviving such a procedure could be a source
     of pride: Samuel Pepys, who endured a horrifically painful extraction,
     carried one of his kidney stones with him for years: it was the size of
     a tennis ball, and he enjoyed showing it off to his friends. (Pepys, vol.
     10, pp. 172–3.)

1   '. . . drawn up his will . . .' Kenelm's will is now TNA, PROB/11/325,
     ff. 109v–111v; there is a copy in BL MS Additional 38175, ff. 52–60.
     Kenelm's handwriting really is a pleasure to read, especially by the
     standards of many seventeenth-century scrawls, and its whorls and
     abrupt shifts of size and direction seem to capture something of his

irrepressible exuberance: even Aubrey noted that he 'wrote a delicate hand'. (2015, vol. 1, p. 325.)

1   '. . . packed with reminders . . .' The nature and contents of these rooms is suggested by the inventory drawn up after Kenelm's death: see British Library MS Additional 38175, ff. 48–51.

2   '. . . George Hartmann . . .' Hartmann posthumously edited Kenelm's collections of culinary and alchemical recipes for publication: in the preface to the latter he called Kenelm 'that Famous Man, and great Privy Councellor of Nature' whom 'I had the Honour and Happiness for several years to serve, beyond the Seas, as well as in England, and to attend on him more particularly in the Production of many of his incomparable experiments'. (*Receipts*, sig.A2^v.)

3   '. . . a series of intense religious scenes . . .' Sadly these paintings have now been lost: Kenelm described them in detail to the Italian art theorist Giovanni Pietro Bellori in the 1640s, when providing the factual basis for Bellori's brief biography of van Dyck. Had they survived we might have a more rounded sense of van Dyck's achievement – he too was a fervent Catholic – whereas he tends to be associated overwhelmingly with courtly portraiture. (Bellori, p. 219; see Wood, 2001.)

3   '. . . plaster casts . . .' See Aubrey, 2015, vol. 1, p. 331.

4   '. . . the new collection . . .' It was partly the hope of recovering these volumes that compelled him to leave London and journey back towards France even in such ill health. Many of these volumes were claimed by the French Crown after Kenelm's death on the basis of the *droit d'aubaine,* a law designating all belongings of any foreigner who died in France as the property of the state. Some were bought back by Kenelm's relative George Digby, second Earl of Bristol, for the enormous sum of 10,000 crowns, but many remain in French libraries today (see Delisle). The books that remained, most of which are now in the Bibliothèque Nationale in Paris, included the gorgeously illustrated Book of Hours which guided Kenelm through his daily prayers. (Bibliothèque Nationale, Paris, MS Latin 1158; see Leroquais, vol. 1,

pp. 72–5.) There is also in Paris the amusing example of a collection of medieval Latin philosophical treatises (MS Latin 8802), in which Kenelm's handwriting on the flyleaf announces, 'Hic est liber publicae Bibliothecae Academiae Oxoniensis' – 'this book belongs to the public library of the university of Oxford'!

4 '. . . liberall to deserving persons . . .' Aubrey, 2015, vol. 1, p. 326.

5 '. . . never failing companions . . .' *Loose Fantasies*, p. 172.

7 '. . . the tools he had assembled . . .' The detailed inventory of his kitchen is in BL MS Additional 38175, ff. 50–51.

7 '. . . fully functioning laboratory . . .' See Aubrey, 2015, vol. 1, pp. 327–8: 'Since the restauration of Charles II. he lived in the last faire house westward in the north portico of Covent Garden . . . he had a laboratory there.'

7 '. . . greate writeinge chayre . . .' See BL MS Additional 38175, ff. 48–50.

8 '. . . a piece of metal . . .' See Scarisbrick, p. 106.

Excursus: The Brazen Head

16 '. . . *From The Famous Historie of Fryer Bacon* . . .' See Anon., 1627, sigs. C2–C3. Roger Bacon was a Franciscan friar, and one of the foremost intellectuals of the thirteenth century. During the sixteenth and seventeenth centuries, many scholars and scientists came to see him as a visionary genius, far ahead of his time, for his work in mathematical optics and his emphasis on an experimental method. After being introduced to Bacon's works in his student days, Kenelm formed a fascination with them that lasted his whole life: he not only consumed Bacon's writings greedily, but formed a grand plan with two of his friends to edit all of them, though sadly it came to nothing. Bacon's technical ingenuity and propensity to dabble in alchemy and other occult arts, though, earned him a place in the popular imagination as

a conjuror and a necromancer. The clash between these views of him was summed up in the title of a work that the Elizabethan scholar and magus John Dee planned to write: *The Mirror of Unity, or Apology for the English Friar Roger Bacon; in which it is taught that he did nothing by the aid of demons but was a great philosopher and accomplished naturally and by ways permitted to a Christian man the great works which the unlearned crowd usually ascribes to the acts of demons.* (See Shumaker, pp. 116–17.) The story of the brazen head appeared in a popular compendium detailing Bacon's various magical feats, published in the very year that Kenelm prepared to depart for the Mediterranean: already deeply interested in this figure, who seemed to point at once towards an enlightened future and a benighted past, and who attracted both admiration and fearful mockery, there can be no doubt that Kenelm read it avidly. (See Molland; Eamon, pp. 47–53; Power, pp. 669–70; Kenelm Digby to John Selden, 11 February 1637, Bodleian MS Selden *supra* 108, f. 78; and the letters between Kenelm, Selden and Gerard Langbaine: Bodleian MS Selden *supra* 109, ff. 376, 380, 434, 444; Bodleian MS Ballard 11, f. 22.)

Chapter 1

20 '. . . *any stain or blemish* . . .' *Loose Fantasies*, pp. 5, 12, 20–21. Faustina is a stock character in the narrative – the aged go-between, most famously embodied by the Nurse in Shakespeare's *Romeo and Juliet* – and is not based on a specific historical individual.

20 '. . . a goodly handsome person . . .' Aubrey, 2015, vol. 1, p. 325.

22 '. . . a cornerstone of the annual calendar . . .' See Cressy, p. 146.

22 '. . . thy holy name . . .' Sparke, sigs. N–N4.

22 'yearly and forever' . . . 'from the mouth of the Furnace . . .' King, p. 70; Sparke, sigs. A6–A6v. See Cressy, ch. 9; Hutton, ch. 39, esp. p. 395; Ferrell, ch. 3.

23 '. . . wandred a while . . .' Carleton, p. 274.

23 '. . . in his late twenties . . .' Everard was probably born in 1578, but the exact date of his birth is uncertain.

23 '. . . taken prisoner . . .' See Nicholls, p. 19. According to one report, published in 1627, the company met at Everard's lodging, and he had organised a hunting party to act as a cover story for their gathering, 'though his mind was Nimrod-like upon a farre other manner of hunting, more bent upon the blood of reasonable men than of bruit beasts'. (Carleton, p. 273.) Nimrod was the Old Testament king traditionally said to have hunted humans for sport: for the remainder of this work, Kenelm's father is referred to as 'Nimrod Digby'.

24 '. . . and we do . . .' Cobbett, vol. 2, pp. 187–8, 193.

25 '. . . almost of nothing else . . .' See Edwards, pp. 216, 218, 225–6; Nicholls, pp. 19–20, 52; Fraser, pp. 225–6, 229–32; Morris, p. 88. The remarkable story of Everard's final words was told by Sir Francis Bacon, who was present at the execution, and reported by Wood, 1817, vol. 3, p. 693.

25 '. . . Tata, Tata . . .' See Fraser, p. 230.

25 '. . . 'as complete a man . . .' Morris, p. 88.

25 '. . . the handsomest Gentleman in England . . .' John Aubrey to Anthony à Wood, 6 July 1672, Bodleian MS Wood F 39, f. 178; cited in Aubrey, 2015, vol. 2, p. 1448. The sources for these judgements were hardly neutral, it has to be said: they derive from a visit that Aubrey made to Kenelm's son John in order to discover further details about Kenelm's life some years after his death, and the younger Digby was presumably keen to suggest that he came from a long line of handsome men.

25 '. . . a Person of extraordinary strength . . .' Aubrey, 2015, vol. 1, pp. 324–5.

26 '. . . in natural duty to me . . .' Kenelm treasured this letter, keeping it by him throughout his life in a splendid silken bag: it was printed fifteen years after his death as part of a collection of documents relating

to the Gunpowder Plot, with an entire appendix of Everard's prison writings. (Barlow, p. 259.)

26 '. . . unto the third and fourth generation . . .' Exodus 20, Verse 5 (King James version).

26 '. . . let their name be blotted out . . .' Psalm 109, Verses 9–10, 13. In the 1630s, Kenelm was instrumental in convincing Coke's daughter, Lady Purbeck, to convert to Roman Catholicism: while this fitted in with Kenelm's own convictions, it is pleasing to imagine that he took a grim added pleasure in winning over the daughter of the man who had so gleefully convicted his own father.

26 '. . . three thousand pounds per Annum . . .' Clarendon, 2009, p. 438; Aubrey, 2015, vol. 1, p. 328.

27 '. . . within its confines . . .' Kenelm's mother devoted herself to a life of cloistered piety after Everard's death, but both she, and the house in which Kenelm spent much of his youth, never entirely lost their association with violent conspiracy in the eyes of suspicious Englishmen: as late as 1633, a boy questioned 'about Lady Digby's house at Gothurst . . . said that Lady Digby had a load of armour and powder brought to her house'. (*CSPD*, 1633–4, 74.)

27 '. . . pillars and friezes . . .' See Pevsner et al, pp. 59, 335–6. Extensive later additions were made to the house in the eighteenth and nineteenth centuries, and it has now been divided into private residences.

27 '. . . the ruins of it . . .' British Library MS Additional 41,846, f. 77. These words are from a speech that Kenelm delivered before the recently restored monarch, Charles II, at the very end of his life, calling for the toleration of Roman Catholics.

28 '. . . in the lineaments of their faces . . .' Kenelm discussed this point in his major philosophical work, the *Two Treatises* on body and soul, while discussing the characteristics of animals, which 'passeth by generation to the offspring, which is a thing so common, even in mankinde, as there can be no doubt of it'. His immediate interest was whether intellectual rather than treasonous traits might be inherited:

'The children of great Mathematicians, who have been used to busie their fantasies continually with figures and proportions, have been oftentimes observed, to have a naturall bent unto those sciences.' (*Two Treatises*, 328.)

29 '. . . Catholic doctrine and practice . . .' Foley, 1.462–4. Gerard describes Mary's father, William Mulsho, as 'a thorough heretic' – that is, a committed Protestant – who was interested only in hoarding up a fortune for his daughters, and claimed that no one else in her family had any Catholic leanings.

29 Later in life, just as Kenelm was emerging into the public realm in the early 1620s, Fisher was involved in a series of prominent public debates with Bishop William Laud and King James himself regarding the validity of the Catholic and Protestant Churches. See Wadkins; Milton, 1995, pp. 163–8.

29 '. . . herb and vegetable garden . . .' See Pevsner et al, p. 337.

30 '. . . continued a prettie while . . .' Bodleian MS Ashmole 174, f. 77.

30 '. . . to the country . . .' *Loose Fantasies*, p. 11.

30 '. . . to meet and talk . . .' *Loose Fantasies*, p. 12.

31 '. . . upon the earth . . .' Kenelm Digby to his three sons, 18 May 1633; 'Letter-Book', p. 123.

31 '. . . litle moule upon her cheeke . . .' Kenelm Digby to an unnamed friend, 11 September 1633; 'Letter-Book', p. 147; Kenelm Digby to his brother, 17 June 1633; 'Letter-Book', p. 83.

31 '. . . my childish yeares . . .' Kenelm Digby to his brother, 24 June 1633; 'Letter-Book', pp. 144–5.

32 '. . . vertues of an heroyke mind . . .' Kenelm Digby to his brother, 24 June 1633; 'Letter-Book', p. 144.

32 '. . . the measure and cadence of Romanzes . . .' Kenelm Digby to Tobie Matthew, 15 September 1641, British Library MS Additional 41,846, f. 56ᵛ.

32 '. . . most pleasingly affable to all . . .' Kenelm Digby to his three sons, 18 May 1633; 'Letter-Book', p. 128.

32 '. . . never flame burned clearer . . .' Kenelm Digby to his brother, undated; 'Letter-Book', p. 138.

32 '. . . peacefull friendship . . .' Kenelm Digby to his three sons, 18 May 1633; 'Letter-Book', p. 122. Kenelm's constant stress on the deep friendship that he and Venetia shared is particularly notable because historians have often argued that the modern ideal of marriage as a relationship between individuals founded on mutual respect was forged among ordinary Puritans in the seventeenth century, who argued for spiritual (if not actual) equality between husband and wife, while Catholics saw marriage as, at best, a necessary evil to be pursued solely for procreation (Todd, pp. 96–101, 104). Theirs, though, was a marriage of true friends founded in their shared Catholicism.

33 '. . . her sleepe and rest . . .' Kenelm Digby to his three sons, 18 May 1633; 'Letter-Book', pp. 123–4, 128.

33 '. . . she never forgate . . .' Kenelm Digby to his three sons, 18 May 1633; 'Letter-Book', p. 131.

34 '. . . the studied eloquence of Philosophers . . .' Kenelm Digby to his brother, 17 June 1633; 'Letter-Book', p. 84.

34 '. . . her behaviour and presence . . .' Kenelm Digby to his three sons, 18 May 1633; 'Letter-Book', p. 131.

34 '. . . an extraordinary beauty . . .' Clarendon, 2009, p. 438.

34 '. . . neither too hott, nor too pale . . .' Aubrey, 2015, 1.330–31.

34 '. . . the loveliest and the sweetest creature . . .' Kenelm Digby to his brother, 17 June 1633; 'Letter-Book', p. 83.

35 '. . . markes upon her bodie . . .' Kenelm Digby to his three sons, 18 May 1633; 'Letter-Book', p. 129; Kenelm Digby to his brother, 17 June 1633; 'Letter-Book', p. 83.

35 '. . . these colours expresse it not . . .' Kenelm Digby to his three sons, 18 May 1633; 'Letter-Book', pp. 129–31.

36 '. . . observe all passage . . .' *Loose Fantasies*, p. 35.

36 '. . . himself and his children . . .' Kenelm Digby to his brother, 23 May 1633; 'Letter-Book', p. 451.

36 '. . . a respectable woman of fortune . . .' It is also suggested in the *Loose Fantasies* that there was some personal animosity between her and Sir Edward Stanley – 'some unkindness' that had occurred – and that she planned to marry Kenelm to the daughter of Venetia's hosts, the Fortescues; but there is no other evidence for either possibility. One of Venetia's sisters married one of the Fortescues' sons.

37 '. . . the angry faucon . . .' Kenelm Digby to his brother, 24 June 1633; 'Letter-Book', p. 143.

37 '. . . some affrighting dream . . .' *Loose Fantasies*, pp. 35–8; Kenelm Digby to his brother, 24 June 1633; 'Letter-Book', p. 143.

38 '. . . in their eyes . . .' Kenelm Digby to his brother, 24 June 1633; 'Letter-Book', p. 143.

38 '. . . the most famous love scene . . .' *The Aeneid*, Book IV. Kenelm's version lacks the atmosphere of Virgil's nightmarish sex scene in which lightning flashes, and nymphs ululate on the mountaintops, while Dido and Aeneas are busy in their cave.

39 '. . . very cunning at his weapon . . .' Morris, p. 88. John Aubrey wrongly believed that Kenelm's father was the author of a Latin philosophical discourse, and a pioneering work on the art of swimming: these were in fact by another Everard Digby, the Cambridge philosopher, who was a distant relation (2015, vol. 1, p. 325).

39 '. . . not naturally addicted to it . . .' See [Walsingham?], p. 70; *Loose Fantasies*, p. 32.

39 '. . . horny with frequent Praying . . .' Aubrey, 1972, pp. 101–2.

39 '. . . his medical practice . . .' see Macdonald, 1981, pp. 31, 59–61, 69.

39 '. . . He had known the Digbys . . .' Napier's casebooks show that he visited Gayhurst in 1599 and also treated Everard for an unspecified condition in early 1604, a year before his execution: Bodleian MS Ashmole 415, f. 12v; Bodleian MS Ashmole 228, f. 179.

40 '. . . whole cloak-bags . . .' See Lilly, p. 79; Kassell, p. 71. In one of his casebooks Napier records a particular visit on which Kenelm borrowed several of his books: see Bodleian MS Ashmole 213, f.73ᵛ.

40 '. . . addicted to all maner of learning . . .' Bodleian MS Ashmole 213, f.25.

40 '. . . Parson Sandie . . .' The reason for this nickname is unclear: Dr Lauren Kassell, the foremost authority on Napier's life and work, speculates that it derives from his family's roots in Sandy in Bedfordshire, but notes that this sits oddly with Napier's own birth in Exeter (private communication). I am grateful to Dr Kassell for this and other information on Kenelm's interactions with Napier.

40 '. . . curable or incurable . . .' Aubrey, 1972, pp. 101–2.

41 '. . . the exact configuration of the planets . . .' See Bodleian MS Ashmole 174, f. 75; Bligh, p. 71.

41 '. . . under the dominion of Venus . . .' Kenelm Digby to his brother, 17 June 1633; 'Letter-Book', p. 83.

41 '. . . a life carefully recalled and ordered . . .' See Macdonald, 1981, pp. 16–19, 156–7, 189–90, 210; Macdonald, 1986, pp. 67–8; Chapman; Curry, pp. 1–44; Newman and Grafton, pp. 11–12.

44 '. . . *whose name she knew yet not . . .*' *Loose Fantasies*, pp. 32, 39, 43, 47.

44 '. . . the plotters' plan . . .' See Smith, 2004.

45 '. . . brokering peace and achieving religious unity . . .' See Patterson, 1997.

45 '. . . fell ill of typhoid fever and died . . .' See Strong, 1986.

46 '. . . a sightseeing tour to Valladolid . . .' Diary of John Phelips, Somerset Record Office, DD\PH/211/16–34; van Eerde, p. 61; Bodleian MS Ashmole 174, f. 77.

47 '. . . the English College . . .' See Williams, 1986.

47 '. . . bleeding, supine Christs . . .' See Mendoza.

47 '. . . did not weare a gowne there . . .' Aubrey, 2015, vol. 1, p. 325.

48 '. . . a great friendship . . .' Aubrey, 2015, vol. 1, p. 325.

48 '. . . was wont to invite him . . .' Aubrey, 2015, vol. 1, pp. 302–3.

48 '. . . all the mathematicians of his time . . .' Wood, 1817, vol. 2, pp. 541–2. See Foster, 1981; Curtis, pp. 142–3, 236; Feingold, 1984, pp. 73, 82, 106, 157–8.

49 '. . . taught Sidney mathematics . . .' See Aubrey, 2015, vol. 1, p. 303; Kuin, pp. 561–2.

49 '. . . one of the finest private collections . . .' Allen had worked tirelessly, following the dissolution of the monasteries by Henry VIII, to salvage all the manuscripts he could from the wreckage of the religious houses, and obtained others from any available source. See Watson.

49 '. . . the writings of Roger Bacon . . .' Allen owned works by Bacon on a vast range of topics: from mathematics, the art of perspective, logic and metaphysics, to the nature of meteors and dreams. His collection also contained at least one astrological treatise and as many as five on alchemy and the philosopher's stone: Bodleian Library, Digby MSS 72, 76, 77, 119, 190, 204, 218. See the details in Hunt and Watson. Those who borrowed Bacon manuscripts from Allen included the Christ Church mathematician Thomas Payne, and the philosopher Thomas Hariot, who was one of the first men (and certainly the first in England) to look at the moon through a telescope, doing so earlier even than Galileo. (Feingold, 1984, p. 158; Clucas, p. 183; Edgerton, p. 226.)

50 '. . . took him as a conjuror . . .' Wood, 1817, vol. 2, p. 543.

50 '. . . accounted the same thing . . .' Aubrey, 2015, vol. 1, p. 303. Aubrey goes on to tell a particularly wonderful story of the fear that Allen's reputation could inspire. While Allen was staying with a friend in Herefordshire, 'he happened to forgett his Watch in the Chamber-windowe. (Watches were then rarities).' The maids entered to clean the room, and, 'hearing a thing in a case cry Tick Tick Tick', they 'presently concluded that this was his Devill', and threw it out of the window and into the moat to drown it. Fortunately for Allen the watch caught on a sprig of elder and was saved from its watery fate, but for the servants this happenstance only 'confirmed them that 'twas the Devill'. (Aubrey vol. 1, pp. 303–4.)

51 '. . . up his staires like Bees . . .' Aubrey, 2015, vol. 1, p. 303; Foster, 1981, pp. 99n.2, 126n., 178.

52 '. . . I had forgot the Fart . . .' Aubrey, 2015, vol. 2, p. 915.

53 '. . . depravation of manners . . .' Hall, 12.104, 115.

53 '. . . his greater future good . . .' [Walsingham?], p. 71; Foster, 1986, pp. 1–5. A decade or so after his Mediterranean Voyage, Kenelm himself would be hauled before the Star Chamber, the highest court in the land, on suspicion of sending his own sons 'into forreigne partes' to receive a Catholic education: Star Chamber Proceedings, 25 May 1636, TNA PC 2/46, p. 194.

53 '. . . am to begin my journey tomorrow . . .' Kenelm Digby to Richard Napier, 30 March 1620, Bodleian MS Ashmole 240, f. 131.

53 '. . . persons of quality that inhabit there . . .' *Loose Fantasies*, p. 43.

54 '. . . divided the nation . . .' See Malettke, esp. pp. 424–5; Dubost.

55 '. . . a fitter field for our wars . . .' *Loose Fantasies*, pp. 43–5, 47, 52–3.

56 '. . . the danger of her fury . . .' *Loose Fantasies*, pp. 56–7.

56 '. . . jealous of his affection . . .' *Loose Fantasies*, pp. 60, 65.

57 '. . . any diminution of sorrow . . .' *Loose Fantasies*, pp. 60–61.

57 '. . . by the Grandees . . .' Aubrey, 2015, vol. 1, p. 330–31.

58 '. . . the fire that was in his chamber . . .' *Loose Fantasies*, pp. 62–7.

58 '. . . ever more salacious details . . .' While living in Paris near the end of his life, he still sometimes 'bragged' that he was once 'sent for to the first Lady of Italy in a sack': British Library MS Additional 74237 Q, f. 70. The document containing this claim consists of three unbound sheets of paper, on which are written twenty-two short anecdotes relating to English Royalist exiles in Paris, recorded on 30 April 1659. No fewer than six of these are descriptions of Kenelm, a clear sign of his fame and the abundance of gossipy stories that still circulated around him at the end of his life. Some of them are wonderfully frivolous – the time that he grew a beard, becoming so handsome in the process that another nobleman's wife fell instantly in love with him, or the time that he fought a duel unarmed and disabled his opponent with a kick to the stomach. Some are more intellectually serious, with the last entry on the list quoting Kenelm on the behaviour of amber rubbed against straw as evidence for the 'emission of Attoms'.

58 '. . . preferable to the simple truth . . .' There are reasons to believe that Kenelm read great works of literature in the same way that he himself hoped one day to be read. On his travels he bought and enjoyed a copy of *Fiammetta*, a story by the great Italian writer Giovanni Boccaccio, in which a lady recounts her love for a merchant who runs off to Florence and falls in love with another woman. He was particularly struck by the depiction of an older woman lamenting her lover's departure, and it helped inspire the Queen of Attica's grief at Theagenes' supposed death: he described the work, in a handwritten note on the inside cover, as 'a lively description of a malicious and luxuriant woman that is in her declining yeares'. (Digby's note on the flyleaf of Boccaccio, 1557, British Library classmark C.134.a.9.) In this note he directly connected the *Fiammetta* to 'the tale of the widdow and the scoller' in Boccaccio's greatest work, the *Decameron*. In this gruesome and bitter fable, a learned young man falls for a rich widow who humiliates him by making him spend a night freezing in the snow, and he exacts terrible revenge by luring her to the top of a tower where he leaves her to get scorched by the sun. (Boccaccio, 1972, pp. 585–610.) Like many readers, Kenelm believed that the scholar in this story was based on Boccaccio himself, who was once spurned by a widow. 'The first part,' he wrote, 'was reall; but the scollers revenge (in whom he personateth himself) but fained.' He loved literature that offered its reader a pleasurable intermingling of autobiography and fantastic invention.

Chapter 2

60 '. . . *grew very affectionate to him* . . .' *Loose Fantasies*, pp. 59, 74.

60 '. . . drew a huge cheer . . .' See Cressy, p. 147. This tradition began only in the reign of Charles I, after 1625; effigies of Guy Fawkes did not begin to be burned until the nineteenth century.

61 '. . . among the more brutish cannibals . . .' See Cressy, p. 149.

61 '. . . entering Tuscany from the north . . .' This was the preferred route of English Catholic travellers, despite the claim that Theagenes travelled 'over the sea': see Stoye, p. 74; Bossy, p. 137.

62 '. . . many stately Pallaces . . .' Dallington, p. 9.

62 '. . . to the rest of Europe . . .' Howell, 1642, p. 105.

62 '. . . the art of sodomitry . . .' Nashe, p. 345. The Englishman corrupted by Italian licentiousness became such a cliché that it spawned a proverb: *Inglese Italianato è un diabolo incarnato* – 'an Italianate Englishman is the Devil incarnate'. (See Ascham, p. 26; Warneke, pp. 56, 106–8; Chaney, 1998.)

62 '. . . dissolut courses, and wantonnesse . . .' Howell, 1642, p. 106.

62 '. . . gave him letters of introduction . . .' Lord John Digby's admiration for Matthew, despite their opposed religious beliefs, was demonstrated when he was sent on his next diplomatic mission after Madrid. In the spring of 1621, some months after Kenelm arrived in Italy, he was sent by James to Vienna to discuss the opening crises of the Thirty Years War with the Emperor. He specifically requested that Matthew accompany him, on the basis of the latter's linguistic and political skills.

63 '. . . boastingly profess . . .' Henry Wotton to Sir Thomas Edmondes, 3 August 1607, in Pearsall Smith, vol. 1, p. 395.

63 '. . . do much harm . . .' Henry Wotton to the Earl of Salisbury, 5 September 1608, in Pearsall Smith, vol. 1, p. 434. Wotton was James I's ambassador to Venice, and one of the most important Italianate Englishmen, with a particular expertise in the country's architecture.

63 '. . . his friend Sir Francis Bacon . . .' See Chaney, 1985, pp. 264–7; Jardine and Stewart, pp. 492–3.

63 '. . . a particular connoisseur of painting . . .' Kenelm met Gage a few months after he arrived in Florence, while the latter was passing through en route to Rome, where he had been sent by James I to conduct secret negotiations with the Pope: see Revill and Steer, pp. 143–6; Barnes. The negotiations with the Pope concerned the

prospective marriage of James's son, Charles, to a Catholic princess, which is discussed in the next chapter.

65 '. . . wrought with knots and flowers . . .' Dallington, pp. 11–12; see Stoye, p. 71.

65 '. . . the prime Italian dialect . . .' Howell, 1642, p. 104.

65 '. . . illustrations and illuminations . . .' For the Dante commentary see Bulgarini; Kenelm's copy is British Library shelfmark 1479.b.6(7). The manuscript is Francesco Petrarca, *Sonetti e Trionfi*, now Bodleian MS Digby 141. It was particularly valuable because of its provenance: Kenelm claimed in a note on its flyleaf that it had once belonged to Aeneas Piccolomini, who became Pope Pius II in the fifteenth century, and had originally been copied 'by the hand of Andreoccius Gerardus, a knight of Siena, for his recreation att his houres of vacancy'. See further Mann, pp. 440–42; Rhodes.

65 '. . . during the Black Death . . .' Petrarch first wrote this passage, in a fit of sudden grief, on the guard-leaf of the splendid copy of Virgil's poetry that he had inherited from his father, and it was later incorporated into editions of his works: see Wilkins, pp. 23–4, 76–8.

65 '. . . famous due to my poems . . .' Bodleian MS Digby 141, f. 176; 'proprijs virtutibus illustris, et meis longum celebrata carminibus' (my translation).

65 '. . . his most treasured papers . . .' His handwritten version is in British Library MS Additional 41,846, ff. 102–3.

67 '. . . wandering simulacra . . .' See Wootton, pp. 157–62; Drake and O'Malley, pp. 36–7.

67 '. . . other geometric figures . . .' Galileo, p. 238. The work in question, *The Assayer*, was finally published in 1623, a few months after Kenelm left Italy. Its developing content was widely known due to the widespread debates in the years prior to its publication: see Redondi, pp. 28–67; Biagioli, pp. 267–311; Wootton, pp. 161–70.

68 '. . . pored over Galileo's works . . .' He acquired a rare manuscript copy of Galileo's book on the nature of tides, another work in which

the great man argued for a Copernican universe. '*Discorso del flusso e reflusso del mare, del sig. Galileo Galilei, primario filosofo e matematico del ser. Gran Duca di Toscana . . .*' (Bodleian Library, Digby MS 133, ff. 1–21.) One of Kenelm's earlier biographers speculates that he might have met Galileo personally (Petersson, p. 54): this is tempting to believe, but sadly improbable. Kenelm fulsomely praised Galileo in his later philosophical writings, even when disagreeing strenuously with him. 'Here we must crave patience of the great soule of Galileo (whose admirable learning all posterity must reverence) whiles we reprehend in him, that which we can not terme lesse then absurd.' (*Two Treatises*, pp. 83–4.) Since he was never shy of flaunting his personal connections, Kenelm would surely have mentioned a meeting had it occurred.

68 '. . . chemical medicine . . .' See Clericuzio, pp. 61–2.

68 '. . . devoted to its lore . . .' See Ernst; Baldini. After Maffeo Barberini became Pope in 1623, he grew terrified of widespread astrological predictions of his death, which led him to employ the controversial occult philosopher Tomasso Campanella: the two men locked themselves in a closed room at the moment of particular celestial peril, purified the air with perfume and smoke, and set up a symbolic representation of the heavens using torches. When Barberini finally cracked down on astrology it was not because he saw it as superstition, but because it was horribly efficacious: one contemporary justly described him as a Pope 'who banned others from astrology while being highly skilled in it himself'. Astrology was not escapist magic but a highly political science. (Ernst, pp. 263–71.)

68 '. . . patterns of apparently random dots . . .' See *Tractatus de arte Geomantiae*, Bodleian Library MS Digby 50, inscription on flyleaf. This manuscript was copied by the obscure translator Hugo Sanctallensis, and contained handwritten annotations from the late fifteenth century: see Haskins, pp. 77–9; Carmody, pp. 172–3; Charmasson, pp. 97–8, 108, 231.

70 '. . . some great point in theology . . .' Montaigne, pp. 222–3; Capatti and Montanari, pp. 38–40, 108–9.

70 '. . . heer choyse musique . . .' Tobie Matthew to Dudley Carleton, 19 August 1608, TNA, SP Tuscany 2/210; Stoye, p. 79.

70 '. . . gobbled avidly . . .' There is a recipe for 'thick mallow soup' in the first great Italian cookbook, Bartolomeo Scappi's 1570 *L'arte et prudenza d'un maestro Cuoco.* (Scappi, pp. 573–4.)

70 '. . . known as *khobbeiza* . . .' See Capatti and Montanari, p. 18; Lando, p. 164; Wolfert, p. 290. The mallow, though an everyday plant, never entirely lost the exotic and dangerous associations of its origins as a vegetable eaten mostly by Muslims and Jews, and was sometimes accorded special powers. It often cropped up in magical recipes, including one for a potion containing egg white, parsley seed, and the juice of radishes and mallows which claimed to allow a person to walk into fire uninjured, while Cleopatra was said to have eaten Jew's mallow soup each day in order to retain her beauty. (Partington, pp. 50, 53.)

71 '. . . soft and moist within . . .' *Closet*, pp. 246–7. It is tempting to imagine a connection between these intensely sugary mallows and modern marshmallows, but there is apparently none: while the term 'marsh mallow' to describe the variety of the plant that grew in swampy areas is attested by the Oxford English Dictionary as early as the tenth century, it is not at all clear how, or why, it started to be used in the nineteenth century to refer to a gelatinous confection.

71 '. . . pain in Urining . . .' *Closet*, p. 247.

71 '. . . violent or venereall exercise . . .' Ascham, f.29ᵛ; Peacham, p. 231. While there is no reason to believe that Kenelm was unfaithful to Venetia in Tuscany, he had good cause to avail himself of the medicinal virtues of sugared mallows in the years following her death, when he seems to have contracted venereal disease and suffered other sexual disorders. In the late 1630s he consulted his friend Theodore Turquet de Mayerne, who was James I's doctor and the greatest chemical physician of the age, and who prescribed treatment and an aphrodisiac.

(Mayerne's notebooks: British Library Sloane MS 1992 ff. 21–2; Sloane MS 2022 f. 107; see Trevor-Roper, 2006, pp. 23–9, 343, 356–7.) The treatment clearly did not have the desired effect, since in the late 1640s Kenelm wrote a luridly detailed letter to his friend the Roman scholar Cassiano dal Pozzo, describing his continued genital malfunctions and discussing possible chemical remedies. (Kenelm Digby to Cassiano dal Pozzo, 8 January 1647, Biblioteca dell'Accademia Nazionale dei Lincei e Corsiniana, MS Dal Pozzo XXXVII, ff. 362^r–363^v.) I am grateful to Kristina Ogilvie for illuminating discussions of seventeenth century sexual disorders.

72 '. . . the just measure of perfection . . .' Lloyd, p. 581.

73 '. . . fanned out like a scallop shell . . .' Dallington, p. 26; Stoye, p. 126.

73 '. . . the fairest and purest . . .' See Weiss; Stoye, p. 79.

73 '. . . countless learned academies . . .' There were as many as 800 of these institutions, varying in size and seriousness, active across Italy in the seventeenth century. The first academy in Siena was the *Intronati* (the 'thunderstruck' or 'stupefied'), founded in the 1520s.

73 '. . . interpreting Plato's wisdom . . .' See Panofsky, ch. 5; Chambers, esp. p. 13; Hankins; Samuels, pp. 607–8; Cochrane, pp. 4–8, 31.

73 '. . . the modern Tuscan tongue . . .' See Grayson; de Gaetano, pp. 69–86.

74 '. . . the beloved's smile or tears . . .' Salvini, vol. 1, p. 80; vol. 2, p. 16; Nardo, pp. 213–14.

74 '. . . lovers of knowledge . . .' See Maylender, vol. 2, pp. 432–4.

74 '. . . the Digby family coat of arms . . .' British Library MS Additional 41,846, f. 140: '*Ultima oratione da me detta nel'academia de Filomati di Siena quando me haveano dato per nome il fiorito . . .*'

75 '. . . the series of rich courses . . .' The *Filomati* sought to differentiate themselves from other learned academies by taking as their model not the Athenian academy of Plato but the more austere norms and morals of ancient Sparta. This did not suggest great gastronomic ambitions: the tough, uncompromising Spartans were hardly renowned for their

fine dining, and their characteristic dish was a decidedly dubious black broth, which tasted vile to anybody not born and raised in their city. (Cochrane, pp. 24–5; Quiviger; Plutarch,1.241.)

75 '. . . the similarity of watermelon and pork . . .' See Dati, vol. 3, part II, pp. 83–99, 152–64; vol. 3, part I, pp. 81–104; Nardo, p. 213.

75 '. . . a topic that gripped Kenelm . . .' British Library MS Additional 41,846, ff. 118–41.

76 '. . . astronomers, philosophers and poets . . .' British Library MS Additional 41,846, ff. 118–9, 121: '*Nel resto è di due spetie; l'una animata dalla viva voce, che procede dal petto per la lingua e per gli altri istrumenti necessarii alla favella, in parole articulate e distinte; e l'altra, cio è la scrittura, chef a l'officio della parola, come muta etacita, separata da parte fuora di noi, della quale la mano è l'istromento.*' (My translation.) Specifically he cited the astronomical poet Manilius, the philosopher Boethius, and the epic poems of Virgil and Ovid. See Peacock, pp. 233–4. The discussion of light may also have emerged from more recent engagement with Florentine science, since the nature of light was one of the topics on which Galileo had ventured daring new thoughts: he was convinced that it was a physical substance, composed of atoms or corpuscles, and had long been fascinated with a luminous rock found in Bologna known as the 'solar sponge', which emitted light without heat. See Redondi, pp. 44–9.

76 '. . . worth in letters . . .' Pistolfilo, unpaginated dedication; Gabrieli, 1957, pp. 27–9. 'Pallas' refers to Athena, Greek goddess of both wisdom and war.

78 '. . . a long time dangerously sicke . . .' Bodleian MS Ashmole 174, f. 78.

79 '. . . those with troubled minds . . .' See Roberts; Macdonald, 1981, p. 187.

80 '. . . land of Araby' . . .' Matar, 1998, pp. 89–98.

80 '. . . his physic, and his mathematics . . .' 'Fama Fraternitatis,' trans. Thomas Vaughan, cited from the appendix to Yates, 299; Woodward, pp. 30–33.

81 '. . . no other knows this Secret . . .' *A late discourse*, pp. 11–12. Digby described the powder and recounted its origins as a gift from this Carmelite in a speech that he delivered near the end of his life before the medical faculty of the university of Montpellier, which was one of the greatest centres of medical learning in Europe, and had particularly pioneered the use of chemical treatments: see Brockliss and Jones, pp. 127–34.

81 '. . . mere legerdemain . . .' See Debus. The origins of the salve were often attributed to the controversial German physician and alchemist Paracelsus. It came to particular prominence in the 1620s thanks to the publication of a Latin treatise arguing for its efficacy by the eminent Flemish physician Johannes Baptista van Helmont. In 1627, the year of Kenelm's departure for the Mediterranean, van Helmont publicly recanted his account when it was attacked by the Jesuits as heresy and sorcery, hence it was highly topical and disputed during these years (see Waddell).

81 '. . . convinced of its efficacy . . .' It is all too clear, to sceptical modern eyes, why the weapon-salve apparently worked so well. Kenelm advised the wounded patient 'to cast away all your Plaisters, onely keep the wound clean, and in a moderate temper 'twixt heat and cold' while the powder was applied to the injury. (*A late discourse*, pp. 9–10.) Given that seventeenth-century plasters and poultices, in keeping with the soundest medical wisdom, often involved applying substances like mustard, mouldy bread, or even fresh dung to open wounds in order to drive out bad humours, there is little wonder that a wound that was simply cleaned and kept warm while the healer fiddled about with his sympathetic powder on the other side of the room had a better chance of healing fully.

81 '. . . a Daemon or Angel . . .' *A late discourse*, pp. 3, 152.

81 '. . . God's active role in the world . . .' This was at once a very ancient and a very modern belief: atomism had been advanced in various forms by Greek philosophers and in the Latin epic poem *De rerum*

natura, by Lucretius, which was rediscovered in the fifteenth century and debated with particular intensity in Florence (see Brown). As atomist ideas were revived and elaborated in the sixteenth and seventeenth centuries, some denounced them as atheistic and others, like Kenelm, sought to reconcile them with Christian tenets, however unorthodox: he cited Lucretius as an authority on the very first page of his *Two Treatises*. (See Passannante, and the essays collected in Lüthy et al; for Galileo's own interests in and inclinations towards atomism see Camerota.)

82 '. . . making it whole . . .' *A late discourse*, pp. 23, 133–6.

82 '. . . in greater detail . . .' The strangeness of this combination was as challenging to Kenelm's contemporaries as it is to modern eyes. His book on the weapon-salve was among his most popular and influential among learned readers, going through twenty-nine English editions and being swiftly translated into English, German, Dutch and Latin. At the same time, it was mocked as ridiculous, and did Kenelm's reputation some damage among the wider public. In his mock-heroic poem *Hudibras*, the Restoration wit Samuel Butler poked fun at a character called Orsin. 'Learned he was in Medc'nal Lore/For by his side a Pouch he wore/Replete with strange Hermetick Powder,/That Wounds nine miles point-blank would solder,/By skilfull Chymist with great cost/Extracted from a rotten Post.' (Butler, 35: First Part, Canto II, ll. 223–8.) The weapon-salve became sufficiently famous that it featured on the Restoration stage in John Dryden's rewriting of Shakespeare's *The Tempest*, in which a character is cured by the application of an unguent to his sword. (See Bynum.)

83 '. . . known in great actions . . .' *Loose Fantasies*, p. 73.

84 '. . . shaped his course the same way . . .' *Loose Fantasies*, p. 74. India was often associated with magical practices by learned Europeans of Kenelm's day: John Aubrey reported 'wonderful stories of Bannians [Hindu traders] in India, *viz.* of their Predictions, Cures, &c., of their Charming Crocodiles, and Serpents: And that one of them walkt over

an Arm of the Sea; he was seen in the middle, and never heard of afterwards.' (1972, p. 83.)

85 '. . . magical characters . . .' *Loose Fantasies*, pp. 78–84.

86 '. . . the spirit vanished . . .' *Loose Fantasies*, pp. 84–7.

86 '. . . with which he controlled spirits . . .' See Hedrick. Behind both Kenelm's Brahman and Shakespeare's magus, both of whom use their books to force spirits to do their bidding, lies a much longer tradition, originating in the sapphire-bound book which the Archangel Raphael was said by Jewish sages to have given to Noah, containing the know-ledge of the stars and the art of mastering demons. (Graves & Patai, 113.) Other particularly relevant parallels include Atlante, maker of magic castles and illusions, who appears throughout medieval tales and in Ludovico Ariosto's wildly popular Italian romance *Orlando Furioso* (1532), and the malevolent Archimago in Edmund Spenser's *The Faerie Queene* (1590–96), who also conjures a replica of a beautiful maiden animated by a sinister sprite.

87 '. . . *they arrived safe* . . .' *Loose Fantasies*, pp. 94–5.

88 '. . . *slide away with least noise* . . .' *Loose Fantasies*, pp. 101–2.

89 '. . . 'a convenient house near the Ambassador's . . .' *Loose Fantasies*, p. 89.

89 '. . . four years his senior . . .' See Sumner, 1986; Tibbutt, pp. 5–7. Kenelm's close and easy relationship with these two men would be lifelong: in the late 1630s he exchanged a series of lengthy letters with George Digby on religion which were later published, and they constantly exchanged books. In August 1662, nearly four decades after they met in Madrid, Kenelm wrote a letter to George Digby, who by then was the second Earl of Bristol, in which he described running into Lewis Dyve 'casually att the bowling greene at Whitehall'. (Sherborne Castle Letter Book, Sherborne Castle, f. 197.)

90 '. . . any proposed marriage . . .' See Redworth.

90 '. . . charged at them . . .' *Loose Fantasies*, pp. 89–90.

91 '. . . flew into his neighbour's face . . .' *Loose Fantasies*, pp. 91–3.

91 '. . . by a mischaunce . . .' Bodleian MS Ashmole 174, f. 78.

92 '. . . clouds of sorrow . . .' *Loose Fantasies*, p. 94.

92 '. . . a kind of astonishment . . .' James Howell to Thomas Savage, 27 March 1623, in Howell, 1650, p. 59.

93 '. . . he rehearsed the ways . . .' See Sharpe, 1992, pp. 4–5.

94 '. . . with any great lustre . . .' Wotton, pp. 78–9. This biography was written by the same Henry Wotton who had been ambassador to Venice and reported on English Catholics in Florence. After listing the cascade of titles bestowed on Buckingham, Wotton concluded with the words, 'Here must I breath a while' – even to list his achievements was an exhausting enterprise.

95 '. . . prodigious comet . . .' Rushworth, p. 304.

95 '. . . more than any other man . . .' See Lockyer, p. 43.

95 '. . . solicitous to bring it to pass . . .' Clarendon, 1888, vol. 1, p. 14.

96 '. . . symmetry and gracefulnesse . . .' The context of this observation was a remark that Kenelm made in a letter to Tobie Matthew, describing a particularly beautiful woman at court. 'In short, the composure of her body, both for symmetry and gracefulnesse; may be the touchstone with her sexe, as the Duke of Buckingham was to ours.' (Kenelm Digby to Sir Tobie Matthew, 29 August 1641, BL Additional MS 41846, f. 42ᵛ.)

96 '. . . becomingness of his person . . .' Clarendon, 1888, vol. 1, p. 10.

96 '. . . his ability to adapt . . .' Buckingham's wife was a Catholic, and Kenelm would have heard of the antics of his mentally ill brother, Viscount Purbeck, who was treated by Richard Napier in the early 1620s for his violent fits, during one of which he smashed all the windows in a London house and cried out that he was a Catholic. (Macdonald, 1996, pp. 74–6.)

98 '. . . rocky and dangerous roads . . .' See the contemporary account by Wynn.

98 '. . . from the saddle of his horse . . .' See Wotton, p. 87.

98 '. . . withdrawal and restraint . . .' See Redworth and Checa.

99   '. . . had his portrait painted . . .' See Brotton, 2006.

99   '. . . as near the Roman form . . .' James I to the Prince and Duke, 17 March 1623, in Hardwicke, vol. 1, pp. 406–8; see Tyacke, p. 114; Patterson, 1997, pp. 323–4; Cust, 2007, pp. 35–6.

99   '. . . much advance any business . . .' *Loose Fantasies*, p. 97.

100   '. . . also in Welsh . . .' *Two Treatises*, p. 255. The book that the priest wrote about his endeavours with this man, which is Bonet 1620, is a landmark in the history of sign language.

100   '. . . *out from the servants mouth . . .*' *Two Treatises*, pp. 48–9. His experiences in the country also allowed him to continue ruminating on the natural antipathies that can exist between both objects and people: he recalled an instance 'in Spaine, of a Gentleman that had a horrour to garlike, who (though he was very subject to the impressions of beauty) could never weane himselfe from an aversion he had settled him to a very handsome woman, that used to eate much garlike'. (p. 332.)

101   '. . . worthy to be put in a new romance . . .' James I to Prince Charles and the Marquess of Buckingham, 27th February 1623, BL Harleian MS 6987, f. 13; cited from Bergeron, p. 151.

101   '. . . the Knights of Adventure . . .' Letter from Edward, Viscount Conway, TNA SP 14/139/26.

101   '. . . to undoe Enchantments . . .' Cherbury, p. 118.

101   '. . . for admitting Charles to her presence . . .' James Howell to Thomas Porter, 10 July 1623, in Howell 1650, p. 64.

102   '. . . only to be rebuffed . . .' See Mabbe, pp. 83–4; Redworth, p. 98. This work, written at the end of the fifteenth century by Fernando de Rojas, was wildly popular, especially so in Kenelm's milieu: it was translated into English around this time by another member of the Earl of Bristol's retinue, James Mabbe, who was also a Catholic: see Smith, 2009, pp. 108–11; Pérez Fernández.

102   '. . . an immediate rapport . . .' See Woolf, 1993, p. 245.

102   '. . . in foreign surroundings . . .' See Foster, 1978.

102 '. . . com to this Court . . .' James Howell to Thomas Porter, 10 July
1623, in Howell 1650, p. 63. These men included such hybrid figures as
Endymion Porter, who was half Spanish and had accompanied Charles
and Buckingham on their secret journey as their servant (Huxley).

103 '. . . drier and dustier pursuits . . .' *Loose Fantasies*, p. 102; see
Donagan, p. 323.

103 '. . . soon besotted with him . . .' *Loose Fantasies*, pp. 101–7.

104 '. . . took his close friend's side . . .' See Birch, 1848, vol. 2, p. 399.

105 '. . . sorrow and despair . . .' *Loose Fantasies*, p. 107.

105 '. . . diverse others in this Court . . .' Howell to Kenelm Digby,
undated, in Howell, 1650, p. 85.

105 '. . . the handsomest Coin . . .' Wynn, p. 339.

105 '. . . sundry different operations . . .' *Two Treatises*, p. 207.

105 '. . . to enable his departure . . .' See Redworth, pp. 134–6.

106 '. . . the glorious navy that was committed to them . . .' *Loose Fantasies*, p. 109.

Chapter 3

108 '. . . *wishes for the greatest light* . . .' *Loose Fantasies*, pp. 114–15.

108 '. . . with his owne hand and sword . . .' Bodleian MS Ashmole 174,
f. 79; British Library MS Additional 41,846, f. 77.

109 '. . . guided his hand aright . . .' *A late discourse*, pp. 104–5.

109 '. . . from her own mouth . . .' *Loose Fantasies*, p. 111.

110 '. . . so forward and so improper . . .' *Loose Fantasies*, pp. 111–19.

112 '. . . a Magician and a Sorcerer . . .' *A late discourse*, pp. 5–11; Bacon,
p. 258. Bacon died the following year, in 1626, when he caught pneu-
monia after packing a chicken with snow to experiment with the effects
of freezing, and his discussion of the sympathetic powder was published
posthumously in 1627. Kenelm stressed that Bacon had learned of it
from him in order to emphasise that he, not the famous scientist, was

first responsible for bringing the secret of cures at a distance into England.

112 '. . . a prime man in the powder treason . . .' John Chamberlain to Dudley Carleton, 20 December 1623, in McClure, vol. 2, pp. 530–31.

113 '. . . had children by her . . .' Aubrey, 2015, vol. 1, p. 326.

113 '. . . come not neare to brave Venetia Stanley! . . .' Aubrey, 2015, vol. 1, p. 331; 'Panders come Away,' ll. 2, 32, in Hales and Furnivall, pp. 104–5.

113 '. . . to make his peace with him . . .' British Library MS Additional 74237 Q, ff. 70–71.

114 '. . . a potential enemy to King and country . . .' See Wiener; Lake, 1989.

114 '. . . being allowed to creep back in unopposed . . .' See Walsham, esp. p. 44.

115 '. . . escape from the Papist yoke . . .' See Cressy, ch. 6; Cogswell, 1989a.

115 '. . . baying for war with Spain . . .' See Cogswell, 1989b.

115 '. . . traduced in most men's opinions . . .' *Loose Fantasies*, p. 110.

116 '. . . to attend his mother on her deathbed . . .' See Gardiner, 1871, pp. v–xiv; Sharpe, 1978, pp. 220–22, 230–31.

116 '. . . denounced the Spanish as dishonourable liars . . .' See Russell, pp. 145–203.

116 '. . . on the verge of entering the war . . .' See Parker, 1987, pp. 71–5; Cogswell, 1989, pp. 240–47. Mansfeld was himself a Catholic but had no compunction about waging war against his co-religionists when the price was right.

118 '. . . any employment about him of any trust . . .' John Chamberlain to Dudley Carleton, 20 December 1623, in McClure, vol. 2, pp. 530–31; James Howell to his father in Howell, 1650, p. 281.

118 '. . . continue to languish in Dorset . . .' Kenelm Digby to John Digby, Earl of Bristol, Sherborne Castle Letter Book, ff. 223–4; British Library MS Additional 9806, f. 1; see Gardiner, 1871, pp. xxv–xxvii.

120 '. . . seen walking atop the floodwaters . . .' Father Cyprien of Gamache, *Memoirs of the Mission in England of the Catholic Friars*, in

Birch, vol. 2, p. 302; Havran, p. 278. Catholics took these apparitions as a sign of God's wrath; Protestants, somewhat more mystifyingly, as a sign of heavenly favour.

120 '. . . duly sent to the Tower of London . . .' See Sharpe, 1978, pp. 232–3.

122 '. . . equally welcome on both sides . . .' *Loose Fantasies*, p. 125.

122 '. . . if he had knowne she was bestowed . . .' Kenelm Digby to his three sons, 18 May 1633; 'Letter-Book', p. 125.

123 '. . . never permitt me to be absent . . .' Kenelm Digby to his three sons, 18 May 1633; 'Letter-Book', pp. 125–6; *Loose Fantasies*, pp. 138–9.

125 '. . . *Theagenes acknowledged ingenuously that he was* . . .' *Loose Fantasies*, pp. 140–42, 163.

126 '. . . to mark the anniversary of her birth . . .' See Cressy, *Bonfires and Bells*, ch. 8, csp. pp. 134–6; Woolf, 1985.

126 '. . . farre more profitable . . .' [Scott?], pp. 34, 43; Lake, 1982; Adamson, pp. 167–9.

127 '. . . the vast Spanish Armada . . .' See Rodgers, 2004. Various scholars advanced historical claims for English ownership of the seas around England and beyond: the polymath and occultist John Dee went the furthest, making unprecedented argument for England's dominion over most of the seas in the northern hemisphere, and calling for the creation of an English navy that could make good these claims. (See Sherman, ch. 7; Armitage, ch. 4.) The anniversary of the Armada was yet another marked ever deeper into the nation's psyche with widespread annual celebrations: see Cressy, ch. 7.

127 '. . . almost brought him on his knees . . .' Anon., 1642, pp. 7–8; Appleby, esp. p. 224; Rodger, 1997, pp. 361–2.

127 '. . . *to folowe his Noble Steps for Gold and Silver* . . .' Drake, 1626; see Hodgkins, esp. p. 447. This volume was edited and compiled by Drake's nephew and namesake.

127 '. . . written by Sir Kellem Digbie . . .' National Library of Wales Classmark E5/4/22; for the original and its authorship, by either Drake or Humphrey Gilbert, see Quinn, vol. 1, pp. 170–75.

127 '. . . his owne eminent talents . . .' British Library MS Additional 41,846, f.76ᵛ. Raleigh was also brought back from the grave by the pen of Thomas Scott, in his 1626 work *Sir Walter Rawleighs Ghost, or Englands Forewarner*, in which the great hero's spectre justified himself and denounced the perfidiousness of the Spanish, particularly their ambassador to England, Gondomar. ([Scott?], 1626; see Beer.)

128 '. . . an enthusiastic amateur cook . . .' Kenelm would have been well aware of Raleigh's culinary pursuits, since he had established his kitchens in his house at Sherborne, which was given to the Earl of Bristol when he fell from grace, and Kenelm visited it frequently. (See Mercer, pp. 27–9; Hill, p. 220.) Raleigh's kitchen has now been reconstructed at Sherborne as a tourist attraction.

128 '. . . executed in 1618 for treason . . .' See Shirley; Hill, pp. 145–9, 206–7. When Kenelm himself was later imprisoned by order of Parliament in the early 1640s in Winchester House, he 'practiced Chymistry' there and 'made artificiall stones' as well as distilling medicines such as 'tincture of strawberries' for the cure of kidney stones, in direct emulation of Raleigh's alchemical imprisonment. (Aubrey, 2015, vol. 1, p. 327; Kenelm Digby to Robert Harley, 1 February 1642, Longleat House, Portland Papers vol. 2, f. 69.) Kenelm also directly copied and adapted Raleigh's most famous recipes: when a description of Raleigh's infamous cure-all, the 'Great Cordial', was published in 1664, its author quoted Kenelm's suggestion that he add 'the Flesh, the Heart, and the Liver of *Vipers*' to the recipe. (Le Febvre, p. 14.)

128 '. . . read it with gusto . . .' See Alexander, 2006; Patterson, 1984, p. 171.

128 '. . . a gallant, and a perfect gentleman . . .' *Two Treatises*, p. 413. In the preface to another of his later works, Kenelm specifically praised 'The Arcadia of Sir Philip Sidney (of whom I may say as St Augustin

did of Homer, that he is passing sweet and delightful, even in his vanities).' (*A Treatise*, sig.A3ᵛ.)

129 '. . . the ancient glory of our predecessors . . .' Bidwell and Jansson, vol. 2, p. 409.

129 '. . . tried and failed to remedy . . .' See Oppenheim, pp. 184–215; Peck, 1990, ch. 5.

129 '. . . to re-edifie and reform them . . .' [Scott?], 1624a, 36–7.

130 '. . . carrying away rich spoils . . .' See Hammer; Allen. Essex was yet another Elizabethan grandee revivified by the pen of Thomas Scott in these years: his 1624 work *Essex his Ghost Sent from Elizian* presented the spectre of the executed Earl recalling the glories of 1588 and demanding renewed anti-Spanish action. ([Scott?], 1624b.)

130 '. . . no more Drakes in England . . .' de Castries, vol. 3, p. 31; see Andrews, 1991, p.1; Grosart; Rodger, 1997, pp. 357–9.

131 '. . . a forced loan levied on his subjects . . .' See Adams; Cogswell, 1984, 1986; Rodger, 1997, pp. 360–61; Cust, 1987; Christianson.

131 '. . . rather than face the imperial general . . .' See Parker, 1987, pp. 77–8.

132 '. . . to aid the blockade of La Rochelle . . .' See Parker, 1987, pp. 76, 105.

132 '. . . limped back to England in disarray . . .' Cogswell, 2004.

133 '. . . these two wars so wretchedly entered into . . .' Clarendon, 1888, vol. 1, p. 51.

133 '. . . to take ships belonging to the enemy . . .' See Stewart; Andrews, 1964.

133 '. . . hundreds of French and Spanish ships . . .' See Kepler.

133 '. . . had been Sir Philip Sidney's muse . . .' Warwick's mother, Penelope Rich, was the inspiration for Sidney's beloved in his famous sonnet sequence Astrophil and Stella, which in turn helped inspire Kenelm's decision to rename Venetia 'Stelliana' when he wrote *Loose Fantasies* (see Hudson).

133 '. . . he fared no better than Buckingham . . .' See Craven, pp. 465–70; Cogswell, 1989, pp. 75–7, 96–8; Brenner, pp. 155–6, 252–3.

134 '. . . blaming one another bitterly for the debacle . . .' Bard, 1984, 1995.

134 '. . . gain himself honour and experience . . .' *Loose Fantasies*, p. 161.

135 '. . . the rich trades in gold and slaves . . .' It was later rumoured that Kenelm's 'first intentions were to go to Guinea to take some islands and found colonies, but the merchants of the East India Company objected'. (*CSPV*, vol. 21, p. 211.) Given that there is no firm evidence for this plan, it is more likely that it was a rumour that Kenelm put out to conceal his plans, not a genuine possibility.

135 '. . . crossed the seas in vast numbers . . .' See Andrews, 1972.

136 '. . . in his chambers in Gloucester Hall . . .' See Cormack, pp. 118, 124–7.

136 '. . . practical guides to seamanship . . .' See Rose; Waters, vol. 2, pp. 457–79.

136 '. . . nothing at all to any purpose . . .' Smith, 1627, p. 59; Digby, 1680, p. 90, no. 210. Smith was writing from first-hand experience: now best known to posterity as the supposed lover of Pocahontas in the New World, he had spent his younger years prior to his more famous escapades in Virginia as a soldier of fortune in Europe, including his own stint as a Mediterranean privateer aboard a French merchant ship, and a period as a slave in the Islamic world followed by a daring escape. (Smith, 1630, pp. 3–6, 21–34.)

137 '. . . gleane a moderate one out of them . . .' Kenelm Digby to his brother, 23 May 1633; 'Letter-Book', p. 451. Edward Stanley died while Kenelm was away at sea, and Kenelm acted as his executor, a sign of how fully the old man had come to rely on his son-in-law's financial acumen by the time of his death: see *Historical Manuscripts Commission* Thirteenth Report, Appendix, Part IV (London: Eyre & Spottiswoode, 1892), p. 384.

137 '. . . a learned family in Glamorgan . . .' See Williams, 1983.

138 '. . . as ample as any had ever granted . . .' 'A Note of Several Interruptions in the Beginning and Prosecution of my Voyage,' in *Loose Fantasies*, p. 211.

139 '. . . but one barrel of gunpowder . . .' 'A Note of Several Interruptions in the Beginning and Prosecution of my Voyage,' in *Loose Fantasies*, p. 212.

139 '. . . the malignity of fortune . . .' *Loose Fantasies*, p. 163.

141 '. . . I could get no good men . . .' 'A Note of Several Interruptions in the Beginning and Prosecution of my Voyage,' in *Loose Fantasies*, pp. 211–12.

141 '. . . 'extravagant' and 'unreasonable' . . .' Ford, pp. 5–6; British Library MS Egerton 2541, ff. 90–91, 95ᵛ.

141 '. . . such a grant to Sir Kenelm . . .' *CSPD*, 1627–8, pp. 377–8, 407.

142 '. . . some former patentes given to knightes and gentlemen . . .' Kenelm Digby to Robert Cotton, 11 July [1627], British Library MS Cotton Julius C.III, f. 140. Cotton already knew Kenelm sufficiently well by this point to have given him a valuable mathematical manuscript: see Roberts and Watson, p. 175.

142 '. . . many doubting Persons . . .' Kenelm Digby to the Masters, Wardens and Assistants of Trinity House and their reply, 1627, Pepys Manuscripts, Magdalene College, Cambridge, MS 2867, p. 188.

143 '. . . noe frequent Case . . .' The Masters, Wardens and Assistants of Trinity House to Kenelm Digby, 1627, Pepys Manuscripts, Magdalene College, Cambridge, MS 2867, p. 189. The precedent to which they referred was the voyage of Sir James Lancaster to the East Indies in the early 1600s: see Markham. This was a sufficiently important point of precedent that Samuel Pepys had these letters transcribed into his voluminous collection of naval records.

144 '. . . all duty, obedience and respect . . .' Ford, pp. 5–6.

144 '. . . not stay at all upon this occasion . . .' Kenelm Digby to Edward Nicholas, 21 December 1627, TNA SP 16/87.

145 '. . . not to win and preserve it? . . .' *Loose Fantasies*, p. 162.

145 '. . . secluded herself from the world . . .' Kenelm Digby to his three sons, 18 May 1633; 'Letter-Book', p. 124.

Chapter 4

150 '. . . *patience in their sufferance* . . .' *Loose Fantasies*, pp. 165–6.

151 '. . . the 'eastward end' of Cyprus . . .' *Journal*, pp. 3–4.

152 '. . . tracing their outlines in ink . . .' *Journal*, p. 5; National Library of Wales MS Peniarth 417, ff. 3–4; Huntington Library MS EL 6858, p. 3.

152 '. . . carefully planned . . .' *Loose Fantasies*, pp. 213–14.

152 '. . . inexperienced gentleman captains . . .' Hodges and Hughes, p. 52. These are the words of the naval officer and sometime privateer William Monson.

154 '. . . This was a sweet captain! . . .' Hodges and Hughes, pp. 52–3; Rodger, 1997, pp. 396–8. 'Rhodomantade', a term meaning a vainglorious braggart, entered English from French in the 1590s.

155 '. . . *so, you go well* . . .' Smith, 1627, pp. 59, 3, 5. The publication of Smith's book was explicitly intended to assist with 'the Present Occasion' – the wars with France and Spain.

155 '. . . receded into the distance . . .' See *Journal*, pp. 1–2.

155 '. . . to be observed in the ship . . .' *Journal*, p. 2.

155 '. . . the vessels of all Protestant nations . . .' In 1627, the year before Kenelm's departure, Spanish ships and Dunkirkers between them seized 150 Dutch and English ships. In the course of 1628 this rose to 245 ships, more than in any previous year. See Baetens, pp. 62, 75; Israel, pp. 192–3.

156 '. . . 5 sailes coming towardes us . . .' Tonnage, the standard measure for a ship's size, referred not to its actual weight but to the approximate weight of the cargo that it could carry: see Lane, 1964.

156 '. . . apprehended and interrogated . . .' See *Journal*, pp. 1–5.

157 '. . . wee gave over our chace . . .' *Journal*, pp. 5–6.

157 '. . . there is no rule for it . . .' Smith, 1627, p. 56.

158 '. . . before we could discover land . . .' *A late discourse*, pp. 51–2.

158 '. . . the warmer Mediterranean waters beyond . . .' *Journal*, p. 6.

158 '. . . the Barbarie coast . . .' *Journal*, pp. 6–7.

159 '. . . Abyla (or Apehill, as he called it) . . .' Throughout the account of Kenelm's voyage, I have retained his preferred spelling for specific geographical locations when these are easily identifiable by a modern reader, but replaced them with their modern equivalents when his choice is different enough to be unclear.

159 '. . . the terrifying and formless beyond of the Ocean . . .' See Romm, pp. 17–18.

159 '. . . havinge a good hamer . . .' See Sherley, p. 16; Dallam, p. 49. The globetrotting Elizabethan Thomas Coryate went even further, wandering around the ruins at length and measuring them in detail, before he knelt amidst them while his friend Robert Rugge, 'in a merrie humour', touched him on the shoulders with his sword-point and declared him 'the first English Knight of Troy'. ('Master Thomas Coryates Travels', in Purchas 10. 397–8; 405; see Spencer, 1957, pp. 82–5.)

159 '. . . a map for the contemporary world . . .' Many English people also believed, via a false etymology, that the modern Turks were the descendants of the Trojans: like the Trojans the Turks were both impressive and decadent, and the eventual defeat of the mighty Ottomans was reassuringly suggested by the victory of the more austere Greeks at Troy. See Spencer, 1952; Toner, pp. 73–104.

162 '. . . by the afternoon of 20 January . . .' *Journal*, p. 7.

163 '. . . compassion for his countrymen . . .' *Journal*, p. 7.

164 '. . . the most of the Levant . . .' Smith, 1627, p. 46.

164 '. . . infamously powerful currents . . .' These currents were (and are) produced by the heavier and saltier water flowing from the Mediterranean into the Atlantic, while lighter, less saline water flows into the sea from the ocean: see Pryor, pp. 13–16.

164 '. . . forced to abandon their vessels . . .' See Lewis, 1976, p. 144, 151.

164 '. . . veered between Europe and Africa . . .' *Journal*, pp. 7–8.

164 '. . . occasional outbreaks of sickness . . .' People in the seventeenth century, who still attributed the spread of plague and other contagions to vaguely defined 'bad air', were routinely susceptible to the spread of infection and often failed to take the most basic steps to prevent it. The general effects of this poor hygiene were exacerbated aboard ship, where contagious diseases were rife. See Keevil, pp. 149–93; Fury, pp. 209–16.

165 '. . . pain and much weakness . . .' *Journal*, p. 8.

165 '. . . in much desolation without any help . . .' *Loose Fantasies*, pp. 166–7; *Journal*, pp. 8–9, 12.

166 '. . . a spacious and pleasant green meadow . . .' *Loose Fantasies*, p. 166.

166 '. . . *honourable and just* . . .' *Loose Fantasies*, p. 167.

167 '. . . scored on to his memory . . .' Years later, Kenelm recorded the deluded extremes to which people would go in times of 'common Contagion', sometimes carrying about 'a living Toad or Spider shut up in a box' in the vain hope that these poisonous animals might drive out and vanquish the threat of infection, or even a vial of arsenic or other poison, 'which draws unto it the contagious air'. (*A late discourse*, pp. 76–7.) Kenelm also coped with what he had seen by blending his description in *Loose Fantasies* with great literary depictions of such mass sufferings: it resonated particularly with the famous opening of Boccaccio's *Decameron*, which he had read in Italy, and which begins with a vivid account of the plague descending on Florence. For Boccaccio, what was most awful was the way in which the disease destroyed the most basic bonds that held humans together. 'Fathers and mothers,' he wrote, 'refused to nurse and assist their own children, as though they did not belong to them.' (Boccaccio, 1972, p. 9.) Kenelm had also seen the plague that ravaged England in 1625, and which may have made it simpler for him to marry Venetia in secret. This disease too seemed to destroy fellow feeling: the playwright and pamphleteer Thomas Dekker fulminated against the heartless, wealthy cowards who 'sit safe . . . from the Gun-shot of this contagion, in your Orchards and pleasant Gardens'. (Dekker, sig.B^r.)

167 '. . . impressed Kenelm with his unblinking bravery . . .' *Journal*, p. 12, 9. Kenelm was not too distracted by the threat of infection and death to add a patriotic aside in his journal, emphasising his credentials as a national hero. 'By the way this observation is worth noting,' he wrote, 'that, whereas all other shippes did runne from us as fast and as long as they could, I yett never met with any English, were they in never so litle or contemptible vessels, but they steyed for us and made ready for fight.' In the behaviour of the English captains whom he met at sea, the fierce, fearless, proud comportment of heroes such as Drake and Raleigh seemed to live on. Even amidst this crisis Kenelm also kept a sharp and delighted eye trained on the world around him, observing that 'I never yet saw store of porposes playing, but soone a storme ensewed', a mysterious conjunction that deserved to be noted even if it could not be explained.

169 '. . . continue to wreak havoc on the seas . . .' See Wolf, pp. 6–16; Hess, 1978, pp. 164–5; Abun-Nasr, pp. 149–53; García-Arenal and Bunes, pp. 180–92; Garcés, 2002, pp. 21–3.

170 '. . . vanquished the Ottoman navy . . .' Kenelm grew up still hearing stories of this triumph, which prompted endless legends and tales including a poem by King James I himself, and they informed his sense that the Mediterranean was a place where great renown might be obtained.

170 '. . . small-scale skirmishes and plunder . . .' See Hess, 1972.

170 '. . . two of the fatalest and most infamous men . . .' James Howell to Thomas Porter, December 1622, in Howell, 1650, p. 12.

171 '. . . how to saile a ship . . .' Smith, 1630, p. 58. This was an exaggeration, but the contribution of these two men and other European converts was significant. Algiers had been associated with pirates since the days of the Barbarossas, but their sphere of activity had been limited by their low-sided, oared galleys – which were fearsome in battle but could make only relatively short voyages and were entirely unsuited for ocean sailing – and by their lack of technical expertise in

navigation, which meant that they could venture only so far from the shoreline. The pirate raids in the Atlantic and on the English and Irish coasts were substantially enabled by the integration of new European maritime technologies.

171 '. . . his grisly and unrepentant death . . .' One popular ballad about Ward complained that 'Men of his own Countrey/He still abused vilely . . . Some are hewn in pieces small/Some are shot against a wall'. 'The Seamans Song of Captain Ward, the famous Pyrate of the World, and an English man born', cited from Swaen, p. 180. See Anon., 1609; Robert Daborne, *A Christian Turned Turk*, in Vitkus, 2000.

171 '. . . lived like a Bashaw in Barbary . . .' Smith, 1630, p. 59; see Chew, pp. 340–86.

171 '. . . rise to the loftiest of roles . . .' See Trevor-Roper, 1957, pp. 174–6.

174 '. . . captured and sold in its slave markets . . .' See Braudel, 1872, vol. 2, pp. 865–91; Earle, ch. 3; Wolf, pp. 91–198; Garcés, 2002, pp. 15–65; Hess, 1972, pp. 164–77.

174 '. . . the Habitation of Sea-Devils . . .' Purchas, vol. 6, pp. 108–9.

174 '. . . put us into a slavish habit . . .' Poyntz survived hard labour, a stretch as a galley slave following a failed escape attempt, and resisted the amorous attentions of his master's son, before eventually escaping from Constantinople by horse and riding until he made his way back into Christendom at the Hungarian court. Kenelm liked this story enough to buy an expensive manuscript version which he kept in the treasured library that was claimed by the French Crown following his death: see the Narrative of Sydenham Poyntz, Bibliothèque Nationale de France, Paris, MS Anglais 55, ff. 5–8.

174 '. . . labour, and torture in the day . . .' Kellet, p. 39. See García-Arenal and Bunes, pp. 220–38; Colley, pp. 43–72; Garcés, 2002, pp. 66–84.

175 '. . . Huge numbers of slaves . . .' See Davis, 2001, pp. 95, 98.

175 '. . . slipshod, uneven and inefficient . . .' See Clissold; Hebb, pp. 136–70.

175 '. . . in the Gallies of Argeire . . .' Knight, sig. A3; see Starr; Matar, 2001.

175 '. . . to rival the greatest cities in Europe . . .' The great historian of the Mediterranean, Fernand Braudel, rightly claimed that the explosive expansion of the city in the sixteenth century was the closest parallel from the age to the astonishingly rapid growth of metropolises in twentieth-century America. (Braudel, 1972 vol. 1, pp. 59, 232–3; vol. 2, p. 870.)

176 '. . . the great trough of the *Mitidja* plain . . .' See Horden and Purcell, p. 116.

176 '. . . of very cheape price . . .' 'The Description of the Citie of Alger, written by Nicholas Nicholay and how it came into the possession of Barbarossa, and also of Malta and Tripolie', in Purchas, vol. 6, p. 113.

176 '. . . rich and exotic goods from the East . . .' See Davis; Maclean, pp. 42–4.

176 '. . . intricately patterned carpets . . .' See Anderson, 1801, vol. 2, p. 154; Peck, 2005.

176 '. . . the former Roman road . . .' Bourdieu, p. 59, n. 8

177 '. . . exercise the Trade of Merchandise . . .' Nicholay in Purchas, vol. 6, p. 113.

177 '. . . their goods intact . . .' See *Journal*, pp. 13, 9–10.

178 '. . . wee tooke up floting in the water . . .' *Journal*, p. 10.

178 '. . . the ambiguities and swift transformations . . .' See Greene, esp. pp. 115, 133, 135–6, 143, 187–92, 224–7; Abulafia, esp. pp. 470, 476–81, 483–7; Benton; Elliott, 2009; Engels, esp. pp. 53–5.

180 '. . . pointed menacingly out towards the sea . . .' Wolf, pp. 92–3; Hess, 1978, pp. 165–7.

180 '. . . like a great crossbow . . .' This was the comparison suggested by the Spaniard Antonio de Sosa, who was enslaved in Algiers in the late 1570s at the same time as the great novelist Miguel de Cervantes, and knew the city intimately: see Garcés, 2011, p. 104.

181 '. . . a man named James Frizell . . .' *Journal*, pp. 15–16.

Chapter 5

182 '. . . *of many things that were wanting* . . .' *Loose Fantasies*, p. 167.

183 '. . . the more enduringly successful Levant Company . . .' See Epstein, pp. 9–39.

183 '. . . only tenuously associated . . .' See Maclean and Matar, pp. 81–5.

184 '. . . pocketed huge kickbacks from suppliers . . .' See Peck, 1990, pp. 114–17. Astonishingly, Mansell was appointed as one of the commissioners to investigate his own corrupt practices.

184 '. . . he understood the city so well . . .' See Hebb, pp. 88–91, 188–9, 193.

184 '. . . for the benefit of trafficke . . .' See Fisher, pp. 196–7; Wood, 1935, pp. 62–3.

184 '. . . to defend himself . . .' Roe, p. 574.

185 '. . . depended on doing so successfully . . .' Frizell would relinquish his official role the year after Kenelm's visit, but lingered in Algiers until 1643, unable to abandon the precarious thrills that the city had to offer. He also continued to write to Kenelm, updating him on violent uprisings in Algiers five years later: see James Frizell to Kenelm Digby, 20 July 1633, TNA SP 71/1, f. 132.

186 '. . . their good intentions towards me . . .' *Journal*, pp. 15–16.

187 '. . . rapacity of its pirate population . . .' While the attempt to sack Algiers in 1620 had been disastrous, in 1637 the threat of Salé was finally ended when an English fleet sacked the town and released 300 English captives: see Hebb, pp. 237–65.

188 '. . . pigeons, doves and rabbits . . .' See Garcés, 2011, pp. 148, 208; Faroqhi, pp. 207–21.

188 '. . . to refresh and digest . . .' Purchas, vol. 6, p. 115.

188 '. . . fresh air, wine and one's wife . . .' See Montaigne, p. 846; Bamforth. The poet Antoine Gérard de Saint-Amant went even

further, penning an entire poem titled 'Le Melon', extolling the fruit's 'sweet smell of musk and amber' and its intoxicating taste, each bite of which 'tickled my soul'. (Vérane, pp. 102–3: '*Quel doux parfum de musc et d'ambre . . .*'; '*Ce morceau me chatouille l'ame*' [my translations].) Because they were so cold and humid, though, melons were seen as dangerous to naturally cold Northerners when eaten in excess: hence a series of works were published in France, detailing both the medicinal virtues of melons, and the serious risks arising from their excessive consumption (see Pons). These unsettling associations were reflected in one of a series of vivid and haunting dreams that were experienced by the great philosopher René Descartes (whom Kenelm later befriended) as a young man, and which he believed to have been caused by malignant demons. Descartes was walking through an empty college and being buffeted by the wind, when he was hailed by a man who told him to look for Monsieur N., who had something to give him. 'Monsieur Descartes imagined that it was a melon that someone had brought from some foreign land', and later he decided that the fruit signified 'the charms of solitude, but presented through purely human enticements'. (Adam and Tannery, vol. 10, pp.180–5: '*M. Desc. s'imagina que c'étoit un melon qu'on avoit apporté de quelque païs étranger*' [my translation]; see Gabbey and Hall, pp. 657–63.) Curiously, the poet Andrew Marvell, whom Kenelm also met in later life, made the same association between melons and solitude: imagining the happiness of ambling 'in Paradise alone', he wrote, 'Stumbling on melons, as I pass,/Insnared with flow'rs, I fall on grass'. ('The Garden', ll.39–40, in Marvell.)

189 '. . . carved and spun entirely from sugar . . .' Sugar was first introduced into Europe from the Arab world, and the art of sugar sculpture was perfected in North Africa before also filtering into Europe. It was practised to a particularly high degree in Italy, where major sculptors like Giambologna would be commissioned to produce works in sugar as well as bronze and marble, so Kenelm may have seen it there during

his travels. Such edible artworks gradually became more popular in England in the course of Kenelm's lifetime: at one banquet in the 1660s, a model of a stag was created from sugar with an arrow sticking from its side and filled with wine, which ran out like blood when a lady plucked the arrow forth, and a sugar model of a ship fired tiny cannons at a castle; the ladies were given eggshells filled with rosewater to toss at one another and sweeten the stink of gunpowder. Sugar was seen as marvellous and mysterious – Michel de Nostradamus, better known for his cryptic prophecies, wrote an entire book on the substance in the sixteenth century – and Kenelm was particularly fond of it in his own recipes. He provided a recipe for a sweetened cream called 'Cresme Fouettee', for example, which was to be continually sugared as it is eaten. 'You should have the sugar-box by you, to strew on sugar from time to time, as you eat off the superficies, that is strewed over with sugar.' (See Mintz, pp. 23–6, 79–82, 86–90, 96–105; Watson, 1978; Hall, 1996, pp. 174–5; Wheaton, pp. 39–40; *Closet*, p. 140.)

189 '. . . noe Christian hath bin the like . . .' Kenelm Digby to Venetia Digby, 26 May 1628, copy, Derbyshire Record Office, Matlock, document ref. D258/12/34.

189 '. . . four grains of Ambergreece . . .' *Closet*, p. 135. Ambergris was a product of a whale's digestive system, but its unexplained arrival and strange mixture of qualities made its origins a source of much speculation, and it was used in perfumes, medicines and magical concoctions as well as in foods: see Read, esp. p. 224.

189 '. . . as if it too were alive . . .' *Two Treatises*, p. 235.

191 '. . . 'Indians' from Brazil and Mexico . . .' Garcés, 2011, pp. 124–5; Dallam, p. 84; Parker; Vitkus, 2003.

192 '. . . many stupendous and sumptuous edifices . . .' Knight, p. 32.

193 '. . . terrifyingly familiar, not horribly other . . .' See Lewis, 1973, esp. pp. 140–41; Helgason.

193 '. . . strange and fascinatingly novel . . .' See Garcés, 2011, p. 185; Kahane, et al, esp. pp. 38–45; Schuchardt.

193 '. . . token, of change in Religion . . .' Kellet, p. 41.

194 '. . . Slaves of all religions and nationalities . . .' See Friedman, pp. 55–90; Davis, 2003, pp. 103–35.

194 '. . . I am of that country's faith . . .' These lines are from Philip Massinger's play *The Renegado*, performed in 1624 and published in 1630. The play testifies to the public fascination with the North African world in the years surrounding Kenelm's voyage: its action centres around a Venetian nobleman named Vitelli who travels, disguised as a merchant, to Tunis, where he hopes to free his sister who has been enslaved by the viceroy of the city; the renegade of the title is the Venetian Antonio Grimaldi, who turned Turk some years before, and is eventually redeemed when he assists in the escape. This account of changing religion is uttered by Gazet, Vitelli's servant, who embodies the ceaseless flow of goods and commodities into and out of the city, setting up a stall in the marketplace from which he sells 'all neat and new fashions', from 'choice China dishes' to 'pure Venetian crystal of all sorts'. (Massinger, 1.2.111–13; 1.3.1–3; 1.1.24, 32–3, 36–7; see Vitkus, 2003, pp. 158–61; Robinson.)

194 '. . . both on Land and Water . . .' Kellet, p. 35.

195 '. . . went by the name Ka'id Muhammad . . .' Garcés, 2011, p. 43; Garcés, 2002, pp. 74–5. Many members of the Jewish community played a crucial role across the Mediterranean as go-betweens, where they linked cultures that would otherwise have remained distinct and shaped themselves adroitly to the demands of particular circumstances (see Arbel). Jews were still officially barred from England during Kenelm's early life, though he may have heard tale of a particularly notable figure who encapsulated the protean abilities of North African Jews that he would later encounter first-hand: Samuel Pallache, a man who drifted in the course of his life between service to the Sultan of Fez, the Kings of France and Spain, and the Dutch Republic, spent a period in the Mediterranean as a privateer before being arrested and put on trial in London in 1614, the year that Kenelm first emerged into

public life under the Earl of Bristol's patronage. See García-Arenal and Wiegers, esp. pp. 88–94.

195 '. . . aggressive raids on the Spanish coast . . .' See Harvey, pp. 291–331; García-Arenal.

195 '. . . the perfidiousness of the Turks and Jews . . .' *Loose Fantasies*, p. 213.

197 '. . . *lived there in miserable servitude* . . .' *Loose Fantasies*, p. 167.

197 '. . . great number of Bathes . . .' Purchas, vol. 6, p. 113; Wolf, p. 94; Braudel, 1972, vol. 1, p. 475.

198 '. . . who bathed and scrubbed his body . . .' See Garcés, 2011, pp. 254–5.

198 '. . . often made experience in those countries . . .' *Two Treatises*, p. 243. Digby wrote these words fifteen years after his experience of the baths, when he was writing his great philosophical work, the *Two Treatises* on the nature of body and soul, while imprisoned by the Long Parliament in Winchester House on the south bank of the Thames. The memory of the Algerian steam-rooms must have felt like a particularly welcome escape from the straitened circumstances in which he found himself.

199 '. . . real qualities existing in the world . . .' This was in keeping with Galileo's arguments that he was developing while Kenelm was in Florence: in *The Assayer*, Galileo wrote, 'First I must consider what it is that we call heat, as I suspect that people in general have a concept of this which is very remote from the truth. For they believe that heat is a real phenomenon, or property, which actually resides in the material by which we find ourselves warmed.' But, he went on to argue, we should not project our sensory experiences on to the world in this fashion. 'Hence I think tastes, odours, colours and so on are no more than mere names so far as the object in which we place them is concerned, and that they reside only in the consciousness. Hence if the living creature were removed, all these qualities would be wiped away and annihilated. But since we have imposed upon them special

names . . . we wish to believe that they really exist as actually different from those.' (Galileo, p. 274.) Effectively, Galileo is arguing here that when a tree falls in the forest and no one is there to hear it, it does not make a sound; or, as Kenelm might have put it, the baths in Algiers were not hot in any meaningful sense when they were empty, since there was no one there to feel their heat. Galileo attributed the position he attacked to the ancient philosopher Arisotle, and to the Jesuits who clung doggedly to his outdated wisdom; while Kenelm largely agreed with Galileo's account of the senses, he sought in his own philosophical writings to reconcile this cutting-edge theory with a continued respect for Aristotle's wisdom, formulating a volatile concoction of the new and the old. (See Mercer, 1993, pp. 62–6.)

199 '. . . hath the prospect of the Sea . . .' Knight, p. 32.

200 '. . . a goshawk flying near . . .' Garcés, 2011, pp. 118, 193.

200 '. . . the women have no souls . . .' Dallam, p. 15.

200 '. . . a life of enforced invisibility . . .' See Faroqhi, pp. 101, 110; Hess, 1978, p. 176.

200 '. . . view and discourse with them . . .' *Two Treatises*, p. 214.

201 '. . . might pass on to their children . . .' Another example that caught his attention in the same passage of the *Two Treatises* in which he recalled the two-thumbed women was that of a cat which had its tail cut off and then supposedly gave birth to kittens with no tails.

201 '. . . a particular curiosity to see them all . . .' *Two Treatises*, p. 214.

202 '. . . Lineaments of a Ship under Sail . . .' Aubrey, 1972, p. 83.

202 '. . . become governor of Connecticut . . .' He and Kenelm would later strike up a close and unlikely friendship based on a shared love of alchemy that transcended their opposed religious beliefs, but it was their youthful travels in the middle sea that fuelled their early enthusiasm: see Winthrop, 1864, pp. 263–78; Woodward, pp. 30–33; Kamil, pp. 470–507. When the two corresponded in the 1650s, Winthrop tried to tempt Kenelm to New England to help form a scientific academy, while Kenelm tried to lure him back to England to help effect a general

reform of alchemy, and inspired Winthrop's serious interest in the weapon-salve: see Kenelm Digby to John Winthrop Jr, 31 January 1654/5 and 26 January 1656, in Winthrop, 1849, pp. 5–6, 15–18; Woodward, pp. 195–6, 264–5.

203 '. . . ancient and sacred texts . . .' See Holt; Toomer, 1996; Feingold, 1996.

203 '. . . by force of arms . . .' Purchas, vol. 9, p. 114; Milton, 1953–82, vol. 1, p. 299; see Matar, pp. 86–7.

203 '. . . studied some Arabic while he was there . . .' See William Lyford, dedicatory epistle to George Digby, in Pinke, sig.A2ᵛ; Toomer, 1996, pp. 97–8.

203 '. . . a great student for the Arabick Language . . .' Hartlib Papers, 29/2/10A; Matar, p. 84. Italy was at the vanguard of Arabic studies in Europe: a complete Qur'an was printed in Venice as early as 1538, and in Tuscany in the 1580s the Medicean oriental press was founded, printing mathematical and philosophical works in Arabic. This stopped operating in 1614, but its types survived and were used to print Arabic books into the 1620s (see Toomer, 1996, pp. 20–24). If Kenelm encountered these printing presses while in Italy, it may have inspired his own attempt, in the early 1630s, to purchase the Arabic type owned by the eminent English Arabist William Bedwell, for printing books in the language; Kenelm also offered the huge sum of £500 for Bedwell's unpublished Arabic lexicon, a sign of his serious and continued Arabic interests. See John Clarke to Barnabas Oley, 29 June 1632, Cambridge University Library MS.Dd.3.12, ff. 75–6; Hamilton, pp. 49, 93.

203 '. . . ye Persian Arabian or Greeke Language . . .' See Ferrier, p. 51.

203 '. . . his optimism began to fade . . .' The great Dutch scholar of Arabic, Jacob Golius, was travelling in the Mediterranean at the same time as Kenelm and managed to obtain a large and varied collection of Arabic books, which formed the basis of his later studies: on his travels he met John Winthrop Jr, and later became acquainted with

Kenelm himself. See Golius; Brugman; John Winthrop Jr to Jacobus Golius, 20 November 1639, in Winthrop, 1944, pp. 155–6.

204 '. . . renowned for their learning . . .' Garcés, 2002, pp. 84–8, 92–9.

204 '. . . the miserable depths of their captivity . . .' Garcés, 2011, pp. 50–51, 175–6, 223.

204 '. . . the convent library of El Escorial . . .' They remain in the library there today. See Hartlib Papers, 39/3/25A; Matar, pp. 84–5; García-Arenal and Wiegers, pp. 79–82; Justel Calabozo.

205 '. . . Arabic volumes on mathematics . . .' One of these was a commentary by Ibn al-Haytham on the works of Euclid, the ancient founder of geometry.

206 '. . . copied out only the year before . . .' St John's College, Oxford, MSS 33, 72, 103, 107, 122, 145, 175; Savage-Smith et al, pp. 3–10, 54–6, 63–70, 85–7, 89–92; Bodleian MS Arch. Selden A.8; Haywood, pp. 77, 82–9; Toomer, 2009, vol. 2, pp. 590, 622 n. 230. One of Kenelm's contemporaries believed him to have bought these manuscripts in Constantinople, but in fact he never set foot there: Johannes de Laet to William Boswell, 30 January 1640, BL Ms Additional 6395 (Boswell Papers), f. 56; the reported place of purchase is mistakenly reported as fact by Toomer, vol. 2, p. 590.

207 '. . . how best to trim one's fingernails . . .' St John's College, Oxford, MS 175, ff. 44, 74; Savage-Smith et al, pp. 5, 135–8; I follow the translations of the poems given in this volume by Geert Jan van Gelder.

208 '. . . a force of 15,000 men . . .' *Journal*, pp. 16–17.

210 '. . . pardoned the rest . . .' *Journal*, p. 17.

212 '. . . upon his triumphant return . . .' *Journal*, pp. 17–19. This is the modern equivalent according to the National Archives' historical currency converter. The hope that reimbursement would be forthcoming was a vain one: Kenelm was still petitioning the perennially cash-strapped English government for reimbursement twenty years later, and never received it. See Hebb, p. 162.

212 '. . . all the English captives that remained here . . .' In fact, several hundred English slaves remained in Algiers, and the treaty in which he took such pride did little to stem their influx: corsairs tended not to pay too much attention to such agreements, and another 300 English people were captured in the next year alone.

212 '. . . a pile of letters . . .' *Journal*, p. 19.

212 '. . . in miserable servitude . . .' Kenelm Digby to Edward, Viscount Conway. 22 March 1627/8, TNA, London, SP 71/1, f. 82.

213 '. . . acts that burnished his honour . . .' See Cust, 1987, pp. 16–17, 30–31, 39–40, 55.

213 '. . . crabbed, incomprehensible handwriting . . .' See Cogswell, 1989, pp. 80–82.

214 '. . . what had passed there . . .' *Journal*, p. 19.

214 '. . . an appropriate moment for a new start . . .' *Journal*, p. 19. It was only gradually, in the course of the seventeenth century, that the Continental habit of beginning the year on 1 January became the norm.

215 '. . . the improvisatory gabble of the *lingua franca* . . .' Kenelm Digby to Venetia Digby, 26 May 1628.

215 '. . . regions, and nations of the worlds . . .' The traveller in question was named Pietro della Valle, and he made his journey a decade before Kenelm: see Dursteler, pp. 1–2.

215 '. . . a ramass of rogues of every nation . . .' See Fisher, p. 156.

216 '. . . whether she would safely receive them . . .' The letters to Venetia have not survived, but when he wrote to her on 26 May, he began the letter: 'I hope that longe ere this you have receaved my two large letters that I writt to you from Argires by Mr George Vernon whom I sent purposely to the kinge to give his Majestie account how I had settled the peace there with that state and redeemed all the English captives that were there, and what extreame miseries I had sustained though of sicknes and mortalitie amonge my men before I came in theire.' (Kenelm Digby to Venetia Digby, 26 May 1628, copy, Derbyshire Record Office, Matlock, document ref. D258/12/34.)

217 '. . . no man or woman ever saw her all the while . . .' Kenelm Digby to his three sons, 18 May 1633; 'Letter-Book', pp. 124–5.

217 '. . . meditating and reading of spiritual bookes . . .' Kenelm Digby to his three sons, 18 May 1633; 'Letter-Book', p. 125.

217 '. . . sett them downe in her owne hand . . .' Kenelm Digby to his brother, 17 June 1633; 'Letter-Book', p. 85.

217 '. . . mortification, penance and devotion . . .' Untitled and undated meditation in 'Letter-Book', p. 98.

218 '. . . excellently well tempered . . .' Kenelm Digby to his three sons, 18 May 1633; 'Letter-Book', pp. 131–2, 125.

Chapter 6

219 '. . . *enemies, of humanity and clemency* . . .' *Loose Fantasies*, p. 168.

220 '. . . I apprehended very much . . .' *Journal*, p. 19.

220 '. . . an unprecedented degree of artillery . . .' The large square sails contrasted with the slim triangular design that was peculiar to Arab craft, and many of the new ship designs combined sails of both shapes. See Parry, pp. 53–68; Guilmartin Jr, pp. 194–220, 221–2, 253–73.

221 '. . . a new standard for speed and efficiency . . .' See Parry, pp. 67–8.

222 '. . . parted very well satisfyed . . .' *Journal*, p. 21.

222 '. . . swordes and halfe pikes . . .' *Journal*, p. 21. The 'falconet' and the 'murderer' were both small and portable pieces of artillery: the first had a bore of around two inches and fired a six-pound ball, the second was slightly smaller and more typically used to repel boarders.

223 '. . . towards the southern tip of Sardinia . . .' *Journal*, pp. 19–22.

223 '. . . mullets and excellent fish . . .' *Journal*, pp. 22–3.

224 '. . . Spanish goods loaded at Naples . . .' The vast kingdom of Naples (which included Sicily) was under Spanish control at this point, giving the King of Spain an enormous foothold in the Italian peninsula. This

also meant that as Kenelm sailed around the southern shores of Italy, he was particularly likely to meet with Spanish vessels which he could legitimately take as prizes.

224 '. . . fortune was not on Kenelm's side . . .' *Journal*, pp. 23–4.

225 '. . . past Cape Passero . . .' *Journal*, pp. 24–7; *Loose Fantasies*, pp. 5, 127.

226 '. . . done by me as I did by him . . .' *Journal*, pp. 26–7.

227 '. . . the Venetians their soveraignes . . .' Sandys, p. 5.

228 '. . . split between Ottoman and Venetian rule . . .' Venice itself was transformed by its constant contact with the East, its churches and minarets often taking on a decidedly Ottoman look and bringing Islamic fashions and techniques into the very heart of European commercial life: see Kissling; Howard, esp. pp. 36–42.

228 '. . . between the Islamic and Christian worlds . . .' Braudel, 2002, p. 119.

229 '. . . made instead for Cephalonia . . .' *Journal*, pp. 27–8.

229 '. . . reminded one visitor . . .' 'Master Thomas Coryates Travels to, and Observations in Constantinople and other places in the way thither, and his journey thence to Aleppo, Damasco, and Jerusalem', in Purchas, vol. 10, pp. 389–91.

229 '. . . winds trapped in the hollow caves and caverns . . .' Heylyn, p. 266.

229 '. . . guarded a monopoly over trade . . .' See de Divitiis, pp. 141–4.

230 '. . . known simply as the 'Currant Islands' . . .' See Fusaro, esp. pp. 150–51; Wood, 1935, pp. 66–8.

230 '. . . which draweth hither much traffick . . .' Dallam, p. 19; Sandys, p. 5.

230 '. . . two thirds of the seven-million-ton crop . . .' Thomas Roe to George Calvert, January 1621, in Roe, p. 10.

230 '. . . thus addicted to that miserable Isle . . .' Lithgow, p. 65.

231 '. . . partly a battle over currants . . .' See Brenner, pp. 63, 67–9, 206, 209, 220–21, 227–8, 231–3, 237, 283–4.

232 '. . . come ashore without licence . . .' Sandys, p. 6.

232 '. . . representing the scarcity in the island . . .' *CSPV*, vol. 21, pp. 73–4.

233 '. . . provided and furnished a house for me . . .' *Journal*, pp. 28–9.

233 '. . . and formed the base of the dye . . .' See Sandys, pp. 4–5.

234 '. . . drink with safety large draughts of it . . .' *Closet*, p. 123.

234 '. . . some Rhenish wine and the yolk of an egg . . .' *Closet*, p. 155.

234 '. . . the empty skin cast aside . . .' He strewed currants liberally into a variety of other dishes, often demonstrating the fusion of sweet and savoury that was still so common in Kenelm's day, and can appear so nauseating to modern palates: for instance currants in a bone-marrow and bread broth, paired with boiled capon *à Milano*, sprinkled on to spinach pasties and veal kidneys on toast with a liberal dose of sugar. See *Closet*, pp. 145, 166–7, 171, 198.

234 '. . . the merchants who had made him welcome . . .' *Journal*, pp. 28–30.

236 '. . . the splintery and barnacle-roughened hull of the ship . . .' See Bard, 1984, pp. 28–9, 35; Rodger, 1997, p. 406.

236 '. . . to give warning unto all others . . .' This is the explanation from the *Sea Dialogues* of Nathaniel Boteler, who had served on Warwick's 1627 expedition: see Hodges and Hughes, p. 54.

237 '. . . might be thrown in his face . . .' *Journal*, pp. 30–32.

237 '. . . mortifies me exceedingly . . .' *CSPV*, vol. 21, pp. 81–2.

237 '. . . a voyage of just six hours . . .' See *Journal*, p. 62.

238 '. . . dismissed as his behaviour deserved . . .' *CSPV*, vol. 21, p. 112.

239 '. . . such as were under my power . . .' *Journal*, pp. 33–4.

240 '. . . the strong possibility of it going astray . . .' The two letters have not survived, and whether they originally reached Venetia is unclear. Kenelm was well aware of the practical hazards that letters had to overcome in an age that lacked an organised and reliable postal service, especially when they were sent from deep into Europe or beyond. As he later put it in a letter to Tobie Matthew, 'I have observed in such letters as I have written from Greece, Afrike, and other remotest parts

of the world, to my frendes in the country; that their hazard and slownesse of going (to the proportion of the distance) from Alexandria or Tripoli to London, hath not bin so great as that little, fagge end of their way from thence to Oxford, for example. Now here I learn *come tutto il mondo e paese*; all places fare alike, and haue a *rapport* to one an other. The negligence of a drunken carrier there, and the hazardes of his greasie pouch; are here balanced with the dosednesse of starved water bearers, and their torne wallets.' (Kenelm Digby to Tobie Matthew, 29 August 1641, BL Additional MS 41846, f.37ᵛ.)

240 '. . . I alsoe make them feare mee . . .' Kenelm Digby to Venetia Digby, 26 May 1628.

241 '. . . even before his return . . .' See Cust, 1986. Kenelm's hopes were in fact realized, despite Venetia's isolation, though it is unclear whether this happened before or after his return: this letter survives only in one of the copies that was made of it, in the papers of a provincial nobleman in Derbyshire. Its place of survival, however, also shows that once Kenelm had sent a letter, he gave up control over how it was received. The man in whose possession it ended up, Sir John Gell, was a fierce Puritan who became commander-in-chief of the parliamentary forces in Derbyshire, Staffordshire and Warwickshire during the Civil War, and he saved the letter alongside many rabidly anti-Catholic tracts. A later hand, probably in the eighteenth century, added at the top of the letter the words, 'A Letter from Sir Kenelme Digby to his Wife giving an Account of several Piracys committed by him in the Mediteranean 1628', suggesting that it was read in the most unflattering light.

241 '. . . leaving the Currant Islands in his wake . . .' *Journal*, pp. 32–4.

241 '. . . the Ile of Ithaca . . .' *Journal*, p. 34.

242 '. . . *with his own admiral ship against that of the enemy's* . . .' *Loose Fantasies*, p. 168.

243 '. . . deployed to devastating effect . . .' The years before Kenelm's voyage saw various works on the art of gunnery published in English,

and its exponents compared the art favourably with music, medicine, astronomy and mathematics: see Digges; Smith, 1927b. Gunnery was of interest not only to soldiers but also to philosophers like Kenelm, for what it taught them about the physics of objects in motion, and debates about the mathematics and physics of cannon-fire, played an important part in the Scientific Revolution. (See Hall, 1952, esp. pp. 33–5; Henninger-Voss.)

243 '. . . a whole medieval bestiary of death-dealing power . . .' See Monson.

244 '. . . now nothing but boges and pondes . . .' Dallam, pp. 28–29.

244 '. . . before sackt by the Turkish Pyrats . . .' Robson, p. 11.

244 '. . . dangerous for strangers to come on shore . . .' 'Part of a Letter from William Biddulph, from Aleppo', in Purchas, vol. 8, p. 256.

244 '. . . known to block the sun and its healthful rays . . .' See Mather, pp. 17–19.

245 '. . . Reddie to leape upon one of us . . .' Dallam, p. 30.

245 '. . . pull up the corps and eat it . . .' Biddulph in Purchas, vol. 8, p. 257.

245 '. . . boggs, foggs and Froggs . . .' Mundy, p. 19; see MacLean, 2007, pp. 195–215.

245 '. . . Armenians and all Europaeans . . .' 'Collections out of divers Mahumetan Authors in their Arabicke Bookes', in Purchas, vol. 9, p. 103.

246 '. . . accesse and recesse to this Citie as Travellers . . .' Biddulph in Purchas, vol. 8, p. 271.

246 '. . . the outlet for goods from Aleppo . . .' It continued to serve as the main port for Aleppo until the outbreak of the Second World War. See Masters, 1999, pp. 29, 36; Masters, 1987; Wood, 1935, p. 24; Mather, chs. 1–3, esp. pp. 93–6.

247 '. . . no fewer than eleven cannons . . .' *Journal*, p. 35.

248 '. . . the most feared Christian corsairs . . .' The knights were initially based in Rhodes, but moved to Malta when that island was taken by the Ottomans in 1522.

249 '. . . the vessels of Protestant nations . . .' See Earle, chs 5–9; Greene, esp. pp. 95–8. Just a few months after Kenelm's encounter with the Knights of Malta, in August 1628, an English ship named the *Sampson* carrying the ambassador Thomas Roe back to England from Constantinople was attacked by several Maltese galleys and fought a fierce battle in order to escape (see Strachan, 1969). Whether the Knights mistook the *Sampson* for a Turk or simply thought that English heretics were fair game, this was a world in which the line between friend and foe was prone to bend and blur.

250 '. . . what he would find at the port . . .' *Journal*, pp. 37–8.

250 '. . . long prospective glass . . .' Kenelm owned two of these glasses, which he left in Paris after returning to England at the Restoration, and specifically bequeathed to George Digby in the codicil that he added to his will: BL Additional MS 38175, f61^r.

251 '. . . that might happily oppose me . . .' *A Relation*, pp. 10–11.

251 '. . . as many as six or seven hundred men . . .' These were probably overstatements that Kenelm made in his journal to magnify the challenge that he faced, but only just.

251 '. . . no fewer than seventy Turkish vessels . . .' See Guilmartin, pp. 232–4; Parker, 1988, pp. 87–9.

251 '. . . to maximise its speed and deadliness . . .' See Lane, 1973, p. 374.

252 '. . . the rich trade that was beneficial to all . . .' The French had been the first, around 1536, to elbow their way into the Ottoman trade that the Venetians had fiercely guarded since the late Middle Ages, and the Venetians and French in turn strove fiercely and ultimately ineffectually to exclude the English, who established trade and diplomatic relations in the early 1580s. It was in the interest of the Ottomans to play the three off against one another. The truly decisive shift, which the English, the Venetians and the French had tried collectively but ineffectually to resist, had already occurred in 1612 when the Dutch obtained 'capitulations' (as the right to trade was known) from the Sultan, and it was this new sea power that would roar into a position

of supremacy that they would retain for the remainder of the century, though this was by no means obvious in 1628. See Steensgaard; Horniker; Maclean and Matar, pp. 91–3; Murphey, pp. 39–41.

252 '. . . more than share with them in that Soveraignty . . .' Sandys, p. 2; Muir, pp. 119–34.

253 '. . . operated from the Dalmatian coast. . .' The Uskoks were Christians based on the Dalmatian Coast (in modern-day Croatia): they saw themselves as Crusaders against the Turks, much like the Knights of Malta, but as their attacks on Muslim ships endangered Venetian trade with the Ottomans, Venice also sought violently to suppress them and denounced them as pirates, leading them to attack Venetian vessels as well: hence commercial relations could trump religious allegiance. See Tenenti, 1967, pp. 3–15; Bracewell.

253 '. . . a forest teeming with bandits . . .' Tenenti, 1967, esp. pp. 18, 51, 56–86 (quotation at 61).

253 '. . . their prowess as both sailors and merchants . . .' See Tenenti, 1973; Tucci. While the loss of dominance at sea has often been described as the general decline of Venice and its importance in Europe, it makes more sense to see it as a reconfiguration of the city-state's priorities: they expanded their territories on the Italian mainland and pursued other forms of wealth in response to the rise of piracy and the relative decline in maritime trade (see Martin and Romano).

253 '. . . the enemy of all mankind . . .' See Heller-Roazen.

254 '. . . actions that he considered great and just . . .' See Kelsey, pp. 95, 136, 171, 217, 393–5; Fuchs, pp. 139–51.

254 '. . . you are an emperor . . .' Augustine, p. 148; see Pérotin-Dumon. Kenelm was deeply interested in Augustine's works throughout his life, citing him constantly and contributing a preface to Tobie Matthew's translation of Augustine's great autobiographical work, the *Confessions* (see BL Additional MS 41,846, ff. 104–5).

254 '. . . no ships durst ever attempt them . . .' *Loose Fantasies*, p. 168.

255 '. . . tearing, raking, and bilging the ships . . .' This was the accurate conclusion of the English naval commission of 1618: see Hale, pp. 405–6; Cipolla, p. 86.

255 '. . . to acquaint them who I was . . .' *Journal*, p. 38; *A Relation*, p. 10.

257 '. . . other than friendly relations with you . . .' *CSPV*, vol. 21, pp. 136–40.

257 '. . . a tactic designed to needle his adversary . . .' This does not necessarily mean that the challenge was not sincere: later in life, Kenelm duelled with and killed a Frenchman who besmirched the honour of Charles I, and was temporarily banished from France for his troubles (see *Honour*). In trying to make the conflict between him and Antonio Capello a matter of personal honour, Kenelm's behaviour was in keeping with Charles's own self-destructive tendencies, and he hoped that if word of his aggressive but gentlemanly conduct reached England, it would meet with the King's approval.

257 '. . . with all my might . . .' *Journal*, pp. 38–9.

258 '. . . the heavy dews in these parts . . .' *CSPV*, vol. 21, pp. 137–8.

258 '. . . a firestorm of cannon and gunshot . . .' *A Relation*, p. 12.

259 '. . . cannon-fire echoing about the bay . . .' *Two Treatises*, p. 251.

259 '. . . split into wretched pieces by the artillery . . .' This was the description of the Venetian writer Paolo Paruta in his work *Dell. historia venetiana'ella guerra di Cipro*, as translated and cited by Hale, p. 324. An arquebus was a long handheld gun, the ancestor of the musket and the rifle, often used in naval battles.

260 '. . . then to endanger our Countrimen . . .' *A Relation*, pp. 11–12.

262 '. . . their riggings and masts shredded . . .' *CSPV*, vol. 21, p. 138.

262 '. . . in a verie abject manner . . .' *Journal*, p. 39.

262 '. . . the first to fire a shot in anger . . .' *CSPV*, vol. 21, p. 138.

263 '. . . to attempt things with much disadvantage . . .' *Loose Fantasies*, p. 169.

264 '. . . it filled his nostrils . . .' Obtaining gunpowder had been one of the challenges that Kenelm had to overcome before departing, since

all the gunpowder in London had been bought up by the Duke of Buckingham's men and he was forced to wait for supplies to arrive from Amsterdam. He was convinced after defeating the Venetians that he could have 'soone ended the quarrell with them' and won an even more resounding victory 'if our powder had not beene very bad, for we had none but Dutch Powder'. (*Loose Fantasies*, p. 212; *A Relation*, p. 12.)

264 '. . . the most mysterious and the most dangerous . . .' Many were so terrified of its devastating force that they believed gunpowder had been invented by Satan himself: see Hale, pp. 397–99. Gunpowder making was becoming big business in the seventeenth century, but it remained rooted in arcane mysteries and secrets deeply connected with alchemy, passed from master to apprentice and jealously guarded. See Buchanan, 2005.

264 '. . . more dreadful than those made by Nature . . .' Plot, pp. 236–7; see Partington, pp. 64–79. Kenelm later saw in gunpowder a reflection of the volatility that he sensed lurking within his own disturbed self: just as 'in a mill where they make gunnepowder' a small grain sometimes 'taketh fire and, consuming it selfe, bloweth up all that is about it', so did the rush of thoughts about his own brain 'of a soddaine entangle them selves in the worke they were about' and he 'was fain to give over, lest my distempered head as well as they should fly in peeces'. (Kenelm Digby to his brother, 25 May 1633; 'Letter-Book', p. 461.) This letter shows that Kenelm was intimately familiar with the practical details of gunpowder production, describing the exact moment at which the powder is 'readie to corne' – that is, to form small black grains – and has to be removed quickly to avoid the risk of accidental explosion, which can occur 'when the sound of the hammer will grow shrill'.

Chapter 7

267 '. . . *to attempt things with much disadvantage . . .*' *Loose Fantasies*, p. 169.

268 '. . . the good laws and statutes of this realm . . .' Gardiner, 1889, p. 66.

268 '. . . a high-profile case argued during 1627 . . .' See Kishlansky, 1999.

269 '. . . to pursue war at all cost . . .' Gardiner, 1889, p. 68.

269 '. . . presented to Charles by the end of May . . .' It was delayed by prolonged negotiation as the Petition passed through the House of Lords: the Earl of Bristol, who had been restored to his seat there and was continuing his personal war with the Duke, was instrumental in ensuring that an accommodation with Parliament was reached, and that the petition was not thrown out as Buckingham's allies demanded. Only after the petition was passed did Buckingham finally take steps to repair his relationship with Bristol, as their former clashes were increasingly irrelevant to current events and the Duke needed to placate his powerful enemies. On 23 June 1628, an order was given to begin paying to Bristol the arrears of a pension granted to him by King James, a sign of his return to favour. See Guy, pp. 302–3; Russell, p. 391.

270 '. . . the laws and customs of the realm . . .' Gardiner, 1889, p. 70. See Russell, pp. 323–89; Guy; Reeve.

271 '. . . their former pride . . .' *A Relation*, pp. 12–13.

271 '. . . The English are staying here . . .' *CSPV*, vol. 21, pp. 138, 146, 147.

272 '. . . the egges that his pigeons were then sitting upon . . .' *Two Treatises*, p. 251. When the vice consul told Kenelm of these broken eggs he 'lamented exceedingly; for they were of that kind, which commonly is called Carriers, and serve them dayly in their commerce betweene that place and Aleppo'. The carrier pigeons of Scanderoon were famous, and remarked upon by almost every English traveller. Their

feet would be dipped in vinegar to keep them cool, and to discourage them from taking refuge in the sea from the hot sun. These birds were not only valued but cosseted and cherished, which might explain the vice consul's lamentation at their loss: Thomas Dallam met a merchant at Scanderoon who seemed to love his pigeons, clutching one to his breast upon its safe arrival with the words, 'Welcom, Honoste Tom.' (Dallam, p. 32; see Russell, 1756, vol. 2, p. 203; Biddulph in Purchas, vol. 8, p. 260; Mather, p. 19.)

272 '. . . all our marchants were putt in prison . . .' *Journal*, p. 39.

272 '. . . no longer be short of money . . .' *CSPV*, vol. 21, p. 147.

272 '. . . to a sharpe itch . . .' *Journal*, p. 40.

273 '. . . love and quietnesse . . .' *Journal*, pp. 40–42.

274 '. . . an Havania passed uppon them . . .' Kenelm Digby to Sir Peter Wyche, 23 June 1628, TNA SP 97/14.

274 '. . . aske reason for the Captaines insolency . . .' Kenelm Digby to Sir Isaac Wake, 24 June 1628, TNA SP 99/30. More so than the austere Wyche, Kenelm had reason to see Wake as a kindred spirit: he was an urbane and learned man, formed by his long years in Italy, and was rarely happier than with his nose stuck in some book treating 'political and civill matters'. He also cut a fine figure in the world: one contemporary described him swanning about after he took up his new and prestigious ambassadorial appointment, 'laying it on with great ostentation' and 'flaunting feathers and the like' – all at his wealthy wife's expense. Wake was also, however, a seasoned practitioner of the diplomatic arts, a practised loiterer in corridors and whisperer in ears, and he was especially attuned to the importance of diplomatic letters. See Stoye, pp. 99, 110, 112–13; McClure, vol. 2, p. 558.

275 '. . . bread baked as thinne as strong paper . . .' *Journal*, pp. 42–4. This last dish, which particularly caught Kenelm's eye, was probably *gözleme* – unleavened bread named after the bubbles of air baked within it which seemed to wink as it was eaten (*göz* meaning 'eye' in Turkish). This was a rich banquet, suitable for a visiting foreigner: meat was

usually eaten only at weddings and other special occasions in the
Turkish countryside. See Faroqhi, pp. 205–7, 210.

275 '. . . the banqueting halls of Algiers . . .' Kenelm's eagerness contrasted
with the attitude of his compatriots who travelled to this region and
had nothing but contempt for the food and the table manners of
ordinary Turks: William Biddulph called their diet 'not sumptuous',
while Thomas Coryat seemed strangely, almost personally, affronted
by the poor quality of their 'sluttish butter', 'the most filthie and
unsavourie that is made in any other part of the world, for besides
that it is defiled with many haires, it is also stained with many colours'.
Samuel Purchas claimed that the Turks had other strange and revolting
culinary beliefs: 'Rice is esteemed a great delicacie, by reason of their
Tradition, that it came of Mahomets sweat.' (Purchas, vol. 8, p. 265;
vol. 10, p. 437; vol. 9, p. 100.)

276 '. . . brave great and stately cittie . . .' *Journal*, p. 46. Kenelm's men
informed him that this was the city Alayassa, once known as Laodicea
ad Mare.

277 '. . . spreading across the Mediterranean at terrifying speed . . .' See
Burke.

277 '. . . the pirate Digby . . .' *CSPV*, vol. 21, pp. 147, 163, 244, 380, 391–2,
412.

277 '. . . seven eventful and often terrifying years . . .' Roe had lived an
extraordinary globe-trotting life even before his appointment to the
Ottoman Porte. As a younger man he had sailed to Guiana on an
expedition orchestrated from the Tower of London by Sir Walter
Raleigh in search of the legendary El Dorado. In 1615 he travelled
to India as James I's ambassador to the Mughal emperor Jahangir,
with whom he became good friends during a four-year stay. Even by
the standards of Ottoman politics, the years of his Turkish embassy
were tempestuous: in 1622, mere months after his arrival, the Sultan,
Osman, was murdered by his janissaries and replaced by his mad uncle
Mustafa, who eventually abdicated and was replaced by Murad IV,

Osman's fourteen-year-old brother. These swift changes were accompanied by the executions of a series of advisors and military commanders: as Roe put it in a bewildered letter, in the first fifteen months of his posting, 'I have seene three emperors, seaven great viziers, two capten bassas, five agas of the Janissaries, 3 treasorers.' This bloody merry-go-round continued throughout his time there – 'a stage of variety', Roe wryly noted, which might provide 'fit matter for Ben Jonson'. (See Roe, pp. 178, 126; Strachan, 1989, *passim*, esp. pp. 134–88.)

277 '. . . but our poor merchants suffer . . .' Roe, p. 827. Later in the voyage Kenelm discussed his victory at Scanderoon with the English vice consul on the island of Delos, and heard 'that he was at Smyrna when the newes of it came to our ambassador Thomas Rowe (then there) and to the consull and English marchantes, all who made much joy at it'. (*Journal*, p. 56.) This man was trying to flatter Kenelm, and probably tried to conceal from him the anger and distaste that was Roe's true response to the news.

278 '. . . for a letter of mart . . .' Roe, p. 821. Roe's fervent Protestantism and hatred of Catholics was reflected in the diplomatic postings that he was given after his return from Turkey: he saw the Thirty Years War, then in its tenth year, as a struggle between the militant forces of God and the Catholic Antichrist, and he spent the years after his return from Turkey in Northern Europe, trying to push England into more active defence of the Protestant cause, which was embodied by the heroic Swedish King, Gustavus Adolphus.

279 '. . . before that of all the rest . . .' *A late discourse*, pp. 27–33; Herodotus, p. 185.

279 '. . . store of flying fishes . . .' *Journal*, pp. 45–7.

279 *A late discourse*, p. 32; *Journal*, p. 47.

280 *A late discourse*, p. 31.

280 '. . . what apprentice, knows not Heliodorus? . . .' Hall, 1808, vol. 9, p. 148. This remark was by Bishop Joseph Hall, the same man who was

such a vociferous opponent of young Englishmen travelling into Catholic Europe for their education. The circumstances in which the *Æthiopica* was rediscovered were dramatic enough that they could themselves have been drawn from a romance – the work languished in obscurity for centuries until a manuscript was rescued from the wreckage of a monastery in Budapest in 1526 after the city was sacked. See Forcione, pp. 49–87.

280 '. . . the Elizabethan soldier-poet Sir Philip Sidney . . .' Sidney entirely reworked his own romance, *Arcadia*, after reading the *Æthiopica*, giving the revised version a much more pronounced maritime and Mediterranean setting, as well as dramatically increasing its narrative complexity: see Skretkowicz, 1976; 2010. Kenelm's decision to rename Venetia 'Stelliana', after the mysterious heroine of Sidney's sonnet sequence, *Astrophil and Stella*, shows that he read Heliodorus through the prism of Sidney's writings.

281 '. . . conferred upon her daughter similarly white skin . . .' The story of a white woman born to black parents fascinated writers in Kenelm's time who tried to understand the basis of racial difference (see Spiller, pp. 79–111). Kenelm himself remained extremely interested in such tales, which suggested 'the marvellous effects that the imaginations of Mothers work upon the bodies of their children'. He mentioned another version of the story concerning 'the Queen of Ethiopia, who was delivered of a white boy, which was attributed to a Picture of the Blessed Virgin, which she had always near . . . her bed'; and 'another of a woman who was brought to bed of a child all hairy, because of a portrait of Saint John Baptist in the wilderness, where he wore a Coat of Cammels hair'. Typically, Kenelm neither rejected these tales as implausible, nor accepted them as inexplicable marvels, but tried to place them on a firm and up-to-date philosophical footing, arguing that, when a person is passionately excited by an object, his or her spirits are 'mingled with the petty body or atoms of the long'd-for-thing', and, in the case of pregnant women, these atoms are led 'to

the same part of the body of the Infant, as well as to his imagination'. (*A late discourse*, pp. 103–4, 101.)

281 '. . . frozen for ever in place . . .' Kenelm wrote a strange, haunting and frivolous poem to his friend James Howell in which he reported this 'towne neare Tripoli in Barbary turnd with all the things in it into Stone': in it he described 'A towne turnd stone with all the Utensells/ Belonging to the place, Men, Women, Doggs/Catts, Batts, horse, Mule, sheepe, Kine, oxe, Asses, Hoggs/Butter and cheese with the cheese nattering Mouse/Not a flea left, nor a backbiting lowse'. (Beinecke Library, Yale University, Osborn Shelves B52, vol. 1, f. 105; I am grateful to Claire Preston for this reference.)

282 '. . . small bodies or Atoms . . .' *A late discourse*, pp. 32–3.

282 '. . . began to emit an acrid stink . . .' Kenelm characteristically saw this potential crisis as an opportunity for ingenious experimentation, noting that 'after I had trycd many other wayes in vaine, I found that putting some litle peble stones and gravell, and hanging some lead, in the jarres, it continued perfect good'. *Journal*, p. 48.

282 '. . . redeemed some 20 or 30 Christian slaves . . .' John Winthrop Jr to John Winthrop Sr, 28 July 1628, in Winthrop, 1929, p. 403.

282 '. . . commanded a fearsome force . . .' Kenelm was saved from this threat, which never materialised, by the larger struggles going on in France for political power, including supremacy over the navy. The years preceding his voyage had witnessed the rise to prominence of the man who would cast his shadow over French political life for decades, Armand Jean du Plessis, Cardinal Richelieu. In the early 1620s, Richelieu had begun pushing the French Crown to develop a navy to match the English and Spanish fleets, and in 1626 the office of *grand-maître de la navigation et commerce* was created for him. The focus of the newly augmented navy, however, was in the first instance the conflict with the English at La Rochelle. Richelieu was determined to exert his personal authority over naval affairs, and this locked him into a power struggle with the Duc de Guise, that ultimately led to the

latter being relieved of his command in the Levant during the course of 1628. Richelieu extended his iron grip to include the Mediterranean coast; Guise was increasingly isolated and finally exiled for plotting with Maria de' Medici, preventing him, among other things, from prowling the Mediterranean in pursuit of Kenelm. See James, chs 2, 3, 5, esp. pp. 44–5, 74–6, 93–9.

283 '. . . is most exactly described . . .' *Journal*, p. 50. It is impossible to know just what was in Kenelm's book of maps, precisely because there were so many options: thousands of practical and beautifully rendered maps of the Mediterranean, both as a whole and in its various parts, had been produced across Europe in the preceding decades (see Astengo). The Mediterranean had long been mapped by both Christian and Muslim navigators and cartographers, as a way of justifying and representing a particular view of sacred and political space, and the expeditions and voyages made in and before Kenelm's lifetime had made this a great age of cartography (see Brummett). He would have been well aware of these advances from his student days, since his Oxford mentor, Thomas Allen, was keenly interested in mathematical geography, and taught several of the great geographers of the age (see Cormack, pp. 118, 124–7).

283 '. . . Nature herself playing a witty joke . . .' See Findlen, 1990, pp. 306–7, 311–12, 327.

283 '. . . in great want of water . . .' *Loose Fantasies*, p. 171.

283 '. . . the island of Milos . . .' *Journal*, pp. 51–2.

284 '. . . *to direct this my journey in the right way* . . .' *Loose Fantasies*, p. 3. These are the book's opening words.

285 '. . . terrors as well as possibilities . . .' *Journal*, p. 53. Throughout his life Kenelm was both fascinated by, and sceptical of, reports of these sorts of demons and devils. In the 1630s his friend Wat Montague took him to the famous convent at Loudun in France, where the nuns were taken over by terrifying demonic forces and displayed the horrifying effects to all and sundry. He saw the convulsing of the nuns' bodies,

and the strange red marks spelling out a word on the hand of the prioress, Jeanne des Anges. Kenelm admitted in a report that he sent to his friend, the great philosopher Thomas Hobbes, that the events 'were strange enough to make me suspend judgement', though he perceptively observed 'the satisfaction people may have of thinking themselves monstrous creatures of the Devil'. (Malcolm, vol. 1, pp. 42–9.) In his oration on the Powder of Sympathy, Kenelm described a lady who 'thought herself possessed, and did strange things', inspiring the five young women who attended her to perform similarly 'prodigious actions'. In fact, she was suffering from 'the disease called the Mother' (that is, hysteria) brought on by the death of her husband: these women were not lying, Kenelm believed, but genuinely suffering from entirely natural disorders of the imagination, which they misunderstood as devilish assaults. (*A late discourse*, pp. 93–5.)

285 '. . . curteous & kinde . . .' Sherley, pp. 17–18. Sherley was notable both as an adventurous hero and as a cautionary tale: he had made several privateering voyages in the Mediterranean around the beginning of the century, while his two brothers had gained renown and notoriety for travelling to Persia and negotiating directly with the Shah. Thomas Sherley, though, had spent painful years imprisoned in Constantinople, and had died in poverty a few years before Kenelm's departure, his grand schemes having come to nothing. The Sherleys showed that a life of Mediterranean adventure might win fame, but only of a fleeting and insubstantial sort. See Grogan, ch. 4.

285 '. . . supplye with all necessities . . .' *Journal*, p. 53.

286 '. . . as cheape as larkes in England . . .' *Journal*, p. 54.

286 '. . . groneth under Turkish thraldom . . .' Sandys, p. 7.

286 '. . . concerned with the plight of the Greek Orthodox . . .' See Trevor-Roper, 1978, pp. 216, 230–31, 233. These connections were strengthened by Thomas Roe during his years as ambassador in Constantinople, when he formed a close friendship with Cyril Lucaris, who was patriarch of the Greek Church in the city on and off between

1620 and 1628; Cyril's idiosyncratic version of Greek Orthodoxy was close to Roe's own austere Calvinism. Though his own theological outlook was very different from both of these men, William Laud, who was particularly concerned with the plight of Greek Christians as part of his wider interest in the Levant, established a correspondence with the patriarch through Roe: Cyril sent the treasure of the Codex Alexandrinus, a rare and priceless early version of the Bible in Greek, to Laud as a gift for Charles I – 'the greatest antiquity of the Greek Church', Roe believed – as well as a copy of the Pentateuch (the first five books of the Old Testament) in Arabic with a personal inscription to Laud himself. After surviving the vicissitudes of Ottoman politics for years by the skin of his teeth, finally in 1638 Cyril was strangled at the Sultan's orders and his body was tossed into the Bosphorus. See Strachan, 1989, pp. 170–5; Roe, p. 618; Spinka.

286 '. . . nor have Turkes come to oppress them . . .' *Journal*, p. 54. Sherley estimated this tribute, in terms of the local currency, at '10000 chikinoes by the year' (p. 18). According to Richard Hakluyt, writing a few decades before, a 'Chikino' was worth seven English shillings (or three chikinoes to the pound), making the tribute around £3,000 anually, or around £300,000 annually in terms of modern currency (Hakluyt, p. 294). This is just one example of the fiendishly complicated array of currencies and conversions of which anyone trading in the Mediterranean had to keep track.

286 '. . . never truly probed the basis of his beliefs . . .' *Loose Fantasies*, p. 97.

287 '. . . polarised, Manichean world view . . .' See Clark; Lake, 1987.

287 '. . . in so grievous a manner interrupting prayers . . .' See Birch, 1848, p. 407; Rodger, 1997, p. 407.

287 '. . . he can pray, but tis by rote, not faith . . .' Leyland, p. 154; Kennedy, esp. pp. 171, 174.

288 '. . . *praying together and singing together* . . .' See Ware, pp. 17–19; Greene.

288 '. . . he was our trustie frende . . .' Dallam, p. 4.

289 '. . . I might enjoy solitude and liberty . . .' *Loose Fantasies*, pp. 171–2.

289 '. . . in respect of others that I have seen . . .' *Journal*, p. 54.

290 '. . . loose sheets of borrowed paper . . .' *Loose Fantasies*, p. 172.

290 '. . . stole unexpectedly upon me . . .' *Loose Fantasies*, p. 172.

291 '. . . used by Knights of yore . . .' Cervantes, 1612, pp. 4–5; this is from the first English translation by the Irish Catholic Thomas Shelton. Cervantes wrote another novel, *Persiles y Sigismunda*, which he described as 'a book which dares to compete with Heliodorus' (Cervantes, 1998, p. 5), and the impact of Heliodorus' work is everywhere felt on the pleasurably inchoate ramblings of *Don Quixote*.

291 '. . . none of his conceit or arrogance . . .' Heliodorus, p. 428; see Whitmarsh. I am grateful to Simon Goldhill for discussion of this point.

292 '. . . that picture of love in Theagenes and Chariclea . . .' Sidney, 1973, p. 103.

293 '. . . possessed with this fever . . .' *Loose Fantasies*, pp. 126–7.

293 '. . . at least a mean esteem . . .' *Loose Fantasies*, pp. 140.

293 '. . . fear that they might be true . . .' *Loose Fantasies*, pp. 141.

294 '. . . consequently to our joys in them . . .' *Loose Fantasies*, pp. 152–3.

294 '. . . inciteth any generous heart to do worthy things . . .' *Loose Fantasies*, p. 132.

295 '. . . she was an Angell . . .' Kenelm Digby to his three sons, 18 May 1633; 'Letter-Book', p. 136.

295 '. . . an even and well shaped nose . . .' Kenelm Digby to his three sons, 18 May 1633; 'Letter-Book', p. 130; Kenelm Digby to Tobie Matthew, 29 August 1641, BL Additional MS 41,846, f. 45.

295 '. . . yet more fragrant than the morning air . . .' *Loose Fantasies*, p. 116.

296 '. . . the ground or author thereof . . .' *Loose Fantasies*, p. 63. This monstrous figure is lifted directly from the famous representation of

'Fama' or 'Rumour' in Book 4 of Virgil's *Aeneid*, which was imitated by writers from Ovid to Shakespeare and beyond: see Hardie.

296 '. . . oppress her spirits . . .' *Loose Fantasies*, p. 26.

296 '. . . solitary lamenting by herself . . .' *Loose Fantasies*, pp. 62–3.

296 '. . . the conversation of men . . .' *Loose Fantasies*, p. 68.

Chapter 8

299 '*. . . the dim light of their own feeble nature . . .*' *Loose Fantasies*, p. 155.

300 '. . . upon his humble submission . . .' *Journal*, p. 54.

300 '. . . that he now seeth two thousand yeares ago . . .' Peacham, p. 105.

301 '. . . many Statues of the best ancient sculptours may bee had . . .' [Petty?], vol. 18, pp. 258, 260. This treatise was formerly and errone-ously attributed to John Milton; for the attribution to Petty see Chaney, 1993, p. 720.

301 '. . . the charge of digging and fetching . . .' Roe, p. 16.

301 '. . . on his travels through Italy . . .' Some of the works that Arundel brought back from Rome were obtained in farcical circumstances: a series of antiquities was buried by his servants beneath a thin layer of soil in an ancient site so that the Earl could excavate and 'find' them for himself. The statues in his collection dazzled and unsettled some of his most famous contemporaries with their ghostly white beauty: supposedly Sir Francis Bacon, 'coming into the Earl of Arundels Garden, where there were a great number of Ancient Statues of naked Men and Women, made a stand, and as astonish'd, cryed out, *The Resurrection*'. (Bacon, 1679, p. 57.) See Michaelis, pp. 5–28; Haynes; Howarth, 1985.

301 '. . . a Royall liking of ancient statues . . .' Peacham, pp. 107–8; see Harris, p. 415; Lightbown, 1989; Howarth, 1989.

302 '. . . two patrons who were fierce rivals . . .' Arundel and Buckingham were bitter rivals throughout the 1620s, with the Earl viewing the

royal favourite as an ignoble upstart and allying with Kenelm's relative the Earl of Bristol against him: see Sharpe, 1978.

302 '. . . which are your Lordships service . . .' Roe, p. 495.

302 '. . . I judge only by the eye . . .' Roe, p. 154.

302 '. . . stealing works from under the noses of rival collectors . . .' After surveying the city following his arrival, Petty informed Roe that they should try to procure the huge statues adorning the Golden Gate, which was unused and had fallen into disrepair. Roe was slightly baffled that Petty prized these works so highly since they 'have all suffered much violence, both by weather and spight', but he trusted his new partner's connoisseurship, and started investigating the practicalities of a thoroughly hare-brained scheme, which would require fifty men, and the construction of a huge scaffold. They proposed, in order to overcome local outrage that such treasures were being removed, to bribe a local imam who would denounce the statues as contrary to Islamic proscriptions against images, 'and under that pretence, to take them downe to be brought into some privat place; from whence, after the matter is cold and unsuspected, they may be conveyed'. In this way, Petty and Roe deviously sought to adapt local religious beliefs in the unlawfulness of images to their advantage, mingling piety, art and politics in the most hard-nosed fashion. Ultimately, though, this plan came to nothing: Roe tried bribing an array of Ottoman officials, but once an irate public caught wind of the plans 'none of them dare meddle', and 'the vizier dares not, for his head, offer to deface the chiefest port, so many will clamour against him'. (See Roe, pp. 386–7, 444–5; Howarth, 1985, pp. 89–90; Strachan, 1989, pp. 168–70.) After he left Constantinople to widen his search for aniquities and arrived in Smyrna, Petty discovered that a Monsieur Samson was in the city, and had acquired thirty valuable inscriptions on behalf of the great French scholar, Nicolas Peiresc – but Samson had just been imprisoned on spurious charges, leaving the ancient works unguarded. Petty swiftly agreed a new price, bought them, and

shipped them back to Arundel before Samson was any the wiser (see Miller). Many of the Arundel marbles survive today as the core of the classical collections in the Ashmolean museum in Oxford, and it is easy to forget, gazing at their tranquil and impassive surfaces, that many of them arrived in England through a particular rogue clergyman's talent for theft and skulduggery.

302 '. . . he left his boate to fish for the marbles . . .' Roe, p. 387.

302 '. . . kept long among the living by their famous deedes . . .' Roe, p. 503.

303 '. . . together in a statue . . .' Roe, p. 534.

303 '. . . any Antique Coins or gravings . . .' Ferrier, p. 51.

303 '. . . in search of antiquities . . .' *Journal*, p. 56.

303 '. . . verie good and exceeding cheape . . .' *Journal*, p. 55. Kenelm retained a lifelong interest in wine – not only in quaffing it, but in relation to his chemical pursuits. Soon after his return he began using the fine array of furnaces in his laboratory to experiment with glass-making, adding extra sand to improve the strength and increasing the heat with a bellows. This allowed him to develop sturdy, dark-coloured, globular bottles, which stood flat and made the transport of wine much safer. Near the end of his life, in 1662, Kenelm was formally recognised as the inventor of these 'English bottles', the ancestor of modern wine and beer bottles, by parliamentary order. He might first have realised the need for such an invention when he witnessed the difficulties of loading and transporting the wine that he bought at Mykonos (and he would hardly be the last English person to buy copious amounts of alcohol on this island). See Parliamentary Archives, HL/PO/JO/10/1/314, 'Draft of an act to confirm the invention and manufacture of glass bottles' (I am grateful to Martin Smith for providing a reproduction of this document); Godfrey, pp. 228–30.

304 '. . . all the smallest bits & fragments . . .' [Petty?], vol. 18, pp. 260–1.

305 '. . . with much ease and speede . . .' *Journal*, p. 56.

305 '. . . an intensely physical form . . .' See Barkan, esp. pp. 136–58.

306 '. . . they have all failed in it . . .' *Journal*, p. 57. 'Divers' here means 'diverse', as in 'many people'.

307 Selden, pp. 707–8; Boeckhius, no. 2286; Michaelis, p. 28. I am grateful to Nick Hardy for guidance on the afterlife of this inscription, and Rosa Andújar for help in deciphering it.

308 '. . . purchased shortly before departing . . .' The copy that Kenelm owned has survived, and is now in the library of Wellesley College in Massachusetts: see Moshenska, 2012.

308 '. . . militantly Protestant fervour . . .' See Norbrook, pp. 199–223.

308 '. . . 'majesty and sweetnes of verse . . .' BL MS Additional 41,846, f. 109.

308 '. . . in the proportions of seven and nine . . .' Spenser, Book II, Canto ix, Stanza 22.

309 '. . . drowned in eternall delight . . .' *Observations*, 1643a, pp. 25, 6, 8, 16, 19, 21, 22, 23; see Fowler, pp. 260–88.

309 '. . . a Welsh family known for supporting poets and scholars . . .' See Williams, 1983.

309 '. . . the consuls feare and weakeness . . .' *Journal*, pp. 58–60.

310 '. . . a range of exotic plants . . .' See Macgregor, pp. 7–9.

310 '. . . camels, giraffes and hippopotamuses . . .' See Maclean, pp. 151–4, 158. For some English visitors to the Greek Islands, the local wildlife was a source of intense terror, occasionally with hilarious effect. When Thomas Dallam and his company set up camp on the island of Ganos, one man, a Mr Glover, decided that it would be a bright idea to describe at length the 'strainge varmen and beastes he had sene in that contrie', and 'spoake verrie muche of Aderes, snaykes, and sarpentes' before they went to sleep. Later that night another member of the party, Mr Baylye, got up in the night 'to make water', and felt a tickle along his calves as he returned to the camp. Recalling the chilling bedtime conversation, he cried, 'A sarpante! a sarpante! a sarpante!' His

bedfellows misheard and thought he was crying, 'Assaulted!' Fifteen of them jumped from their beds, grabbed their swords, and began swinging them wildly in the dark to repel the imaginary intruders: by a miracle no one was hurt, and they could laugh when lights were lit and they discovered that Baylye's trailing garter had triggered the near-disaster. (Dallam, pp. 54–6.)

310   '. . . whiles their bodies were covered with the sea . . .' *Two Treatises*, p. 311. Kenelm was interested in exotic creatures such as 'a baboon, that would play certaine lessons upon a guitarre', or the 'strange thinges' told of elephants, but admitted that he had not seen them for himself. In his *Two Treatises*, when he recalled the dogs on Zante and discussed the seemingly reasonable behaviour of animals, Kenelm insisted that despite appearances it could always be understood on purely physical principles, in line with Descartes' claim that a beast is nothing more than a complex machine. If this argument seemed to distinguish animal and human absolutely, in other respects Kenelm was fascinated by the blurry and shifting line between the two. He paid careful attention to the story of a man known as John of Liege, who fled when his village was attacked and 'lived many yeares in the woods, feeding upon rootes, and wild fruites' until he was discovered, 'naked and all over growne with haire, having lost all of his human capabailities'. He was eventually taught once again to speak and act like a human, but reported that whereas in his wild state 'he could by the smell judge of the tast of any thing that was to be eaten', since re-learning language he had 'quite lost that acutenesse of smelling which formerly gouerned him in his taste'. The exercise of language and reason seemed to dull the acuity of the senses. (*Two Treatises*, pp. 319, 247–8.)

310   '. . . warmer than att any time in England . . .' *Journal*, p. 58.

312   '. . . Signior Bego, a local dignitary . . .' *Journal*, pp. 60–63.

312   '. . . infallibly take part with a Christian invader . . .' This was a deeply implausible hope – the Ottoman forces may have been divided, but

there was no prospect of a unified Christian force while Europe was torn apart by war.

312 '. . . how to cure it and make it up very well . . .' *Journal*, pp. 64–5. Tobacco had first been introduced into the Mediterranean and North Africa by the English from the New World. Many, both Christians and Muslims, consumed it avidly; and many others, also both Christians and Muslims, abhorred its pleasures – most notably King James I, who wrote a whole book against the new craze, denouncing its unhealthiness and unpleasant smell. See MacLean and Matar, pp. 203–9.

313 '. . . *which will remain with me forever* . . .' *Loose Fantasies*, pp. 155–6.

314 '. . . they beat and mutilated his frail body . . .' See Bellany. Kenelm met Lambe personally, around the time of his knighthood and before Buckingham's hatred for Bristol drove an insuperable wedge between them: Kenelm later reported to his friend John Finch that he visited Lambe at the Tower of London 'by persuasions of the Duke of Buckingham to convince him of apparitions . . . and Lamb told him that he would show him somewhat. But he did nothing but make him looke in a cynlindricall glasse and brought shapes of some horrid thing with him and bid him see in what terrible shape it rose.' (Finch, vol. 1, p. 62.) Lambe, like Kenelm's teachers Richard Napier and Thomas Allen, was an expert astrologer with an interest in ingenious illusions that earned him a dubious reputation as a sorcerer; but Kenelm found that, unlike his mentors, Lambe bore much of the responsibility for his own reputation since he sought to pass himself off as a true magus.

314 '. . . The Duke shall die like Doctor Lambe . . .' *CSPV* vol. 21, p. 157; Russell, p. 392; Fairholt, p. xv.

315 '. . . killing him instantly . . .' Lockyer, pp. 419–56; Holstun; Cogswell, 2006.

315 '. . . the prince of darkness it self . . .' Wotton, p. 232.

315 '. . . and 'God bless thee!' as he passed . . .' See Holstun, p. 528; Cogswell, 2006, pp. 357–8.

315 '. . . strung up in chains . . .' Lockyer, p. 459.

318 '. . . I shaped my course homeward . . .' *Journal*, pp. 65–70.

318 '. . . strangely compelling power . . .' It is telling that, when Shakespeare wanted to invent an island packed with spirits, spells and mysterious forces in one of his last plays, *The Tempest*, he very deliberately placed it between Tunisia and Italy, in precisely this region. See Hess, 2000.

319 '. . . some other ladyes . . .' *Journal*, pp. 71–5.

320 '. . . the terms of his commission . . .' Ragusa was the name for modern-day Dubrovnik, the city on the Croatian coast that was then the capital of an independent maritime republic.

320 '. . . make their way to the nearest shore . . .' *Journal*, pp. 75–9.

321 '. . . to general astonishment . . .' See Israel, pp. 197–8; Parker, 1989, pp. 102, 106.

322 '. . . a sizeable sum . . .' It is difficult to estimate the modern-day value of pieces of eight but this probably equates to around £500,000 in today's terms.

323 '. . . grosse sands somewhat reddish . . .' *Journal*, pp. 80–91.

323 '. . . sniff its salty tang . . .' This remains a common mode of practical navigation for fishermen, as Nicholas Rodger has helpfully informed me: sailors often know the constitution of the seabed in different parts of the local waters so well that they can estimate their location at any given moment from its colour, texture and smell.

324 '. . . his new-found knowledge . . .' See Feingold, 1991, p. 72.

326 '. . . a rule of great decorum . . .' *CSPV*, vol. 19, p. 21; this was the description of the Venetian ambassador to England in 1625, who further observed, 'The nobles do not enter his apartments in confusion as heretofore, and each rank has its appointed place . . . [the King] does not wish anyone to be introduced to him unless sent for.' See Richards, pp. 73–9.

328 '. . . gouged at one another . . .' See Russell, p. 391; Parker, 1987, pp. 105–9.

328 '. . . an act of political expedience . . .' See Reeve, 1989, pp. 227–74.

329 '. . . as an example to others . . .' *CSPV*, vol. 21, pp. 345, 380–81. Contarini had been further incensed in December, when the account of the fight at Scanderoon that Kenelm had sent back to England was printed. The ambassador called the work 'boastful and mendacious' and insisted that 'Digby falls back upon the pen because of his lack of right and fair dealing': but when he demanded that the account be publicly burned, he discovered that this was impossible. Kenelm's account of Scanderoon had been printed along with the articles of peace agreed with France, giving his words a veneer of respectability and official approval, and making it impossible to burn one without the other. (*CSPV*, vol. 21, pp. 417–18, 437, 443–4, 484.)

329 '. . . forbidding hostilities within the Mediterranean altogether . . .' Privy Council, 190, pp. 222–3; 'A Clause to be inserted in Letters of Marque forbidding hostilities within the Straits', in Marsden, 1915, vol. 1, pp. 456–7.

331 '. . . giving her majesty in her lookes . . .' Kenelm Digby to his three sons, 18 May 1633; 'Letter-Book', p. 131.

Chapter 9

333 '. . . *which my continual thoughts administered me* . . .' *Loose Fantasies*, p. 171: 'Postscript, or Advertisement to the Reader'.

334 '. . . playing the two sides off against one another . . .' See Fincham and Lake.

335 '. . . the true representatives of the reformed English Church . . .' See Russell, p. 410.

335 '. . . was named in 1627 as the new Bishop of London . . .' Laud was not officially installed until the summer of 1628, while Kenelm was at sea.

335 '. . . giving royal approval to the views that terrified so many . . .' See Tyacke, *passim*, esp. p. 161.

336 '. . . this new "Trojan horse" of crypto-Catholicism . . .' See Tyacke, pp. 134–5, 160–61.

336 '. . . Charles vowed not to call another for as long as he lived . . .' See Russell, pp. 414–16; Kishlansky, 1996, pp. 113–15.

337 '. . . maritime law was enormously convoluted and disputed . . .' See Marsden, 1910.

338 '. . . the astonishing sum of £15,000 . . .' This is equivalent to around £1.5 million in modern currency.

339 '. . . Tradescant's growing collection of exotic rarities . . .' Tradescant had himself travelled to Algiers in 1621 as part of the failed mission by Robert Mansell to attack the city, and collected specimens while he was there. As a client of Buckingham's he had also served at the Île de Ré in 1627 before being appointed Keeper of His Majesty's Gardens in 1630. The collection that he built up was expanded by his son and namesake into one of the largest and most famous in the country, and it formed the nucleus of the Ashmolean Museum in Oxford. The published catalogue acknowledged Kenelm as one of the men who had provided rarities. See Tradescant, p. 180; London, pp. 35–6; Macgregor, pp. 7–9, 19.

339 '. . . compleat Gentleman Sir Kenhelme Digby Knight . . .' Peacham, pp. 107–8.

339 '. . . *wine from Crete, and some other things* . . .' CSPV, vol. 21, pp. 554–6.

339 '. . . to make in large quantities . . .' CSPV, vol. 22, p. 63.

340 '. . . confirmed with the Treaty of Susa in April . . .' Sanders and Atherton, p. 3; Parker, 1987, p. 108.

340 '. . . agreed a fragile peace on harsh terms . . .' See Parker, 1987, pp. 79–81. Mansfeld himself had died at the end of 1626 in Bosnia, after disbanding his troops and fleeing towards Venice.

340 '. . . the ships plundered by Digby . . .' CSPV, vol. 22, p. 198.

342   '. . . choice wines and jovial welcome . . .' Howell, 1650, supplement, p. 25; Donaldson, p. 407.

342   '. . . financial help and patronage . . .' The degree of this esteem was confirmed when Jonson named Kenelm one of his literary executors before his death in 1637, and Kenelm took an active role in editing a posthumous edition of Jonson's works: see Dobranski, pp. 113–15.

342   '. . . Witness his action done at Scanderoon . . .' Ben Jonson, 'An Epigram: To My Muse, the Lady Digby, on her Husband, Sir Kenelm Digby', ll. 5, 9–10, 13–14, in Jonson. See Evans; Donaldson, pp. 61–2, 262–5, 411–13.

343   '. . . beaten before . . .' James Howell to Kenelm Digby, 29 November 1629, in Howell, 1650, p. 168. Howell went on to note Kenelm's smaller-scale triumphs since returning: 'I give you the joy also that you have borne up against the Venetian ambassador here, and vindicated yourself of those foul scandals he had cast upon you in your absence.'

343   '. . . the learned circles to which he aspired . . .' Kenelm wrote a sequel to the discourse on Spenser that he had written to Stradling and which he addressed to a member of Jonson's circle, Thomas May, who became a good friend: see BL MS Additional 41,846, f. 109. May later dedicated his 1639 play, *The Tragedie of Cleopatra, Queene of Aegypt*, to Kenelm.

343   '. . . the learning of the ancient world . . .' Selden had never travelled to the Levant himself but was fascinated by its status as the origin of all wisdom. While Kenelm had been at sea, as well as taking a leading role in the parliamentary debates that led to the Petition of Right, he had compiled a learned catalogue of the Earl of Arundel's ancient marbles (Selden, 1628). Kenelm took Selden to Whitehall, along with the Royal Librarian, Patrick Young, and showed them the pillar from Delos with its inscription, which fascinated both men. See Selden, 1653, pp. 707–8; Young, sig. M4r-v; Michaelis, p. 28; Toomer, 2005.

343 '. . . that he had procured in Algiers . . .' Toomer, 2009, vol. 2, p. 590; Feingold, 1991, pp. 71–2.

344 '. . . and adding his own . . .' Laud later gave the collection to St John's College, Oxford, his alma mater. See Wakefield; Savage-Smith et al.

346 '. . . learned and pious men like Kenelm . . .' Laud, pp. 613–16; Lake, 1993.

346 '. . . entirely his and his family's . . .' See Foster, 2004; Aubrey, 2015, vol. 1, p. 327.

346 '. . . a gallery for a library to be built . . .' Kenelm Digby to his three sons, 18 May 1633; 'Letter-Book', p. 128.

347 '. . . that could bind and unloose itself so easily . . .' Kenelm Digby to his three sons, 18 May 1633; 'Letter-Book', p. 132.

347 '. . . in this miserable world . . .' Kenelm Digby to his three sons, 18 May 1633; 'Letter-Book', p. 126.

348 '. . . that I should ever be false to her . . .' Kenelm Digby to Thomas Gell, undated; 'Letter-Book', p. 448.

349 '. . . plunged in all voluptuousness . . .' Untitled and undated meditation in 'Letter-Book', p. 97.

349 '. . . agreed on £750 as the sale price . . .' This is around £70,000 in modern terms.

349 '. . . boatloads driven out of England . . .' See Andrews, 393.n.2. The vessel arrived in Massachusetts by mid-June, having survived storms and seen whales along the way: see Winthrop, 1996, pp. 13–30.

350 '. . . recognised Kenelm's talents and sought to harness them . . .' There was another basis for their affinity. Coke's principal patron for much of his life had been Fulke Greville, Lord Brooke, who had been Philip Sidney's best friend and had been the last of the heroic Elizabethans until he, like Buckingham, was stabbed to death while Kenelm was at sea – not for political reasons, but by a servant disappointed to be left so little in Greville's will. Coke had revered Greville as a man who combined heroism with scholarly nous, and he believed that Kenelm had displayed the same mixture of qualities in the

Mediterranean. See Young, pp. 207–8, 211–12; Farmer. Kenelm was very interested in Greville's poems and plays, and helped Coke prepare them for posthumous publication: see Alexander, 1999, pp. 215–17.

350 '. . . he was astonished to discover . . .' On 18 October 1630, Henry Skipwith reported to Sir Gervase Clifton that the commission was 'a thinge that Sir Kellam Digby never so mutch as once knew of, till the Kinge sente it to him by Mr. Secretary Cooke's servante'. (*HMC*, Report on Manuscripts in Various Collections, vol. 7 [London: HMSO, 1914], p. 398.)

350 '. . . well acquainted with the seas . . .' Draft by Sir John Coke of a letter from the Commissioners of the Admiralty to the Officers of the Navy, 13 October 1630, *HMC, Twelfth Report, Appendix, Part I* (London: HMSO, 1888), vol. 1, p. 413. See Aylmer, pp. 62, 232. It had previously been rumoured that Kenelm would be granted the command of fifteen vessels in order to drive the Dutch out of the valuable fisheries of the North Sea, while Henry Mervyn, the Admiral of the Narrow Seas, found himself in dire financial straits at this time, and considered selling his post to Kenelm: see Thrush, pp. 89–90, 156–7.

351 '. . . found itself at peace with all the world . . .' See Sanders and Atherton, p. 3; Parker, 1989, p. 108.

351 '. . . professed the Protestant Religion . . .' Aubrey, 2015, vol. 1, p. 327.

351 '. . . become a Protestant . . .' *CSPV*, vol. 22, p. 452.

352 '. . . *sprinkled upon Aurora's face* . . .' *Loose Fantasies*, p. 60.

352 '. . . the rage and fury of arms . . .' Clarendon, 1888, vol. 1, pp. 55, 94; see Anselment. The peace that the Emperor had begun to impose in 1629 following the collapse of the Protestant alliance came to an end in July 1630. Protestant prayers were answered when King Gustavus Adolphus of Sweden roared in from the north to join the religious wars in Europe, winning a series of battles over the Catholic armies with tactical brilliance and bravery. There was no longer any need for an Englishman feebly to play the part of a Protestant hero – as Charles and Buckingham

had once sought to do – now that a real one had arrived, and the pressure for English involvement in these wars therefore lessened for the time being. See Roberts, 1967; Parker, 1987, pp. 121–32.

353 '. . . almost into every room in every ship . . .' See Thrush, pp. 34–9, 78; Quintrell; Sharpe, 1992, pp. 97–104; Rodger, 1997, pp. 391–4.

353 '. . . the design, manning and provisioning of the fleet . . .' Kenelm Digby to Sir John Coke, 12 September 1632, TNA SP 16/223/21; Kenelm Digby to Sir John Coke, 12 August 1632, BL MS Additional 64903, f. 22. Kenelm did express concerns about the quality of the new ships and Charles's overly direct role in their design. 'I have heard much whispering,' he wrote to Coke from Charterhouse Yard, 'that the two new ships are likely in their conditions and qualities at sea to fail much of the expectation that hitherto hath been had of them,' and gently expressed the hope that 'when the King hath any more ships to build, he will refer the consulting of their models to the most eminent and able men in that faculty'. (Kenelm Digby to Sir John Coke, 2 January 1633, *HMC, Twelfth Report, Appendix, Part I*, vol. 2, p. 1.)

353 '. . . than any of his progenitors . . .' Clarendon, 1888, vol. 1, p. 95.

354 '. . . great friendship . . .' Aubrey, 2015, vol. 1, p. 325.

354 '. . . a mutual relationship of sympathy and good will . . .' Bellori, pp. 218–19. Granted, this information came from Kenelm himself, so is hardly objective, but the two were certainly fast friends and intimates.

354 '. . . the vast collection from Mantua . . .' See Scott-Elliott; Whitaker; Smuts, chs. 5–6; Strong, 1972; White; Sharpe, 2009.

354 '. . . as an allegorical figure of Prudence . . .' Bellori, van Dyck's first biographer, helpfully explained the significance of the figures surrounding her, which would have been readily apparent to Kenelm's contemporaries, who were used to decoding such paintings. 'Beneath her feet she has a block, and bound to it in the form of slaves are Deceit with two faces; Wrath with a furious aspect; Envy, scrawny, with a mane of serpents; profane Love in a blindfold, with his wings clipped, his bow broken, his arrows scattered, and his torch extinguished.' (Bellori, 219.)

355 '. . . the best swordsman of his time . . .' Aubrey, 2015, vol. 1, p. 368; see Foster, 1982a.

356 '. . . which Allen had helped to found . . .' See Foster, 1982b; Philip, pp. 17, 41. Kenelm also gave the library a valuable load of oak-wood from the estate at Gayhurst to help build its bookshelves.

356 '. . . particularly in the Mathematical Sciences . . .' William Forster, 'To the Honourable and Renowned for vertue, learning and true valour, Sir Kenelme Digbye, Knight', in Oughtred, sig. A3, a translation of a work on technical measuring instruments by the renowned mathematician William Oughtred. This public praise might seem like mere puffery, but Kenelm was privately recognised as an authority on such matters based on his Mediterranean experiences. When the scholar Thomas Lydiat sent a copy of his work on the mesolabe, a form of line-measuring device, to Robert Pink, warden of New College, Oxford, Pink found the technicalities of the work beyond him and suggested sending it instead to some 'expert Mathematicians in London' and named 'Sir Kenelm Digby our noble & learned Benefactor' as one possibility. (Robert Pink to Thomas Lydiat, 30 April 1636, Bodleian Library MS Bodley 313, f. 75; see Feingold, 1984, 82, 151.)

356 '. . . standeth fair with the world . . .' Kenelm Digby to Thomas Gell, undated; 'Letter-Book', p. 447.

357 '. . . enjoying the pleasure of its own wealth . . .' Clarendon, 1888, vol. 1, p. 95.

357 '. . . impregnated of a horrid tempest . . .' Hutchinson, p. 279.

357 '. . . that she had bin fast asleep . . .' Kenelm Digby to his three sons, 18 May 1633; 'Letter-Book', p. 132.

358 '. . . could not choose but pray . . .' Kenelm Digby to his brother John, undated; 'Letter-Book', p. 141.

358 '. . . as a holy relike of her . . .' Kenelm Digby to his three sons, 18 May 1633; 'Letter-Book', p. 130.

359 '. . . began to paint her there and then . . .' See Sumner, 1995.

359 '. . . I see her and I talke with her . . .' Kenelm Digby to his brother John, 23 May 1633; 'Letter-Book', p. 450; Kenelm Digby to his brother John, undated; 'Letter-Book', p. 138.

360 '. . . original from her birth and conception . . .' Kenelm Digby to his three sons, 18 May 1633; 'Letter-Book', pp. 134–5, 130.

360 '. . . desolation, lonelinesse and silence . . .' Kenelm Digby to his brother John, 7 October 1633; 'Letter-Book', p. 85.

360 '. . . I have raked together . . .' Kenelm Digby to his brother John, 25 May 1633; 'Letter-Book', pp. 460–61.

360 '. . . all dusty and foule . . .' Kenelm Digby to his brother John, 7 October 1633; 'Letter-Book', p. 86.

360 '. . . going abroad to take the ayre . . .' Kenelm Digby to his brother John, 15 October 1633; 'Letter-Book', p. 88; Kenelm Digby to his three sons, 18 May 1633; 'Letter-Book', p. 133.

361 '. . . reconciled with the ancient authority of their Church . . .' See Finocchiaro, pp. 288–93; Wootton, pp. 223–4. Most famously René Descartes, with whom Kenelm later enjoyed a relationship of mutual respect, decided to suppress his work *Le Monde* when he heard of Galileo's condemnation.

361 '. . . placed at the head of the English Church . . .' His appointment was formally confirmed in November 1633.

361 '. . . aggressive disregard for the feelings of local communities . . .' See Walter.

362 '. . . signes of sorrowe for his beloved Wife . . .' Aubrey, 2015, vol. 1, p. 327.

362 '. . . portrait a navigational instrument known as an armillary sphere . . .' This instrument is in the form of a celestial globe, made from metal rings. The presence of a sunflower in the other portrait of Kenelm may have been van Dyck's choice, since the painter used it in a self-portrait from around the same time as a symbol of the subject's fidelity to his monarch. It may also, however, have been a nod to Kenelm's occult and scientific interests: the inexplicable ability

of this flower to follow the trajectory of the sun across the sky was often numbered among the occult relationships binding together the cosmos, that so fascinated Kenelm in his account of the powder of sympathy. See Brown, 1982, pp. 144–50; Brown and Vlieghe, pp. 30, 89, 244–5; Peacock, pp. 273–8; Fehl, pp. 53–63.

362 '. . . now worne out . . .' Kenelm Digby to Sir John Coke, 23 May 1633; 'Letter-Book', p. 446.

362 '. . . available to a wider public . . .' See Ames-Lewis.

362 '. . . the Professors' good conversation . . .' Aubrey, 2015, vol. 1, p. 327.

362 '. . . New Oven to bake pies in . . .' 'Inventory of Digby's Laboratory at Gresham College, Hartlib Papers, 16/1/6B; Feingold, 1984, pp. 181–3; Hill, pp. 37–49, esp. pp. 47–8; Appleby; Dobbs.

363 '. . . that she would steale a Leape . . .' Aubrey, 2015, vol. 1, pp. 327, 332. Rumours of poisoning often attended prominent deaths in the seventeenth century, especially after the sensational case in 1613 in which James I's then favourite, the Earl of Somerset, was convicted along with Frances Howard, his mistress, of poisoning Thomas Overbury as part of their plot to secure an annulment for her marriage. Among the charges hysterically levelled at the Duke of Buckingham in the 1620s was the claim that he had poisoned James I. In Kenelm's case, his known proclivity for poisonous vipers as an ingredient in medicines and cosmetics – the main addition that he made to the recipe for Walter Raleigh's famous cordial was 'the Flesh, the Heart, and the Liver of *Vipers*' – may have worsened his reputation in the public eye; but in fact vipers were an established and expensive component in elite medicine, especially in Italy, where Kenelm may first have encountered their use during his travels. Sometimes recipes specified vipers from North Africa or the Middle East, so it was an ingredient associated with the world of his Mediterranean travels. See Le Febvre, p. 14; Findlen, 1994, pp. 240–44; Aubrey, 2015, vol. 2, pp. 1213–14.

364 '. . . heartfelt and extravagant accounts . . .' These are collected in BL
    Additional MS. 30259. The strangest and most haunting of these
    poems, by the minor playwright Joseph Rutter, is written as if in
    Kenelm's own mourning voice: a strange act of ventriloquism, which
    might seem to modern eyes like an inappropriate violation of individual
    grief, but was clearly acceptable to Kenelm as an act of empathy. ('A
    Pastorall Elegie in the person of Sir Kenelme Digby, on the death of
    his noble Lady, the Lady Venetia Digby, f. 14.)

365 '. . . fitter to shadow out her mind than her shape . . .' Kenelm Digby
    to his three sons, 18 May 1633; 'Letter-Book', p. 129.

365 '. . . an inconsiderable atome . . .' Kenelm Digby to his brother John,
    24 May 1633; 'Letter-Book', p. 454.

Epilogue

367 '. . . only as far as Sittingbourne in Kent . . .' See Bayle, vol. 4, p. 596;
    Petersson, p. 303.

368 '. . . his servants George and Anne Hangmaster . . .' See British
    Library, MS Additional 38175, ff. 60–62.

368 '. . . drawings of tombstones and inscriptions . . .' Aubrey, 2015, vol.
    1, p. 329.

369 '. . . firmnesse, and beauty . . .' Howell, 1642, pp. 208–9. See Wall,
    pp. 159–61; Summerson, 1964, 1990; Duggan.

369 '. . . like a primitive Tuscan temple . . .' See Summerson, 1964,
    pp. 174–6. Interestingly, this was the first church to be built entirely
    from scratch in England since the Reformation (that is, not built on
    the site of an earlier church). In the eighteenth century Horace Walpole
    claimed that the Earl of Bedford, who owned the land and master-
    minded the building of Covent Garden, told Jones that he had to build
    a chapel for the local parishioners, 'but added he would not go to any
    considerable expense. "In short," said he, "I would not have it much

better than a barn." "Well! then," said Jones, "You shall have the handsomest barn in England." ' (Cited by Summerson, 1964, p. 173.)

371 '. . . valiant efforts by recent historians . . .' For the most sustained of these defences of the King see Kishlansky, 2005.

372 '. . . he had fathered six sons and outlived all but one . . .' Kenelm Digby to Cassiano Dal Pozzo, 4 August 1648, Biblioteca dell'Accademia Nazionale dei Lincei e Corsiniana, Rome, Archivio Dal Pozzo MS IV, f. 97: 'Mi resta adesso un solo, di sei figlioli.' Cassiano had one of the finest museums, libraries and art collections in Rome in his palazzo on Via Chiavari. Kenelm's friend John Evelyn visited the year before and described 'a great Virtuoso one Cavalliero Pozzo, who showed us a rare collection of all kinds of Antiquities, [and] a choice Library', but noted, 'That which was most new to me was his rare collection of the Antique Bassirelievos about Rome, which this curious man had caus'd to be design'd in divers folios.' (Evelyn, vol. 2, p. 277.) This was Cassiano's *museo cartaceo* or 'paper museum': he had used a significant portion of his fortune to send artists out into Rome and the surrounding countryside to draw gorgeous, meticulously rendered pictures of every species of plant and vegetable, every chunk of ancient marble or fragment of inscription, that they found there, while other artists sent similarly intricate depictions of rare items from around the globe. He gathered these images into a series of huge volumes – at least twenty-three in number – in which the countless minute wonders of the natural world were depicted: resplendent, meticulous depictions of broccoli and pineapples, flamingos and pineapples, coral and fungi, no object too mundane or grotesque to be captured in its particular being. Cassiano, like Galileo, had been a member of the Accademia dei Lincei, which supported the great scientist throughout his life; but the academy was much concerned with alchemy and occult phenomena from its foundation, and Cassiano shared this fascination. He and Kenelm exchanged a long series of letters, largely on alchemical topics, which are now in the Biblioteca

dell'Accademia Nazionale dei Lincei e Corsiniana in Rome. See Haskell, pp. 98–116; Stranding; Freedberg, pp. 15–77; Clericuzio and da Renzi.

372 '. . . he had become a Catholic again . . .' Kenelm announced his reconversion in a letter to Laud, and his friend the Archbishop sent a long reply, regretting but respecting his decision: see Laud, pp. 611–13.

372 '. . . a large mastiff on a leash . . .' Finch, p. 61.

372 '. . . the management of the splendid navy . . .' Kenelm wrote to John Coke regarding the new Ship Money fleet, which Charles funded by means of a controversial tax, causing huge resentment that ultimately helped provoke the Civil Wars: Kenelm believed that the fleet 'will have the power to keep the balance even', maintaining a fragile equilibrium among the competing naval powers even if it 'do no more than sail up and down'. He also advised Coke regarding John Selden's newly published book, *Mare Clausum*, which argued that the King of England was sovereign ruler of all the surrounding seas. See rough draft of a letter from Sir John Coke to Kenelm Digby, dated 1639 [written 1634/5], British Library MS Additional 64921, ff. 63–4; Kenelm Digby to Sir John Coke, 25 August 1635, 14 September 1635, British Library MS Additional 64910, ff. 65–6, 90–91; Fulton, 209–377; Toomer, 2009, vol. 1, pp. 388–437; Muldoon.

373 '. . . strong bonds between England and the Continent . . .' See Albion; Lister; Lightbown, 1981.

373 '. . . prominent conversions to Catholicism . . .' See Dubois. Among the most high-profile of these converts was his friend Wat Montague, to whom Kenelm wrote long letters advising him how best to defend his defection to Rome: Kenelm Digby to Walter Montague, 18 October 1636, Houghton Library, Harvard, MS Eng 382; Kenelm Digby to Walter Montague, 15 November 1636, Smith College Library, MS Misc. 820. In the mid-1630s Kenelm also helped to convince an English lady in Paris to join him in going over to Rome: this was Francis

Coke, Viscount Purbeck (see *Conference*). Her father, Sir Edward Coke, forced her to marry the Duke of Buckingham's mentally disturbed brother, and she was later accused of adultery with Sir Robert Howard and convicted; she fled to France disguised as a page-boy, where Kenelm met and admired her. He may also have taken a private pleasure in helping convert the daughter of the lawyer who had prosecuted his own father with such cruel vigour.

373 '. . . baste roasting meat with egg yolks . . .' *Closet*, pp. 131, 169. A book of the Queen's recipes was published in 1655 under the title *The Queens Closet Opened* (see Knoppers). This in turn inspired the title given to Kenelm's posthumously published cookbook, *The Closet of Sir Kenelm Digby, Open'd.*

373 '. . . Kenelm's closest friend and mentor . . .' In his philosophical notes Kenelm's friend John Finch called White 'a person whose memory can never be forgotten, since eternized by the pen of the glory of our nation, Sir Kenelm Digby; a gentleman so generally accomplished that 'twere an insult to raise his applause from any particulars'. (Finch, vol. 2, p. 502.)

373 '. . . the most powerful man in France . . .' Kenelm received 'a most courteous letter of thanks' from the Cardinal in return for these books. (Kenelm Digby to Richard Smith, 7 February 1639, Archives of the Archdiocese of Westminster, Series A, vol. 29, no. 77.) He also bought romances in Paris for his friend Edward Conway – son of the Secretary of State to whom he had once written from Algiers, and a fellow bibliophile – enquiring whether he wanted them bound 'for curiosity and cost, or whither the vulgar meanest binding will serve your turne'. See Kenelm Digby to Edward, Viscount Conway the Younger, 30 June 1636, TNA, SP 16/344/58; Smith, 2012.

374 '. . . seemed to confirm their worst fears . . .' See Hughes; Hibbard, 1983; Questier, 2006.

374 '. . . placed in charge of collecting the funds . . .' See Hibbard, 1982; 1983, pp. 102–3.

374 '. . . labour lustily for the advancement of Popery . . .' Browne, sig. A4ʳ; see D'Ewes, pp. 291–96, 393, n. 16.

375 '. . . which had begun to trouble him . . .' Aubrey, 2015, vol. 1, p. 327; vol. 2, p. 1209; Kenelm Digby to Robert Harley, 1 February 1642, Longleat House, Portland Papers vol. 2, f. 69.

375 '. . . neere two hundred sheets of paper . . .' *Observations* 1643b, p. 11.

375 '. . . the ancient wisdom of Aristotle . . .' See Mercer, 1993, pp. 62–6.

375 '. . . a performance of undiplomatic and unprecedented daring . . .' Aubrey, 2015, vol. 1, p. 328. See Gabrieli, 1954; Sells, pp. 77–91. Kenelm's diatribe was swiftly translated into English and circulated: see 'The Negotiation of the Honᵇˡᵉ Sʳ Kenelm Digby, Resident for yᵉ late Queen at Rome, as it was by Himself Presented by way of Addresse to Pope Innocent yᵉ Xᵗʰ, Faithfully Translated out of the Italian Manuscript', Archives of the Archdiocese of Westminster vol. 30, no. 100. Kenelm's time in Rome was not entirely wasted, for as well as striking up his alchemical friendship with Cassiano dal Pozzo, he also exchanged letters and books with the learned Vatican librarian, Lucas Holstenius, met the Jesuit polymath Athanasius Kircher, who showed him how to resurrect plants from their ashes, and even learned a new recipe for making 'a *Pan Cotto*' or cooked bread 'as the Cardinals use in Rome'. The recipe in question suggests boiling 'lumps of fine light-bread tosted or dried' in mutton broth for hours, and flavouring it afterwards with spices and orange juice. See Kenelm's letters to Holstenius in Vatican Library MS Barb. Lat. 3631; Blom; Rietbergen, pp. 256–335; *A discourse*, 1661, p. 75; *Closet*, p. 157. I am very grateful to Nick Hardy for advice and guidance regarding Holstenius and his connections with Digby.

376 '. . . famous through all Europe . . .' Bernadino Guascino to the Grand Duke of Tuscany, 30 June 1646, in Crinó, 208. (My translation.)

376 '. . . afforded freedom of conscience . . .' See Worden; Collins; Tutino.

376 '... my lord Protectors goodnesse and justice ...' Kenelm Digby to John Winthrop Jr, 26 January 1656, in Winthrop, 1849, pp. 15–18. Kenelm's friend Samuel Hartlib similarly wrote to Robert Boyle, 'I suppose you have heard, how that Sir Kenelm is in very good favour with the lord protector; his sequestration is taken off.' (8 or 9 May 1654, in Boyle, 2001, vol. 1, p. 175.)

376 '... the newly founded library at Harvard ...' It was later rumoured that Kenelm would make a longer voyage still, sailing to Connecticut to start a learned alchemical academy with Winthrop (see Mortimer, sig.a–b3). The books given to Harvard – all but one of which were destroyed in a fire in the eighteenth century – are mentioned in the same letter to Winthrop, in which Kenelm sends his thanks 'to the President and fellowes of your college for the obliging Letter they have bin pleased to send me', and detailed in the book list enclosed with Kenelm's letter to Hugh Peters, Beinecke Library, Yale University, Osborn Files 4407; see Wright, pp. 41–2.

377 '... Norwegian and Danish alchemists ...' Knowledge of Kenelm's alchemical activities in the 1650s has recently been expanded by the discovery in Strasbourg of a new body of manuscripts relating to this period of his life: see Principe, 2013. Kenelm's Scandinavian connections are demonstrated by the letters to him from F. Schaub in 1661, sent from Horten in Norway (British Library MS Additional 41,846, f. 80), from the Danish alchemist Bartholus Herland, alias Severinius, in 1663 (British Library MS Sloane 2870, ff. 151, 153) and the Danish natural philosopher Olaus Borrichius in 1663 (Royal Society, London, EL/B1/103).

377 '... the great Pierre de Fermat ...' The letters are reproduced in Wallis; see Stedall, esp. pp. 317–19.

377 '... the newly founded Royal Society ...' Kenelm delivered a paper on the vegetation of plants before the newly founded Royal Society, which became the first paper that the Society officially asked to be published, and he distributed copies to all the fellows. In this work

Kenelm argued, for the first time in history, that plants took in sustenance of some sort from the air around them – an early, uncertain step towards understanding photosynthesis. See *A discourse*, 1661; Birch, 1756–7, vol. 1, pp. 13, 41; Evelyn, vol. 3, p. 294. This work was notable not only for its scientific ambition but for Kenelm's determination to discuss 'the mysterious contemplation of the resurrection of dead and dissipated bodies, and how they may continue the same individuation, and be again the same identical body, after so many strange changes, and having put on so many different habits and shapes'. He claimed to have successfully achieved palingenesis, the rebirth of creatures from their ashes – in the case of crayfish, placing their crushed roasted fragments in water and coaxing them back to life with oxblood – but here his work in the laboratory clearly crossed over with the obsession with continuity and regeneration that he had first developed after Venetia's death. (*A discourse*, 1661, pp. 3–4, 83–5; see Janacek.)

378 '. . . a bust of Venetia herself . . .' See Burch.

378 '. . . a sacred duty to do so when she is dead . . .' The phrase derives from the Roman poet Statius.

379 '. . . glowing with a fiery rednesse . . .' Evelyn, vol. 3, p. 454.

380 '. . . our deservedly famous Countryman Kenelm Digby . . .' Ferrar's epitaph cited in Wood, 1817, vol. 3, p. 369; Boyle, 2000, vol. 13, p. 227. Kenelm lent Boyle manuscripts and advised him on alchemical matters: see Principe, 1995. In one of his chemical works Boyle included a respectful reference to Kenelm's assistance when he wrote the manuscript draft but omitted it in the published version, a sign of how swiftly his reputation declined: see Boas, pp. 161–2.

380 '. . . widely read and debated across Europe and New England . . .' The prominent Puritans named Increase and Cotton Mather, father and son, owned and cited Kenelm's *Two Treatises* and his observations on Thomas Browne's *Religio Medici*: see Wright, pp. 142, 179.

381 '. . . Dame Venetia's Bust standing at a Stalle . . .' Aubrey, 2015, vol. 1, p. 333.

ACKNOWLEDGEMENTS

The years that I have spent getting to know Kenelm Digby have been a joy and a challenge in their own right, but they have also been the most delightful of pretexts: they have given me an excuse to travel to many of the wonderful places that Kenelm visited or in which documents relating to his life have ended up, and to speak with many fascinating people who have generously shared their expertise relating to his diverse areas of interest.

For making materials available and sharing expertise I would like to thank the staff of the British Library, Cambridge University Library, the Bodleian Library, several branches of the Bibliothèque Nationale de France, the Vatican Library, the National Library of Wales, the National Archives at Kew, the New York Public Library, the Huntington Library, the Houghton Library at Harvard, the Beinecke Library at Yale, the Biblioteca dell'Accademia Nazionale dei Lincei e Corsiniana (especially Allessandro Romanello), the Bibliothèque Saint Genviève, the library of the Royal Society, the Derbyshire Record Office, the Somerset Record Office, the Kent History and Library Centre, the library of the Wellcome Trust, Lambeth Palace Library, the library of the Society of Antiquaries, the Archives of the Archdiocese of Westminster, the Pepys Library of Magdalene College, Cambridge, the library of Worcester College, Oxford, the library of St John's College, Oxford, the library of Wellesley College, the staff of the Mortimer Rare Books Room at Smith College (especially Barbara Blumenthal), Kate Harris at Longleat House, and Ann Smith at Sherborne Castle, who shared with me her unparalleled knowledge of the various branches of the Digby family and their histories. I would particularly like to thank Sandy Paul and the expert staff of the Wren Library and the Trinity College Library.

I owe an enormous debt of gratitude to those friends, colleagues and scholars who have shared knowledge of and enthusiasm for Kenelm and his world: Claire Preston, Kevin Jackson (with whom I still hope to cook some Digby dinners), Jeff Dolven, Reid Barbour, Alan Stewart, Dan Carey, Molly Greene, Michael Hunter, Rhodri Lewis, Nick McDowell, Katie Murphy, Scott Mandelbrote, Gavin Alexander, Steve Connor, Simon Goldhill, Leah Whittington, Antonio Clericuzio, Andrew Zurcher, Lauren Kassell and Nicholas Rodger (who helpfully confirmed that cannons firing with black powder easily could shatter glass and pigeon eggs on a far-off shoreline). Anne-Laure Meyer knows Digby's surviving traces better than anyone, and has been unfailingly generous with her knowledge. I would particularly like to thank Sir Noel Malcolm, for his encouragement and frequent provision of possible leads and intriguing titbits. Nigel Smith remains my principal inspiration for exploring a seventeenth century rarely found in textbooks, and a valued teacher and friend.

ACKNOWLEDGEMENTS

The depressing and increasing corporatisation of the English universities has made me ever more aware of my privilege in being able to research and write this book in the surrounds of Trinity College, Cambridge, a place where ideas are still valued for their own sake. I would like to thank the Master, Fellows and staff of the college for helping to make it so. To have had such splendid colleagues in English – the late Anne Barton, Angela Leighton, Adrian Poole, Anne Stillman, Anne Toner, and Ross Wilson – makes me luckier still. I am indebted as well to my students, often first sounding-boards for undeveloped ideas, and especially those who have tolerated idiosyncratic reading lists and even found themselves writing literature essays on Digby's cookbook. My colleagues in the early modern period could have been deliberately assembled as a crack team designed to advise on Kenelm's many facets, and I am grateful to the vast knowledge and good humour of Nick Hardy, Sachiko Kusukawa, Dmitri Levitin, David McKitterick, Richard Serjeantson, and Alex Walsham.

I would never have studied the literature and culture of the early modern period had it not been for the teaching of Sean McEvoy, who remains a dear friend and inspiration. Life in Cambridge has been enriched, enlivened, and made joyous by the friendship of Leo Mellor, Sophie Read and Edward Wilson-Lee. I have become thoroughly used to running most of my thoughts past David Hillman, with whom I have shared so much in so relatively short a time.

I have been fortunate to have had research assistance at crucial moments from three young scholars at the beginning of their glittering careers: Cassie Gorman, Andrew Sanchez, and Ted Tregear. I have benefited from responses to work in progress from a number of conference and seminar audiences: thanks to all those in Cambridge,

Oxford, York, Princeton, London and Galway who asked questions and made comments.

My research has been generously supported at different points by the Vice Chancellor's Fund of the University of Cambridge, an Early Career Fellowship from the Centre for Research in the Arts, Social Sciences and Humanities (CRASSH), a small research grant from the British Academy, and, repeatedly, by the Fellows' Research Fund of Trinity College. Its completion was aided enormously by a research fellowship from the Leverhulme Trust. I am enormously grateful to all of these bodies. For supporting and encouraging other aspects of my work on Digby I would like to thank Jacqueline Baker, and all those with whom I have worked at the BBC. Some of the material used in this book also forms the basis of my article 'Kenelm Digby's Interruptions: Piracy and Lived Romance in the 1620s', *Studies in Philology*, vol. 113 (2016) © North Carolina University Press.

I have been tremendously fortunate to have had, in Luke Ingram, someone who was a dear friend for a decade before he became my literary agent. I am grateful to him for constant support and advice, as well as to the entire staff of the Wylie Agency, especially Sarah Chalfant. In Tom Avery I have been blessed with an editor whose enthusiasm for the project was immediate and unwavering, and who has shepherded and shaped it expertly through its development, his comments both exacting and acute. I am hugely thankful to him, and to all the staff at William Heinemann, especially Emma Finnigan, Nicky Nevin, Jason Smith, Anna Watts, and my lynx-eyed copy-editor Mary Chamberlain. Cherrell Avery produced a wonderfully elegant recreation of Digby's monogram at short notice.

A Stain in the Blood is in fact not my first but my second attempt to tell an exciting story set in the seventeenth century: my first was completed in 1989 when, as a five year old, I wrote a long story about Roundheads and Cavaliers, which was 'published' thanks to the enthusiasm of my teacher at Coombe Road School in Brighton, Lynn Hawkin, and the typewriter of the headmaster, Adrian Marshall. It took me a fair while to find my way back to this period of history, but the mixture of politics, culture and language that still fascinates me is a direct legacy of my childhood. My parents, Chana and Raf, and my siblings, Ruby and Gabe, are largely responsible for this aspect of me, and for so many others, and they continually remind me that ideas and convictions are the basis of a life well lived.

When Kenelm Digby decided to leave England for the Mediterranean late in 1627 he left his wife and two small children behind. I have been more fortunate in being able to bring my family along on the travels I've made in his wake. My wife, Rosa Andújar, has embraced the seventeenth century eccentric hovering in the margins of our marriage, and our common conviction that a busy and challenging life is better than a boring one has sustained me throughout. Her good humour and generosity of spirit are incomparable; her effortless facility in half a dozen languages hasn't hurt either. This book is dedicated to her, with love. Our son Alejandro (who was never at risk of being named Kenelm, despite some mischievous suggestions), and our daughter Beatriz, might not ultimately remember the Digby trips on which we have taken them in their early years, but they show every sign of developing a taste for adventure that I hope they never relinquish, and each day with them brings new joys.

INDEX

Page numbers in *italics* indicate illustrations.